THINKING FROM THE HAN

non-dualism?
Self
Truth
Transcendence

53

149→

THINKING

FROM THE

HAN

*Self, Truth, and Transcendence
in Chinese and Western Culture*

David L. Hall and Roger T. Ames

STATE UNIVERSITY OF NEW YORK PRESS

Published by
State University of New York Press, Albany

The cover is a painting by the contemporary Chinese artist,
Qi Baishi 齊白石 entitled "Refusing a Drink No. 2" 邻飲圖之二
and is reproduced with the permission of the National Gallery
of Prague (Národní Galerie v Praze). We are grateful to Dr. Lucie
Borotová for her guidance in touring the Prague collection, and
introducing this painting to us.

For information, address State University of New York Press,
State University Plaza, Albany, N.Y., 12246

Production by Cathleen Collins
Marketing by Fran Keneston

Library of Congress Cataloging in Publication Data

Hall, David L.
    Thinking from the Han : self, truth, and transcendence in Chinese
and Western culture / David L. Hall and Roger T. Ames.
        p.   cm.
    Includes bibliographical references and index.
    ISBN 0-7914-3613-6   ISBN 0-7914-3614-4 (pb)
    1. Philosophy, Chinese.   2. Philosophy.   3. Philosophy,
Comparative.   4. East and West.   I. Ames, Roger T., 1947–
II. Title.
B126.H255   1998
181'.11—dc21
                                                        97-24491
                                                          CIP

10 9 8 7 6 5 4 3 2 1

For Eliot Deutsch:
. . . in wanting to establish himself
he establishes others;
in wanting to succeed himself
he helps others to succeed. (*Analects* 6.30)

Contents

Prologue

This volume, *Thinking from the Han: Self, Truth, and Transcendence in Chinese and Western Culture*, completes a trilogy on comparative Chinese and Western thought whose first volume, *Thinking Through Confucius*, was published in 1987. The second volume, *Anticipating China: Thinking through the Narratives of Chinese and Western Culture*, appeared in 1995. During the more than ten years of collaborative effort that led to the production of these volumes, comparative philosophy within the Western philosophical community has gained momentum, moving from the status of a marginalized enterprise to an interest pursued by increasingly serious philosophers. This is due partially to the improvement and availability of translations, and to an exponential rise in our general understanding of the history, politics, art, and religious sensibilities of the major alternative cultures. Partially, and this is true with respect to China in particular, it is a consequence of pragmatic pressures to interact with those cultures that have begun to emerge as economic and political powers.

As we have indicated in the past, our comparative efforts have constituted attempts to raise to the level of consciousness, those habitual attitudes and assumptions that preclude Western thinkers from understanding China on its own terms, and to offer, quite tentatively, some revised categories that may permit a richer understanding. From the beginning we have been pleased with the reception our work has received within the community of comparative philosophers and sinologists. Those inclined to appreciate our work (several of them our graduate students) have done so in the manner that means most—that is, by further refining and expanding upon our ideas. Our critics, too, have served us well by usually stating their differences in a balanced and fair manner, thereby challenging us to attempt greater clarity and cogency. Perhaps most often, our readers have combined these responses, expressing a critical appreciation of what we have been trying to do.

The benefit we have received from both defenders and critics will, we hope, be evident throughout the following pages. In many instances we have been able to engage our supporters and critics in an explicit manner. There are, however, two thinkers whose works provide alternative perspectives to that which we represent, and who we have been unable to discuss in the body of our work. We should like to consider them briefly at this point as a means of clarifying the sense of our overall project.

The first is Alasdair MacIntyre, who has pondered the project of substantial cross-cultural engagement, and who, having expressed reservations about its very possibility, suggests a way out of incommensurability.

MacIntyre begins his reflection with a caution that, we believe, is well placed. In earlier published work, *A Short History of Ethics* (1966), he argues that comparative philosophy was possible because there are general qualities of the human virtues specifically, and the human experience more broadly, that can be identified and isolated without reference to particular cultures. MacIntyre now believes this assumption that there are universally human, culturally neutral grounds to which we can appeal as a basis of comparison is a mistake, since any neutral vantage-point from which to evaluate competing theories "will be so bare a level of characterization that it will be equally compatible with far too many rival bodies of theory."[1] Alternatively, any account that is rich enough to be relevant to the theories at issue would not be innocent, presupposing something of the theoretical stance of the tradition from which the analysis and evaluation begins. MacIntyre's conclusion, then:("There is just no neutral and independent method of characterizing those materials in a way sufficient to provide the type of adjudication between competing theories of the virtues which I had once hoped to provide and to which some others still aspire."[2]

In the absence of some external standard for adjudicating truth-claims between rival theories such as Aristotle and Confucius, they are incommensurable in a Kuhnian sense of this term. It needs to be noticed that MacIntyre's examples of cultural incommensurability continue to be largely drawn from scientific models/Despite the fact that MacIntyre is well aware that the Confucian moral vision depends little on what we would take to be theoretical or conceptual claims,[3] he is still insistent that the comparison be pursued if at all at this level because the ultimate goal of such comparison is to determine the truth or falsity of claims made.

A further element in MacIntyre's argument is that translation and exposition present us with what seems at first blush to be a vicious rather than a hermeneutical circle: You cannot translate unless you understand the target culture, and you cannot understand the target culture unless you can translate it. But MacIntyre does allow that there might be Cicero-like scholars who can move comfortably back and forth between traditions and their languages to separate out what is translatable from what is not. In fact, MacIntyre's ultimate resolution of the incommensurability problem is dependent upon the skills and cultural sensibilities of just such comparativists. It is only when these same scholars recognize the inevitability of their rejecting the target culture because of their own presuppositions—that is, the inevitability of incommensurability—that the conversation seems to move ahead. But since the dialectical engagement made possible by appeal to mutually acknowledged principles cannot take place, the victim in the recognition of this incommensurability is the strong sense of truth that can hold irrespective of one's point of view.

MacIntyre allows that there is an alternative to holding out for the strong sense of truth: to allow some pragmatic, context-bound notion of truth negotiated out of contingent circumstances—what he would call with some disdain, the affliction of "pragmatic aestheticism"—to stand in for the traditional notion of rational justification. But this is not acceptable.

Still, there is, by MacIntyre's lights, a way forward. If, thanks to the comparativists, we are enabled each to understand the other on the other's terms, and then, armed with this clear sense of rival systems, challenge the most problematic and vulnerable representation of our own position with the history we have available to us of the target culture, we open up a space for a conversation that preserves rational engagement. The vulnerability of our own tradition is a sign of sincerity. We must allow for possible fallibilism within our own tradition, not necessarily as a belief, but at least as strategy for encouraging worthwhile conversation in which rational beings can change their minds.

There are ironies in MacIntyre's approach, some of which he does not miss. The way in which he chooses to frame the project of comparison, as he himself would expect, is grounded in certain Aristotelian assumptions about conceptual schemes and standards of evidence that do, for

him, make fruitful comparison between traditions excruciatingly difficult. He cannot (and will not) take leave of Aristotle, and the high
standards of rational encounter dictated by the Philosopher, and as a
consequence, he has set for himself an all but impossible task.

A first irony is that, in spite of himself, MacIntyre throughout his
essay, identifies and expounds upon interesting and important points
of comparison between Aristotle and Confucius on virtue—the role of
theory and *telos* in Aristotle, for example, guarantees a strong sense of
the unity of virtues, while the absence of such commitments on the
part of Confucius make this kind of unity less likely. It would seem
that MacIntyre understands Confucianism better than his own approach would allow.

A second irony is that MacIntyre's formulation of the problem and
his way out of incommensurability is a solid demonstration that his
resolution will not work. MacIntyre's insistence upon rational engagement as the *sine qua non* of responsible philosophy and his dismissal
of any alternatives to rational engagement as a blanket "pragmatic
aestheticism" stops any fair comparison with the Confucian tradition dead
in its tracks. MacIntyre generously allows that this kind of "smorgasbord
of theoretical standpoints laid out before a clientele of metaphysical and
moral consumers"[4] (traceable, who would suspect, to nineteenth-century
Protestant Christianity!) is "very different from the sense of aesthetic
order that Hall and Ames understand as underlying Confucius' social and
political theory and cosmological vision."[5] MacIntyre understands us to
be presenting a Confucius whose practice of the virtues has claims that
"are universal, even if the universal envisaged is very different from, for
example, an Aristotelian conception of rational universality."[6] The irony,
hopefully addressed by our continuing attempt in this book to produce
a clearer interpretation of the differences between the philosopher Confucius and rational engagement, is that we must demure, and allow that
very probably Confucius (and pragmatists like us) in fact would be more
sympathetic with "pragmatic aestheticism" than with any sort of univer-
salist position. The pragmatic, historicist approach that we have appealed
to throughout our comparative collaborations does not have the exclusive
universal pretensions that have made cross-cultural engagement so difficult these many centuries. That is, we do not and need not choose
between asserting culturally neutral, supposedly universal claims on the
one hand, or, for derivitively universalistic reasons, surrendering to in-

commensurability on the other. The third position is to see these traditions as historical narratives that, at a practical, concrete level, intersect and even overlap. At this level, comparisons can be formulated and understood that are productive in identifying alternatives to familiar modes of expression and action.

We have discussed our own approach to comparative method in some detail in the second chapter of *Anticipating China*. We refer the reader to that source for further explanation into the contrast between views of the sort MacIntyre entertains and those we espouse. The essential difference lies, as we have indicated, in the degree of rational articulation one considers desirable when making comparative judgments. If one holds, as do we, that to be useful in cultural conversation, language must remain productively vague, then desire for conceptual clarity may be found antithetical to the most satisfactory forms of cultural interaction. After all, the sense of community we Anglo-Europeans feel with our fellows depends upon the invocation of vague terms such as "freedom," "justice," "democracy," and so on, which, if stipulated overmuch, can only advertise irresolvable differences of opinion and occasion unwinnable debates. Meanings jointly entertained are negotiated less through theoretical discussion and debate and more through practical and behavioral interactions. Such interactions depend upon the rich vagueness, rather than any narrow precision, of linguistic expression. Our celebration, throughout our work, of the value of "vagueness" is intended to promote the move from mere "intercultural conversation" to practical engagements among individuals of alternative cultures.

The second scholar we should like to consider briefly is Geoffrey Lloyd. Lloyd is well known for his careful studies of ancient Greek thought. He is presently engaged in an exciting collaboration of his own with Nathan Sivin, one of our more distinguished sinologists, on comparative treatments of Greek and Chinese science.

In his review of *Anticipating China*,[7] Lloyd found what he considers two serious faults with our work. The first concerns what he perceives to be a narrowness of focus. We concentrate, says Lloyd, too much upon "philosophical" sources and not enough upon, for example, mathematical and medical treatises. His suggestion is that our conclusions might have been different had we cast our net more widely. His second criticism is that we stress too much the value of individual thinkers—Pythagoras, Zeno, Confucius, Xunzi, and so on. He suggests that we are thereby presenting the old-fashioned "Great Man" approach to intellectual history. With respect to this second point Lloyd is insistent that "questions to do with circumstances in which individuals and groups aimed to impress their contemporaries and gain prestige need to be recast in social institutional terms."[8]

These criticisms highlight a central issue in our pragmatic method. Were we attempting to present pictures of classical Western and Chinese societies *in situ* and in all their complex detail, Lloyd's reservations would be most justified. But the issue, as we have repeatedly urged throughout our work, is one of the distinction between merely *historical* and *historicist* projects.

In the first place, our concentration upon so-called "philosophical" sources is in fact a concentration upon those ideas and practices that have shaped general cultural attitudes and institutions. We might indeed have explicitly included other cultural interests in our work were it our project to offer a complete cross-section of cultural aims, interests, and institutions. But we wished, rather, to celebrate the *most productive* ideas and activities—those that have shaped the dominant sensibilities of Chinese and Western cultures. It is our claim, subject to pragmatic test, that we offer a judicious selection of just such ideas.

Secondly, our pragmatic approach is indifferent to the issue of whether one casts one's discussions in terms of texts or social institutions. We are concerned with the delineation of cultural *importances*. In particular, our question is: "What are the major obstacles, expressed as attitudes and assumptions, that prevent a better appreciation of Chinese cultural sensibilities when viewed from a Western perspective?" In attempting to respond to this question we have searched out those *important* ideas and assumptions that constitute roadblocks to our understanding, and then sought to clear them from the path leading to China.

The pragmatist is certainly not a proponent of a Great Man approach to cultural interpretation. For the pragmatist (as perhaps for any careful thinker), names such as "Pythagoras" and "Xunzi" cannot be thought merely to designate specific historical individuals. Such names are always complex propositions that sum the ideas and influences to which their names effectively refer. Indeed, it is a truism that, considered in terms of effective ideas, "Pythagoras" is shorthand for the Pythagorean community, and equally truistic that, as we have stressed throughout our work, that "Confucius" names a corporate personage. In fact, as perhaps China's most influential thinker, Confucius is still very much alive in the ways of living and thinking of a vast population.

Perhaps Lloyd's failure to come to terms with the pragmatic method comes from an unwillingness to understand the term "pragmatism" in more than a casual throw-away sense. The pragmatist is not a theoretician concerned with a coherent "vision" of this or that. Neither is he a sociologist concerned to detail the issues, ideas, and institutions that constitute the form of a particular society. Nor is he, for that matter, the scrupulous historian energized by the discovery of exceptions that challenge the rule or details that fall outside dominant patterns. The pragmatist by no means intends to deny the value of these enterprises. The pragmatic thinker wishes, rather, to take as his project the highlighting of those species of importance that shape the general thrust of events.

The facile belief that we can succeed in translating ourselves into another culture before we have done the hard work of ridding ourselves of habitual attitudes and assumptions that preclude our understanding of an exoteric culture has seriously impeded the development of comparative philosophy. Thus, without the attempts to clear away, in John Dewey's phrase, "the useless lumber that blocks our highways of thought," the historian, or sociologist, or ethnologist cannot avoid being victimized by precisely those offending attitudes and assumptions assayed by the pragmatist.

We look forward to the day when the projects of the sort MacIntyre and Lloyd endorse can in fact be more successfully performed. Indeed, it is our sincere hope that our work can, in some small way, prepare the path for such efforts.

We should say something about the relation of this work to its predecessor. In the first and last chapters of _Anticipating China_, we offered parallel accounts of the development of classical Western and Chinese cultures, respectively. In telling the story of the origins and development of Western culture from the Homeric to the Augustinian periods, we attempted to highlight the important ideas and doctrines that would most seriously contrast with the cultural dominants emergent in Han China. Our articulation of "Han Thinking" has benefitted greatly from the resort to these contrasts. In the middle chapter, we attempted to build a methodological bridge that would facilitate movement back and forth between the two cultural sensibilities. Any readers of this present work who find themselves puzzled by our methods of construction and critique are urged to consult that discussion.

In this book we deal with three subjects that we think can serve to focus comparative discussions. Two questions arise when reflecting upon our particular choices. The first is, "Why these three as opposed to any number of others?" The answer to this is quite straightforward: Our experience has shown that "self," "truth," and "transcendence" encapsulate any number of topics and issues that have occasioned mutual misunderstanding between Chinese and Western interlocutors. We believe that, considered together, they permit perhaps the most efficient advertizement of the barriers existing between China and the West. By implication, of course, the reformulations made possible by the recognition of these barriers, will best enhance the possibility of sound communication.

A second question concerning the shape of our project may be asked in this manner: "Haven't we stacked the deck by using obviously Western terminologies in identifying the subjects of our work?" This question gains pertinence when one realizes that we shall be at odds to radically revise Western-based notions of "self" and "truth" in order to make them at all applicable to Chinese sensibilities. Moreover, we shall continue to deny that there is any such thing as strict "transcendence" in mainstream Chinese culture.   (?)

Our explanation is again simple: In building a bridge you must begin where you are, and we are not on the bridge over the river Hao. In fact, if we could effectively begin on the Chinese side, we wouldn't need the bridge at all. Hopefully, and this has indeed been our experience over the last several years, we will find ourselves increasingly in the position of meeting in the middle our Chinese colleagues who are themselves in the business of building bridges.

A final word about the individual to whom this book is dedicated. Eliot Deutsch may not be aware of this, but it was he who was responsible for bringing the two of us into collaboration. As editor of *Philosophy East and West*, he generously agreed to publish the first comparative essays of David Hall. Upon reading these essays, Roger Ames recognized an individual who was dealing with issues similar to those with which he was concerned. Contact was made; discussions ensued. And the rest is (a somewhat chequered but personally enjoyable) history.

There are countless other personal reasons why each of us is pleased to dedicate this work to Eliot, but we cannot omit the recognition that we have this collaborative reason for doing so, as well.

In the preparation of this book, we have utilized materials from the following previously published work:

Hall and Ames, "Confucian Friendship: The Road to Religiousness," in *The Changing Face of Friendship*, ed. Leroy S. Rouner (Notre Dame: Notre Dame University Press, 1994).

Ames, "Rites as Rights: The Confucian Alternative," in *Human Rights and the World's Religions*, ed. Leroy S. Rouner (Notre Dame: University of Notre Dame Press, 1988).

Ames, "Taoism and the Androgynous Ideal," in *Women in China*, ed. Richard W. Guisso and Stanley Johannesen (Youngstown, N.Y.: Philo Press, 1981).

Hall, "Dancing at the Crucifiction" in *Philosophy East and West* 39:3.

Hall, "The Way and the Truth," in *A Companion to World Philosophies*, ed. E. Deutsch and R. Bontekoe (Oxford: Blackwells, 1997).

We would like to acknowledge the assistance of Daniel Cole in preparing the index, done as always to his high standards.

David L. Hall
University of Texas at El Paso

Roger T. Ames
University of Hawai'i

PART I

Metaphors of Identity

CHAPTER ONE

The Problematic of Self in Western Thought

SELF, HISTORY, AND CULTURE

All of the important notions characteristic of Western cultural self-consciousness are "vague" in the sense that they are open to rich and diverse interpretations.[1] This is the case with respect to the term "self" and allied terms such as "person," "personality," and "individual." A perusal of the meanings for these terms in the *Oxford English Dictionary* (OED) demonstrates this fact rather well. Indeed, beyond the strictly denotative senses found there lie the semantic complexities associated with the use of these terms in variant theoretical contexts.

Even if such genetic analyses were helpful, we would gain nothing by searching out the origins of the term "self," for, as we are darkly told at the beginning of the OED entry, its etymology is "obscure." We are dependent, therefore, upon the history of the semantics of the concept and its referents, whose philosophical transmutations over time have been further ramified by the accreted significances of "soul," "mind," "person," "human being," "agent," and associated terms.

Normally, a dictionary is meant to include alternative meanings in order to facilitate the selection of the best definition relative to context. In our hyperconscious late modern period, however, this aim has been subverted in favor of the recognition that all of our interpretative categories are semantically vague complexes whose associations can neither be reduced to a coherent or internally consistent meaning, nor exhaustively isolated by appeal to their respective context-relative

3

meanings. In the absence of narrow and arbitrary stipulations, such categories are intransigently ambiguous.

Not only is there little consensus as to the correct meaning of any given term, most of us who have no specific theoretical motivations seem quite content to hold central cultural notions such as "freedom," "power," "nature," "knowledge," and "love" together in gloriously inconsistent clusters. With each use of such terms we are, willy-nilly, alluding to the entire cluster of associations, for the most part unaware of the logical tensions that might exist among the variant meanings.

What *meaning* can a cluster have if the semantic elements are mutually inconsistent and yet, in some complicated manner, can be shown to possess their meaning by virtue of the clustering process? We can answer this question only by reconsidering the meaning of "connotative sense." For vague terms are shaped by their overlapping contexts.

The meaning of a semantically vague term results from aesthetic juxtapositions that highlight the tensions of contrasting senses that form an aesthetically complex, but often logically inconsistent, context. Our puported understanding of such terms might better approximate the experience of "appreciation" than the grasp of certain cognizable import. Such enjoyment or appreciation of the meaning of vague concepts challenges the coherence of the agent of understanding, who can can truly accommodate the incoherence, incongruence, and inconsistencies embedded in vague notions only if she owns the same complexity as the notions themselves.

Thus the primary semantic associations, when they qualify the experience and practice of individuals, destabilize the self by shaping actions and appreciations in disparate, richly vague, manners. Such destabilization threatens the existence of any coherently defined ego or personality construct characterizing a core self. We are our (often conflicting) desires, our (often contradictory) beliefs, and the (often discordant) activities they enjoin. Aristotle's doctrine remains intact: There is a real sense in which we become that which we know.

This situation places us in a better position to understand at least one aspect of the Chinese cultural sensibility. For what we have achieved involuntarily as a consequence of the failure of any single definition or interpretation to realize consensual status, the Chinese have traditionally affirmed as the ground of their intellectual and institutional harmony—namely, the recognition of the copresence of a plurality of significances with which any given term might easily resonate. The difference is that the Chinese understanding of self is not threatened, but deepened by this fact.[1]

In this work we wish to search out relevant meanings of "self" and its cognates in order to approach the Chinese senses of self as it is disclosed in terms such as "self" (*ji* 己), "person/s" (*ren* 人), "I/we/us" (*wo* 我), and, most importantly, *ren* 仁. We shall also be concerned with the distinctive sense of self-reflexivity in the Chinese tradition, as in "self-so-ing" (*ziran* 自然), "self-cultivation" (*xiushen* 修身), and so forth.

Before we do this, however, we must assay the principal meanings of self in the Western tradition. This requires that we attempt to escape the bounds of the dictionary and move among the uncollected, initially uncoordinated senses of things. Ironically, we can only evoke a viable sense of self by presenting a cluster of associated meanings that, even though they lack logical or semantic coherence, nonetheless name the vague reality we have become.

Within the Western philosophical tradition, subjective consciousness in the strictest sense is likely a modern invention.[2] Of course, the less stringent sense of self as agent or knower who acts or understands in the outer world of things and events is of much earlier origin. One may, with some plausibility, trace the *historical* origins of the concept of the self within Anglo-European culture. The historical vagueness[3] of "self," a consequence of the development of contrasting understandings of the notion by appeal to several distinct historical narratives, provides some evidence for the culture-bound character of the concept. We shall further highlight this boundedness below when we consider alternative Chinese understandings of "selfhood."

We have argued elsewhere that in the Western tradition, our cultural self-understanding has been importantly influenced by analogy with the cosmogonic motivation of construing order from out of chaos.[4] This motivation has operated to shape our myths, religions, laws, and institutions. Equally it is evident in the development of the Western philosophical dialectic that effectively began with the systematization of thinking by appeal to logical definition as a means of bringing order into our perceptions and imaginations.[5] One way of recounting the narrative of our developing intellectual culture is by indicating the specific manner in which we have established the meanings of important notions such as "God," "Nature," "Power," "Law," "Freedom,"—and, of course, "Self."

Broadly speaking, there have been four primary semantic contexts that have shaped alternative meanings of terms such as "individual," "human being," "personality," and "self." In our previous work, these contexts were termed the materialist, formalist, organicist, and volitional models.[6]

The neurophysiologists' construal of human behavior in terms of neuronal firings, or the sociobiologists' characterization in terms of genetic determinants, or Sigmund Freud's reduction of human experience and expression to libido, and of human culture to sublimated products of libidinal sexuality, along with the behaviorists' reckoning of human individuality by appeal to contingencies of reinforcement in local environments, establish a materialistic-mechanistic axis of interpretation in Western culture. This axis goes back through the latter to Thomas Hobbes, who conceived of individuals as bodies swirling in social space, and to ancient materialists such as Democritus who believed that human beings were mere collocations of atoms who "emerged from the ground like worms, without a maker and for no particular reason."[7]

At the opposite extreme lies the characterization of personality by appeal to mind, consciousness, or reason. Plato's explanation of *psyche* in terms of the guidance of the rational element, Hegel's claim that "the real is the rational," and Husserl's delineation of the Transcendental Ego as a formal and noncontingent structure defining the apriori character of both mind and self, are points on a line constituting the rational axis of interpretation. Obviously, idealist and phenomenological understandings are not commensurable with materialist interpretations.

In addition to these explanations that emphasize the physical or mental individuality of the self, there are two models that stress the self as a function of social and or political contextualization. Aristotle's organic naturalism conceived the human being as a language-bearing creature whose experience is constituted by interactions with other persons. The person as biological and social organism is ensconced in a sociopolitical context itself construed in organic terms. The chief defining characteristic of this organism is its principal aim, which Aristotle conceived to be "happiness." This view has since received elaboration and nuance in the pragmatic vision of George Herbert Mead and John Dewey. For these thinkers, persons emerge in the mutually constitutive relationships which ultimately define both self and social ambiance. This social view is found in a variety of forms in sociology, social psychology, and political science.

The Sophistic tradition persists in the twentieth century as a vision that characterizes knowledge as a function of rhetorical persuasion, and personality as a function of self-creativity and persuasive power. This perspective has both "political" and "literary" versions. It is political to the extent that it promotes the ruler-ruled relationship as the context within which meaningful human existence is to be found. Powerful persons are authentic by virtue of the fact that they establish the context of meaning; the ruled are those who operate within this context. This perspective originated in early Greek thinkers such as Protagoras and Thrasymachus and has been perpetuated in modern times by certain strands of existentialism. Michel Foucault's critique of the conspiracy of knowledge and power in social institutions is an instance of this approach. Derrida's virtuosic deconstruction of the coherence of the canonical texts instances this volitional turn in contemporary philosophy in its literary guise. Here person and text are mutually defining, providing the dynamics of self-creativity involved in authoring both self and text.

The four principal models just rehearsed may be capsulized as follows: The self is either a physiological mechanism swirling in social space, *or* a mind or consciousness detachable from its bodily housing, *or* an organic, socially interactive, goal-achieving organism, *or* a willing, deciding, potentially self-creating agent whose meaning is determined by persuasive agency.

The ages-long transmogrifications of the Western notions of self from Homer to the present has been told as a psychic journey from the Many to the One, from the disparate and unfocused actions, dispositions, and understandings that variously expressed the human mode of being in its world to the unity of the human being individuated by mind, will, purposive functioning, or physical substrate. This press toward unity has finally created a new plurality, a plurality of ways of characterizing the unity of the person. These alternative models of unity may be seen to rehearse the four primary semantic contexts described above.[8]

Lately, this cultural adventure seems to have turned about, and has begun to retrace its path, moving now from unity to plurality. The late modern self well might be the original disparate self—but with a remarkable difference. What is left over from the failed project of the Enlightenment that sought in the unity of rational self-consciousness the highest expression of human sensibility is not, of course, the unity of the self but its *self-consciousness*. Ironically, the content of this consciousness is of the self as a candidate for a variety of distinctive interpretations. Thus the desire for wholeness and unity, already definitive of the Western adventure by the close of the Hellenic period, cannot be said to have realized its goal in modernity. The modern self collapsed as soon as it was formed, its very apotheosis signaling its demise.

This fragmentation can be further detailed by recourse to a second set of variables. For in addition to the broad distinctions between the characterizations of self associated with the four principal philosophical traditions, there is the distinct manner in which each tradition comes to interpret the tripartite structure of the *psyche* elaborated in the philosophic syntheses of Plato and Aristotle. The elements of reason, appetite, and will (thought, action, and passion) grew to be so much a part of the problematic of selfhood that some characterization of them appears in almost any full-scale treatment of personality, ancient and modern. We find more than echoes of this psychic structure in Augustine's treatment of the *imago dei*, in Kant's critiques of the aesthetic, moral, and scientific spheres of value, and in Hegel's dialectical analysis of consciousness as In-Itself, For-Itself, and In-and-For-Itself, as well as in Freud's psychoanalytic categories of ego, superego, id.[9]

It is a truism of the interpretation of ancient Greek culture that the analogy established between *kosmos* and *polis* had its origins in the sense of *kosmos* initially referenced to social and political structures. The verb, *kosmeo*, "to set in order," was used in a number of quite ordinary contexts from the household to the military before it came, as a noun, to be used, initially perhaps by Pythagoras, as a characterization of the natural world. *Kosmos* came into being modeled upon social organization. The cosmos is the *polis* writ large, just as the *polis* is the soul writ large. This structure is adumbrated already in the senses of person or individual suggested by the Homeric texts. The terms Homer used to refer to the essential, living aspect of the individual human being were variously *psyche, noos*, and *thymos*. There is in the beginning no reason to posit a self-conscious being aware of its various functionally specialized potentialities.

The analogical relationships among *psyche, polis*, and *kosmos* were exploited in the mature phases of Greek philosophy to develop the general structures of aesthetic, political, ethical, and metaphysical understandings. The same process is to be seen with respect to the cosmological employment of the concept of *dikaiosyne*, "justice," which was a term of art in the courts before Anaximander applied the notion to the interaction of opposites within the Boundless.

In the discussion of putatively naturalistic concepts, therefore, one does well to seek a social and cultural ground for the tools permitting their articulation. This principle must be applied, above all, to any consideration of the meaning of self within the Western tradition. *Psyche* developed in Plato as a tripartite structure owning the functions of spirit (*thymoides*), appetite (*epithymia*), and reason (*nous*). These notions were manifest in conventional contexts associated with disparate and uncoordinated human activities and expressions, and only later came to possess an essentialistic reference to psychic structure. Aristotle used these same notions in his organization of the disciplines into theoretical, practical, and productive.

One of the most telling developments in the creation of a coherent conception of self comes about with the transition from the Greek to the Judaeo-Christian cultural context. As has been argued by a number of different scholars, until the Stoics' and Augustine's ruminations upon the soul's relationship to God, the notion of will (*voluntas*) was not a part of the conception of personality.[10] The notion of "will," after all, requires a sense of over-against-ness that derives from a central power—God as Divine Caesar—who represents absolute authority. Another way of saying this is that to own *intention*, one must be *in tension* in some significant manner.

We have said enough to demonstrate the plausibility of the thesis that, from the sense of a chaotic matrix of shifting uncoordinated and unintegrated vital functions, to the expression of the tripartite structure in Plato and Aristotle, to the final articulations of the three modes of functioning as reason, passion, and will, Greek, Roman, and Judaic elements of Anglo-European cultural traditions contributed the contingent factors that eventuated in the modern conception of the self.

Whatever permutations of the self one might wish to highlight, the three general notions expressed by terms such as knowing, acting, and feeling will be involved at some level. No coherent analysis of these terms is possible, of course, for there have simply been too many theoretical proposals offered with respect to these modalities of psychic activity to make any final analysis either possible or even desirable. Nonetheless, a general analysis will serve to provide a background against which we might highlight the fragmentation of the modern self and the late modern celebration of that fragmentation as a means, finally, of preparing ourselves to understand the Chinese senses of self.

A major presumption of our tradition has been that legitimate knowledge must have resort to concepts or principles involving class concepts that have the effect of denying the idiosyncratic character of particulars. Whether knowing is said to precede or to be consequent upon praxis, it has, nonetheless, a shaping character since the practical forms of construing the world are reflections of the theoretical forms of shaping antecedent chaos in terms of the structures of mythopoetically described cosmos. The first philosophic question, the question to which *physis* was the answer, is: "What kinds of things are there?" Understanding the world in terms of a *kind* or *kinds* of things is the paradigmatic expression of knowledge in our tradition. It is this that introduces the notion of natural kinds characterized in terms of essential properties. This development has led us to ask after the meaning of an essential human nature, which grounds the core meaning of the self. Platonism finds this core self in a formal rationality, while Aristotelian naturalism finds it in the knowledge of ends or aims defining the nature of the human organism.

"Action" has its origins in the heroic model characterized by appeal to the *agon* or contest, which involves the assertion of an agent of such quality or magnitude as to certify either the agent's strength or courage in the face of the strength of an "other." This model derives from the Homeric tradition and continues to serve as one of the crucial interpretations of action in our tradition. An alternative model, paradigmatically expressed by St. Augustine in the fifth century, involves obedience to the all-powerful Will of God. The elements of *greatness* and *humility*, or excellence and deference, define the modalities of human action. In either case, there is the notion of assertion, be it that of the hero or the Divine agent.

The Greek concept of *agon* or contest that defined the context for the heroic notion of the individual did not provide a stable, continuous focus of authority in tension with which the notion of will could be established. That notion did not originate in our tradition until action was interpreted in relation to an authoritative Divine will. Modernity, then, charts the detachment of that notion from its theological context and the association of action with the volition of autonomous human beings. It is this that insures that *self-assertion* will constitute one of the principal defining characteristics of the modern age.[11]

The element of "feeling" is more diffuse in its signification than the other two modes of psychic expression. Perhaps it is best focused by the notion of "desire." The difficulty in understanding the mode of desiring lies in a failure to grasp its psychological underpinnings. Desiring is a wanting and, as the ambiguous word, "want" suggests, it is predicated upon a lack. When Plato defined *eros* as the "stepchild of abundance and need," he captured the essentials of passion. Absence of the desired object leads to desire. The presence or possession of the object (ostensibly the goal of desiring) mitigates or cancels the desire. We want what we do not, perhaps *cannot*, have.

One of the serious problems associated with the element of desiring concerns the contradiction between the need to possess a desired object and the even more primordial need to create an *object* out of that which is desired. The poignancy of the Platonic reading of desire is that, in objectifying and then possessing the goal of our desiring, we cancel the desire. This self-contradictory character of desiring is, of course, a major theme in most Buddhist and some Western psychologies.

Desire, as a category serving to shape our understandings of the self, has also received an important materialistic interpretation in terms of the notions of *pleasure* and *pain*. Materialist or mechanistic philosophies interpret desire as the motivation to promote pleasure and avoid pain. From the early hedonistic philosophies to the latter day Freudians and behaviorists, the self is seen as contingent upon its more or less successful attempts to maximize pleasure and minimize pain.

This broad survey of the contextualization of the self from out of the classical cultural resources highlights the elements which the Age of Enlightenment will take up in its effort to build the subjective autonomy and rational self-consciousness of the modern self. For we do not have a real concept of the self until we arrive at subjective, self-conscious ex-perience as the principal medium of self-articulation. This is, as we have said, a peculiarly modern occurrence in the West.

THE MODERN SELF

In tracing the complexities of the modern development of the self, one normally begins with Descartes' diremption of mind and body, which permitted a means of maintaining the material character of body as a part of physical nature while making room for strictly mentalist explanations. The development of materialist science from Galileo, Boyle, and Newton provided the grounds for physical reductionisms of positivism and behaviorism in which the self or personality is construed in terms of matter and motion. After Kant, mentalist explanations employed the explanatory matrix of the value spheres that, as we have seen, were analogous to the psychic modalities of reason, volition, and feeling.

One way of telling the story of the strictly modern self is by rehearsing the reading Hegel provided of Immanuel Kant's philosophic program.[12] According to Hegel, Kant's three critiques were in fact conscious attempts to ground the autonomy of the value spheres of art, science, and morality. Taking the analogy from Plato, Kant recognized that reason, passion, and (in the post-Augustinian age) will, as modalities of human experience, were focused by the cultural interests of science, art, and morality. The three critiques provided an account of the nature and limits of rational inquiry vis-à-vis the investigation of intellectual and practical culture.

Hegel claimed, however, that Kant was not sufficiently aware of the threat to the cultural autonomy of the value spheres. He decided that it was his mission to provide a philosophic rationale for the protection of these individual and cultural interests. Hegel's speculative system rehearsed in the most complete form the means of coming to cultural self-consciousness. With the advent of this exercise in cultural self-articulation, which involved the mediation through cultural forms of the various modalities of self-expression, the modern self, at least in principle, realized its apotheosis.

It was certainly the case that the modern world had already manifested other agents of self-interpretation. Descartes is often singled out as the first truly *modern* philosopher by virtue of his discovery of rational subjectivity; Francis Bacon may be said to provide a supplement to Descartes' project through the elaboration of the self as assertive agent and as a shepherd of technological progress. David Hume found in the passions of pride and envy, love and hate, the source of self-awareness and the meaning of individuality. Baudelaire, ringing the aesthetic variation of Hume's economic interpretation, stressed the creative, novelty-seeking artist as the paradigm of selfhood.

These thinkers could easily be understood as having stressed the importance to self-understanding of the elements of reason, volition, and passion respectively. But there is a sense in which, the obvious limitations of Hegelian philosophy to the contrary notwithstanding, the full conscious recognition of the complexity of the self is a post-Hegelian phenomenon that depends in some skewed manner upon the grandiosity of the Hegelian project.

The assault upon the Hegelian project came from numerous quarters, of course, but none was so devastating in its consequences as the critique offered by Søren Kierkegaard. It is one thing, said Kierkegaard, to realize in some abstract and speculative manner a vision of the harmony of the value spheres and of the modalities of self-expression that resonate with them, and quite another thing to come to grips with the concreteness of temporal experience. At the level of lived experience there seems no way of overcoming the concrete conflicts between the knowledge-bearing institutions, the propertied interests, and those technological activities that order the instrumentalities of society. Life is one thing; philosophy another.

Hegel's resolution of the diremption of the value spheres was a resolution in theory. It was comprehensive in itself, but remained essentially unrealized in the sphere of praxis. Other proposed resolutions, such as those offered by the Marxists or existentialists, constitute attempts to promote resolutions in practice. Even here, however, we are often offered mere *theories* of practice. Further, these practical approaches are both reductive and partial. That is, they require that personal and institutional choices be made that exclude real alternatives without providing an adequate rationale for this exclusion.

For example, though Marx's indignation at the alienated condition of the newly emergent proletariat was a justifiable decrying of the reduction of the self to the interests of property acquisition and ownership, the Marxian alternative errs in the opposite direction by collapsing the distinction between the theoretical and practical spheres in a manner that effectively cancels the life of disinterested intellectual activity. Relevance is gained at the cost of comprehensiveness.

There appears to be no means of establishing a preference of one view over another. If we are to be reasonable, however, we cannot simply be content with settling upon whichever theory or mode of praxis best suits us. The dominant views of the self, derived from the specialized, reductive, construals of selfhood in accordance with the rational, volitional, and affective paradigms are, of course, mutually incompatible. Further, that incompatibility has practical consequences by creating active tensions within each self-conscious self.

Faced with the alternatives of either narrowness or incoherence, the only rational choice seems to be that of attempting to avoid inconsistencies by tentatively accepting one of the various modalities of self-expression as the focus of one's sense of self. Even if this were possible, however, it would only result in externalizing the otherwise internal conflicts that come from attempting to modulate the tripartite self. The more individuals refuse to recognize the need to supplement within themselves the full range of the modalities of self-expression, the greater will be the conflict of ideologies and institutions within a society. Thus the so-called rational response to a pluralism of understandings and practices turns out, finally, to be rather *unreasonable*.

Perhaps the most reasonable approach to the plurality of beliefs and practices, though this may hardly seem satisfying, is simply to accede to the relativist *in theory*, while attempting to go one's own way in practice. Practical commitments do not gain any clarity or cogency by being supported by dogmatic claims to the truthfulness of a theory said to support or entail them. This is especially so if these claims are made in the face of a number of alternative theories. And any attempt to separate theory from practice in any final way assumes, illegitimately, that the vagueness of our understandings will not affect our actions. This is, of course, altogether naive.

MIXING METAPHORS: THE VAGUENESS OF THE SELF

In late modern culture, to be a self is to be incoherent or narrow; moreover, to *have* a self in these times is to recognize that our incompleteness, or our incoherent forms of self-articulation and expression, leads to a sense of fragmentation, manyness, and internal contradiction. Whether this condition is experienced as alienation, or as a complex aesthetic satisfaction, is the question that currently divides we late moderns.

Late modern theories offer an alternative to both narrowness and the negative construal of incoherence through a transfer of the criteria of relatedness away from the logical or rational to the aesthetic. On these terms, what was once unacceptable because expressive of divisiveness, inconsistency, and incoherence, is desirable because of its expression of aesthetic contrast and intensity. This reversion to what we have called "first-problematic thinking" issues in a correlative interpretation of the self.[13]

In this sort of interpretation, the paradigm of self-understanding has shifted from an ego-based, substance view, to that of the person as process. And the processive understanding of the self permits the serial realization of conflicting modalities of self-expression. The self as process is concerned with its potentially multifaceted "career" rather than its self-identity at any moment. This career is one in which various dimensions of expression are possible.

The denial of authorial presence, the absence of the omniscient narrator, and the general suppression of linear narrativity in fiction, along with the celebration of multiple personality constructs, the announcement of the "death of man" in the human and social sciences, all challenge the modern concept of the self as free, subjective, autonomous consciousness.

Each of these phenomena is an expression of the general disillusionment with the so-called "philosophy of presence" that according to Heidegger, Derrida, and the poststructuralists, has dominated philosophic discourse from the beginnings of Greek philosophy. The desire to make Being present through the beings of the world, to advertise the logos, essence, or logical form of that which is conceptually entertained, has created a profound bias toward the recognition of the sameness of the otherwise different, the pattern in the flux of passing circumstance.

With the failure of the philosophy of presence, however, comes the new project of thinking based upon the claims of difference. With respect to the self, one thinks difference by attempting to think the becoming of the self. By attempting to think *self-difference* rather than *self-sameness*, one denies the need for a *logos*, pattern, or structure that makes the self present to itself. In place of such a *logos* one celebrates the ever-not-quite, the always-only-passing, character of experience.

Though the project of thinking about change is no more easily realizable today than when Parmenides and Zeno advertised its rational impossibility, something has been gained by virtue of the critiques of Kierkegaard and others. At least this much is different: Whereas after the Parmenidean gambit, the principals of our cultural articulation chose reason and *logos* over the intuition of process and becoming, contemporaries faced with that same choice today are apt more readily to forego strict rationality if it precludes access to the temporal, processive, character of concrete experience.

This turn toward processive understandings of selfhood may be illustrated in many ways. Indeed, the appeal to notions of self as process is characteristic of both the metaphysical and nominalist strains of contemporary philosophy. The most elaborate analysis of self-as-process is to be found in those philosophies influenced by Henri Bergson, A. N. Whitehead, and Charles Hartshorne. According to the philosophy of process expressed by Whitehead, the self is a temporal route of occasions of experiencing. One could think of a string of beads strung out in time— but with the string removed. The transitory drops of experience con- stituting the actual occasions comprising the career that is, in fact, the self, are loosely tied together through the inheritance by the present occasion of relevant data from its predecessor. But without any notion of a substrate or core defining the permanent features of the self, the conviction that there must be a strict continuity of the self through time is called into question.

On this view, the self is constituted by its becoming, both in the sense that individual selves come into being and pass away, and in the sense that the career of such occasions that comprises the self through time is itself a process of becoming. Though understandings of the self, such as are presented by so-called process philosophers, are perhaps overly burdened by recourse to abstract metaphysical constructions, they do serve to indicate the turning away from substance views of selfhood that characterizes a large number of contemporary Western philosophies.

The turn toward processive understandings of selfhood may be found in distinctly nonmetaphysical thinkers as well. Richard Rorty, for example, has recently elaborated what he takes to be an argument of Donald Davidson[14] by contrasting the Freudian understanding of the relations of reason to the passions with traditional understandings from Plato to Hume. Far from claiming with Plato that reason is at war with the passions, or, with Hume, that "reason is, and ought only to be the slave of the passions, and can never pretend to any other office but to serve and obey them,"[15] Freud affirmed a continuity between "conscious" and "unconscious" that placed these two aspects of the personality on a par. Thus, the unconscious is as likely, or unlikely, to be rational as is the conscious mind.

On this view, the unconscious is no seething cauldron of chaotic passions, but is as coherent as is the conscious mind. The belief in such coherence is a consequence of the fact that the effects of the unconscious upon the conscious presumed by the Freudian vision requires that the former, as fully as the latter, be "a coherent and plausible set of beliefs and desires."[16] This coherence allows it to serve as a context within which matrices of desires and beliefs alternative to those abiding at the conscious level are to be found. These alternative networks form candidates for alternative selves that can, and often do, compete with the conscious self.

If we describe a self as a coherent set of beliefs and desires, and we allow for alternative sets of such beliefs abiding within a single person, then we have a new model for accounting for so-called "irrational behavior." Such behavior indicates that more than one set of beliefs and desires may serve as the reference for explaining a given act or set of behaviors. The interpretation of the unconscious then, is that it "can be viewed as an alternative set, inconsistent with the familiar set that we identify with consciousness, yet sufficiently coherent internally to count as a person."[17]

On this reading of the self, there is no war of reason against the passions, but a complex set of interactions between competing sets of beliefs and desires. This quasi-Freudian description of the human being is a primary illustration of the decentering of the self common to late modern thinkers. Such decentering well illustrates the vagueness of selfhood presupposed in our discussions to this point. Among the hyperconscious intellectuals of late modern culture, self-awareness becomes the awareness of a number of potential ways of being. Further this notion of the decentering of the self is a variant of the process view sketched earlier, since the designation of *the* self requires resort to a shifting set of references. By contrast to the Whiteheadian view in which the self is a route of occasions strung out in time, this revised version of Freud suggests that the self is an aggregate of sets of beliefs and desires existing contemporaneously.

Another sign of the fact that "difference" reigns with respect to our understandings of the self is the manner in which characterizations of the self have become fragmented and compartmentalized in the name of specialization. For example, the conception of the person most emphasized in John Rawls' writings is deemed "moral," or "political," as opposed to religious, scientific, legal, or philosophical. Rawls' conception of the person is a normartive conception,

> one that begins from our everyday conception of persons as the basic units of thought, deliberation, and responsibility, and adapted to a political conception of justice, and not to a comprehensive doctrine. It is in effect a political conception of the person, and given the aims of justice as fairness, a conception suitable for the basis of democratic citizenship. As a normative conception it may be distinguished from an account of human nature given by natural science and social theory.[18]

More and more we find such stipulations among theoreticians. There is the increased recognition that theories are stipulative contexts that deal with partial perspectives on subjects that may be thought to receive "comprehensive" treatment elsewhere. Of course, there are increasingly few resorts to such comprehensive theories, and the few that are offered are met with the suspicion currently directed at metaphysics and speculative philosophy in general. As a consequence, the self is fragmented both within and without. This is but to say that the self is conceptualized as processive and/or internally diremted, or is parcelled out among any number of specialized theories in a manner that prevents any sense of the whole, if such a whole there be.

The embarrassment of modernity lies in the obvious failure of the creators and purveyors of intellectual culture to demonstrate the efficacy of reason in establishing a consensual basis for our scientific, social, and political institutions. One of the casualties of this project has been the notion of "rational self-consciousness" upon which the free, autonomous activity of the modern self was to have been predicated.

Late modernism celebrates aesthetic criteria of evaluation, such as intensity and contrast. Both the self created by recourse to these criteria and the self engaged in employing these criteria are functions of the creative juxtapositioning of intensely contrasting features developed from traditional modalities of self-articulation. Instead, however, of seeking a rational accommodation, the elements of the self are held together by the claims of aesthetic enjoyment.

The late modern self returns to its origins in aesthetic plurality, but it arrives with the gift of reflexive consciousness. In the beginning, human beings *were* selves but they didn't *have* their selves. At present, a plural, aesthetic self has an awareness both of its plurality and of the insistent particularity of the elements which variously focus that plurality. As we shall soon see, this aesthetic consciousness rehearses something like the Daoist vision of no-soul, or no-self (*wuwo* 無我 or *wuji* 無己) that rejects the unitary self, and affirms the self as a locus of sometimes consistent, and sometimes less than consistent, experiences.

The above rehearsal of the relevance of the four primary semantic contexts and the tripartite structure of the soul for understanding discussions of the meaning of the self may be fruitfully supplemented by a consideration of the issues of sex and gender.

In the West there is a strong tendency to construe important contrasts as disjunctive by virtue of the pervasiveness in our culture of dualistic contrasts rooted in the being/not-being problematic. This problematic has its strongest illustration in the logical contrast of "p" and "not-p." This linguistic pattern is an important signal and/or determinant of the manner *in which* contrasting pairs are construed.

This is easy enough to see with respect to the semantic variations played upon the gender distinction. Materialists, from Lucretius to Freud, are hard put to characterize anything like a significant relationship between male and female and must either deal with them as two separate beings (the Lucretian option) or, as with Freud, in terms of the female as an incomplete male. From the Lucretian perspective,

> . . . frame unto frame they wildly lock,
> Mingling the moisture of their mouths, and e'en
> Draw in each other's breath, as teeth on lips
> They madly press; yet all in vain, since naught
> Can they remove therefrom, nor penetrate
> Body in body, and thus merge in one.[19]

If the nature of things is defined by atoms and empty space (being and not-being), then any two beings separated by not-being can never overcome the separation, can never "penetrate body in body, and thus merge in one." In a materialist world, all relationships are finally extrinsic.

Aristophanes' familiar myth of the round men makes the problematic of sexual separation quite clear: after Zeus divides the round men, each sundered part seeks its complement. The consequence in the beginning is disaster, since once the pairs struggle to reunite, they smother one another or prevent their complements from getting nourishment. Zeus seeks to solve the problem through the invention of the orgasm. Now pairs unite for but a little while, and then are able to go about the business of the day. The implication of this colorful myth is that love drives us to seek unity, while physical sex permits us to maintain autonomy.[20] Plato's response to the myth of Aristophanes is to find unity by abstracting from difference. Gender is a bodily affair; the rational *psyche* is asexual. In Plato's heaven, as in that of St. Paul, "there is neither marrying nor giving in marriage."

Volitional understandings of the sexes are defined by the power relationship. The interactions between male and female are construed as struggle for dominance. Love is seen as seduction in which one party gains victory over the other. It is not always the female who surrenders. As much romantic poetry suggests, the power of female beauty is often the occasion of male surrender.

The materialist finds no unity possible; the formalist finds unity without ultimate difference. The volitional thinker maintains the relationship of dependence of the ruled upon the ruler. (Though as Hegel's famous discussion of the master/slave relationship suggests, the ruler/ruled relationship is often one of mutual dependence.) On the organicist model, there is a recognition of functional difference in which a degree of complementarity is achieved through procreation, the nurturing of children, and the functional specialization of household and public institutions. In the Western tradition, this model has traditionally been thought most promising for defending parity and the complementarity of the sexes.

There are attempts among some contemporary Western thinkers to appeal to models which promote complementarity. The mystical *coincidentia oppositorum* associated with Nicholas Cusanus, and the androgynous models associated with the ancient Gnostic myths, and the modern Jungian *anima/animus* characterization of personality, stress such complementarity. But, for the most part, these models have received inadequate philosophical elaboration.

Western thinkers may easily forget the importance of the male/female distinction since our thinking is arguably shaped by a reduction of one of these genders (almost always the female) to the other, and a subsequent resort to a putatively neutral, but certainly gender-biased, language of theory.

Summarizing our argument thus far: The fundamental senses of self in the Western tradition appeal to at least three sets of distinctions: The first utilizes the four primary semantic contexts defined by the metaphors of matter, mind, organism, and will. The second involves three psychic modalities of thinking, acting, and feeling that constitute the tripartite functioning of *psyche*. The third involves the gender distinction.

We have not sought to provide detailed examples of the various theories that specify the senses of self in our tradition. Our concern has been to celebrate the fundamental categories that ground more specific theories. For it is at this, quite general, level that one can best understand the theoretical distance that exists, for the most part, between Chinese and Western philosophical understandings. And if it is found to exist here, one must expect equally profound differences when these general categories are employed to build more specific theories. In what follows we shall attempt to develop the Chinese understanding of selfhood against the background of the three sets of distinctions assayed above. In so doing we shall be able to demonstate the pragmatic value of our, thus far, quite general approach.

Our argument is that, in our efforts to understand the Chinese, we must be cautious in applying home-grown concepts and categories such as we have just considered. It is easy enough to show that comparative philosophy aimed at understanding the Chinese sensibility has not, to this point, been able to accomplish this adequately. By writing large Western philosophical speculations concerning the meaning of self, we are attempting to remain alert to the major sorts of roadblocks that stand in the way of an appropriate appreciation of Chinese sensibilities.

(Our task, therefore, is to indicate the irrelevance of the philosophic inventory rehearsed above to Chinese understandings of self. First, the four primary semantic contexts will be shown to provide misleading categories that we shall have to qualify as carefully as possible in our attempts to understand Chinese notions of self. Secondly, with regard to the tripartite structure of the psyche, we shall find, particularly within Daoism, something like a reversal of the sense of these modalities that will require a significant transvaluation of the categories of thinking, acting, and feeling. Finally, in the last chapter of this part, we shall examine the distinctive manners in which the gender question has been treated in China and the West, and attempt to show some of the consequences of these different treatments for understanding the contrasting senses of self in China and the West.

CHAPTER TWO

The Focus-Field Self in Classical Confucianism

THE "SELFLESS" SELF

If, as we shall argue, the interpretative vocabulary associated with Chinese constructions of what we would identify as "self" or "person" is radically distinct from that drawn from the primary semantic contexts forming the major interpretative constructs in our tradition, we must acknowledge that we are in a difficult situation. The best way of indicating the nature of this situation is to say that, if we are to be strictly limited to the interpretative categories associated with the Western theories of the self, the Chinese are, quite literally, "selfless."

We begin our discussion with this rather extreme bit of rhetoric because it helps to focus the differences both Chinese and Westerners have always understood to qualify their distinctive modes of self-understanding. One of the most prevasive characterizations of the Chinese people is the degree of their "selflessness," their "self-abnegation." Such characterizations are not generally meant to convey the inappropriateness of applying Western understandings of "person" and "self" to the Chinese. Rather, the assumption is that the Chinese have selves pretty much as we do, but have chosen to yield them up in the service of the society or state. Much can be gained, perhaps, by beginning our discussion with what we take to be the rather faulty rationale behind the assumption that the Chinese are necessarily self-abnegating—that they are those sorts of beings who are primarily motivated by the need to suppress their interests on behalf of the well-being of the group.

In arguing against this interpretation, we will suggest the more important sense of "selflessness" as applied to the Chinese suggests the irrelevance of any notion of self defined primarily in terms of: (1) rational consciousness, (2) physiological (neurochemical; sociobiological) reduction, (3) volitional activity, or (4) organic (biological and social) functioning. Since these elements illustrate the dominant models that ground our Western senses of self, the Chinese may, at least from a Western perspective, be considered quite literally, "selfless." Moreover, it is the confusion resulting from the misapplication of these irrelevant categories that has led scholars so often to see the Chinese as "selfless," self-abnegating creatures whose "consciousness," "will," "desires," and "aims" are wholly absorbed by the society, community, or state of which they are a part.

Much, if not most, of the contemporary commentary available on Chinese attitudes to individual human rights assumes that selflessness in this sense of self-abnegation is a traditional Chinese ideal. Donald J. Munro, for example, argues that:

selflessness . . . is one of the oldest values in China, present in various forms in Taoism and Buddhism, but especially in Confucianism. The selfless person is always willing to subordinate his own interests, or that of some small group (like a village) to which he belongs, to the interest of a larger social group.[1]

R. Randle Edwards combines the presumption of a Chinese homogeneity with his observation of preestablished social patterns to reinforce Munro's interpretation of this supposed Chinese ideal:

most Chinese view society as an organic whole or seamless web. Strands in a web must all be of a certain length, diameter, and consistency, and must all be fitted together in accordance with a preordained pattern. . . . The hope is that each individual will function as properly as a cog in an ever more efficient social machine.[2]

Both Munro and Edwards construe the Confucian model as a collectivism in which individual interests are insignificant except when they are of service to those of the group.

It can be, of course, be argued that Chinese understandings of self do not entail a strong notion of "individuality." The Western notion of the separate, distinct, individual in its various forms is anathema to the Chinese. We should not, however, think that because we most often associate self-actualization with individuated existence, there can be no appreciation and personal enjoyment of an alternative understanding of uniqueness among the Chinese.

The term "individual" can mean either one-of-a-*kind*, like a human being, or *one*-of-a-kind, like Turner's "Seastorm." That is, "individual" can refer to a single, unitary, separate, and indivisible thing that, by virtue of some essential property or properties, qualifies as a member of a class. By virtue of its membership in a kind or class, it is substitutable. Thus, all individuals are equal before the law, loci of human rights, and entitled to equal opportunities; each is one of God's children, and so on. It is this definition of individual that generates notions such as autonomy, equality, liberty, freedom, will, and so on. Such a self relates to its world only extrinsically.

Individual can also mean *unique*. A unique individual has the character of a single and unsubstitutable particular, such as a work of art, that might be formally comparable to other such works, but that remains, nonetheless, qualitatively unique. This sense of individual does not entail assumptions about class membership. Under this definition of individual, equality can only mean parity. It is this sense of "unique individuality" that is helpful in understanding the traditional Confucian conception of self.

In the model of the unique individual, determinacy lies in the achieved quality of one's multivalent relationships. A person becomes recognized, distinguished, or renowned by virtue of communal deference to the quality of one's character. Much of the effort in understanding the traditional Confucian conception of self has to do with clarifying this distinction between autonomy and uniqueness. While the definition of self as irreducibly social certainly precludes autonomous individuality, it does not rule out the second, less familiar notion of uniqueness expressed in terms of *my* roles and *my* relationships.

Attributing the ideal of self-abnegation to the Chinese tradition involves importing both the public/private and the individual/society distinctions. To be selfless in the sense presupposed by some commentators on Chinese culture requires that an individual self first exist, and then that it be sacrificed for some higher public interest. And the suggestion that there are higher interests on the part of either person or society covertly establishes a boundary between them that justifies an adversarial relationship. The interpretation of these commentators does not support the claim that a person in the Chinese tradition is irreducibly social; ironically, it vitiates it.

This attribution of selflessness to the Chinese tradition, both ancient and modern, seems to arise out of a misunderstanding of the relationship between "selfishness" and "selflessness." To eschew selfish concerns does not necessarily lead to self-effacement. Paradoxically, it is selfishness in the usual sense that can lead to the loss of self. After all, if one attempts to take more than one's share of the resources of a society, that action impoverishes the modes of interaction that alone are capable of engendering the communication of shared meanings. Without such communication, individuals are cut off from the community of participation and communication that alone can serve to humanize. Aggressive autonomy leads to alienation. It is only if one has a view of society as constituted by already individuated, particularized members that one can promote the sort of autonomy that we often see in Western democratic societies.

In the Confucian model where the self is contextual, it is a shared consciousness of one's roles and relationships. One's "inner" and "outer" (neiwai 內外) selves are inseparable. Here, one is self-conscious, not in the sense of being able to isolate and objectify one's essential self, but in the sense of being aware of oneself as an locus of observation by others. The locus of self-consciousness is not in the "I" detached from the "me," but in the consciousness of the "me." This involves an image of self determined by the esteem with which one is regarded in community, an image of self that is captured in the language of face and shame.[3]

Mark Elvin is especially sensitive to the importance of unique place in the traditional Chinese world:

> The Chinese believed, by and large, in a unique personal existence, no doubt fortified by the concept of a structure of kinship ascendants and descendants, stretching indefinitely forward into the future, in which the individual occupied his unique place.[4]

This Chinese conception of unique place stands in contrast to the autonomous individuality that attends the isolation of the soul from other souls,

and from the illusory world of sensual perception. The uniqueness of the
Chinese person is immanent and embedded within a ceaseless process of
social, cultural, and natural changes.

Another way of making our case is to look at the cluster of Chinese
terms that characterize the self in terms of the relationship between "self"
(*ji* 己), "other" (*ren* 人), and as a cultivated "authoritative person" (*ren* 仁).
Our argument will be that *ren* 仁 is what Confucius means by "self." But
if *ren* 仁 is "self," what then of *ji* 己, which we conventionally render "self"
in a seemingly standard self/other (*ji/ren* 己/人) distinction? In the
Analects we read:

> Yan Yuan inquired about *ren* 仁. The Master replied, "Self-
> discipline (*keji* 克己) and practicing the rites will make one *ren*.[5]
> If for the space of a day one were able to accomplish this, the
> whole empire would turn to him as a model of *ren*. Becoming
> *ren* is self-originating (*youji* 由己)—how could it originate with
> others?"[6]

We must remember that Confucian distinctions such as "self/other"
are mutually entailing and interdependent correlatives, and are not dualistic in the sense of representing some underlying ontological disparity.
Yin 陰 is always "becoming *yang* 陽," and *yang* is always "becoming *yin*,"
just as "day" is a "becoming night" and "night" is a "becoming day." For
the *ji/ren* distinction, "oneself" is always a "becoming other," and an
"other" is always "becoming oneself."

The function, then, of disciplining *ji* through ritual practice is to take
up the appropriate place (*wei* 位) for oneself in relationship to other
persons in community. This is *not* to say that *ji* defines a disjunctive relation between self and other. Confucian language suggests that relations
of self and other are intrinsic and thus constitutive of self.[7]

We shall elaborate upon this issue later on when we consider a more
constructive notion of selfhood in the Chinese tradition, but we should
at least note here that the model of society that sustains an appropriate
sense of individuality is one that achieves a balance of what Whitehead
has called "individual absoluteness" and "individual relativity."[8] Such a
model construes the relatedness of individuals to social groupings in such
a manner as to enrich and intensify the self-actualizing potential of the
individuals.

It is commonly noticed that in China, from ancient times to the
present, conflicts are generally dealt with through informal mechanisms

for mediation and conciliation as close to the dispute as possible.[9] Ideally, society has been regulated through ritually defined relationships, and thus has often required relatively minimal government. It is this same communal harmony that defines and dispenses order at the most immediate level that is also relied upon to define and express authoritative consensus without more obvious formal provisions for effecting popular sovereignty. Clearly, to the extent that the Confucian model is a project of cultivation directed at self-realization, the social and political order is derived from the participants themselves, who cannot thereby be construed as self-abnegating. While it is true that, on the traditional Chinese model, self-realization does not permit a high degree of individual autonomy, it does not follow that the alternative to autonomy is capitulation to a general will. Rather, Confucian "personalism," to use Wm. Theodore de Bary's felicitous term,[10] involves benefiting and being benefited by membership in a world of reciprocal loyalties and obligations which surround and stimulate a person, and which define one's own worth.

THE MINDLESS SELF

G. W. F. Hegel was typical of nineteenth-century Western thinkers when in his *Philosophy of History* he said of China:

> Its distinguishing feature is, that everything which belongs to Spirit—unconstrained morality, in practice and theory, Heart, inward Religion, Science and Art properly so called—is alien to it.[11]

This presumption is grounded in a particular sort of disposition that first equates subjective autonomy with "mind" or "spirit" in the essentially Platonic sense of the term, and then finds the Chinese lacking in autonomy and individuality because they lack those characteristcics so defined.

Jacques Gernet makes the distinction between the traditional Chinese notions of self and familiar Western concepts by rejecting the relevance of the mind/body, and reason/experience disjunctions for the Chinese experience:

Not only was the substantial opposition between the soul and the body something quite unknown to the Chinese, all souls being, in their view, destined to be dissipated sooner or later, but so was the distinction, originally inseparable from it, between the sensible and the rational. The Chinese had never believed in the existence of a sovereign and independent faculty of reason. The concept of a soul endowed with reason and capable of acting freely for good or for evil, which is so fundamental to Christianity, was alien to them.[12]

If we look within the Chinese tradition for a correlate of "mind" and "rationality," we discover a cluster of three important terms—*xin* 心, *li* 理, and *zhi* 知. The term *xin* 心, often translated as "heart-mind" refers indifferently to activities we would classify as thinking, judging, and feeling, and arguably reflects all three modalities of the tripartite model in an undissected form. Prior to the entrance of Buddhism into China, *xin* is most successfully translated as "heart-mind" or, appropriately privileging physiological function over anatomy, "feelings."[13] The translation of *xin* in classical Confucian and Daoist texts exclusively as "mind" would almost certainly misdirect the Western reader.[14] The most important inference about the meanings of *xin* is that none of them, even after the Buddhist incursion, suggests a basic mind-body dualism. This dualism was systematized in the Platonic corpus, further ramified by Christian theologians, and finally, after Descartes, became one of the most influential problematics of modern philosophy.

Taking the nondualistic character of *xin* into account, there is no justification for interpreting any Chinese notion of selfhood along the formalist lines as they developed in the West. The self cannot be dichotomized. The "purity" of mind abstracted from context, therefore, cannot be maintained.

The second notion, then, that might be supposed to tend toward mentalist interpretations of the self is the Chinese term most often associated with reason and reasoning, *li* 理. In the absence of an ontological tradition, the act of understanding and articulating the *dao* of things—*daoli* 道理, literally, the dynamic patternings in the ways of things—cannot have ontological reference. In general, to be *heli* 合理— to be "in accord with *li*"—is to be reasonable or rational. *Dilixue* 地理學 in modern Chinese is "the investigation of the patterns of the earth," and

is a translation of what we term "geography." "Psychology" is translated as
xinlixue 心理學, which means "the investigation of the patterns of the
heart-mind." To be *heli* means for the heart-mind to be functioning in a
fully integrated way within its various physical and psychological
contexts.

Li 理 has also often been translated "principle," generating
considerable confusion on the part of a generation of Western interpreters of Chinese, encouraged as they are to assume that *li* must, at some
level, be transcendent. But *li*, as a "making sense of things," cannot be
understood as a process of seeking principles as determining sources of
order, or of discovering essential categories inclusive of particular things.
Li involves an analogical activity that constructs categories (*lei* 類) anal-
ogically, then traces, again by analogical means, correlated details that
manifest patterns of relationships immanent within things and events.
This sort of reasoning depends upon noninferential access to enlarged
and deepened patternings. Inclusion or exclusion of items within a
"category" is not associated with notions of logical type or class—the
sortings are analogical, not logical.[15] Chinese reasoning is radically situated and cannot be interepreted as residing in a transcendental or superordinated self.

The third term, *zhi* 知, is conventionally translated "to know, to
realize, to be wise, wisdom," and is to be distinguished in several ways from
knowing as a primarily theoretical activity. First, the etymology of *zhi* 知,
according to Bernhard Karlgren, is probably the combination of "person"
(*ren* 人) and "mouth" (*kou* 口)=㠯, suggesting that *zhi* is a sociological
rather than psychological event. *Zhi* is a communal achievement that
emerges out of effective communication.

Zhi is always characteristic of a particular, unfolding human situation
that cannot be reduced to mental states. It is not an abstractive process,
but a profoundly concrete activity that seeks to maximize existing possibilities and contributing conditions. Knowing is getting the most out
of any situation. It is to "*actualize*" or "*realize*" the world. As such, the
"realizer" is not independent of the realized circumstances, but rather is
a constitutent element in the creative enterprise of making a world.

Zhi is often understood as "foreknowledge" because of this strong
performative connotation. It is not access to some revelatory source, but
rather the ability to anticipate a particular future, and the strength of
character to consolidate the human community in such a manner as to

make it happen. That the presence of some achieved authoritative person (ren 仁) is a precondition for zhi is suggested by the fact that ren and zhi are so often found together in the formative Confucian texts. The robust relationships that are entailed by ren are necessary conditions for the communal harmony that produces zhi.

Another association with zhi is "enjoyment." Knowledge and happiness are mutually entailing. Thinking and feeling are not separate, but occur together as the concrete human expression of the resolutely contextualized "heart-mind." Zhi, like li and xin, is thus radically situated, integrating the human world and its natural, social, and cultural environments.

THE BODILESS SELF

There are two problems in attempting to discern the relevance of the materialist paradigm to the understanding of the meaning of the self in the Chinese cultural tradition. The first concerns the degree to which the Chinese have developed anything like an atomistic or materialistic understanding of the world. The second is the extent to which Chinese intellectual culture has been shaped by the dialectic of a mind-body dualism. We have commented sufficiently upon the absence of a mind/body dichotomy in the previous section. In the following discussion, we shall see that the perception of the body in the broad sweep of the Chinese tradition precludes anything like a materialistic or atomistic interpretation, as well. Having done this, we shall have demonstrated the need for real caution in the application of either formalist or materialist assumptions in the interpretation of Chinese understandings of "self."[16]

The Chinese conception of body is integrally related to the fundamental project of "cultivating oneself" (xiushen 修身), where shen in this expression has strong physical connotations in referring to "one's person." In the Great Learning, one of the Confucian Four Books, we read:

> From the Son of tian down to the commoner, all should take self-cultivation as their foundational concern.

The expression and "performance" of the body, like other Confucian preoccupations such as the practice of ritual, the playing of music, the writing of calligraphy, or the composition of literature, is a medium for self-articulation. Thus, in classical China, human realization is the fashioning and configuring of one's *entire* person: *ren* 仁, 道, 空

The centrality of ritual practice (*li* 禮) in Confucianism is clear when we begin from Confucius' premise that personal accomplishment is measurable in terms of the quality of the relationships that one is able to effect. It is "ritualizing," taken in its broadest sense, that enables persons to assume roles which define their appropriate relationships with others. It is a social syntax that enables them to communicate with others, and in so doing, to constitute themselves as a matrix of relationships. The interlocking pattern of relationships, where focused and individuated, is the particular person, both psychic and somatic. The "field" that both constitutes and is constituted by these foci is the community.

These ritualized roles and practices, never separate from the physical body, shape and are shaped by the community in which they are performed, and provide the community with both its identity and its character. The terms for body (*ti* 體) and ritual (*li* 禮) are cognate, sharing as they do the core idea of articulated form.

The language used to describe ritual practice is suggestive of the intimate relationship between one's physical figure, and one's interpersonal and social configuration. Ritual action is not only *synchronic*, in the sense that it is constitutive of a given social present; it is also *diachronic*, since a community's cultural memory is this body of formalized actions that displays the cumulative investment of meaning and importance (*yi* 義) of one's precursors in the cultural tradition. Ritualized roles and institutions, as a corpus of meaning-invested practices, preserve and transmit cultural significance. For this reason, the performance and embodiment of the ritual tradition both socializes and makes one a member of a community. Ritual informs the particular person with shared values and provides one with the opportunity to integrate in a way conducive to the maintenance and enrichment of community. And the lived body is the concrete and particular medium through which the substance of the tradition is expressed. It is this shared, participatory harmony at all levels, physical as well as psychical, that Confucianism seeks to cultivate as productive of human enjoyment.

Ritual practices are not simply standards of appropriateness sedimented within a cultural tradition that serve to shape and regulate its participants; they have a significant creative dimension since what distinguishes ritual from rule or principle as a source of order is that ritual practices not only *inform* the participants of what is proper, they are also *performed* by them. They are formal structures that, to be efficacious, must be personalized to accommodate the uniqueness and the quality of each participant. In this sense, ritual actions are a pliant body of codes for registering, developing, and displaying one's own sense of importance. The relationship between ritual practice and body is apparent in the way that ritual articulates a boundary "skin" at the interface between interior and exterior, between person and community.

A physical notion related to the Confucian way (*dao* 道) in expressing the classical Confucian concept of natural order is *wen* 文, meaning "to enscribe," "pattern," and "patterning." Just as the firmament displays its elegance as a celestial pattern (*tianwen* 天文), so the human world as "the heart-mind of heaven and earth" expresses its accomplished patterns as culture (*wenhua* 文化). *Wen* is "pattern" where aesthetic value and meaning are co-present. *Wen* is writing, both in the sense of literature (*wenxue* 文學) and the written word (*wenzi* 文字). It is elegance (*wenti* 文體) and style (*wenfeng* 文風); it is education in the humanities (*wenjiao* 文教); it is civilization (*wenming* 文明). *Wen* 紋 are the wrinkles on an older person's face that reflect character and experience. It is the creative and expansive civil side of being human (*wen*) in contrast with the destructive and delimiting yet ineluctable military occupations (*wu* 武). In short, *wen* encompasses those refining vocations of the human being that, in Confucian terms, make one most fully human.

These various processes of refinement covered by the term *wen* share the same cultural dynamic as ritual action. That is, the creative product is the consequence of the play between one's personal uniqueness and some continuing historical structure or aesthetic convention. New cultural models are continually emerging as qualitatively achieved persons who personalize formal ritual practices, write commentary on some canonical text, or create some particular variation on a conventional example of calligraphy or a painting prized by the tradition.

The physiological language that is used as categories to describe and evaluate the formation of Chinese characters, establishes a rather overt analogy with the ritually engaged body. Like a "literary corpus" or "a body of rituals," the written character is an articulated model that registers and expresses the growth and refinement of the participating calligrapher. There is a supporting kinesthetic structure—a skeleton, if you will—that defines the underlying form. But these "bones" (*gu* 骨), invested with a communally shared meaning, carry the lived body of the artist. The "flesh" (*rou* 肉) and "sinew" (*jin* 筋) of the brushstroke disclose the substance and shape of the Chinese character. The "blood" (*xue* 血), "pulse" (*mo* 脈), and "life breath" (*qi* 氣) of the stroke reveal movement, balance, rhythm, and action.[17] The formation of the character itself is a ritual performance, at once appropriating and disclosing meaning. It is communicative, and reflects both the quality of its performer and its audience. Like the lived body, the character is a transformative configuration.

Ritual practices, and the lived body (*shen* 身) through which they are expressed, are necessary conditions for the Confucian vision of communal harmony because they not only allow, but actually require, full personal participation in their performance. "Propriety," a frequently encountered alternative translation for ritual action, reflects the expectation that the performance of ritual action is an appropriation for oneself of formalized patterns of action through which to express one's own meaning. The creative complements of ritual practice entail both an "appropriating from" and a "being appropriate to." The achieved social harmony is predicated on the premise that people are unique, and that they must orchestrate themselves into relationships that permit expression of this uniqueness.

Ritual practices are invariably unique not only because they require personalization, but because they display the qualitative differences of the performers. The significance of ritual practice and its potential to produce social harmony is a direct function of the cultivated quality of it several participants:

> What does one who is not authoritative in his person have to
> do with ritual performance or with music?[18]

Community characterized through the combined creativity of its members is programmatic and open-ended; it exists neither as an immediate reality nor as a fixed ideal. It is rather an aesthetic achievement, contingent upon particular ingredients and inspiration. Like a true work of art, it cannot be produced by the mere application of a formula or a blueprint.

What is most fundamentally and significantly human in the Confucian tradition are the seemingly indeterminate possibilities for growth, cultivation, and refinement. The natures of certain things will perforce remain relatively constant. But the human being, that entity most given to cultivation and refinement, is dynamic. The relatively constant tendencies that constrain the creative project of personal development are one's natural and cultural legacy. But it is against this legacy that one displays one's humanity.

THE AIMLESS SELF

Another model often incautiously applied in explanation of the Confucian conception of self is that of the Western metaphor of organism.[19] In the West, the term "organism" is primarily resourced in the philosophy of Aristotle, whose use of the model of biological organism provided the structural coherence of his thinking.

Aristotle thought of an organism as a vital whole whose parts acted in accordance with an organizing *telos* or aim. The root meaning of organism was established with reference to the biological sphere then analogized into the other aspects of Aristotle's system. Thus, in investigating a particular subject, it is the function, purpose, or goal inherent in the activities exemplified or enjoined with respect to that subject that serves to organize the investigation. In the study of the ethical activity of the human being, one is concerned with the purpose of the individual, broadly defined as "happiness." In political discussions, one asks after the purpose of the *polis* as an institution meant to guarantee justice and parity.

The fruitfulness of the organic metaphor in Western scientific and philosophic speculations has made it a tempting candidate for use in comparative Chinese-Western discussions. Prominent among those who have appealed to the notion of organism to account for important aspects of the classical Chinese cultural sensibility are Joseph Needham[20] and Benjamin Schwartz.[21]

Needham's use of the term "organism," however, is somewhat Pickwickian. Though he appeals variously to thinkers such as Leibniz and Whitehead to support his discussions, it turns out that Needham's understanding of "organicist thinking" vitiates a principal component of the model. According to Needham,

> When Leibniz speaks of the difference between machines and organisms as lying in the fact that every monad constituting the

organism is alive and co-operating in a harmony of wills, we
are irresistibly reminded of the "harmony of the wills" so characteristic of Chinese associative thinking.[22]

But elsewhere Needham is at pains to deny the strictly teleological
character of Chinese organic thinking, claiming that the Chinese
required no "guiding principle," and that "to them . . . cooperation of the
component parts was spontaneous, *even involuntary*, and this alone was
enough."[23] Effectively, then, whatever Needham means by "organicism"
must exclude the central characteristic of the principal meanings of
"organicism" in the classical West—namely, that of a guiding teleology.

Needham is clearer about the sense he gives to the organic model
when, referring to the *Yijing* (*Book of Changes*) as a "cosmic-filing system,"
he wonders: "Was the compelling power which it had in Chinese
civilisation due to the fact that it was a view of the world basically
congruent with the bureaucratic social order?"[24] It seems clear, as we have
argued in another context,[25] that Needham has applied the notion of
organism to the Chinese sensibility in an ambiguous way by not giving
an adequate account of the significant differences between biological
"organism" and bureaucratic "organization."[26] It is the latter sense that
more closely approximates the model to which the classical Chinese
appeal in understanding the world about them.

Benjamin Schwartz's offers a qualified agreement with Needham's
claims that the Chinese have an organismic worldview, and at times
presses much farther in the direction of more classical Western understandings of the organic model. But, finally, Schwartz makes the same
move as does Needham, affirming the prominence of the "bureaucratic
model" and the "state analogy." Applauding Needham's characterization
of the *Yijing* as a "cosmic filing system," Schwartz adds: "Indeed, one might
say that the 'state analogy' may be much more important as a paradigm
of Chinese holism and organicism than the biological organism."[27]
Schwartz follows Donald Munro in challenging the suitability of Needham's use of the organic metaphor, preferring the family metaphors
pervasive in the early cosmologies, and defining of the specifically genealogical cosmogonies.[28]

When, shortly, we come to suggest a model for the construal of
Chinese understandings of selfhood, we will discuss the relevance of
sociopolitical constructs such as state, bureaucracy, and so on, in terms of
what we, along with Munro, take to be the basic metaphor from which

understandings of self, society, and the external surround may best be understood. Our "focus-field" conception of the self, which we shall discuss in some detail later, is fundamentally a familial model. It is not one, however, that presupposes a strictly organic model of the family.

We endorse Needham's claim that the organismic interpretations of neo-Confucianism likely were derived from a "bureaucratic" and "administrative" model. We also believe Munro correct in claiming that familial relations constituted the ground for Chinese understandings of the world about them. Familial order is fundamental in determining at least the Confucian sense of self. And the bureaucratic structure and the state itself are extensions of familial order. That is to say, the self is primarily focal within the family field. The other fields by which the individual is contextualized are continuous with the family model. One may recall, for example, that among the Confucian "five relationships," the relation of father and son is employed to explicate the relation of ruler and people, as well as ruler and *tian* 天 The relationship between *tian* as the firmament and *di* 地 as the earth is defined in traditional lexicons as a "father and mother" relationship.

THE NONWILLING SELF

A final Western candidate for interpreting the Chinese conception of self is the metaphor of "volitional activity." It is perhaps easier to establish the inappropriateness of this metaphor, largely because there is a greater consensus upon the merely contingent character of the notion of "will" in the Western tradition. As we discussed at some length in *Anticipating China*,[29] a number of scholars, arguing from a variety of perspectives, have concluded that the concept of "will" in its recognizable forms emerged out of the debates associated with the Stoics of the early centuries of the common era and received its first subtle presentation in the work of St. Augustine. After Augustine, the interpretation of the "spirited" faculty of the Platonic *psyche* in terms of volitional categories came to dominate philosophic speculation.

There are two implications of the metaphor of volitional activity that bode ill for its use as a means of understanding Chinese conceptions of the self. The first is that volition as an individuating principle leads to the construal of beings as agents characterized in terms of power relations. The will, directed outward, leads to a linear expression of efficacy that makes it difficult to achieve real harmony without recourse to a greater will that forces consensus. Volitional activity is born from out of an *agon*, a struggle of one agent against another. The sort of interactions that are likely to take place among selves characterized by the dominance of volition would be truly counterproductive in a society grounded in communal forms of ritual practice.

Disc.mivd   A second implication of the volitional metaphor is to be found in the implicated notion of "decision." Freedom of the will is expressed through the ability to decide among alternatives. The ethics that derives from the notion of volition permits the dissociation of decisional acts from ideas and dispositions. One can choose contrary to that which one knows to be the "right" way; likewise, one can decide against the dispositional leanings that otherwise might sway one. Any interpretation of the self that would lead to the separation of idea and action, or action and disposition, would be highly controversial among the Chinese.

As Herbert Fingarette has observed, the absence in the classical Chinese tradition of any individual faculty of will distinct from the act of willing suggests that, for Confucius at least, no distinction is drawn between intentionality and what is intended. That is to say, there is no "will" separate from what one wills. Under this assumption, both intentionality and specific intentions are, like one's self, social facts. What the self wills and *how* it wills are mutually determining. Thus, as an ongoing process specific to social, cultural, as well as natural conditions, human action is patterned by contingency.

Zhi 志 is the the term conventionally translated with the Western concept of "will." Etymologically, *zhi* combines *xin* 心 "heart-and-mind" with "to go to" (*zhi* 之) or "to abide in" (*zhi* 止), and means "to have in (heart) mind" or "to set one's heart on." In the classical *Shuowen* lexicon, *zhi* is glossed as "meaning" or "idea" (*yi* 意). It means what one has in (heart)mind. It is much closer to the notion of "disposition" than the concept of "will."[30]

The term *de* 德, most often translated "virtue," might more closely approximate the sense of "will." The Latin *virtus* carries the senses of "excellence," "potency," or "power." *De* also refers to "favor" or "bounty" extended outward, and further, the gratitude it evokes as a response. That is, *de* constitutes social patterns of both excellence and deference.

The classical Chinese language tends to locate action within a situation as a whole, rather than within a discrete unit or agency. For example, *shi* 勢, conventionally translated as "power" or "force," locates this energy as an aggregate tension that includes but is not limited to the specific parties in a dispute. It is the "force of circumstances."

Similarly, *de* encompasses both determining agency and its effects. On this basis, we might want to suggest "virtuality" in the archaic sense of "having inherent virtue or power to produce effects" as our working translation of *de*. In the *Shuowen* lexicon, *de* is defined as "to ascend," "to climb," "to arise," or "to presence" (*sheng* 升).

Knitting the various strands of the philological data together, it would seem that *de* denotes the emergence of particularity as a determining focus of the field that contextualizes it. The range of its particularity is variable, contingent upon the way in which it is interpreted both by itself and by other environing particulars. That is to say, its context in whatever direction and degree, can always be construed inclusively or exclusively as either "us" or "other." This "arising" is not random and chaotic. Rather, there is an appropriate direction which the particular pursues, negotiated between its own agency and the flux of its context. The particular is a compositor, always composing its world. Its direction is appropriate to the extent that it enriches the particularity of the constituent elements of its context. This interplay is that of deference to recognized excellence. The coherence and regularity observable in one's world emerges as a vector negotiated out of the interplay between oneself and the elements of one's context. The influence of the arising particular is dependent upon the range and quality of its self-construal. Any particular can become coextensive with other particulars insofar as they defer to it. This can involve the inclusion of an increasingly broader field of "arising" within the sphere of one's own particularity. This then is the "getting" or "appropriating" aspect of *de*—*de* 德 as *de* 得.

SELF AS FIELD AND FOCUS

Having questioned the appropriateness of each of the four Western root metaphors of self associated with the primary semantic contexts of Western thought, we can now make some constructive comments that adumbrate a notion of self arising from the Confucian problematic.

Our focus-field model of the self must be understood in terms of what we have elsewhere termed, *ars contextualis*.[31] Chinese thinkers, both Confucian and Daoist, most often employ an approach to philosophic understanding that is in striking contrast to the two dominant modes of

Western speculation. Among the majority of classical Chinese thinkers, there is resort neither to *ontologia generalis*, a "general ontology," nor to *scientia universalis*, a "science of universal principles." It is the "art of contextualization" that is most characteristic of Chinese intellectual endeavors. The variety of specific contexts defined by particular family relations, or sociopolitical orders, constitute the fields focused by individuals who are in turn shaped by the field of influences they focus. *Ars contextualis*, as a practical endeavor, names that peculiar art of contextualization that allows the focal individual to ally herself with those contexts that she will constitute and that in turn will constitute her.

Ars contextualis suggests a "this-that" rather than a "one-many" or "part-whole" model. Since there is no overarching context determining the shape of other contexts, the world is an open-ended affair comprised by "thises" and "thats" construable from any number of distinct perspectives. There is no One behind the many; there are, rather many ones, many particular foci that organize the fields about them. The art of contextualization involves the production of harmonious correlations of the myriad unique details (*wan wu* 萬物 or *wan you* 萬有) that make up the world.

It is through patterns of deference to recognized excellence that an individual extends himself to encompass a wider range of "presencing" or "arising." In Confucianism one understands this deferential activity in terms of *shu* 恕, which involves the analogical operation of taking up the stance of an other.[32] As this takes place, the possibilities of its conditions and its potency for self-construal are proportionately increased. When *de* is cultivated and accumulated such that the particular is integrated efficaciously into its environments, the distinction between *dao* and *de*, as field and focus, collapses and the individuating capacity of *de* is transformed into its integrating capacity. That is to say, the focus of *de* extends without discontinuity to embrace the indeterminate field of its context. *De* is both particular and its particular field—that is, the field as construed from its perspective. It is both *focus* and *focused field*.

Perhaps a concrete example would clarify this rather abstract discussion. The political, religious, and intellectual traditions of China have been regularly defined in terms of "supreme personalities." Given the aesthetic order characteristic of the Confucian worldview, the ruler or the magistrate or the father or the canonical text derives its authority from being a focusing center, and having implicated within it the order of the whole field of relevant details: in the case of the ruler, his subjects; in the case of the canonical text, its commentaries; and so on. The attraction of the center is such that, with varying degrees of success, it draws into its field and suspends the disparate and diverse centers that constitute its world. Although the family, the society, the state, and even the tradition itself, as the extended field is indeed ambiguous *as a field*, the vagueness of the abstract nexus is focused and made immediate in the embodiment of the field by the particular father, the communal exemplar, the ruler, the cultural hero. It is by virtue of the embodiment of the respective worlds in the supreme personality that this person can lay claim to impartiality such that the actions of the ruler or magistrate or father are appropriate (*yi* 義) and accommodate the interests of all concerned, rather than being self-interested (*li* 利).

Just as notions such as *dao* 道 or *tian* 天, encompassing within themselves the existing world order, are described in terms of impartiality, so the "Sage-ruler" or "Son of *tian*" (*tianzi* 天子) with similar compass, is devoid of selfishness. As long as the center is strong enough to draw the deference of its environing spheres of influence, it retains its position of authoritativeness. Such authoritativeness results in both an acknowledgement of that center as center, and active participation in reinforcing it. Standing at the center, the ruler acts imperceptibly, constituting a bearing for the human order, yet appearing to be himself neither mover nor moved.[33]

The description of self elaborated by the social psychologist George Herbert Mead provides a suggestive vocabulary for exploring the field-focus model of self. In describing the integrity of the social self, Mead claims:

> The "me" represents a definite organization of the community there in our own attitudes, and calling for a response.... The "I"... is something that is, so to speak, responding to a social situation which is within the experience of the individual. It is the answer which the individual makes to the attitude which others take toward him when he assumes an attitude toward them.... The attitudes he is taking toward them are present in his own experience, but his response to them will contain a novel element. The "I" gives the sense of freedom, of initiative.[34]

To isolate self (*ji* 己) from other (*ren* 人) would be tantamount to insisting that what Mead *really* means by "self" is the isolated "I."

As reinforcement for the fundamental nondiscreteness of self, it has often been pointed out that in the classical Chinese language, there is no distinction between the first person singular, "I," and the first person plural, "we." An "I" is always a "we." Equally significant, if we can take Mead's language one step further, is the absence, at least in the early corpus, of any explicit and consistent distinction between the subjective "I/we" and the objective "me/us." The "I/we" is embedded in the "me/us." Further, according to Mead:

> The unity and structure of the complete self reflects the unity and structure of the social process as a whole.... The organization and unification of a social group is identical with the organization and unification of any one of the selves arising within the social process in which that group is engaged, or which it is carrying on.[35]

Mead here expresses very well the interpenetration of self and society. And he does not in the least shrink from the dramatic implication of this mutuality for the question of the locus of the person.

> If mind is socially constituted, then the field or locus of any individual mind must extend as far as any social activity or apparatus or social relations which constitute it extends; and hence that field cannot be bounded by the skin of the individual organism to which it belongs.[36]

The locus of a mind is coterminous with its field of social activity and relations. In the Chinese perspective, the person extends as far as the roles that define her and through which she expresses herself. Any use of the term "mind" might seem inappropriate with respect to the Chinese model, but Mead moves far in the direction of ameliorating any confusion that might result from the use of the term:

> The unity of mind is not identical with the unity of self. The unity of the self is constituted by the unity of the entire relational pattern of social behavior and experience in which the individual is implicated, and which is reflected in the

structure of the self; but many of the aspects or features of this entire pattern do not enter into consciousness, so that the unity of mind is an a sense an abstraction from the inclusive unity of the self.[37]

Here Mead leaves open the question as to just how important the category of mind might be in the interpretation of the interrelations of self and society. It is clearly significant in the Western tradition. Essentially the same vocabulary of selfhood might be found applicable to the Chinese tradition, but with less recourse to abstracting from the inclusive unity of the self.

We include this brief account of Mead's notions of self to indicate our indebtedness to the general thrust of his theory. The locus of the self as a field of social relations constituting and constituted by the person is fundamental to our understanding of Chinese conceptions of selfhood. But we would also caution that there are limitations on the appeal to Mead's vocabulary. For, as fruitful as it clearly is for understanding self in a social context, even Mead's treatment is too closely tied to the dialectic associated with dualistic theories. Mead's creative integration of doctrines drawn from the behaviorist Wilhelm Wundt, on the one hand, and his Idealist teacher, Josiah Royce, on the other, present us with a theory still replete with the sort of tensions expressed in more obvious forms of dualist theory.

The focus-field model results from understanding one's relation to the world to be constituted by acts of contextualization. The self is focal in that it both constitutes and is constituted by the field in which it resides. The field is the order constituting its relevant environs. By definition, the focal self cannot be independent. The structure and continuity of the focal self is immanental, inhering in and continuous with its context. And since the field is always entertained from a particular perspective, the self as focus shares the particularity, indeed uniqueness, of the particular perspective. The openness of the self is guaranteed by the indefinite reservoir of potential perspectives offered by familial, social, cultural, and natural environs.

CHAPTER THREE

The Focus-Field Self in Classical Daoism

Before we consider the Daoist contribution to the understanding of self, it is necessary that we at least briefly indicate what we shall mean by the term "Daoism." For, unlike Confucianism, so-called philosophical Daoism, *daojia* 道家, does not name a school constituted by a founding thinker who might be said to have directly influenced the principal members who came after him. Daoism is an *ex post facto* creation of subsequent editors and historians, first named as a school by Sima Tan 司馬談 in the second century B.C.E. In fact, Sima Tan in his "Preface of the Grand Historian" uses the expression "*daode*" to refer to the Daoist School. The expression "Lao-Zhuang" first occurs in the postface to the *Huainanzi*, a Daoist text compiled *circa* 140 B.C.E.

In the following discussion, we shall for the most part limit ourselves to the *Daodejing* 道德經, and to what are generally considered to be the authentic writings of *Zhuangzi*.[1]

THE TRIPARTITE *PSYCHE* AND THE *WU* 無-FORMS OF DAOISM

Classical forms of Confucianism and Daoism are normally distinguished by claiming that Confucians focus upon issues relevant to a ritualized human society, while Daoists concern themselves with the natural ambiance. Such a distinction has but qualified merit. Though the familial or bureaucratic metaphor employed by the broad Confucian tradition is most relevant to the concerns of social structure and harmony, Han

45

speculations led to the extension of this metaphor to the broadest of "cosmological" issues.[2] In a similar manner, the more naturalistically inclined Daoists begin with the "Six Realms"—heaven, earth, and the four directions—but were quite capable of bringing their model to bear upon concrete social and political concerns in a variety of both constructive and critical manners. Indeed, the *Daodejing* is generally considered to be a political manual dealing with the proper guidance of society.

Were we to search for something like a central insight or commitment giving rise to the most general speculations associated with the two visions, we might find that there is, in fact, a single thread running through them both. The central focus of both Confucian and Daoist ways of thinking is the form of engagement we would call *deference*. Deference involves a yielding (and being yielded to) grounded in a recognition of a particular focus (*de* 德). Deferential acts require that one put oneself in another's place.

In Confucianism, deference (*shu* 恕) operates within ritual patterns (*li* 禮) shaped by familial relationships extending outward into society and culture. By contrast, Daoism expresses its deferential activity through what we shall call the *wu*-forms: *wuzhi* 無知, *wuwei* 無為, *wuyu* 無欲 —that is, "no-knowledge," a sort of knowing without resort to rules or principles; "no-action," or actions in accordance with the *de* 德 ("particular focus") of things, and "no-desire," or desiring that does not seek to own or control its "object" (which, in effect, makes it an "objectless desire"). In each of these cases, as in the case of Confucian *shu*, it is necessary to put oneself in the place of what is to be known, to be acted in accordance with, or to be desired.

In the following we shall be articulating the sense of deference common to the main traditions of philosophical Daoism, principally those associated with the names of Zhuangzi and Laozi. Our chief aim is to demonstrate how a Daoist understanding of deferential activity presupposes, as does the Confucian, a focus-field model of self.

Since the *wu*-forms bear some skewed resemblance to the faculties of the tripartite *psyche* that has played such an important role in Western modes of speculations since Plato, we shall begin with an attempt to point up the contrasting problematics underlying the distinctive interpretations of *knowledge*, *action*, and *desire* in classical Daoism and dominant strains of the Western tradition.

The heritage of the self construed as a tripartite structure is one of conflict—the soul at war with itself. In Plato, the primary conflict is between knowledge and ignorance. Allied with this conflict internal to reason itself is that occasioned by the appetitive and the spirited elements. This conflict is ramified with the confluence of Hebraic and Hellenic sensibilities. It is well expressed in the words of St. Paul, "The good that I would do, I do not do; the evil that I would not do, that I do," and receives perhaps its profoundest expression in Augustine's *Confessions* in the form of a war between passions and the will—the former demanding the satisfactions of desire, and the latter seeking obedience to the Will of God.

> But I wretched, most wretched, in the very commencement of my early youth, had begged chastity of Thee, and said, "Give me chastity and continency, only not yet." For I feared lest Thou shouldest hear me too soon, and cure me of the disease of concupiscence, which I wished to have satisfied rather than extinguished.[3]

Another variant of the soul warring with itself is found in Hume's famous claim that reason is a slave to the passions. This variant forms the basis of traditional interpretations of Freudian psychoanalytic theory with the conflictual dynamics of id, ego, and superego.[4]

If these psychic conflicts are analogized to the social ambiance, they are expressed in even more recognizable forms as the division between theory and practice that has characterized so much of our intellectual culture, and as the search for scientific objectivity that has urged a separation of reason and the passions. In addition, conflict between the dynamics of power and justice in political culture is a consequence of writing large the tensions between volitional and rational components of the soul.

These permutations of the soul at war are so deeply embedded in our own intellectual culture as to be presupposed in much of our analysis of alternative cultural sensibilities. This has led to serious problems when attempting to understand the dynamics of Chinese models of the person, and the relation of that model to its larger social and cultural context.

The first thing to be said is that the psychic dynamics of the tripartite self are not present in classical Chinese culture. A signal of this fact is that there is no fundamental mind-body dualism with which to contend. After all, it is this dualism that sets up the principal conflict within the self between reason, on the one hand, and the affective and volitional components, on the other.

There is, indeed, a kind of conflict associated with Daoist models of self-realization, but in the absence of the mind-body dichotomy the principal tensions are not internal to the self. Since the division among the affective, volitional, and the rational components is not a structural distinction made in the classical Chinese tradition, the paradoxical notion of a self at war with itself doesn't make as much sense in the Chinese as in the Western tradition.

The principal reason, of course, that the Chinese self is not internally conflicted is that there is nothing strictly internal to the self. The Daoist self is a function of its relations with its world. Just as the Confucian self is determined by deferential activity (*shu* 恕) guided by ritually structured roles and relationships (*li* 禮), so the Daoist self is determined by its deferential activities guided by *wuzhi*, *wuwei*, and *wuyu*.

It is also crucial to understand that, as in the case of Confucianism, there is no separable volitional function in Daoist models of self. Elsewhere we noted that the notion of will did not develop until quite late in the Western tradition.[5] In our discussion of the "nonwilling" Confucian self above, we questioned whether such a development took place in the mainstream of Chinese intellectual history. And without a notion of will, the actions of an agent must be characterized in a manner that does not have recourse to models of decision-making based upon a reflection among alternatives.

The notions of *shi* 是 and *fei* 非, conventionally translated as "right" and "wrong," and as "this" and "not-this," are the elements that serve as alternatives in modes of argumentation in the *Zhuangzi*. But there is no faculty of willing or intentionality that leads us to choose one alternative over the other. The performative function of language reflected in the normative implications of *shi* and *fei* means that in naming (*ming* 名) a world, we are commanding (*ming* 命) this world into being.

The conflict associated with the Daoist self obviously cannot be between heart and mind. The goal of cultivation of the self for the Daoist is to move from activities of knowing, feeling, and action shaped by construal, to those shaped by deference. But it would be inappropriate to see the underlying conflict as one between a disturbed aspect of heart-mind (*xin* 心) and a calm aspect. It is unlikely that we should find Hamlets or St. Pauls prominent among the Chinese.

If the problematic of unrealized selfhood does not entail the self divided against itself, what *is* the source and nature of the disturbance that the Daoist discipline is meant to overcome? If it is not referenced primarily within the soul, it can only be a disturbance in the relationships among those things which constitute the context of self-realization.

> The stillness of the sage is not a matter of his saying: "It is good to be still!" and thus he is still. He is still because none of the myriad things are able to agitate his heart and mind.... If water becomes lucid when still, how much more so his spirit. The heart and mind of the sage is so still—the mirror of heaven and earth, the looking glass of the myriad things.[6]

It is precisely *not* through an internal struggle of reason against the obstreperous passions or will, but through mirroring the things of the world as they are in their relatedness to us, that we reach a state in which "none of the myriad things is able to agitate" our hearts and minds. In other words, we defer to the integrity of those things that contextualize us, attempting to establish a frictionless relationship with them. The notion of *jing* 靜 "stillness, tranquility" that is often used to characterize this posture, is not passivity, but an ongoing, dynamic achievement of equilibrium. We must recall that all correlative pairs entail their opposites in the sense that *jing* is "tranquility-becoming-agitated," or "tranquility-within-agitation." Tranquility (*jing* 靜) stands in a dominant relationship to agitation (*dong* 動) rather than excluding it utterly. The same qualification has to be brought to bear on other familiar pairs which might otherwise mislead us, such as vacuity (*xu* 虛) and fullness (*shi* 實), and clarity (*qing* 清) and turbidity (*zhuo* 濁), for example.

We have said enough to call into question the relevance of the tripartite model of the self to classical Chinese contexts. The Chinese do not "slice the pie" as is done in the West; effectively, there are no faculties of knowing, doing, and feeling that can be distinguished one from the other; and there is no division between the modalities of reason on the one hand, and appetite and will on the other. This is the case because, as we have stressed, there is no mind-body dualism to generate such a division. Further, the processive and relational character of the self precludes the existence of any substrate self that could house separate faculties.

Having said this, there are terms such as *zhi* 知, *wei* 為, and *yu* 欲 that initially seem to correlate rather closely with what we call knowing, acting, and desiring. If the Daoist self is not divided in the manner of the Western model of the tripartite soul, how are we to account for these three modalities? The *wu*-forms must be thought of simply as activities that establish the deferential relations that give rise to the self at any given moment. They are not faculties; they form no coherent psyche.

Wuzhi 無知, as "no-knowledge," means the absence of a certain kind of knowledge, the sort dependent upon ontological presence. Knowledge grounded in a denial of ontological presence involves the sort of acosmotic thinking that does not presuppose a single-ordered world and its intellectual accouterments.[7] It is, therefore, *unprincipled* knowing. Such knowing does not appeal to rules or principles determining the existence, meaning, or activity of a phenomenon. *Wuzhi* provides one with a sense of the *de* of a thing, its particular focus, rather than knowledge of that thing in relation to some concept or universal. Ultimately, *wuzhi* is expressed as a grasp of the *daode* 道德 relationship of each encountered item that permits an understanding of the totality construed from the particular focus (*de*) of that item.

Knowledge, as unprincipled knowing, is the entertainment of the world on its own terms without recourse to rules of discrimination which separate one sort of thing from another sort. The *Huainanzi* 淮南子, a Han dynasty eclectic text with a strong Daoist coloration, reports on this kind of mirror-like "knowing":

> Therefore, the sage is like a mirror—
> He neither sees things off nor goes out to meet them,
> He responds to everything without storing anything up.
> Thus, he is never injured through the myriad transformations
>   he undergoes.[8]
> Is it not the case with him that to gain is to lose
> And to lose is to gain![9]

> It is because the mirror and water do not, in anticipation, equip themselves with cleverness, that the shapes they come into contact with cannot but show themselves as they are: square, round, bent and straight.[10]

Rules of thumb, habits of action, customs, fixed standards, methods, stipulated concepts, categories, commandments, principles, laws of nature, all require us to "welcome things as they come and escort them as they go." Having stored past experience and organized it in terms of fixed standards or principles, we anticipate, celebrate, and recall a world patterned by these discriminations. The sage, however, mirrors the world, and "neither sees things off nor goes out to meet them." As such, he "responds to everything without storing anything up." This means that he mirrors the world *at the moment*, without overwriting it by the shape of a world passed away, or by anticipations of a world yet to come.

Daoist literature is preoccupied with the possible fragmenting and ossifying effect of language functioning as precedent (*gu* 故).

> One who understands the workings of *tian* and the workings of humankind is the highest understanding. One who understands the workings of *tian* lives life naturally; one who understands the workings of humankind uses what is known to him to cultivate what is not. To live out one's natural lifespan without being cut off mid-course is to have an abundance of understanding. But there is a problem with all of this. Understanding is understanding about something, and that something is never fixed. … And so there can only be genuine understanding when there is a genuine person.[11]

The application of language and concept arrests the fluidity of an ever novel flow of events. When our experience is mediated through language, we in varying degree deny the uniqueness of particular phenomena by imposing a given structure and patterned regularity upon the world around us. The alternative is to reflect events as they are in our dynamic relationship to them, without distortion.

There is a rather dramatic difference in the meanings of the mirroring metaphor in Chinese and Western cultures. In the West, the mind as the mirror of nature has been based upon understandings of the world as patterned by unchanging essences. Mind and nature mirror one another by possessing an essential structure in common. Indeed, Plato's doctrine of "recollection" insists that it is precisely by virtue of the fact that the mind is a storehouse of the essential patterns resourced in an unchanging world of forms that we may be called rational creatures. The mirroring activity associated with the Daoist *wu*-forms is a form of activity that allows things to be themselves both in their transitoriness and their particularity. It is the things themselves as individual events and processes, and the orders construed from their particular perspectives, that are reflected in the mirroring process.

Wuzhi 無知, or "knowing without principles," is tacit and, though inexpressible in literal terms, may be communicated though parabolic and imagistic language. A Confucian critic challenged the Daoist claim that begins the *Daodejing*—"*Dao* can be spoken of, but it is not constant *dao*" —by asking: "If constant *dao* cannot be spoken of, how is it that the author of the *Daodejing* used several thousand characters in speaking of it?" The Daoist replied: "I make for you a beautiful embroidery of drakes and pass it along to you for your admiration. I cannot, however, show you the golden needle by which it was made."

Such parabolic language is distinctive in an acosmotic context since metaphor and imagery do not presuppose a literal ground. Parabolic language is constitutive of discourse itself. Language is, from the beginning, a language of difference and particularity. It is this language that permits the communication of the results of *wuzhi*.

Wuwei 無為, often translated (unfortunately) as "no action" or "non-action," involves the absence of any action that interferes with the particular focus (*de* 德) of those things within one's field of influence. Actions untainted by stored knowledge or ingrained habits are unmediated, unstructured, unprincipled, and spontaneous. As such, they are consequences of deferential responses to the item or event in accordance with which, or in relation to which, one is acting. These actions are *ziran* 自然, "spontaneous," "self-so-ing." They are *nonassertive* actions.

It would be a mistake to interpret the modes of disposition named by the *wu*-forms as passive. The deferential activities underlying these modes are shaped by the intrinsic excellences of those things calling forth deference. Deference is a yielding to recognized excellence (*de* 德). The assumption must be that the Daoist sage sees beneath the layers of artifice that mask the naturalness of persons and things and responds to the excellence so advertised. Further, deference is a two-way street. The excellence of the realized Daoist calls forth deference from others. The *wu*-forms operate within a context of yielding and being yielded to.

The "grand analogy" in the *Daodejing* is: *Dao* is to world as ruler is to people. As the discernible rhythm and regularity in the world around us, *dao* is nonimpositional. "*Dao* is constantly non-assertive (*wuwei*) yet there is nothing which is not done."[12] In government, impositional power is a major concern, so the consummate political model in Daoism, corresponding to *dao*, is described as *wuwei* and *ziran*:

> The most excellent ruler: The people do not even know that
>   there is a ruler.
> The second best: They love and praise him.
> The next: They stand in awe of him.
> And the worst: They look on him with contempt.
> Inadequate integrity in government
> Will result in people not trusting those who govern.
> So hesitant, the ruler does not speak thoughtlessly.
> His job done and the affairs of state in order,
> The people all say: "We are naturally like this (*ziran*)."[13]

Spontaneous action is a mirroring response. As such, it is action that accommodates the other to whom one is responding. It takes the other on its own terms. Such spontaneity involves recognizing the continuity between oneself and the other, and responding in such a way that one's own actions promote the well-being both of oneself of the other. This does not lead to imitation but to complementarity and coordination. Handshakes and embraces are actions that presuppose a recognition of the stance of the other, and complete that stance. When the music starts to play and your partner opens his arms, the dance proceeds as a dyadic harmony of nonassertive actions.

An individual trained in *taijiquan* 太極拳 will recognize in the so-called "push-hands" (*duishou* 對手) exercise a basic illustration of *wuwei*. Two individuals facing one another perform various circular movements of the arms while maintaining minimal hand contact. The movement of each individual mirrors that of the other. *Wuwei* is realized when the movements of each are sensed, by both parties, to be uninitiated and effortless.

Presumably one can employ such mirroring responses in "the art of rulership," providing a sort of nonconstruing model for the guidance of the state. Such is the testimony of the *Daodejing*:

> Thus, the sage says:
> I am nonassertive (*wuwei*)
> And the people transform themselves;

I cherish stillness,
And the people attune themselves;
I do not intervene,
And the people are prosperous of their own accord;
I am objectless in my desires,
And the people retain their natural genuineness of their own
    accord.[14]

Under the proper ordering of the sage:
He constantly causes the people to seek "unprincipled
    understanding" and to be objectless in their desires,
And as for the erudite—they wouldn't dare to do anything.
In simply acting non-assertively,
Everything is properly ordered.[15]

Perhaps the best characterization of the term *wuyu* 無欲 is "object-less desire." Since neither unprincipled knowing nor nonassertive action can in the strict sense *objectify* a world or any element in it, the desiring associated with the Daoist sensibility is objectless. The enjoyments associated with *wuyu* are possible without the need to define, possess, or control the occasion of one's enjoyment.

Thus, *wuyu*, rather than involving the cessation of desire through possession and consummation, represents the achievement of *deferential desire*. Desire, based upon a mirroring understanding (*wuzhi*) and a nonassertive relationship (*wuwei*) is not shaped by the need to own, control, or consume, but simply to celebrate and to enjoy. Desire is for those things desirable in part because they *stand to be desired*. But those things that stand to be desired must themselves be deferential, which means that they cannot *demand* to be desired. For to demand to be desired is to seek a kind of seductive control over the desirer. In a world of events and processes in which discriminations are recognized as conventional and transient, desire is predicated upon the abilities to "let be" and "let go." It is in this sense that *wuyu* is a nonconstruing, objectless, desire.

The Daoist problematic does not concern *what* is desired but the manner of the desiring. Objectless desire always allows for letting be and letting go. Enjoyment for the Daoist is realized not *in spite of* the fact that one might lose what is desired, but *because of* this fact. The world is a complex set of processes of transformation, never at rest. *Wuhua* 物化,

"the transformation of things," means that one can never pretend that what we seek to hold onto, has any permanent status.

In Plato, the desire for knowledge is the only thing that can define both embodied and disembodied existence; it is the only desire that can be permanent, eternal. In Daoism, transient desire is the only desire that lets things be, that does not construe the world in a certain manner, that does not seek to apply the brakes on a world of changing things.

The key to understanding the *wu-forms* lies in the contrast between "objects" and "objectivity." From a Western epistemological perspective, both the *Zhuangzi* and the *Daodejing* presuppose what we in the West would term a realist perspective.[16] Beyond the confusions introduced by language, and by our own distorted perceptions and tendentious categorizations, there is a real world. Our task is to entertain that world as objectively as possible.

The problem begins when we believe that the objective world is a world of objects, of concrete, unchangeable things which we encounter as over against us; things that announce themselves to us by saying "I object!" For the Daoist, the objective world *cannot be* objective in this sense. It is a constantly transforming set of events or processes that belie the sorts of discriminations that would permit a final inventory of the furniture of the world.

> Maojiang and Lady Li were beauties for human beings, but fish upon seeing them would seek the deeps, birds on seeing them would fly high, and deer upon seeing them would dash off. Which of these four understands what is really handsome in this world![17]

The moment we begin to discount these other views of Lady Li, we have drained a great deal of significance from our understanding of beauty by setting up exclusive standards that determine not only the truly beautiful but the unacceptably ugly. Further, these *fixed* standards, whether of beauty or goodness or justice, are the means of creating a world of fixed objects.

Paradoxically, for the Daoist, the real world is objectless. The sage envisions a world of transforming events that she *may*, for whatever reason, choose to freeze momentarily into a pattern of discrimination, but that she recognizes, when she sees clearly, as beyond such distinctions.

There is nothing which is not a "that," and nothing which is not a "this." Because we cannot see from a "that" perspective but can only know from our own perspective, it is said that "that" arises out of "this" and "this" further accommodates "that." This is the notion that "this" and "that" are born simultaneously. And even though this is so, being born is simultaneously dying and vice versa; being acceptable is simultaneously being unacceptable and vice versa; accommodating right is accommodating wrong and vice versa. It is for this reason that the sage, illuminating this situation with the way things really are rather than going along with discriminations, is also a case of accommodating what is right and what is "this." But "this" is also "that" and vice versa. And a "thises" "that" further has one set of right and wrong while "this" has another. In truth, is there really such a thing as "this" and "that" or not?

> Where neither "this" nor "that" has an opposite
> Is called the hinge of *dao*,
> And as soon as the hinge is fitted to its socket
> It can respond endlessly.[18]

The function of a hinge is not to rise above the two sides, but to swing back and forth between them. It is a metaphor that recalls the opening and closing of the "heavenly gate" (*tianmen* 天門) and the moving back and forth between *yin* 陰 and *yang* 陽 that pervades the literature, from *Yijing* 易經 to *Guiguzi* 鬼谷子. In the ongoing process of change, the hinge is at the intersection between the formal, rhythmic aspect and the propensity of circumstances. It is the vantage point that allows full access to the possibilities inherent in one's situation.

The *wu*-forms all provide a way of entertaining, of deferring to, an objectless world. Thus the sage is concerned with that sort of knowing, acting, and desiring that does not depend upon objects. This point is crucial to the Daoist understanding of the self. For the discriminated self of the sort recognized in the contemporary Western world comes into being through encountering other things that effectively stand over against, "objecting" to the burgeoning self. Selves cannot exist without others. In Daoism the self is forgotten to the extent that discriminated objects no longer constitute the environs of the self.

The consequence of this transformed vision is that knowing, acting, and desiring are no longer based upon *construal*. Principles and fixed standards lead us to construe the object of our knowledge by recourse to such principles. An item becomes one of a *kind*, or an instrument for the achievement of an end. Feeling ourselves in tension with objectified others leads us to act in an aggressive or defensive manner to effect our will. Desire motivated by an object leads us to seek possession of that which is desired, allowing it significance only insofar as it meets our needs. A self intoxicated by objects narrows, truncates, and obfuscates the world as it is. On the other hand, unprincipled knowing, nonassertive action, and objectless desire have this in common: To the extent they are successful, they enrich the world by allowing the process to unfold spontaneously on its own terms, while at the same time, contributing themselves fully to it. We may say that implementation of the *wu*-forms allows us to leave the world as it is. But we may say this only if we recognize that "world" in this context means myriad spontaneous transactions characterized by emerging patterns of deference to recognized excellences.

If the Daoist sage leaves the world as it is, it is because he has in some sense lost an objectifying self and found the deferential self. In the *Zhuangzi*, the distinction between these two selves is marked linguistically. The original embedded self is *wu* 吾. The self that has fallen into the habit of objectifying its world, as well as itself, is *wo* 我. That is, the construing self is *wo*; the deferential self is *wu*.

Wo, as the self unaware of the effect of its discriminations, may strive to achieve the status of *wu*, a self not only aware of the transitory relevance of any sort of discriminations, but capable at times of attaining that "soft focus" that allows her to mirror the world as it is. This *real* world is an indefinite complex of overlapping orders, which may be entertained from an indefinite number of perspectives, each perspective characterized by a particular focus that calls for a deferential relation between the *wu*-self and the things, events, or processes constituting these foci.

> Ziqi of the southern suburb sat in a meditative posture leaning on an armrest. He breathed deeply with his head raised toward the sky, and achieving a trance-like state, seemed to have lost his sense of "other." Yancheng Ziyou, standing in attendance before him, said, "Where are you? Can you really

make the body like rotting wood and the heart-and-mind like dead ashes? The person meditating now is not the same one who was meditating a time ago."

Ziqi replied, "Yan, marvelous that you should ask such a question! Were you aware that just now 'me' left 'I' behind? You have heard of the piping of humankind and yet not that of the earth. Or perhaps you have heard of the earth's piping and yet not that of *tian*?"[19]

It is the construing *wo*-self that is lost. The person leaning on the armrest is now a deferential *wu*-self who, apparently has moved beyond the conventional, discriminating, language of humankind, and has listened to the piping of *tian* which consists of "blowing out a myriad different things, causing each of them to be itself, and all of them to take what they want."[20]

DAO 道 AND DE 德: DIFFERENCE AND DEFERENCE

We have been speaking of the *wu*-self as nonconstruing and, ultimately, nondiscriminating. It is important to recognize that the refusal finally to discriminate does not leave us with the bland oneness of a "night wherein all cows are black." The aim of Zhuangzi's Daoism is, in fact, quite the opposite. The Daoist wants to attend to "the piping of *tian*" that blows through things in different ways, allowing each to be itself. The Daoist celebrates the bottomless complexity of particulars.

The posture permitting one to distinguish the differences among things without making invidious distinctions is that suggested by the tern *qi* 齊, "parity." The title of the second chapter of the *Zhuangzi* is "*qiwulun*" 齊物論, which means "a discourse (*lun* 論) on parity (*qi* 齊) among things (*wu* 物)." Our discussion of the *de* of individual things as particular foci would indicate that "parity" is a better translation of *qi* than "equality." Thus a more apposite rendering of the sense of "*qiwulun*" might be, "The Mirroring Which Allows Things to Be Seen in Their Parity." The sage does not so much insure parity among things, as he mirrors it.

The term *qi* does not entail notions of identity that are assumed in familiar understandings of equality. According to the *Shuowen* lexicon, *qi* describes ears of grain that have grown to the same level. According to

Bernhard Karlgren, *qi* is both homophonous and cognate with *qi* 妻, which means "consort" or "legal wife," the one wife who has the same social status as her husband. Rather than equality, *qi* carries the senses of "on the same footing," "affinity," "resemblance," and "analogy," all of which seem to better capture the sense of *qi* since they allow for distinctive differences among items that nonetheless, exist on a par with one another. Understanding the Daoist's mirroring of things, therefore, will lead us to ask after the manner in which he or she comes to appreciate the distinctive *de* that forms the basis of its parity with all other things. This is one insight into the Daoist understanding of difference.

There are two additional points that need to be made here: First, this notion of parity does not vitiate our claim that, given the uniqueness that each particular entails, all relationships in the classical Chinese worldview are resolutely hierarchical. The husband and legal wife, although having social parity, still stand in an hierarchical relationship one to the other, depending on the specific issue under review. In terms of the education of the young child, for example, the wife has dominant responsibility; later education becomes the main responsibility of the husband.

Secondly, the mirroring relationship that the knower has to the known does not on any account mean passivity, any more than noncoercive action means doing nothing or objectless desire means being emotionally barren. On the contrary, knowledge being performative, the knower collaborates with what is known to shape a world, and the quality of the knowledge is a function of the success of this collaboration.

As we shall see, Daoist notions of difference contrast dramatically with the sense of "ontological difference," one of the popular themes in speculative philosophy since Heidegger. Heidegger claimed that a distinctive error of almost the entire philosophical tradition in the West involved forgetting the difference between Being and beings. Jacques Derrida has recently won some philosophic fame by drawing out some of the implications of this claim.

Derrida's well-known critique of logocentrism and "the language of presence" (language whose meaning is a function of the presencing of Being through the beings of the world) suggests that one may ask after the differences among beings without appealing to any ontological contrast. On such a reading there is no ontological ground. There is no *Being*; there are only beings. By contrast, the radically *ontological* view originating in Parmenides presumes that "Only Being is..." The question of difference resolves itself into a difference between Appearance and Reality, between the Way of Truth and the Way of Opinion. In reality, there is only the ontological ground. There are no beings; there is only Being.

Between this radical acosmology and radical ontology there lies the position that has dominated traditional Western metaphysics. This position eschews (or attempts to eschew) the single-sidedness of either radical solution. Being is privileged over both beings and not-being. God may serve as creator who brings the beings of the world from the emptiness of not-being.

A fourth possibility regarding the understanding of *difference* lies in that metaphysical nihilism that claims that Not-being is the ultimate. Beings are illusory as is, a fortiori, Being-Itself. On this view nothing exists. There can be no true difference(s), only Indifference. The question of difference arises with respect to the contrast between the merely apparent beings of the world and the Nihil that guarantees their illusory status. Such nihilism is the reverse of the Parmenidean vision, and leads to what may be called the *dis*ontological question: "Why is there Nothingness rather than Being or beings?"

These four possible manners of construing the question of difference vis-à-vis the question of Being, beings, and not-being, provide a resource not only for the assessment of alternative views with Western culture, but for the interpretation of cross-cultural phenomena and for the assessment of the relevance of those phenomena for issues within the Anglo-European context. Our grasp of the Daoist understanding of difference will be greatly facilitated by appeal to this typology.

The most provocative characterization of "*dao*" in the *Daodejing* is as both "nameless" and "nameable."

> *Dao* can be spoken of, but it is not constant *dao*;
> The name can be named, but it is not the constant name;
> The nameless is the beginning of the heavens and the earth;
> The named is the mother of the myriad things.
> Dwell constantly in nothing in order to observe its mysteries;
> Dwell constantly in something in order to observe its
>   boundaries.[21]

If *dao* per se is the "way" of things, construed as all of the processes of becoming,[22] then nameless and nameable *dao* characterize the functions of "not- (or 'non-') being" and "being" respectively, as abstracted from the process of Becoming-Itself. *Dao* is the *That Which*. That which *is* and that which *is not*, are the polar elements of Becoming-Itself.

It would be easy to misunderstand this interpretation as claiming a far greater coherence for the Daoist vision than is likely. One must look carefully at the meaning of *wu* 無 in this context. As Angus Graham has argued, "Being" and "Not-being" have strikingly different associations than do the notions of *you* 有 and *wu* 無.[23] For example, *wu* means "have not," "there is not," which readily contrasts with the sense of not-being as "nothing" or "no entity." The sense of *wu* is of the absence of concrete things. The correlative sense of *you* in this context is the presence of these same concrete things. Further, this sense of "presence" and "absence" has to be qualified by the fluid, processional character of *dao*, making something present always a "becoming absent," and something absent a "becoming present."

If one looks at Daoism with the appropriately adjusted senses of "being" and "not-being," the notion of *dao* as the "That Which" loses its ontological tone. There is only "this" and "that." To translate this idea as "Only beings are" is quite appropriate provided one not look for any Being standing behind or beneath or beyond these beings, and provided one not interpret "are" in any strong existential sense. The best manner of avoiding such a confusion is simply to say, since there are only "thises" and "thats," the locution "Only beings are" is more aptly expressed as "beings only" or "these beings."

Beings are "thises" and "thats." *Dao*, construed as That Which Is and That Which Is Not, as nameable and nameless *dao*, characterizes the process of existence and experience as Becoming-Itself. This reflexive notion, however, does not name an "It" that becomes; rather, the locution "Becoming-Itself" refers simply to the unsummed processes of becoming per se. It is these processes that are reflected in the notion of *dao*.

What this means, of course, in relation to our typology of ways of entertaining the notion of difference, is that Daoism expresses a radical acosmology. The Daoist is an *acosmotic* thinker. If we wish to understand the sense in which difference is to be understood relative to the parity of things, therefore, we must restrict ourselves solely to the question of the differences among particular things.

Each particular element in the totality has its own *de* 德. As we have said, *de* is best understood as a particular focus that orients an item in a field of significances such that it achieves its own intrinsic excellence. The *de* of an element provides the perspective from which it construes all other items in its environs. In this manner each item, with respect to its *de*, names and creates a world. *Dao* and *de* are related as field and focus respectively. The relations of *dao* and *de* are holographic, which means that each element in the totality of things contains the totality in an adumbrated form. The particular focus of an item establishes its world, its environment; the totality as a noncoherent sum of all possible orders is adumbrated by each item.

The *Zhuangzi* contains a passage in which this notion of "locus" or "place" is presented as being integral to what it means to know:

> Zhuangzi and Hui Shi were strolling across the bridge over the Hao river. Zhuangzi observed, "The minnows swim out and about as they please—this is the way they enjoy themselves."
>
> Huizi replied, "You are not a fish—how do you know what they enjoy?"
>
> Zhuangzi returned, "You are not me—how do you know that I don't know what is enjoyable for the fish?"
>
> Huizi said, "I am not you, so I certainly don't know what you know; but it follows that, since you are certainly not the fish, you don't know what is enjoyment for the fish either."
>
> Zhuangzi said, "Let's get back to your basic question. When you asked '*From where* do you know what the fish enjoy?' you already knew that I know what the fish enjoy, or you wouldn't have asked me. I know it from here above the Hao river."[24]

Graham, in interpreting this passage, observes that the expression *anzhi* 案知 can mean both "how do you know..." and "from where do you know..." But Zhuangzi is not just depending upon this linguistic ambiguity in order to win a sophistical argument. He has a more philosophic point to make: He wants to deny any sense of the act of knowing that would make the knower independent of the world known. For Zhuangzi, knowledge is a "realizing" of a world in the sense of "making it real." And the knower and the known are inseparable aspects of this same event. Agency cannot be isolated from action. As Zhuangzi says elsewhere, "There can only be genuine understanding when there is a genuine person."[25] Where you are and how you know are one and the same. Knowledge is always proximate, and a condition of an experience rather than an isolated experiencer. Zhuangzi's experience with the fishes is a situation, and the situation has priority over any abstracted agent. Situation makes Zhuangzi's world continuous with the world of the fishes, and as such, his claim to knowledge is a claim to having been there.

Being continuous with the fishes and collaborating with them in the experience does not deny the fishes their difference. In fact, it is only through Zhuangzi's deference to their difference that the experience can be optimally fruitful, and he can really come to know these particular fishes.

The Daoist tradition is critical of the Confucian willingness to limit its concerns to the human world alone. It does not reject the "extension" of oneself in the development of one's humanity (*ren* 仁), but seeks to go further in extending oneself to all things by "acting authentically and without coercion" (*wuwei* 無為). The Daoist texts, like their Confucian counterparts, see resistence to the emergence of a discriminating self as a precondition for integrative natural action and the extension of *de* 德 that follows from it. In a *Zhuangzi* parody on Confucius:

> Yan Hui said, "I have made progress."
> "How so?" inquired Confucius.
> "I have sat and forgotten (*zuowang* 坐忘)."
> Confucius, noticeably flustered, inquired: "What do you mean by 'sitting and forgetting?'"
> "I have demolished my appendages and body, gotten rid of my keenness of sight and hearing, abandoned my physical form, and cast off knowledge, and in so doing, have joined the Great Thoroughfare 大通," said Yan Hui. "This is what I call 'sitting and forgetting.'"[26]

Perhaps the most helpful metaphor available in the Daoist texts to elucidate this notion of "joining the thoroughfare" is that of the tally. The *Daodejing* states:

> The sage, holding onto the left half of the tally
> Does not demand payment from others;
> The person with potency (*de*) takes charge of the tally;
> The person without potency looks to collecting on it.[27]

The meaning of this rather obscure passage is made clear in the fifth chapter of the *Zhuangzi*, the title of which is "*De* Satisfies the Tally (*dechongfu* 德充符)." This chapter is a series of anecdotes about mutilated cripples who, under normal circumstances and under the sway of conventional values, would be ostracized from their communities. Their mutilated physical forms, often with the inference that they are the result of amputatory punishments, would be certain grounds for societal rejection. Having overcome discreteness and extended their *de* to contribute to and integrate themselves with the community, however, they "satisfy the tally" with their *de* and not only blend harmoniously with their societies, but further come to exercise considerable influence in establishing the importances of their respective worlds. The extent and quality of their *de* is such that they are important factors in the ongoing process of defining values and establishing an aesthetic and moral order.

In the Daoist tradition, the extension of one's *de* is described in more pervasive terms than in the Confucian literature. As in the Confucian tradition, at times such a person becomes the embodiment and protector of the human order, a styler of new culture and a source of new meaning. But the Daoists take it beyond this into the natural world. The *zhenren* 真人, the Daoist version of the consummating person, embraces the *de* of the natural as well as the human environment. By becoming coextensive with the *de* of the ox, for example, Cook Ding in butchering its carcass is able to penetrate its natural lineaments and interstices without distraction, and hence is able to become an efficacious butcher;[28] by becoming coextensive with the *de* of the wood, Carpenter Ching is sensitive to the quality and potential of his materials without distraction, and hence is able to become an efficacious craftsman.[29] The absence of a "disintegrating" discrete self makes these exemplars open to the *de* of their natural environments, so that the environment contributes to them, making them potent and productive, and they contribute to their environments, interpreting and maximizing the possibilities of those things which constitute their world.

The dynamic nature of this process of extending one's *de* is underscored in the vocabulary that defines the Daoist tradition. The person of insistent and productive *de*, for example, is called *zhenren* 真人, "the authentic person." The character, *zhen* 真, meaning "authentic" or "genuine," is classified under the radical *bi* 匕, which means *hua* 化, "to transform." In the *Zhuangzi*, the process of existence itself is referred to as the "transformation of things" (*wuhua* 物化). As the Daoist *zhenren* extends himself to become one with his natural environment, he becomes increasingly deferential to the transformation of things. To the extent that he embraces the *de* of his totality within his particularity, he is integrated and efficacious at whatever he does. His hands express the clay, and the clay expresses his hands.

We have perhaps said enough to illumine the manner in which the Daoist belief in the "the parity of things" celebrates the *differences* that obtain among the items of the totality. The manners in which all things are *similar* is easily stated: Although the *de* of things are always hierarchical, they have parity in the sense that each *de* is necessary for every other *de* to be what it is.

Daoism expresses acosmotic thinking in its most consistent form. With no Being behind the beings of the world, the way of things is both continuous and radically <u>perspectival.</u> There can be no standards *that is the world.* such as the "Great Chain of Being" or the "Ladder of Perfection" establishing ontological hierarchies. What we have, in the final instance, is both the uniqueness of each perspective (*de*) and parity among them (*qiwu*).

Above all, the Daoist self is *deferential.* Deferring to the way of things as they truly are involves the sort of mirroring responses discussed above in terms of the *wu*-forms. In the first place, mirroring such a world involves, in fact, a mirroring of an indefinite number of worlds since each item is the particular focus of a world. In his commentary on the *Daodejing,* Wang Bi 王弼 states that "the myriad things manage and order themselves."[30] In ordering themselves, they thereby order a world. Mirroring the individual things in their distinctive particularities involves, therefore, mirroring a complex set of overlapping orders, each with its own ✓ distinctive center.

Obviously, the construing self could not but treat such a world as chaotic in the extreme. The deferential self, on the other hand, sees these overlapping orders as a richly spontaneous array of patternings. The familiar account of Lord Hundun that closes the Inner Chapters of the *Zhuangzi* is appropriate here:

> The ruler of the North Sea was "Swift," the ruler of the South Sea was "Sudden," and the ruler of the Central Sea was "Chaos." Swift and Sudden had on several occasions encountered each other in the territory of Chaos, and Chaos had treated them with great hospitality. Swift and Sudden, devising a way to

repay Chaos' generosity, said: "Human beings all have seven orifices through which they see, hear, eat, and breathe. Chaos alone is without them." They then attempted to bore holes in Chaos, each day boring one hole. On the seventh day, Chaos died.[31]

The construing self, acting in accordance with the world shaped by its seven orifices, closes down the spontaneity of the unordered totality.

But why shouldn't one wish to bring order out of Chaos?[32] A reasonable question, indeed, if chaos is the confusion and disarray that Western mythology describes. But if chaos is a noncoherent sum of all orders, then imposing order on it means simply selecting one of a myriad candidates for order and privileging that one over the rest. If chaos is the indeterminant element that guarantees novelty and uniqueness, disciplining it through the imposition of a single order would make life repetitive and predictable.

Obviously something more needs to be said concerning how one might go about actually mirroring the parity of all things. After all, the practical effect of giving each thing its due, when that means allowing it to focus a world from its own peculiar perspective, would seem to be potentially disastrous. Indeed, the extent to which the Daoist may be said to be successful on his own terms may be reasonably questioned. We can, however, attempt at least to follow the "logic" of the Daoist position. *That is all that we can do with such an imaginative philosophy.*

First, the "mystical" experience of the Daoist sage, rather than that of Oneness with all things, is closer to an experience of the particularity of all things. The experience of oneness relevant to the Daoist, therefore, is of *this one* and *that one*. The Daoist does not become one with all things; rather, as a deferential self, he may at least approach becoming one with *this or that thing*. In effect, the sage becomes one with *all* other things only through celebrating his or her *continuity* with other things based upon an intuition of parity.

But if the world is not a single, unitary cosmos, with rules and standards and laws finally determining its order, if the world, on the contrary, is the noncoherent totality of all possible orders, how does the deferential sage survive deferring to chaos? Ostensibly, the sage must discriminate as much as we ordinary folk. The difference that makes all the difference is that the sage recognizes the arbitrariness, transitoriness, and merely conventional status, of such discriminations.

Only thises and thats exist as truly discriminable items. When discriminations are made, as perforce they must be, one treats, or "deems" things in the mode of a transitory discrimination. This involves the utterance of a "That's it!" which deems something to be the case. Angus Graham has noted that the *Zhuangzi* never does say that everything is one *Right!* (except as one side of a paradox). He always speaks subjunctively of the sage treating as one.[33] The same may be said concerning all deeming. The sage discriminates as she deems necessary, always acting in a deferential mode. But such discriminations are qualified in two important manners: First, the sage recognizes that such discriminations are conventional and transitory. Secondly, to the extent possible, she engages these discriminated items in the modes of unprincipled knowing, nonassertive action, and objectless desire. In this manner, she is able to mitigate the pejorative effects of the discriminations.

The Daoist posture of mirroring the world cannot be either dialectical or analytic, since both analysis and dialectic require a putative whole, the former in order to divide into parts, the latter in order to form the opposing parts into some synthetic whole. Neither the "ten thousand things" nor the self that plies its way among them, may be summed to a coherent whole. The Daoist way is *analogical*. That is to say, it involves *Yes.* the correlation of elements with presumed similarities of structure, character, or function without the necessity to assume a holistic context. *?chaos* Such a method emphasizes the ad hoc nature of any sorts of discrimination or organization.

The employment of correlativity without the necessity to posit a cosmic whole as background of one's ruminations is a defining characteristic of philosophical Daoism.[34] From that insight follows the irrelevance of dialectical and analytic modes of discourse. And from the irrelevance of the dialectical and analytic modes of discourse follows the implausibility of precise concepts, or of univocal language. From the irrelevance of conceptual language derives the impossibility of having objects or explanations of those objects that own any final integrity or comprehensiveness. This means that neither the world nor the self can constitute a coherent unity.

We have seen thus far that the Daoist self expressed in terms of the *wu*-forms engages the world in a mirroring manner that accepts order to be a function of the focal activity of each item in the totality of things. In such a world, order is the same as chaos: Order in any general sense is an indefinite, sum of overlapping orders. *All this is basically Zhuangzian Daoism, rather than Laozian Daoism.*

SELF, HUMOR, AND THE
TRANSFORMATION OF THINGS

We have tried to understand the focus-field self in classical Daoism by articulating some of the consequences of the sage's act of mirroring that allows things to be seen in their own order(s). One way of doing this is to ask, as we have just done, "What sort of being is it who engages a world constituted by a complex set of overlapping orders shaped by the individual perspectives, or particular foci (*de* 德), of each of 'the ten thousand things'?" Responding to this question has led us to the notion of the deferential self characterized by the modes of engagement we have identified as *wuzhi*, *wuwei*, and *wuyu*.

Another fruitful route toward understanding the Daoist version of the deferential self is by noting that the employment of the *wu*-forms as means of mirroring the world as it is, has direct consequences for establishing the "mood," "temperament," or "humor" with which the Daoist engages the ten-thousand things.

According to the *Zhuangzi*, the Daoist deferential self is characterized by a lighthearted mood of "free and easy rambling."[35] Such a mood is often contrasted with the more serious-minded Confucian, and is perhaps even more dramatically contrasted with the "high seriousness"[36] of the Anglo-European culture.

The dominant sensibility of Western philosophy is imbued with a commitment to a single-ordered world, hierarchically arranged, with human beings near the top of the ladder ("a little less than the Angels"). The high-seriousness of the Western person is an appropriate response to the fixed and permanent status of his world. Daoists, by contrast, respond to a more horizontal world of things possessed of an indefinite number of orders. Their's is thus a more flexible, lighthearted, response. We propose to pursue this contrast between the "serious" and the "lighthearted" as means of highlighting the distinctive character of the Daoist self.

On the cover of Hans Lenk's delightful collection of philosophical humor entitled, *Kritik der Kleinen Vernunft*,[37] there is a unicorn with its celebrated single horn fully as long as its torso. Its foreleg is raised in a classic pose. A saddle blanket on its back carries the portrait of Descartes. The caption reads: *"Du denkst, also bin ich."*

The humor of this statement lies in the claim (*pace* Descartes) that there are serious incongruities between the character and intent of rational thinking, and the more bizarre entailments and accoutrements of

that process. The rational cogito that permits arguments for the existence
of God, the self, and the world, and for the regularities of the world-order,
must be allied with the means of entertaining extrarational phenomena.

This rendering of the consequences of Cartesianism illustrates one
of the more popular interpretations of humor. On this view, humor results
from a clearer recognition on the part of an individual that allows him
to assume a superior stance with respect to the humorous object, person,
or event. Thus, the humorist does not primarily comment upon the
constitutively humorous character of existence and circumstance, but,
rather recognizes the laughable state into which others have fallen in their *?*
attempts to be serious. In this instance, philosophy itself may be said to
be humorous by virtue of its everlastingly unsuccessful siege upon the in-
finite, the sole motivation of which is to kidnap truth and bring it home
"dead or alive."   *Not necessarily Daoist.*

One may surely find a rather different sort of humor in Daoism
by virtue of its recognition that the incongruities of life and circumstance
are built into the character of the world. The Daoist recognition of the
penultimate, transitory state of all final discriminations does not, fundamentally, serve a didactic program meant to reveal to the uniniti- *?*
ated the truth of the Daoist perspective. After all, things are not truly
humorous if we are merely making fun of those who do not see the world
as we do. For the Daoist who mirrors the parity of things, there can be
no final distinction between joker and "jokee." Humor must be based
upon parity, and this means that the joke is always pretty much on
everyone.

This suggests that there are two levels of humor in Daoism, only one
of which is finally endorsed by the deferential self. One level results from
revealing to the unaware the transitory character of the sorts of distinctions and discriminations often made and presumed to be firm
characteristics of the way of things. The other, truer, source of Daoist
humor lies in the recognition that the myriad things require us, as
deferential selves, to take stands and make commitments that cannot but
lead to substantive incongruities. In other words, there are incongruities
that cannot be resolved even by the increased awareness of the sage. The
deferential sage has no means of escape from this condition. Nor does he
wish to escape.

In contrast to the lightheartedness of Daoism, mainstream Western
theories of humor may be found to be based upon some rather *serious*
assumptions. If the end of philosophic enquiry is final understanding

of the way of things, then humor is a penultimate affair at best. The only philosophic positions that allow constitutive incongruities are those that permit the coexistence of a plurality of ways of focusing the world. Of course, merely recognizing these incongruities will not in itself be humorous. This recognition must involve an awareness of the (transitory) commitments involved in the deferential acts of the self in its exercise of *wuzhi, wuwei,* and *wuyu.* If the commitment is merely to *the fact that* the world is incongruous, there can be no real humor, for this is simply another theoretical claim that renders the world a *seriously* plural affair.

To be constitutively funny, humor cannot simply be the consequence of one person's insight into incongruities unperceived by another. Thus all didactic humor is suspect. For, if the lesson is one that the teacher, but not the poor student, knows in advance, where does the true humor lie? Didactic humor is always tainted with *cruelty.*

What this means of course is that didacticism is ultimately an extremely serious affair. And surely the most serious of all didactic thinkers are the ideologues and theorists who believe themselves to have rather important lessons to teach. Armed with the principal weapons of reason, construction, and critique, such individuals express themselves in the mood of unrelenting seriousness, killing in advance any opportunity for the recognition of humor. Theory construction subsumes incongruities, sometimes outright contradictions, under a single putatively more coherent theory. Critique directly challenges the distinctions that lead to the incongruities among things, thereby dissolving the problem.

Of course, in their attempts to employ criticism and construction to cancel incongruities, theorists create new incongruities. Since no single theory has ever won the day, and since we are possessed of such a large number of conflicting theories, theoretical activity, degenerated now into a highly relativistic enterprise, itself easily becomes an object of humor. But the situation of theoretical relativism hardly seems to be legitimately funny.

Relativists can easily develop incongruity criteria for humor, but are not so apt to find any place to apply these criteria since the relativities they chart are almost always theoretical, rather than ontologically constitutive of the way of things, and are seldom thought to involve practical consequences. That is to say, relativists do not normally wish to claim that the world itself actually exists in a number of different ways, but only that we have a number of different theories of the way of things, and that there is no satisfactory means of deciding that gets at the way things really are. Secondly, a consistent relativist must claim that nothing *practically* follows from her relativism but inaction. If one tacitly or explicitly commits to one of a number of ways of acting, relativism has been *practically* abandoned. Thus, the issue of relativism in Western philosophy is mainly a red herring. Most individuals who espouse relativism at the level of theory, abandon it when practical commitment is called for.

Philosophical Daoism avoids relativism by asserting a ground for parity by virtue of the continuity among things, associated with Zhuangzi's "transformation of things (*wuhua* 物化)." *Dao* is the total process of becoming that constitutes the ways of things. These things form worlds characterizable from the perspective of each and every item in the total process. Given the uniqueness of all things as a starting point, particulars must, with reference to any given issue, stand in hierarchical relationships. This is the ground of deference. All things defer, in this way or that, to all other things. This is why a correlative *yin-yang* vocabulary usually works to articulate relationships. We say "usually," because, given the porous nature and attendant vagueness of particular things and events, there are occasions on which the *yin-yang* language is not functional: "What *yin-yang* does not fathom is called inscrutable (*shen* 神)."[38]

The transformation of all things entails two important consequences: First, there are always myriad alternative postures that challenge the ultimacy of one's present configuration. Secondly, the processional nature of experience guarantees that one will in fact actually proceed through an indefinite number of such configurations. The sagely recognition of this fact is the source of Daoist humor at its best.

With Daoism, specifically the Zhuangzian variety, the issue of relativism is usually seen to be irrelevant. Though our assumption that Zhuangzi is a realist would doubtless be challenged by many scholars who would insist that he is an extremely subtle proponent of a kind of skeptical relativism, Zhuangzi's transformation of things seems to commit him to the belief that the world actually exists as a shifting set of ways of being, a myriad set of overlapping worlds, a chaos of thises and thats, a multifarious congeries of orders. Chaos, *hundun* 渾沌, understood as the totality of all orders, names the way of things. Moreover, Zhuangzi seems to believe that there are crucial and direct practical consequences of such pluralism. The deferential self, expressed through the modalities of the *wu*-forms, spontaneously engages in mirroring responses that take into account the *de* of the items or events it encounters.

Thus, Zhuangzi's "relativism" (a misleading description) at the level of "theory" is seriously moderated at the level of practice, since deference entails both *continuity* and *commitment*. There are, therefore, direct practical consequences of mirroring the vast indifferent complex of the ways of things in a manner that allows one to see all things as viable candidates for deferential response.

The paradigm for Daoist humor turns out to be something like this:

If people sleep in damp places, they ache at the waist and end up half-paralyzed, but is this the case with the loach? If they live in the trees, they tremble with fear, but is this the case with the ape?[39]

The paradigm of humorlessness, on the other hand is something like:

What is sauce for the goose is sauce for the gander.

Daoist humor depends upon the coexistence of a plurality of viable world-orders. If *the* World is one, single-ordered, rational, coherent, internally consistent cosmos, then it is singularly humorless. Even if the totality is acknowledged to possess many orders, as long as there is any hint of a logical or axiological priority given to one or some orders vis-à-vis another or others, the ground of constitutive humor is undermined. This is the case because the notion of a privileged order implies a nondeferential, determinative stance that cancels true humor.

For Zhuangzi, it is not simply a matter of taking up a variety of sympathetic stances; one actually becomes all of the potential objects and beings with respect to which such stances may be taken:

Before long, Master Lai fell ill. Wheezing and panting, he was on the brink of death. His wife and children gathered about him and wept. Master Li, having gone to enquire after him, scolded them, saying: "Get away! Don't impede his transformations!"

Leaning against the door, Master Li talked with him, saying: "Extraordinary, these transformations! What are you going to be made into next? Where are you going to be sent? Will you be made into a rat's liver? Or will you be made into an insect's arm?

Master Lai replied, "...Now if a great ironsmith were in the process of casting metal, and the metal leapt about saying: 'I must be forged into a Mo Ye sword!' the great ironsmith would certainly consider it to be an inauspicious bit of metal. Now, if once having been cast in the human form, I were to whine: 'Make me into a human being! Make me into a human being!,' the transformer of things would certainly take me to be an inauspicious person. Once we take the heavens and earth to be a giant forge and transformation to be the great ironsmith, where ever I go is just fine. Relaxed I nod off and happily I awake."[40]

The transformative processes (*wuhua* 物化) are not to be interfered with, but are to be met with _deference_. To this extent, the sage is in agreement with Faust who proclaims to Mephistopheles: "If I ever say to the moment, 'Hold! Thou art so fair!,' then thou canst require my soul of me."[41] What distinguishes the life of the Daoist sage from that of the pleasure-seeking Faust lies in the difference between aggressive desiring and *wuyu* 無欲. For Faust each moment brings a new object of desire to be seduced, consumed, or otherwise enjoyed, and then abandoned.

Show me fruits which rot ere ever gathered from the tree.
And trees that ever bloom anew.[42]

The Daoist neither demands constant transformation for the sake of the ever new, nor does she object to transformation, attempting to apply the brakes and hold onto the moment. The deferential self yields to the ✓ moment, without constraint.   /subtexting/

Daoists such as Zhuangzi are lighthearted by virtue of being freed from the serious responsibilities entailed with "being right" or "having the truth." Were one to seek a coherent theory to house Zhuangzi's teachings, he would risk constructing a platform from which he may proclaim (implicitly) the superiority of those teachings. And if we presume that Daoist humor is used in the defense of a vision of things that necessarily denies the validity of other visions, we have simply rendered humor parasitical upon the defense of a particular way of envisioning things.

The character of lightheartedness lies in a felt incongruity or contradiction. Daoist humor treats these incongruities as existing among things and events that are on a par with the others. The pluralist vision of Daoism plays upon the sense of the contradiction between one perspective and a myriad others: between Zhuangzi and a butterfly; among fishes, birds, cicadas, and turtle doves; between men and monkeys. Lightheartedness is an essential means of teasing one into the recognition of the variety of perspectives permitted by the totality of existing things. The need for allusiveness lies in the fact that one cannot fully appreciate the differences without some sense of the reality of those differences. However, one cannot confront these differences in too direct a manner; they may best be hinted at.

Language is both expressive and allusive. Elliptical uses of language in the expressive mode are translatable into literal locutions. Much didactic humor may be translated in just this way without (didactic) loss. But this can be so only in a world that presumes a single ordered perspective. In a world defined by the vast indifference of Chaos, literal expressions, or metaphorical expressions that may be translated back into literal locutions, are of little account. Allusiveness is essential; nuance is the goal of language. If one wishes to make a statement about something that is irrevocably *vague*, parabolic and metaphoric languages are necessary.

Leibniz held that this world is best because any other possible world would suffer from a greater amount of evil. He believed this because he held that a perfect world would perforce contain "incompossible" items, things that could not logically coexist. This single best world then is patterned by a preestablished harmony of ordering actions and events. Zhuangzi's view, on the other hand, seems to be that there is no one or no thing, neither the Great Clod 大塊, nor *tian* 天, nor *dao* 道, which has decided which among an indefinite number of worlds will be allowed existence. All possible worlds will obtain by virtue of the transformation of things. No world is privileged over any other in the sense that all are required for any other to be what it is, and what it will be. Furthermore, the logical notion of "incompossibility" (which Zhuangzi almost certainly never entertained) is dissolved into a broader notion of "incongruity" that results from the diversity of things, each possessing its particular focus, each owning its claim to deference.

We certainly agree that humor requires commitment to incongruities, but acceptance of the fact of these incongruities by recourse to a *theory*, tames them overmuch. Humor requires that we escape from theory, for theory is nothing more, or less, than a sorting that makes us see things as unequal. What the Daoist requires is an acceptance of the ontological parity of things, and of the necessity for deferential, if transitory, commitments to one or more of the multifarious outcomes in the world.

In the Western context we would call the mood or attitude that results from these two acknowledgements, *irony*. According to Cleanth Brooks, "Irony is the most general term we have for the sort of qualifications that the various elements of a context receive from the context."[43] Theory is always a narrowing of context. True humor, at least in the form of irony, is a celebration of the limitations of embodiment. This is the reason those who insist upon theories that embody intuitions about the way of things within limiting contexts fail to be humorous, even though they themselves may be thought laughable. Only if she can raise to the level of consciousness the fact that visions, theories, worldviews are in their very nature self-limiting, and therefore ironic, can the intellectual escape humorlessness. This point is illustrated quite well in the following lines of Whitehead concerning the need for the philosopher to avoid as much as possible delimitations based upon too narrow a selection of evidence: "Philosophy must not neglect the multifariousness of things. The fairies dance and Christ is nailed to the cross."[44] Most would likely claim that attempting to keep both the serious and the lighthearted aspects of existence together in a single intuition would not allow us much room for laughter. We laugh when we forget the seriousness of things, or as a means of so forgetting. Recall Byron's line, "If I laugh at any mortal thing, 'tis that I may not weep." The closest thing in our own cultural inventory to humor as defined by the Daoist seems to be the ironic sense. Holding in a single intuition both the fairies' dance and the crucified Christ brings a recognition of the ironic character of life and circumstance. In the West, therefore, the highest form of humor involves a recognition of limits. Its precondition is reflexivity; its mode is irony. Philosophic humor is that irony most directly associated with self-referential contradictions or conflicts. What this means is that, however ironic may be life and circumstances, nothing is really very funny.

The key is found in the advice that we must not take ourselves too seriously, or others too lightly. The world is a Vast Indifference, a Blessed Multifariousness. It is unorganized. Living an embodied, contextualized, existence—whether as an eel, an elephant, a turtle dove, or human being—means that we have automatic preferences for construing the world in accordance with the convenience of the sorts of beings we presume ourselves to be. It is not enough to recognize a plurality of ways of being; we must own up to our transient preferences and commitments; they are important for as long as they last. The contradictions they entail are unavoidable. But for every loss there is a gain; nothing is finally tragic.

Though "irony" is the closest term to suggest the Daoist form of humor, it is hardly an altogether appropriate one. There can be no philosophic irony without the dialectic of tragedy and comedy as it developed in ancient Greece.[45] And as no such dialectic is evident in the development of Chinese culture, we probably should not attempt to interpret Chinese humor in ironic terms.

In Zhuangzi's Daoism, the doctrine of the transformation of things precludes the development of a tragic sense. Such a sense is predicated upon *loss*. The transformation of things guarantees that there is no final loss; there are only processes of transformation that allow us to become what we have not yet become. Further, the lightness of Daoist humor is by no means a consequence of focusing upon the fairies' dance in order to avoid the vision of the crucifixion.

There is an ultimate seriousness in the ironic sense that precludes it from expressing the lightheartedness of the Daoist sage. Irony, in Kierkegaard's phrase, "masters the moment," permitting the ironist to accept the tragic way of things without recourse to a mask. The Daoist does not seek to master the moment, but to yield himself up to it through the sort of lighthearted deference with which Master Li, lolling against Master Lai's door, proclaimed, "Extraordinary, these transformations! What are you going to be made into next?"

Zhuangzi's Daoism, purged of any taint of ultimate privilege, expresses the sort of lightheartedness that manifests true humor. For the Daoist thinker would not be undone by the fact that "the fairies dance and Christ is nailed to the cross." He or she knows that we shall each have our turn at the dance, and on the cross. There, by the grace of the Vast Indifference of Lord Hundun and the Blessed Multifariousness of His Realm, we *shall* go. This is the transformation of all things. There is nothing tragic here. No need, therefore, for a comic mask behind which to hide. There is lightheartedness and lightmindedness, and the humor it engenders. This is true humor. And the joke, as always (if we would but recognize it), is on us.

The Daoist and the Confucian understandings, as we have just outlined them, may appear more distant from one another than in fact is the case.

Partly this is so because we have separated our discussions of the basic meanings of selfhood in these two traditions, and have appealed to a different vocabulary. However, we have but to keep in mind that both Confucian and Daoist understandings are based upon *deferential* engagement in order to recall their core similarity. In the following chapter, dedicated to the discussion of Chinese and Western under-standings of sex and gender, we shall be able to draw upon both Daoist and Confucian sources to illustrate the family resemblances of the two traditions vis-à-vis the rather distinct family of Western thinkers.

CHAPTER FOUR

Chinese Sexism

Our argument so far has been that an explanation of the classical Chinese model of self requires an appeal to a significantly different vocabulary from that which has framed those conceptions of self dominant in the development of Western cultures. A failure to appreciate the real degree of difference between prevailing Western assumptions about self and their Chinese counterparts has had important consequences for some issues in cross-cultural studies. Perhaps none of these issues is more significant than that associated with the understanding of sexual difference. We will move now to that subject in an effort to explore the implications of factoring the treatment of sexuality into the question of what it means to be a person.

Given the pervasiveness of the masculine prejudice in Chinese culture, we certainly will not pretend that the Chinese tradition is anything but sexist. We shall argue, however, that the shape that sexism takes in the Chinese tradition is culturally specific and reflects an alternative model for the interpretation of gender differences, a model that might offer a fruitful line of inquiry and practice for Western thinkers.

THE GENDER OF THINKING

A generation of feminist reflection in the West has provided us with the useful distinction between "sex" and "gender." Sexual distinctions between males and females are associated with biological factors such as the possession of XY as opposed to XX chromosomal structures (in human beings), or, more generally, with the production of relatively small or large gametes, respectively, or with differences associated with reproductive physiology and secondary sexual characteristics. "Gender," on the other hand, refers to specific roles and functions performed by men and women in various societies. Whereas sexual differences may be said to constitute a transcultural phenomenon, gender distinctions are held to be culturally specific and often to vary significantly from one social or cultural complex to the next.

The one gender-related trait that seems practically pervasive in the human species is that of the dominance of the male sex over the female, when dominance is construed in broadly political terms. If it can be shown that this dominance is not a definite implication of biologically determined sexual differentiation, or that cultural evolution has reached a point that such natural determinants can be transcended, then social and cultural changes leading to parity between the sexes can more easily be pursued.

At the extremes, many sociobiologists provide the conservative "biology is destiny" arguments. The most familiar argument runs something like this. Females produce a small number of large gametes; males produce a large number of small gametes. The aims of procreation are served best by a male tendency to disperse gametes in as large a population as possible, and by a female tendency to nurture her fertilized eggs. Activities associated with male promiscuity and polygamous sentiments, as well as female domesticity and nuturance, are accounted for in this way. Thus behavioral differences at the cultural level are accounted for by appeal to genetic determinants. Gender is reduced to sex.

At the other extreme are those who argue for the pluralism associated with the original Darwinian vision of the variability of species. In the absence of any essential shared characteristics, there are no fundamental natural kinds. Variations within a species constitute a primary expression of the mutability of species. By analogy, morphologically and genetically grounded variations among the members of a single sex argue against the use of sexual differentiation to ground explanations of behavioral differences. When one adds to the categories "male" and "female" those of "hermaphrodite" and "neuter," and supplements the gender-based notion of "heterosexuality" with that of "homosexuality," the degree of biological and cultural diversity is increased sufficiently to challenge the idea that sexual differences among human beings reflect natural kinds.

Our own, distinctly pragmatic approach to the issues of sexuality and gender is well expressed in the words of John Dupre:

What is unique about human beings is not their tendency to contravene an otherwise unvarying causal order, but rather their capacity to impose order on areas of the world where none previously existed. In domains where human decisions are a primary causal factor, I suggest, normative discussions of what ought to be must be given priority over claims about what nature has decreed.[1]

This is a classic illustration of the claims of *nomos over physis*. We endorse this view as long as it is not (mis)understood in the stereotypically Protagorean form that interprets culture as the imposition of order through expressions of the human will. Viable human order is, as we have argued throughout our published work, an aesthetic achievement constituted by culturally specific activities. Applying this insight to our present subject leads to the following claim: Rather than gender differences being ruled by sexual distinctions, the reverse seems largely to be true.[2]

The outline of our argument is as follows. In Western cultures broadly, the sexual differentiation of male and female has tended to be rooted in dualistic categories that arguably ground the gender distinction. There is first the diremption of the range of possible human traits and dispositions into male and female. Male dominance has then led to the definition of the truly human person in terms that by and large privilege masculine gender traits. The achievement of humanity is thus construed as the realization of maleness. Freedom from male dominance at the level of *sexual* differentiation has not freed the female to realize female *gender* traits, but rather has required that she, like the male, employ the gender roles of the male as the standard.

By contrast, in China the realized person has been broadly defined as an achieved harmony of the full range of human traits and dispositions. Male dominance is a consequence of sexual differentiation into male and female that has tended to exclude the female from the achievement of becoming human. Thus, the male has been free to pursue the task of realizing his personhood though the creation of an androgynous personality.

The distinctive feature of the Chinese conception of gender is that were, *per impossibile*, the female to be allowed freedom to pursue realized personhood, she could do this by seeking a harmony of the same range of human traits that the male employs as standard. Chinese sexism, which denies to the female the possibility of becoming a human being, is brutal in the extreme. However, the model available to avoid continued brutality might be more humane than is the Western model. The status of women in Western cultures might be deemed less humbling, but the means of becoming truly human advertise a more subtle kind of dominance. To be human you must be male.

In her work on the relationship between gender and the Chinese cosmology in which gender relationships are subsumed, Alison Black notes:

> We may legitimately pursue the possibility that some of the basic concerns of Chinese metaphysics and cosmology transcend questions of gender.... It is probably safe to say that the basic polarity is not one of gender. Not only do *yin* and *yang* not *mean* "feminine" and "masculine" etymologically or invariably or primarily, gender in fact depends on too many other concepts in order to develop into something significant itself.[3]

Black then pursues those more fundamental conditions of the culture in which the gender distinction has emerged:

> Is there any governing factor that lends consistency to the transitions and permutations of gender concepts in Chinese correlative thinking? Can we identify *the* basic polarity?[4]

We would argue that the first step in this recovery is to acknowledge that the contrasting senses of aesthetic and rational order described throughout our work help us to understand the distinction between a dualistic and a correlative model for construing gender relations. The cosmological contrasts in the Western tradition have tended toward exclusive dualisms; those in China toward complementary pairings. The basic polarity in China will doubtless involve mutually implicated contrasts ("light" and "dark," "active" and "receptive"). The basic polarity in the West will involve mutually inconsistent pairings. An extremely influential illustration of this is the Pythagorean Table of Contraries as recorded in Aristotle's *Metaphysics*.[5] Characteristic of this set of pairings based upon the contrast of "limit" and the "unlimited" is the radical exclusivity of the categories.

Pythagoras' Table of Contraries

Limit	*Unlimited*
One	Many
Odd	Even
Light	Darkness
Good	Bad
Right	Left
Straight	Curved
Square	Oblong
Rest	Motion
Male	Female

In the left column are listed the formal qualities that are so-called because they are determined by number, the root metaphor of the Pythagoreans. On the right are the inchoate properties or qualities that are indeterminate with respect to number. This suggests the sort of form/matter distinction that will later become central to Aristotle's thinking. To the extent that this sort of classification has been influential, the male/female distinction has been thought to function as the relation of inconsistent elements.

One of the more influential responses on the part of contemporary feminists to this dualistic assessment of sex and gender differences is found in Carol Gilligan's distinction between a "feminine" and "masculine" voice.[6] Gilligan argues, first, that virtue is gendered, and second, that, contrary to the common notion that the female is less developed morally than is the male, the ethic that can be derived from the feminine voice has many qualities preferable to those of the male ethic.

Although Jean Grimshaw is unpersuaded herself that such a masculine/feminine distinction can be meaningfully articulated and sustained, she does provide us with clear language for pursuing the distinction, citing a range of feminists in reconstructing what is fundamentally this same dichotomy between "the maleness of philosophy" and "the idea of a female ethic." Grimshaw presents the following list as six characteristics that advocates of the distinction, notably Jane Flax,[7] would identify as most revealing of the maleness of philosophy:

1. A denial of the social and interactive character of human development; a stress on the separateness or isolation of human beings.

2. Forms of individualism which stress autonomy; for example, the autonomy of the individual will or the autonomy of the knower and the radical separation of the knower from what is known.
3. Oppositions between mind and body, reason and passion, reason and sense.
4. Themes of the mastery, domination and control of the body, the passions or the senses; and fears about loss of control.
5. Fear of women and of anything that is seen to be associated with them: sexuality, nature, the body.
6. Devaluation of all that is associated with women, and a need not to be dependent on it.[8]

Grimshaw then identifies the following three themes as recurring in those feminists who seek to pursue the lineaments of a female ethic:

1. A critique of abstraction, and a belief that female thinking *is* (and moral thinking in general *should be*) more contextualized, less bound to abstract rules, more concrete.
2. A stress on the values of empathy, nurturance or caring, which, again, are seen as qualities that women both value more and tend more commonly to display.
3. A critique of the idea that notions of *choice* or *will* are central to morality, and of a sharp distinction between fact and value; a stress, instead, on the idea of the *demands* of a situation, which are discovered through a process of *attention* to it and require an appropriate response.[9]

Although this contrast between male philosophy and the possibilities for a female ethic seems initially plausible, one may observe that, with respect to the mainstream of Chinese cultural self-articulation, there is a tacit rejection of those characteristics that define the maleness of Western philosophy in favor of what at least initially seems to be those same themes defining of a female ethic. *Ren* 仁, the central virtue of Confucianism, asserts the relationality and interdependence of human beings:

Authoritative persons establish others in seeking to establish themselves, and promote others in seeking to get there themselves.[10]

Daoism and its notion of the "authentic person" (*zhenren* 真人) is a celebration of the pursuit of full contextualization for the always unique person within an ever changing world. On the surface at least, it would seem that the patriarchs of both Confucian and Daoist philosophy expressed themselves in what is being described as a feminine voice, and given the pervasiveness of Confucianism and Daoism in the formative period of Chinese philosophy, it can be fairly argued that the development of Chinese culture has been strongly colored by feminine gender characteristics.

The observation that Chinese philosophy, taken in broad strokes, seems to promote either a sex- or gender-based ethic has at least three immediate implications for this discussion of feminist concerns.

First, given that Chinese philosophy has been no less a male-dominated occupation than Western philosophy, it would seem to support Grimshaw's resistance to the notion that philosophical temperaments and positions are physiologically based. After all, Chinese males seem to embody at least some of the characteristics that feminists who embrace the distinction between male and female gender have assigned to a female ethic. There seems to be something more fundamental than gender-difference at issue. Where "female voice" and "male voice" might be serviceable categories, these categories most definitely seem irrelevant to Chinese society.

Secondly, the Chinese example is surely a caution to those feminists who would promote a female ethic as an adequate resolution to Western sexist problems. If we take the Confucian experience into account, the reign of what is being described as a female ethic, far from precluding sexism, seems to have spawned an alternative, equally pernicious strain.

Thirdly, the specific characteristics that define the so-called maleness of the dominant Western style of thinking, such as autonomy and self-sufficiency, in contrast to the femaleness of a nurturing, caring, tradition, suggests at least one reason why Western philosophy, so defined, has failed to take the Chinese philosophic tradition seriously as real philosophy. And to the extent that the Western tradition has allowed Chinese philosophy a place, it is a place defined through the imposition of the disciplinary categories and standards of Western thought. As long as Western philosophers maintain their commitment to the Enlightenment project that promises it a self-sufficient certainty and that makes alternative traditions interesting only as a source of corroboration, Chinese philosophic and cultural activities will remain on the periphery.

DUALISTIC SEXISM

Above we have suggested that the idea of a sex- or gender-based ethic seems, on the surface, to be consonant with the aesthetic understandings of the Confucian/Daoist tradition. On inspection this turns out not to be the case, as we shall now argue. The primary argument against such compatibility is that the notions of either a sex- or a gender-based ethic reside within a dialectical context predominantly shaped by the recalcitrant male voice. What is at issue here is not simply the sex or gender distinctions, but the more general dualisms associated with the dominant Western tradition of thinking. This dualism begins at the cosmogonic level with the distinction between the procreative relations of Heaven (Male) and Earth (Female) that reflects, ultimately the contrast of Cosmos (rationality, Male) and Chaos (nonrationality, Female), and is instantiated philosophically in the contrasts of the worlds of being and becoming, and of the rational and irrational souls, in Plato. The dualism is of fundamental importance to Aristotelian thought expressed as the form/matter distinction. Its modern avatar, of course, is the mind/body dualism spawned by Cartesian mechanics.[11]

Proponents of a female, or feminine, voice differ as to whether this voice is a function of sex or gender. Some ground this difference in biological nature and its consequences.[12] Others claim only that it is a function of existing social practices and roles.[13]

Jean Grimshaw expresses at least two concerns about the elaboration of a sex- or gender-based ethic. First, whether the male and female voices are natural or cultural, they resist adequate description and remain unclear, a problem that seems related to the empirical observation that however these voices are distinguished, they do not seem to be characteristic of *all* males or *all* females. Secondly, the acceptance of such a distinction, entailing as it does claims so fundamental that women are perceived as reasoning in a way typically different from men, might well reinforce precisely those repressive stereotypes that we are anxious to overcome.[14] If one employs the male/female or masculine/feminine distinctions within a context in which the male voice is independent, autonomous, and self-sufficient, the female voice remains marginalized. This is true regardless of how we elaborate, amplify, and promote the gender traits assigned to the female.

It is clear that both of Grimshaw's concerns are important. First, this dualism threatens to instantiate an unnegotiable set of differences between the two categories. Characteristics of the male voice such as autonomy, independence, and individual freedom render it self-sufficient and exclusive. As such, it stands beyond the influence of the female voice that is at best incidental to it, and at worst, irrelevant. The female voice is derived from it, dependent on it, and inferior to it. As long as the male voice is maintained on its own terms, it continues a standard that, far from being able to tolerate or accommodate the female voice, exercises control over it. Under such a regime, interaction and reconciliation are not possibilities. The priority and strict transcendence of the one over the other precludes any substantive interaction between the two.

The question whether we can adequately discriminate a male and a female, or a masculine and feminine, voice in Western culture has to be addressed historically. While sympathetic to Grimshaw's argument for the richness and diversity of the positions that are being truncated to fit the potted characterization of "maleness," certain minimum generalizations can stand. When Grimshaw searches the inventory of Western philosophic positions, she is able to discover great divides among these positions that would preclude any broad generalizations or assertions. The definitions of reason, mind, and masculinity posited in any univocal sense are open to counter-example. But, even allowing for the richness and diversity of both the Western and Chinese philosophic traditions, and for the presence of both an aesthetic as well as a logical sense of order within both cultures, comparative philosophy does provide us with a perspective from which to generalize meaningfully about dominant features of these philosophic traditions. For example, where major thinkers such as Plato and Kant do have significantly different conceptions of reason, and of the manner in which sexuality affects or is affected by rationality, the gap closes measurably when we compare assumptions about the nature, the place, and the importance of reason in these two Western philosophers with any Confucian representative.

The pervasive nature of Western dualism explains in part the affinity that feminism has with many other marginalized ideologies, such as environmental thought or animal welfare. The resolution of any one of these problems seems in important measure dependent on the resolution of them all.

The bad news, then, is that our particular forms of sexism are culturally entrenched, and cannot be fundamentally resolved without a radical philosophical revolution. A truly nonsexist society cannot exist in the presence of social, political, and religious commitments that still promote dualistic thinking. The best nonsexist society possible under the continuing hegemony of dualistic categories would be achieved through the promotion females to the status of *honorary males*. To a significant degree, this has been the direction of women's liberation in Western society. However, this development entails precisely what Carol Gilligan has worried over—namely, gender sameness at the expense of sacrificing a range of human qualities that ought to be retained. In the presence of dualism, gender parity in difference is not a possibility.

The good news is that the attacks of philosophical positions such as pragmatism, hermeneutics, and various forms of poststructuralist thinking on dualistic thinking mark a significant revisioning of fundamental philosophic assumptions. This turning in Western philosophy seems essential if we are to dislodge the sort of thinking that has funded our Western brand of sexism.[15]

CORRELATIVE SEXISM

In the *Analects*, Confucius states:

> It is only women and morally retarded men that are difficult to raise and provide for. Drawing them close, they are immodest, and keeping them at a distance, they complain.[16]

Reflecting on the predicament of women in the Confucian tradition, the May Fourth author and critic, Lu Xun 魯迅, observes with undisguised cynicism:

> According to the ideas of present-day moralists who have stipulated the definition of chastity, generally speaking a chaste woman never remarries nor does she elope with another man after her husband has died. The sooner her husband dies and the more impoverished her family is, the more magnificent is her chastity. There are two more kinds of rigorously chaste women: the first one kills herself when her betrothed or husband dies, whether she has married him yet or not; the second one, when confronted by a rapist who will defile her, manages either to commit suicide or to have him take her life in the struggle to

resist him. The more brutal and painful her death, the more magnificent is her chastity.... In summary, if a woman's husband dies, she should remain chaste or die with him; if she encounters a rapist she should also die. And when such persons are everywhere praised, morality prevails in the world, and China can still be saved.[17]

From its classical beginnings to the present moment, China was and is a uniformly male-dominated and sexist society. Perhaps the most devastating charge against the tradition is the way in which this bias has insinuated itself into the Chinese language. If we look at the range of characters that have been grouped with the "woman" classifier, *nü* 女, as the signific portion of the graph, we find that, by and large and with some notable exceptions, these characters can be divided into three categories.

The first category is what we might expect: female roles and relationships such as "mother" (*ma* 媽), "aunt" (*gu* 姑), "wife of one's husband's elder brother" (*si* 姒), and "sister-in-law" (*zhou* 妯) are quite reasonably identified as female, where the remarkable and culturally revealing feature is the specificity of the relationship. The second category is a rather damning collection of negative character traits and suspect attitudes that are directly associated with the female gender: "absurdity" (*wang* 妄), "jealousy" (*ji* 嫉), "envy" (*du* 妒), "greed" (*lan* 婪), "lewdness" (*jian* 奸), "flattery" (*mei* 媚), and "slavehood" (*nu* 奴). In the third category, we have innumerable ways of saying "handsome" and "graceful" with subtle nuances: "alluring" (*yao* 妖), "good-looking" (*jiao* 姣), "agreeable" (*wan* 婉), "graceful" (*ting* 婷), and so on, suggesting that physicality was a major consideration in the male evaluation of the female.[18]

It is essential that we begin by stressing the pervasively sexist character of classical and contemporary China because, attempting to distinguish the Chinese form of sexism from that found in our own tradition, we will have to employ the language of interdependence, rather than independence, and of complementarity rather than autonomy. On the surface, such terminology may seem less pernicious than characterizations of sexism and male-dominance in Western societies. As the opening paragraphs of this chapter suggest, and as we shall soon argue, the problem of sexism is as great, or greater, in China than in industrialized Western societies. The primary point we wish to make is that the understanding of gender-construction in China is quite different from that dominant in the West. Grasping that difference will further our appreciation of the distinctiveness of these two cultures.

In the West, gender construction reflects institutionalized male dominance, while in China masculine and feminine gender traits form complementary characterisics that together suggest the range of possibilities for self-cultivation. In spite of the fact that, historically, occupations were clearly demarcated along the lines of sexual differences ("silk worms and the plow") and further, that only members of the male sex were given access to the cultural prerequisites for personal realization, we will see that the correlative model of gender-construction offers the possibility of a "polyandrogyny."[19]

In the classical Chinese tradition, personal realization in both the Confucian and Daoist traditions has been articulated in terms of the cultivation of the full range of gender traits. In Chinese culture, heart-and-mind (*xin* 心) make emotion and rationality co-present and inseparable. The same is true of *yin-yang* gender traits. As a corrective of what we take to be a popular, but nonetheless unfortunate, reading of Daoist philosophy, we will take the Daoist case as our example here.[20] Joseph Needham is typical of contemporary commentators in casting the Daoist-Confucian relation as *yin* versus *yang*:

> Confucian knowledge was masculine and managing: The Taoists condemned it and sought after a feminine and receptive knowledge which could arise only as the fruit of a passive and yielding attitude in the observation of Nature.[21]

Needham is committed to the significance of the "feminine symbol" in Daoism to the extent that on the basis of this interpretation (and seemingly unsupported by any documentable evidence), he suggests that ancient (proto) Chinese society "was in all probability matriarchal."[22]

The popular characterization of Daoism as feminine stresses its emphasis on all that is tolerant, permissive, withdrawing, mystical, and receptive, and advocates feminine yieldingness in all social and political relationships.[23] From a personal perspective, it recommends the observation of nature as opposed to the management of society, receptive passivity as opposed to commanding activity, and freedom from preconceived theories as opposed to an attachment to a set of social conventions.[24] Needham's discussion of the feminine symbol is in tandem with the water metaphor that suggests submissiveness and yielding.[25] That Needham is equating this feminine symbol with *yin* almost to the exclusion of *yang* seems to be his intention when he asserts:

> If it were not unthinkable (from the Chinese point of view) that the Yin and the Yang could ever be separated, one might say that Taoism was a Yin thought-system and Confucianism a Yang one.[26]

On this reading of Daoism (and it is *not* ours), it would be claimed that the *Daodejing* as a text supports the feminine interpretation in the following ways: There is the direct assertion in the text that the feminine overcomes the masculine, and corollary assertions such as soft overcomes hard, weak overcomes strong. Throughout the text, there seems to be an identification between the female reproductive organs and the reproductive *dao*, where, for example, the female vagina is often represented metaphorically as "the river valley," "the gorge," "the gateway of the mysterious womb," "the ravine of the world," and so on.

The key metaphors such as water, the infant, the valley, the mother, and the source, which parallel references to the female, are all defined in the language of feminine gender traits such as softness, weakness, darkness, tranquillity, receptivity. Traits such as these are employed to characterize the ideal ruler.

According to Needham, the *Daodejing* sponsors an ideal ruler who, rejecting the "masculine, managing, hard, dominating, aggressive, rational and donative" attitudes of the rival Confucian and Legalist traditions, opts for the "feminine, tolerant, yielding, permissive, withdrawing, mystical and receptive" approach to social and political order.[27] This interpretation usually centers in protracted discussions of *wuwei* 無為 translated as "non-action," *buzheng* 不爭 as "not contending," *rouruo* 柔弱 as "softness and weakness," *jing* 靜 as "tranquillity," and *xu* 虛 and *wu* 無 as "vacuity," portraying the sage ruler as the embodiment of these qualities.[28]

Needham, in advancing his "feminine" interpretation of Daoism, opens his discussion by lamenting:

> It is necessary to say that, for one reason or another, Taoist thought has been almost completely misunderstood by most European translators and writers.[29]

Ironically, Needham's characterization of Daoism as advocating feminine qualities to the exclusion of masculine ones itself does a serious violence to the texts.

We will argue that the rehabilitation and reinstatement of the feminine traits in the *Daodejing* is compensatory, and that a failure to appreciate this has resulted in a misreading of Daoism as passive, quietistic, and escapist. Against this reading, we contend that Daoism pursues a positive conception of the consummate human being, where attainment of this ideal demands sustained effort and authentication of one's understanding in action. It affirms the reality and the worth of the world as such, and seeks not to escape from it, but to appreciate it in all of its complexity.

The Daoist project entails the emulation of nature's patterned regularity:

> The human being emulates the earth,
> The earth emulates the heavens,
> The heavens emulate *dao*,
> And *dao* emulates what is so of its own accord (*ziran* 自然).[30]

The sense of order pursued by the consummate person has its analog in nature. This attitude is a recognition of the continuity that obtains among all things in the ongoing process and regularity of existence that we call *dao*:

> Thus the sage grasps on to continuity to be the shepherd of the world.[31]

Throughout the *Daodejing*, there is resort to "the Grand Analogy:" *Dao* is to the myriad things as the conduct of the consummate ruler is to the people. That is, there is an immediate correlation between how nature unfolds to maximize the possibilities of its myriad ingredients, and how the ruler ought to conduct the affairs of government. In the language of the *Daodejing*, both *dao* and ruler share the following characteristics:

1. "Doing nothing coercive yet accomplishing everything" (*wuwei er wubuwei* 無為而無不為) 37, 3
2. "Seldom issuing commands" (*xiyan* 希言) 23, 17

3. "Preserving the profoundest depths of vacuity and tranquillity" (*xujing* 虛靜) 5, 16
4. "Being soft and weak" (*rouruo* 柔弱) 40, 27
5. "Not contending" (*buzheng* 不爭) 23, 68
6. "Dwelling below/last" (*juxia/hou* 居下/後) 8, 7
7. "Unworked wood" (*pu* 樸) 32, 28
8. "Not appropriating" (*buyou* 不有) 51, 2

Dao pursues balance and harmony, and when this is upset, it works to restore it. Similarly, the *Daodejing* embraces *yin* characteristics as an appropriate antidote for the imbalance in the human world. The *Daodejing* is not advocating the substitution of *yin* values for the prevailing *yang* ones. On the political level, the *Daodejing* is not advocating the application of *yin*-based techniques to achieve the *yang*-inspired end of political control. Rather, the text pursues both the personal and the political ideal that reconciles the tension of opposites in sustained equilibrium and harmony. Whatever else "grasping on to continuity" might mean, it would seem to imply the interdependence of opposites, and their reconciliation through an achieved harmony that recognizes the value of difference. *Dao* activity is repeatedly described in the paradoxical language of the reconciliation of opposites:

> Radiant *dao* seems obscure,
> Advancing *dao* seems to recede,
> The greatest form is formless.[32]

The consummate person, modeling nature and achieving a posture consistent with the prescriptive *dao*, is also the reconciliation of opposites:

> One who realizes the male and yet preserves the female
> Is the river gorge of the world...
> One who realizes whiteness and yet preserves blackness
> Is the model of the world...
> One who realizes glory and yet preserves tarnishedness
> Is the valley of the world.[33]

We translate *zhi* 知 here as "realize" because of the performative implications of knowing in the classical language. To know the male is to embody it in action. This passage has a parallel elsewhere in the text which reinforces our reconciliation reading:

> The world had a fetal beginning
> Which can be considered as mother of the world.
> Having gotten the mother, thereby know her progeny.
> Having gotten to know her progeny, again preserve the mother,
> And live to the end of your days without peril.[34]

What appears here as feminine symbolism more appropriately represents a reconciliation between the feminine and the masculine. "Mother," for example, is impregnated woman—a union of the masculine and the feminine.

There is a related passage that again describes harmony and productivity as a coalescing of yin and yang:

> The myriad things shoulder the yin and embrace the yang,
> And blending this qi 氣,
> They attain harmony.[35]

Daodejing is, at least at one level, a political treatise, and because of its focus on the person of the ruler, we can claim that at least this person is described in androgynous terms. We can go beyond this and infer, however, that the ruler is perceived as setting the political and social conditions for the pursuit of personal realization generally, and inasmuch as his values serve as models for the empire, such realization is androgynous. Such speculation is not inconsistent with the passages in the text in which the sage-ruler is referred to as the "model of the world"[36] and in which, under the conditions of this model, the people are free to pursue their own realization:

> Thus, the sage says:
> I am nonassertive (wuwei)
> And the people transform themselves;
> I cherish stillness,
> And the people attune themselves;
> I do not intervene,
> And the people are prosperous of their own accord;
> I am objectless in my desires,

And the people retain their natural genuineness of their own
    accord.[37]

The conditions that the ruler desires for the people are the same as those
that he seeks for himself. A consummate person is one who has the tolerance to respond appropriately and efficaciously to any circumstance.

In the dominant models of Western cosmology, individuals move
from "where they are" to "where they ought to be" by siding with the
superior element in a set of dualistic categories. These categories include
God and world, being and becoming, knowledge and opinion, reality and
appearance, spirit and flesh, truth and falsity, and so forth. On the "*dao*"
model, realized individuals become correlates of *dao*, having available to
them the full range of *yin/yang* traits that includes both sides of the divine/
human (*tianren* 天/人) complementarity, both sides of the reason/emotion
(*zhiren* 知/仁) complementarity, both sides of the theory/practice (*zhixing*
知/行), substance/function (*tiyong* 體/用), spirit/flesh (*xinshen* 心/身),
practice/language (*xingyan* 行/言) complementarities.

It is important to realize that all correlative oppositions in the classical Chinese tradition are themselves hierarchical, with the dominant
member usually expressed first: Heaven/human being (*tianren* 天/人),
heart-and-mind/body (*xinshen* 心/身), and so on. What is curious in the
yin-yang case that does distinguish it from standard Confucian correlates
is that *yin* comes first, suggesting that the preferred posture is certainly
androgynous, but with the *yin* character traits being on balance superior
to those associated with *yang*.

In the correlative understanding, gender is more fluid and lacks
exclusivity. Although correlativity more easily promotes the redefinition
of roles and gender characteristics than does the dualistic model, in
practice the weight of tradition is a formidable obstacle to the instantiation of such redefinitions. Still, it is plausible to assume that, in the
absence of transcendental commitments to the contrary, alterations in
practice may be more easily made if there are concomitant changes in
cultural attitudes and practices that reinforce sexual inequalities.[38]

On the Confucian side, different players in the personalization of
gendered roles can express their own uniqueness as persons in a way that
can be compared with the way one "ritualizes" oneself to find a place in
community. Neither human nature nor gender is a given.[39] A person is not
born a woman, but becomes one in practice.[40] And gender identity is
ultimately not one of kind, but resemblance. The sexist problem, then,

will be one of degrees of disparity rather than strict inequality. Males and females are created as a function of *difference in emphasis* rather than *difference in kind*. Richard Guisso suggests as much in defining "difference" in the Chinese culture:

> The essential perception they [the Chinese classics] offer was the most basic of all—that male and female were different, as different as heaven and earth, *yang* and *yin*. The corollary, however, is what distinguished the Chinese view from most others. In an organically holistic universe, male and female were inextricably connected, each assigned a dignified and respectable role, and each expected to interact in co-operation and harmony. The fact remains, however, that the relationship is not an equal one.[41]

In his survey of the *Classics*, Guisso tries to clarify this relationship between subordination and difference:

> [W]hile there may be an implicit connotation of superiority and inferiority in the cosmology, the greater emphasis fell on the difference between male and female. Each sex had a distinct and complementary function and woman's place was neither dishonorable nor necessarily inferior to man's except in so far as earth was inferior to heaven or moon inferior to sun.[42]

Within the correlative model, the richest correlations are those that stand in the greatest degree of contrast. Hence, equality defined in terms of univocity and sameness is a casualty of difference and diversity. At the same time aesthetic coherence demands that there be centers that draw differences into harmony and have implicate within them a sense of a broader field. Corollary to difference then is the necessity of hierarchy. Without hierarchy, there cannot be a center. Creativity is dependent upon the degree of difference that exists between the polarity of male and female, and the tensions that it produces:

> The Confucian solution to male-female conflict was therefore threefold: separation of function, acknowledgement of hierarchy, and the idealistic injunction that mutual love and respect would be infused into the relationship.[43]

The culturally stipulated differences in function stimulates an inter-dependence between male and female that is cumulative and ideally is productive of mutual interest, need, and affection.

In the dominant strains of the Western tradition, even though a woman must resign her difference to become a person, she can still lay claim to an essential humanity that distinguishes her from her context. Essential human nature is a guarantee. Regardless of how degraded woman's role, she is still potentially and irrevocably a human being. The correlative model is more fluid and less stable than the dualistic one. The flexibility that permits a greater degree of creativity in the correlative model also permits a greater degree of abuse and grosser violations of human dignity.

The limits that restrict creativity in the dualistic model also establish boundaries on what is acceptable conduct. For example, the classical Confucian notion that the difference between beast, human being, and gods is simply cultural, means that while those human beings who are important sources of culture have a claim to divinity, human beings who resist enculturation are, quite literally, animals.

In the absence of some essential nature that guarantees the sanctity of all human life, there is justification for worshipping some human beings while abusing others as chattel. In the dualistic model, one may argue that a woman has not been permitted to be a man. In the correlative scheme, females have historically not been allowed to be persons.

Another feature of the correlative model is that the male/female complementarity cannot be divorced from other significant correlations. As Guisso observes:

> If the *Five Classics* fostered the subordination of woman to man, they fostered even more the subordination of youth to age. Thus, in every age of Chinese history where Confucianism was exalted, the woman who survived, the woman who had age and the wisdom and experience which accompanied it, was revered, obeyed and respected...even if her son were an emperor. It is perhaps this fact more than any other, which enabled the woman of traditional China to accept for so long the status imposed upon her.[44]

If we begin from the assumption that humanity is an achievement, age becomes a significant factor. Woman achieves status by growing old.

However, a simple-minded reverence for the aged is not to be encouraged. Confucius himself says repeatedly that age in the absence of achievement should be a source of embarrassment:

> The young should be held in high esteem. After all, how do we know that those yet to come will not surpass our contemporaries? It is only when one reaches forty or fifty years of age and yet has done nothing of note that we should withhold our esteem.[45]

The downside of the respect for cultural contribution and the age that necessarily attends it, however, is that it reduces the relative value of the young, and in extreme cases, has even served as a warrant for infanticide. Still, as a test for the claim that in the classical Chinese worldview, personal realization precedes the gendering of human characteristics, we can ask the question: In those cases when a woman becomes a matriarch, is she evaluated on the same terms as the patriarch, or is some distinctively feminine standard applied?

Another significant difference between dualistic and correlative sexism can be brought into focus by considering the private/public dichotomy. Jean Grimshaw points out that in our Western experience, both women themselves and the sphere of activity (the family and the home) with which they are associated have been devalued: "Masculinity, membership in the community of men, is something over and against daily life, to be achieved in opposition to it, in escaping from the female world of the household."[46]

This does not seem to be the case in the same degree in the Chinese world, where public and private are not severely separated. In fact, in all aspects of Chinese life—social, political, religious—it is the family rather than the individual that constitutes the basic unit of humanity. What is most significant about a person religiously, politically, and morally is derived from his or her participation in a ritually ordered familial world to the extent that, in the absence of family, one has little claim on humanity. A person lives within the interstices of the changing relationships and hierarchical patterns of deference that define family and lineage, and the person's realization is a function of the deepening significance of these same relationships. Without discounting the impoverishing effect of the patriarchal prejudice, we must allow that the relational definition of person in some degree shares both loss and gain in personal worth across the membership of the family unit.

As we saw above, the continuity and the wholeness of the family means that both the feminine and masculine contributions to the familial order are implicated in the person who embodies the authority of the tradition. In the Confucian tradition, the ruler is described not just as the father, but as "the father and the mother" (*fumu* 父母) of the people. Just as ruler *is* empire, so patriarch *is* family. The "roundness" of the realized person is an androgyny that enables him/her to draw on the resources of both male and female gender traits and to respond efficaciously to all circumstances.

There is one final feature of the correlative model that follows from this "achievement" conception of human being. Becoming a human being presupposes a perpetual revolution, an ongoing renegotiation and re-constitution of the roles and rituals that structure society. The portrait of women in history is certainly definitive of the historical situation, but still the uniqueness and fluidity of the present moment do allow in degree for a new configuration of the male/female roles. We must allow that the extent to which biological female has been deprived of meaningful participation in the culture has taken a toll on human possibilities. Stated the other way, a Chinese individual will undoubtably be both different and qualitatively more interesting when women are liberated from patriarchy.

However, there is a persistent worry in the project of woman's lib-eration in a Chinese society. Unlike the dualistic model in which some equality can be sought by recourse to a woman assuming the gender traits of a man, there is no such basis for essential equality in the correlative structure. Hierarchy would seem to be inevitable. The only possibility that might seem acceptable would be a qualitative hierarchy where status is a function of nongendered personal achievement rather than biological sex or cultural gender.

We should stress once more that our motive for articulating this alternative model of gender construction in the Chinese tradition has not been apologetic. Rather, ours is simply an effort to separate baby from bathwater when engaging Chinese culture. One familiar pattern in the literature that reports on gender in China has been to equate traditional Chinese culture with Confucianism, and then to condemn Confucianism because of its unrelenting patriarchy. This is analogous to disposing of all of the accomplishments of liberal democratic thinking—human rights, representative democracy, the modern university, the technologies of mass communication, and so on—because of a recalcitrant sexism within this tradition. Neither traditional Chinese culture nor Confucianism reduce to footbinding, any more than the richness of Western art and music reduce to breast implants.

Our argument has been that an understanding of gender construction and the prejudice that has attended it within Chinese society can be used as a resource for reflecting on our own experience, and further, can be appropriated as a supplemental resource from which a new conception of person can be derived for a new world.

PART II

"Truth" as a Test Case of Cultural Comparison

CHAPTER FIVE

Excursus on Method

THE WAY AND THE TRUTH

One of the more provocative questions raised in the last generation of sinological studies is whether the Chinese have a concept or theory of "truth."[1] While on the surface the claim may appear rather outrageous (surely Chinese tell the truth as often as we, and lie as often), the issue turns out not to be as easily settled as one might think.

In his introduction to *Disputers of the Tao*, Angus Graham distinguishes the central philosophical concern of the emergent literati class in classical China from that of the traditional Western philosopher by saying that their question was "not the Western Philosopher's 'What is the Truth?,' but 'Where is the Way?'"[2] This statement very succinctly contrasts the problematics of Western and Chinese cultures with respect to the issue of how one might orient oneself within the natural and social worlds.

The Western "What" question is usually expressed in something like this manner: "What kinds of things are there?" "What is the world made of?" or simply, "What *is* this?" Such questions have resulted in a catalog of facts and principles that assist one in taking an inventory of the world about us. The Chinese "Where" question, on the other hand, led to a search for the right path, the appropriate models of conduct to lead one along the path, the "way" that life is to be lived, and where to stand.

Each of the two civilizations is also shaped by the other's question as well, but with different meanings attached. In the West we do not ask "Where is the Way?" but "Where *in the world* am I?" Our response to that question has led to a relentless exploration of the worlds beneath, beyond, and about us, always motored by the desire "to boldly go where no one has gone before."

When the Chinese ask the "What" question, they ask "What sort of person am I?," "What is my role?," and respond with the observation that they are in fact social, familial, creatures shaped by custom and ritual, and intrinsically interconnected one with another. They are fathers, sons, brothers, citizens. Further, the Chinese have largely focused upon their "Chineseness," and have developed their world essentially in isolation from those outside the Chinese family. They have had little inclination to explore the world around them. (After all, why should they travel? As *zhongguoren* 中國人, people at the center, they, like the Cambridge don, are already there.) Their special genius has been the articulation of forms of ritual action to structure and stabilize the Chinese community. Such rituals lead to social harmony and the cultivation of the realized person within the Chinese family.

In addition to the "Where" and "What" questions, both Chinese and Westerners have asked "How?" For the Chinese the question is "How, by what means, may this or that be brought into the service of human flourishing?" For the Westerner, the question is "How might I classify or define this and that?" The popular Chinese writer, Lin Yutang, in a book with an appropriately Chinese title—*The Importance of Living*—illustrates the different shape of the "How?" question in China and the West. According to Lin, the reason the biological sciences, for example, never developed in China as they did in the West is that the Westerner, encountering a strange plant or animal will ask "How may I classify this?" while the Chinese will immediately ask "How may this be cooked?"

Chang Tung-sun [Zhang Dongsun] 張東蓀, in an article that first appeared in the thirties, observes:

> In putting a question about anything, it is characteristic of Western mentality to ask "What is it?" and then later "How should one react to it?" The Chinese mentality does not emphasise the "what" but rather the "how." Western thought is characterized by the "what-priority attitude," Chinese by the "how-priority attitude."[3]

In the West, truth is a knowledge of *what* is real and what represents that reality. For the Chinese, knowledge is not abstract, but concrete; it is not representational, but performative and participatory; it is not discursive, but is, as a knowledge of the way, a kind of know-how.

The contrast between Truth-seekers and Way-seekers is really quite significant. Truth-seekers want finally to get to the bottom line, to establish facts, principles, theories that characterize the way things are. Way-seekers search out those forms of action that promote harmonious social existence. For the Way-seekers, truth is most importantly a quality of persons, not of propositions. Truth as "Way" refers to the genuineness and integrity of a fully functioning person.

The apparent fruitfulness of this basic contrast between Truth- and Way-seekers certainly does not in itself answer the question whether it is legitimate to search for a word or words in the Chinese language we would be justified in translating as "truth." Further, if we were to translate some Chinese locution as "truth," we still would have to ask whether the Chinese conceptualize or make up theories explaining this term and account for the phenomena it represents or to which it alludes.

Oddly, it is the question of the presence or absence of formal *concepts* or *theories* of truth that looms largest in this discussion. For merely suggesting, along with Aristotle (*Metaphysics* Book III) that one speaks truly when saying of "something that is, that it is, and of something that is not, that it is not" is stating what is for (nearly) all of us, quite obvious. The interesting and important issues generated by the search for truth are consequences of the strong motivation of Western thinkers to move beyond the obvious and to construct theories. The situation is the same with the seemingly innocent notion of concepts. In a formal sense, a concept expresses the sense of a term. A term is a word with a stipulated meaning. The contexts of stipulation are, ultimately, theories. Thus a concept of truth has its locus within a particular theory.

There is really no useful sense in which we could refer to the statement of Aristotle just cited, taken simply by itself, as stating a concept or a theory of truth. This is the case even though the sentence is often taken as a succinct statement of the correspondence theory of truth. It is only after placing this claim within the context of Aristotle's metaphysical and epistemological assertions that we may say such a thing. In fact, the statement taken from its Aristotelian context and articulated in terms of idealist theory could as easily support a coherence theory of truth.

Even if we are uninterested in the philosophical niceties, we are nonetheless a part of a culture in which phrases such as "the quest for truth," "scientific truth," and "We hold these truths to be self-evident," make good sense to us. And when such rhetoric is unpacked by the experts, we have theoretical discussions of truth aimed at strengthening and justifying this language.

When we look at the Chinese culture, therefore, we do so armed with the assumptions highlighted by the importance Western philosophers have given, both tacitly and explicitly, to the notion of truth. We presume the Chinese must have a concept or theory of truth because we, quite rightly, assume that the Chinese are as concerned as we are as to whether or not dinner is on the table. We further believe (with far less justification) that in the background of this concern is a worry about saying of something that is, that it is. And we then take for granted (this time with no justification at all) that such a worry requires, yet farther in the background, some theory of truth.

It is plausible to suggest that we ought to translate a Chinese term "truth" only if the Chinese have essentially the same beliefs about, and with respect to, that term. This is to say, we might expect the Chinese to assert essentially the same things as we do when we address the term "truth." Let us grant for the moment that we in the West are in fact disposed to envision truth as an abstract concept and to develop epistemological theories underwriting the search for truth, and to justify claims to having discovered it. If the Chinese do not treat the locution(s) in their language that are translated by the term "truth" in the same manner, we are thereby urged to believe that we are dealing with different things.[4]

In the following pages we shall, tentatively, presume that the contrast between Truth- and Way-seekers is at least heuristically valuable, and along with the attempt to determine if there is indeed a viable concept of truth in the Chinese tradition, we shall endeavor to point out the interesting differences entailed by the contrasting interests in the Way and the Truth. In our contrast between the Way and the Truth as goals of philosophical reflection, we do not wish to perpetuate the clichéd interpretation of the West as theoretical and dispassionately reflective, and Chinese thinking as vested in the need for social harmony. From our perspective, the two cultures shared the only sensible goal for social human beings—the attainment of social stability and, possibly, of harmony.

Some comparativists have claimed that the Chinese concern for the Way was a consequence of the breakdown in moral and political order at the very period in which reflective thinking began in China. The Chinese, in contrast to the more speculative Greeks, were concerned with social order and harmony rather than with a dispassionate search for Truth. But, as we have argued in *Anticipating China*, there is every reason to believe that the search for a Truth that could serve as a standard in accordance with which a plurality of distinctive beings might be measured was itself a response to the problem of creating or discovering a social and natural order within which individuals might find a secure and harmonious existence.[5]

The suggestion that the Chinese sought the Way because of their more practical and urgent political and social concerns, while in the West we went adventuring after Truth because we somehow had the luxury to be speculative, is on reflection, highly questionable. A more pragmatic interpretation seems equally plausible. The philosophical discourse shaped in large measure by the search for Truth itself had an ethical and political cast from the beginning.

In pluralistic, ethnically diverse societies, it is not so easy to chart a concrete and specific Way among the many ways suggested by diverse languages, myths, customs, and rituals. Harmony must be sought through ascent to abstract, and ultimately universalizable, principles and standards. The quest for capital "T" Truth serves the aims of social and political stability in both positive and negative manners. Positively, it promises, down the road, a standard of common assent that can ground common values and practices. Negatively, it suggests the necessity of a certain tolerant circumspection in the treatment of those who do not share our present truths.

The prospect of contrasting these two political strategies for attaining social harmony is nonetheless worthwhile. For, simply on the surface, one can see that insisting that China belay its concern for the Way and go marching after Truth may easily threaten the sort of stability which is the hallmark of that civilization. Likewise, an attempt on the part of Western nations to institute a ritual-based culture might well threaten the stability of ideals and institutions in the West.

The series of events that has made the question, "What is Truth?" one of the defining concerns of the Western tradition constitutes a fascinating narrative, not the least because it could all have been different. The complex senses of truth encountered in the *Oxford English Dictionary* divide rather naturally into two categories. There is one class of meanings associated with notions of rectitude, integrity, wholeness, lack of distortion, and so on, and a second class associated with the comparison of what appears to be the case and the reality itself. This second class concerns issues such as "conformity with fact," or "real contrasted with imitation." The first class of meanings resonates with the Way metaphors we associate with the Chinese sensibility: the true course of an arrow, following the true path, having a true heart, and so on.

If we look to the Hebraic tradition at the time of the major prophets (8th–6th centuries B.C.E.), the senses of truth (ᵉmeth, ᵉmuna) are related to wholeness, integrity, and the ability to maintain oneself as healthy and whole in all circumstances. "Truth is that which can be maintained by the soul, that which has the strength to exist and act in the entirety of the soul."[6] The prophet is one whose words, being true, have *efficacy*. "A prophet must be true (ne'ᵉman) in order to be a prophet, to have the necessary strength of soul, that his words shall not fail to take effect."[7]

The sense of truth as "the strength to maintain oneself" contrasts readily with the notion of truth as signaling a correspondence between appearance and reality. Indeed, in the Western tradition, that sense was a gift of the post-Homeric Greeks. Philosophically, it is the Greek *aletheia* and the Latin *veritas*, as influenced by the Greek thinkers, which have come to determine the dominant uses of the terms in philosophical discourse. At the beginning of *Anticipating China*, we told the story of the manner in which second-problematic thinking associated with the presumption of the construal of a single-ordered cosmos from out of chaos provided the grounds for the assumptions of an ordering agency, the belief in an reality/appearance contrast, the preference for being and permanence over becoming and process, and the presumed disjunction between the claims of reason and those of sense experience.[8] It is this complex of beliefs that motivated the development of the distinctive senses of truth in the Western tradition.

Greek understandings of the term *aletheia*, as Heidegger and others have pointed out, suggest the idea of the revelation of something hidden or concealed. And though Heidegger argues that this sense contrasts with the more impoverished notions of truth as "correspondence with facts," it seems clear that the meaning of *aletheia* is consistent with the notion of "encountering reality," or "learning the way things are." Among the Greeks, encounter with reality is first achieved through direct revelation. The *Theogony* begins with the invocation of the Muses:

Hail daughters of Zeus! Give me sweet song,
To celebrate the holy race of gods
Who live forever.[9]

No reality/appearance distinction is asserted. The question of truth or falsity is yet to be raised.

In Homer, roughly contemporary with Hesiod, there is the beginning of a sense of truth as contrasted with "misrepresentation," or "dissimulation." There is a way things are, and a way things are presented. The conformity of the two is truth. But this is focused almost exclusively upon the notion of personal veracity which indicates that truthfulness is a characteristic of individuals.

It might be best to say that this sort of concern was still a matter of wholeness or integrity, and insofar as there was a generalization or abstraction from that concern, it led in the direction of what we might term facticity rather than propositional truth. And the concern with "fact" may be distinguished from the concern with "truth," precisely because at the concrete and specific levels at which one is concerned with facticity, the reflective issues leading to questions of a reality/appearance contrast, or the presumption of the coherence of all factual propositions, are not raised.

The disjunction between reality and appearance is most profoundly expressed in Parmenides' distinction between "The Way of Truth" and "The Way of Opinion." In the discussion of the two ways, Parmenides is addressed by a goddess in this manner:

> It is meant that you learn all things—both the unshakable heart of well-rounded truth and the opinions of mortals in which there is no true belief. But these, too, you must learn completely, seeing that appearances have to be acceptable, since they pervade everything.[10]

Ironically, the structure of Parmenides' poem is not unlike that of Hesiod's *Theogony*. The truth of the two ways is revealed directly by a goddess. We may be dealing here simply with poetic artifice. But the mystical character of Parmenides' doctrines suggests that he may indeed have felt his vision to have had the character of revelation.

It is rather clear that a *rational* distinction between the realm of sense experience and that of reason was rendered propositionally explicit in the paradoxes of Parmenides' disciple, Zeno. The Zenonian paradoxes of motion and change were to serve as one of the principal foils over against which subsequent theories were constructed. The question of how to save the reality of change and motion presented to our senses, and the authority of reason that led to the conviction that the evidences of the senses were misleading, occasioned the development of a series of attempts to deal with the way of things that had as a corollary consequence the perpetuation of the distinction between reason and sense experience, with the latter being placed in a subordinate position to the former.[11] Indeed, the greatest cause of the importance of truth-theory in the classical tradition and beyond has been the institutionalization of a reality/appearance contrast that led us directly, through the use of reason and rationality, or indirectly, through the use of logic, to criticize the evidences of the senses, and to concern ourselves with the establishment of correspondences between reality and appearances.

Xenophanes, an older contemporary of Parmenides,[12] expressly stated that the knowledge of the gods is not revealed by the Muses, but is a result of human reflection upon the world order:

The gods have not revealed all things from the beginning to mortals; but, by seeking, men find out, in time, what is better.[13]

A second development in the classical period that insured a concern for the notion of truth is that of the victory of the belief in a single-ordered cosmos. Of the two sorts of problematics that coexisted at the beginnings of our intellectual tradition, what we have termed first-problematic thinking, involving the belief in many world-orders, gave way early on to the acceptance of "one best world."[14] The second-problematic assumption of cosmological coherence was to serve as the basis for understandings of truth that depended upon the coherence of propositions and states of affairs.

The twin assumptions of a single-ordered world and a reality/appearance distinction guaranteed the dominant understandings of truth in the Anglo-European tradition. In much of our previous work, we have argued that these two assumptions were of no cultural importance in the Chinese tradition.[15] We shall briefly rehearse these arguments in the following pages. Our argument here is that, on these grounds alone, we would not expect to find concern for the notion of truth as correspondence or coherence to be of signal importance in the classical Chinese sensibility.

The story is far more complicated than this, of course, since there has been a perpetuation in our culture of the tradition associating truth with

Way metaphors. Existentialist and pragmatic understandings of truth, as we shall note later in our discussions, are themselves constructed against a background of the implicit or explicit denial of the two principal assumptions that ground dominant theories of truth in our tradition.

In modern Western philosophy, existentialist and pragmatic understandings of truth are concerned with the practical, consequential nature of thinking and acting. Existentialist perspectives often advertise an individualistic stance that does not well resonate with the Chinese sensibility. Nonetheless, the concern for self-cultivation in both Confucian and Daoist traditions is similar enough to the existentialist desire for personal authenticity to permit fruitful comparisons. But it is, most certainly, American pragmatism that provides the best resource for understanding Chinese approaches to the issue of truth. Thus, when in the latter portions of this part we do discuss the terms that function in classical China to do the work of truth-seeking in the West, we shall find that we have shifted to something like a pragmatic understanding of knowledge and truth that has less to do with correspondence or representation than with *inquiry*.

ARS CONTEXTUALIS

We wish to illustrate our claims about the absence of notions of truth in principal visions of classical Chinese culture by recourse to a method that may at first seem rather odd. Elsewhere we have described this comparative method as *ars contextualis*—the art of contextualization.[16] Practicing that method here will involve us in pointing out the shape of a cultural context within which a serious concern for truth would be found. That is, we shall ask "What are the cultural requisites for active speculations concerning truth?" Our intent is to demonstrate that the best way of deciding the issue of the importance or unimportance of a concept or theory of truth in China is to try to see if the cultural requisites permitting the search for truth are importantly present.

We obviously recognize that unreflective translators have presumed to find translation equivalents for "truth" (*dao* 道, *zhen* 真, *li* 理) by isolating a term or text from the cultural context that houses it. But the true guide and measure for any responsible translation or interpretation is the broad cultural context within which a term or argument finds its home. In the following pages, therefore, we have a twofold purpose: First, we want to question the importance in Chinese intellectual culture of the notion of truth in the formal, philosophical, senses that term has taken on in our own culture. We will do this, first, by pointing out the sorts of beliefs and assumptions entailed by the active search for truth, and, then, by suggesting that these beliefs and assumptions are not present in any important sense among the Chinese. Second, we shall be demonstrating what we take to be a fruitful manner of comparing alternative cultures with respect to the broadest range of issues.

Instead of asking directly after an equivalent Chinese term or concept that may be translated "truth," therefore, we shall ask what ideas, beliefs, or practices must be present if a concept or theory of truth of the sort found in the Anglo-European philosophic tradition is to be present. These serve as correlates of the self-conscious articulation of the concept of truth. We shall suggest that these correlates may be used to test whether such a notion is in fact present.

WHAT HAS ATHENS TO DO WITH ALEXANDRIA?

The principal distinguishing features of our method are the following: First, we are concerned with *discourse* rather than language in its formal sense. Thus, we are not concerned with the grammatical or syntactical potentialities of the language, but with the way the language has actually been used. Further, we are concerned with the manner the language has been used in those texts that have reflected the dominant beliefs and practices of the culture. Thus, we are focused upon cultural importances.

We can contrast our distinctly *philosophical* method with two other prominent methods of making cultural comparisons that we shall term the "grammatical" and the "historical." The grammarian is largely interested in the morphological possibilities of the language, quite apart from whether it has actually been employed in a manner that exploits those possibilities. The historian may be interested in the actual ways in which the language has been employed, however rare the instances of this or that usage might have been. Philosophers of culture, such as we purport to be, are interested in the efficacious uses of the language that constitute the dominant cultural sensibility.

There is no problem in distinguishing our method from that of the historian per se. Oddly, there might be some difficulty distinguishing our approach from that of the grammarian. The reason for this lies in the fact that we have over the years had numerous interactions with Angus Graham, perhaps the chief proponent of the grammatical method. These interactions have combined heated debates over method and warm agreements with respect to substantive conclusions. It will be important for us to show why our methodological disagreements with Graham have not carried over into conflicts concerning fundamental conclusions. Otherwise our readers may be confused by our generally positive references to Graham's insights.

In an appendix to his *Disputers of the Tao*, Graham criticizes some of our claims about the Chinese language made in *Thinking Through Confucius*. A discussion of those criticisms will clarify and focus both our arguments concerning the treatment of "truth" in the Chinese tradition, and the contrasting emphases of our respective comparative methods.

At issue is the relative merit of two contrasting emphases with respect to the analysis of Chinese philosophical discourse. Graham held that grammatical analysis provides profound insights into the Chinese language. Our claim, on the contrary, is that the inventory of ideas and principles expressed in the texts and doctrines of the tradition offers the best means of assessing the shape and direction of philosophic thinking. The clashes between Graham and ourselves occur when he appeals to grammatical evidences at those points we believe he should be focusing on the broader cultural context of the philosophical discourse.

Our arguments are philosophical; Graham, often (unnecessarily) cautious about mounting philosophical arguments himself, attempts to ground many of his most important claims about classical Chinese philosophy in what he takes to be the grammar of the classical Chinese language. Our methodological conflicts with Graham have often led us to ask, "What has Athens to do with Alexandria?"

Graham's interest in the morphological and grammatical characteristics at least potentially present within the Chinese linguistic structures led him to defend the flexibility and richness of linguistic and grammatical potentiality against those he believed were attempting to place undue limitations upon the language. At times Graham placed us among the group he accuses of "generalising about Classical Chinese... without reference to its grammar."[17]

Our response is that our disinterest in distinctly grammatical evidence is due to our conviction that the sort of grammatical investigations performed upon the Chinese language in recent years has been both inspired and practiced primarily by Western sinologists. We are, in fact, rather skeptical about the grammatical approach many Western sinologists, Graham being prominent among them, have taken with respect to the Chinese language.[18] Moreover, we would suggest that there is good reason why the Chinese themselves have been less disposed than have their Western interpreters to worry about the morphological characteristics of their language. The rationale is to be found in the distinctive manner in which the Chinese actually employ their language.

As broadly conceived as our comparative method might be, we would contend that it permits greater insight and accuracy with respect to both the translation and interpretation of mainstream philosophic texts. The most direct manner of stating the distinction between Graham and ourselves is to indicate that while Graham is essentially concerned with *langue*, our topic is *parole*. It is language as used within the context of broad cultural assumptions that appear to dominate the tradition that is our primary concern. Further, we are interested in the uncovering of cultural importances. That is to say, we wish to ask after the manner in which the language was *importantly* employed in philosophical practice, and precisely *not* how the language *might have been* employed. This distinction permits us to explain the rather paradoxical fact that though Graham and we are almost always in agreement on substantive issues bearing upon Chinese-Western comparisons, sharp disagreements over method persist.

The claims of ours that most exercised Graham were these: First, that "sentences" in the classical Chinese language are not expressed in propositional (subject-predicate) manner, and that since, in the West, truth is traditionally held to be a characteristic of propositions rather than words or names, the absence of the propositional form is evidence of a disinterest in questions of truth and falsity; second, that in Chinese there is a relative absence of a language of entification and contrary-to-fact conditionals, implying a lack of interest in both scientific and ethical deliberations.

Concerning the issue of propositional truth, Graham, of course, agrees that "Chinese philosophising centres on the Way rather than on the Truth."[19] And we certainly agree with Graham that this claim "has nothing to do with everyday questions of fact."[20] Whether or not dinner is ready is a significant question in both Chinese and Western cultures. But this in itself does not touch the issue of whether a concept of truth is present. Indeed, Graham holds it to be obvious that the Chinese have no concept of truth. His argument is this: In the West we have developed a concept of truth by extending the meanings of "fact" from questions such as "whether the money, as you told me, is already in the bank"[21] to such nonfactual issues as the truth of tautologies, the truth of narratives, and so on.

Thus the semantical range of "true" and "truth" comes to extend far beyond first-order questions of a factual nature to logical, historical, and literary issues that are expressed in propositional form. What this means is that truth comes to be a second-order concern involving the comparison of propositions with states of affairs, or facts. As for the Chinese, Graham notes that

> such words as *jan* [*ran* 然], *yu* [*you* 有], and *hsin* [*xin* 信] would not be expected to, and do not, have the same metaphorical spread as "true".... To say that Chinese philosophers display a "lack of interest in questions of truth and falsity" amounts then to saying that like Western [*sic*] they are not primarily concerned with the factual, but unlike Western [*sic*] they do not use a word that assimilates other questions to the factual. That they would have no concept of Truth would be taken for granted, but is trivial.[22]

Why would we hold this conclusion to be important for an understanding of classical Chinese cultural sensibility while Graham claims it to be trivial? The reason lies in the distinctive foci of our contrasting arguments. Graham is interested in grammatical evidences when making claims about the language; we are interested in the broadest of cultural evidences that shape the construction and expression of values and visions. Thus, the distinctive treatment of facticity in the Western and Chinese traditions noted by Graham is of greater interest to the philosopher of culture than it would be to the grammarian.

Graham argues that, while the Chinese language is uncongenial to subject-predicate sentence constructions, the language may be expressed in what appear to be modern (unquantified) logical forms that themselves can have a truth-value.[23] He wishes in this manner to criticize our claim that, since only propositions of a subject-predicate form are candidates for truth-claims, the absence of such forms in classical Chinese signals an allied disinterest in propositional truth. But this argument from grammatical possibility to philosophical actuality is certainly strained. The question, after all, is not the grammatical possibility of the *langue*, but the actual intent of the *parole*.

In fairness to Graham, we should say that, since he accedes to the absence of the concept of truth in the Chinese sensibility, his primary concern here is to show that the Chinese language is expressible in logical forms that we could interpret in a truth-functional form. But that is certainly not at issue with us. We accept the indefinite flexibility of the Chinese language.

Graham's introduction of Western logical forms to support the grammatical possibilities of Chinese discourse is truly puzzling. After all, those forms are themselves streamlined versions of propositions, and would not have been developed without the model of the subject-predicate sentence. Further, truth functionality is argued for only with respect to sentences and propositions. The distinction often made between a sentence and a proposition—in which only propositions are formally true or false, and sentences have truth-value only insofar as they express propositions—is unimportant here. Nor is the distinction between propositions formally expressed in subject-predicate form, and those, such as "It's hot!," which only imply that form ("It is true that 'It's hot!'") of any significance. Graham's claim[24] that this latter point is relevant to his discussion of the grammatical possibilities of Chinese language is due to a simple confusion on his part. Whether one takes a redundancy or a disquotational view of truth in which "It's hot!" and "It is true that 'It's hot!'" are identical (or at least equivalent) expressions, or whether one sides with more traditional views to the contrary, dealing with truth-claims always involves the explicit or implicit presence of the locution, "It is true that . . ." Truth-claims establish the form of the proposition as "It is true that x." Moreover, as Graham himself explicitly points out, Chinese philosophy was "conducted in a language without the morphological distinctions which call attention to logical relations in sentence structure."[25]

What makes the observation that the Chinese have no concept of truth distinctly nontrivial is that this absence signals an alternative to the basic philosophical assumptions implicated in the belief in a single-ordered world. This belief entails not only the dualistic reality/appearance, knowledge/opinion, kind of distinctions, but a variety of other assumptions correlated with such beliefs. In the course of our discussions in this part, we shall illustrate how one might responsibly move from hypotheses involving the absence of interest in truth in the Chinese tradition, to an understanding of other elements of the Chinese sensibility entailed by this claim. Though the absence of truth in the

Chinese world-view is certainly a trivial claim when used as an overall assessment of the value of the culture, this same assertion is of immense importance in providing access to the manner in which the culture is internally articulated.

Of course, the lack of interest in propositional truth is no more a sign of cultural defect than is the Western stress on the notion of truth as correspondence or coherence at the expense of a concern for the understanding of truth as the way of things. The issue, rather, involves the question of how mutual understandings between these traditions may fare in the absence of self-consciousness about the differences in cultural inventories. It is, after all, clear that Western intellectuals hold a rather qualified respect for Chinese scientific and historiographical methods rooted in traditional values rather than objective standards of evidence. Indeed, the speculation concerning reasons for the retardation of scientific development in China are most often addressed in terms of the relative unconcern of the Chinese for the objective assessment of the natural world. For their part, the Chinese question the moral sensibilities of Western societies who are seemingly unconcerned with the more human tasks of realizing a harmonious way of living.

Graham would find such concerns, particularly the former one, illegitimate insofar as they presuppose some norm for assessing worthwhile cultural development. And we would certainly concur. But concerns of this sort do effectively advertise possible roadblocks to mutual respect and understanding. There is good reason at least to call attention to the presence of potential barriers such as these. Our argument is meant to suggest that, while from the grammarian's perspective the absence within one culture of a concept importantly resident in another may not constitute a serious issue, such a situation provides the philosopher of culture with valuable grounds for making useful cultural comparisons.

Graham criticizes a second claim of ours relevant to the discussion before us. Our assertion that there is relatively little resort to a language of entification and contrary-to-fact conditionals in classical Chinese thought, and that this implies a lack of interest in both scientific and ethical deliberations, led Graham to respond that such argument forms do in fact exist in classical Chinese. But to quote again from *Thinking Through Confucius*, "Our argument...does not depend upon the absence of counterfactuals in the classical Chinese, only the infrequent resort to such locutions in philosophic argument."[26] The Mohists, among others, generated such forms, and during the period of the "Hundred Schools," disputation involving the use of such forms was common. We certainly believe the grammatical form of such locutions exists in Chinese language, but the question is how such forms actually function. Given the contrast between "is" and "is not" on the one hand, and *wu* 無 and *you* 有 as "not being present to hand" and "being present to hand" on the other, a Western counterfactual and a Chinese one would have dramatically different consequences. The Western form is grounded upon a disjunctive logic of "p" and "not-p"; the Chinese form is based upon a logic of presence and absence.

However we are to interpret Mohist argumentative forms, any significant resort to them was clearly short-lived.[27] With the development of the Han synthesis of Confucian orthodoxy, such argumentation fades. As Graham himself concedes,

> It may be admitted that when philosophical argument dies down China does show that aversion to the "either-or" sensibility implied by Hall and Ames's general thesis (that China demands not the transcendence of A but its superiority to and interdependence with B). The final tendency of the schools was toward syncretism; philosophers settle for "I see the whole thing, you are one-sided" rather than "I am right, you are wrong."[28]

Graham misunderstands us when he interprets our statement that "the deemphasis upon scientific and ethical reasoning (in China) is intrinsically related to the relative absence of counterfactuals in the classical Chinese philosophy"[29] to mean that the relative absence of counterfactuals was the cause of the deemphasis upon scientific and ethical reasoning. We definitely do not accede to the linguistic determinism suggested by that criticism. The expression "intrinsically related" in the *Thinking Through Confucius* quote above reflects the interdependence of the two factors, and does not suggest that either is exclusively the cause of the other.

Finally, our argument that abstract nouns are philosophically unimportant in mainstream philosophic discourse in China is also construed by Graham in a manner contrary to our intentions. Graham interprets us as endorsing in an uncritical manner Alfred Bloom's[30] thesis that, stated in Graham's language, "the absence in Chinese of morphological means of distinguishing the noun 'goodness' from the adjective 'good'...hinders the formation of abstract concepts."[31] But this was not our claim. Our assertion, rather is that "the infrequent recourse to abstract nouns and counterfactuals [is] a consequence of the absence of notions of transcendence in the classical Chinese tradition."[32]

Again, ours is not a grammatical argument, but an argument drawn from an investigation of the Chinese cultural sensibility. Our point as stated is that "significant communications depend neither upon the separation of the entertainment of a proposition from the act of judgment that asserts its truth or falsity nor upon the generation of conscious alternatives prerequisite to judgments or actions."[33] As we have already noted above, Graham himself says as much when he accedes to the fact that the Chinese aversion to the "either-or" sensibility is implied by our thesis "that China demands not the transcendence of A but its superiority to and interdependence with B."[34]

While Graham holds the question concerning the relative absence of entification in the classical Chinese tradition to be "an interesting and highly debatable question," he places us among those who offer this generalization "without offering anything concrete for debate."[35] We would claim, to the contrary, that what we offer for debate is quite specific and concrete, though it is in the form of *cultural* rather than grammatical evidence. We concern ourselves with the unimportance of radical senses of transcendence in the development of the classical Chinese sensibility because the entification or the hypostatizing of abstract nouns cannot proceed without an operative sense of transcendence. There is, of course, really no debate between Graham and ourselves on the issue of transcendence. He accepts our view without objection.[36] An interesting implication of this acceptance is found in Graham's treatment of the notion of "essence" in the Chinese language:

> In the absence of an affirmative copulative verb, there is no *being* an ox, any more than there is *being* white, and so no essence intervening between name and object; the term closest to Aristotelian essence, *ch'ing* [*qing*] 情, covers everything in the ox without which the name 'ox' would not fit it, not everything without which it would not *be* an ox. One begins to understand why in Chinese philosophy argumentation is conceived solely in terms of whether the name fits the object.[37]

Once again there seems no substantive disagreement between Graham and us.

Engagaging criticisms of Angus Graham has allowed us to demonstrate that, despite sharp disagreements on method, there is a fundamental agreement between Graham and us on precisely the sorts of issues addressed in this present work. We intend to exploit this agreement in the following discussion by appealing from time to time to the insights Graham educes with respect to the themes of this part.

SOME IRONIES OF THE SEARCH FOR TRUTH

We may turn the question of the presence or absence of truth concepts or theories in China around, and ask, not without some irony, of course: "Is there a concept of theory of 'truth' in the Anglo-European tradition?" The immediate response would have to be "No, there is not *a* concept or theory, there are all too many!"

At the most general level, there are any number of distinctive correspondence and coherence theories. In contemporary philosophy these tend to be variously expressed in semantic theories, redundancy theories, identity theories, disquotational theories, pragmatic theories, and so on. Truth theories are further articulated in terms of operationalist, conventionalist, instrumentalist, and behaviorist categories. Western culture has been so obssessed with the notion of truth, that we find ourselves grossly overstocked with answers to the question "What is Truth?" And we cannot but feel some discomfort in celebrating such a diversity of approaches to the question of how to get things right!

Historically, we have moved from visions of truth that center on notions of "mind" and "experience" to those that focus upon "propositions" and "propositional attitudes." In such views, formal logic provides the model for theoretical speculations.

No matter how logically refined such theories may become, we are still left with the two fundamental notions of "coherence" or "correspondence" as setting the conditions that permit the determination of the truth of a proposition. Thus, the truth condition of the statement "Britain declared war in 1939" is that Britain declared war in 1939. We are back to Aristotle's "saying of what is, that it is," albeit with the addition of some rather sophisticated notions of "fact" or "state of affairs" with which a proposition may be compared. We may equally move from the proposition

"Britain declared war in 1939" to argue in terms of a coherence theory that suggests the necessity of allying that proposition with other propositions that offer support for understanding of the components of the proposition: "Britain," "war," "declaration."

Contemporary speculations have the additional irony that they have avenged themselves upon the world of facts. The commonsense interest in saying of something that is, *that it is*, and then of simply leaving it at that, is hardly permissable since we might be forced to concede with the truth theorists that to say "Britain declared war in 1939" is to say that "Britain declared war in 1939 is a fact." And this is but to say "It is true that Britain declared war in 1939." Facts are facts in the commonsense understanding only if we leave them alone as passive assumptions or assertions.

In their attempt to avoid metaphysical or cosmological assumptions, some contemporary thinkers associated with "identity," "redundancy," or "disquotational" theories of truth seem to have returned to the naive assertions of facticity. Theories such as these do not distinguish between assertions of the sort "The ball is red" and "It is true that the ball is red." The two propositions have the same meaning. Many proponents of such views hold that one may avoid reifying notions of truth in this manner. Thus one need not presume what are taken to be the perniciously metaphysical contexts in which both correspondence and coherence theories are normally embedded. According to these views, questions such as "What is Truth?" are wrong-headed and can only lead into hopelessly complex metaphysical disputes.

But this return to facticity has not avoided metaphysical issues in the manner desired. Indeed, Wittgenstein's ill-fated attempt in the *Tractatus Logico-Philosophicus* to employ an ontology of facts ("The World is the totality of facts, not of things") illustrates the manner in which the sweeping of metaphysical speculations out the front door is so often followed by their blowing back in through the rear. Once raised to the level of consciousness, we are tempted to ask "What makes a fact a fact?" And with this question we return, once more, to questions of coherence or of correspondence that involve "truth-conditions," "states of affairs," "propositional systematicity"—questions that, whether we like it or not, point to the very metaphysical notions that we have attempted to excise altogether. Wittgenstein's rejection of his fact-ontology in his later work, *Philosophical Investigations*, led to his adoption of an essentially pragmatic theory of truth.

The metaphysical issues underlying the Western tendency to conceptualize truth in the manner that it does, either in classical or contemporary idioms, involve two assumptions. These assumptions are (1) the existence of a single-ordered world, and (2) a distinction between reality and appearance. The latter assumption leads to an emphasis upon correspondence notions of truth, while the former underlies discussions of truth as coherence.

CHAPTER SIX

Cultural Requisites
for a Theory of Truth in China

With regard to the presence of concepts or theories of truth in China, our method of contextualization leads us to seek, not some possible candidate for translation, but a context of speculations and practices similar enough to the one that sustains our own truth-seeking activities to signal the presence of a Western-style notion of truth. That is, we are looking, not directly for "truth," but for the understandings and tools that are allied with the search for truth. We shall take this rather unusual approach because it will allow us to chart some distinctive differences between Chinese and Western cultures that otherwise might not be so obvious to us. The result will be that we shall see the interestingly different approaches to a number of issues and activities that the contrast between Truth-seekers and Way-seekers entails.

In the following we shall select five general notions that help set the context within which Western speculations concerning truth proceed. We shall not attempt an exhaustive demonstration that the cultural requisites for a theory of truth are in fact unimportant in classical China, though we, of course, intend to provide enough evidence along the way to render such a claim plausible. We believe that we shall have served the comparative cause quite well if we provide criteria in accordance with which this question may continue to be examined in a detailed and rigorous manner. In the latter part of this chapter we shall consider why something like a pragmatic perspective on truth is helpful in understanding Chinese Way-seekers.

COHERENCE AND WORLD ORDER

Theories of truth grounded in rational coherence depend upon concepts of system and structure analyzable in terms of systematic completeness. A coherence theory of truth depends upon the notion of a system rather than a congeries, or a plurality, of systems. This means that a theory, as opposed to mere reflection, must add up to a system. Truth as rational coherence requires a putatively complete context within which a single proposition may be found to be consistently housed. The stipulation of such a context is in fact nothing more or less than the claim that beyond uncoordinated musings and speculations, there is the possibility of a "logical, coherent, necessary system of general ideas"[1] that provides a coherent matrix to house propositions whose putative truth can be shown to be actual if the propositions cohere.

In Anglo-European philosophy, the most notorious illustration of systematic incoherence is the Cartesian claim that thought and extension form distinct substances. The problem entailed by this claim is to find a coherent system of ideas that provide a context for propositions that house both material and mental subjects and predicates. But as neither mind nor matter can be predicated of the other, propositions combining material and mental subjects and predicates cannot be coherent in themselves, nor can they be considered coherent with respect to the remainder of propositions expressing the logical form of Cartesian philosophy. It is only because of the independent consistency of mental and material propositions to their respective areas of reference that we have put up with the incoherence of the total view. Assessing individual Cartesian insights in terms of the conformity of appearance and reality argues for their truthfulness. Looking at the propositions in terms of their capacity to comprise a system yields less satisfactory results. Partly for this reason, materialistic or dualistic visions have favored correspondence theories, while idealist theories, given their interpretation of the world in single-ordered terms reducible to ideal elements, are naturally suited to coherence views.

We may conclude that the World as some overarching context either in the sense of a Vague General Whole or as the present inventory of beliefs and practices, is essential to any of the concepts of truth associated with coherence criteria.[2]

If one were to seek a coherence theory of truth in China, it would be necessary to argue for the fact that the Chinese are concerned not only with a single-ordered cosmos, as opposed to the claim that the world is but the "ten-thousand things (*wanwu* 萬物 or *wanyou* 萬有),") but also that they are concerned to develop theories in the sense of systematic contexts within which propositions may be housed.

An important demurrer is necessary, however. Though we will argue that coherence in classical China is not a function of a single world-order, it may be shown to exist *secondarily* between rituals as embodiments and evocators of feelings, actions, and dispositions to act, and *primarily* among those feelings, actions, and dispositions themselves. There are notions of "appropriateness or fittingness (*yi* 義)" and "harmony (*he* 和)" in classical Chinese suggestive of the idea of finding one's proper place within a context. Rituals as rules of action and disposition, rather than propositions as candidates for belief, will constitute the erstwhile "objective" elements of a coherent context, providing the place within which questions of "appropriateness" and "inappropriateness," or "harmony" and "disharmony," may be addressed.

Since the classical Chinese have no important regard for a systematically complete contexts such as referenced by the "Cosmos," the "Mind of God," the "Laws of Nature," or the "Repository of Eternal Ideas," all contexts, both textual and social, must be immanent and, in a special sense, open-ended. The focus-field model of order discussed in *Anticipating China*[3] provides one means of thinking of coherence in this sense. While there is no concern for a bounded whole, attention is paid instead to the transactions taking place with respect to a given center or focus. This center is not the focus of a tightly enclosed circle but of a field of interrelated elements that decrease in relevance the farther they get from the center. The concern among the classical Chinese is primarily with mutual resonances of the principal artifacts of the literary tradition. And that tradition cannot be said to transcend the texts in the sense in which an authorial presence, analogized after the model of God as Creator, might be said to transcend the text by virtue of *auctoritas*. The Sages reside in the literature; in fact, they emerge from it. Confucius is created by a commentarial and a social tradition he both serves and helps to produce. He is created by the *Analects* as much as he is creator of the sayings that constitute it.

It may seem misleading to say that there are no overarching contexts in something like the Western sense of "World." The classical meanings of *tian* 天, "heaven(s)," or *dao* 道, "the way or path of things," are more often than not treated as notions bespeaking organic wholeness. However, we have argued elsewhere that it is necessary to pluralize and relativize these notions, and that attempts to render these notions in generic terms is wrongheaded.[4]

Turning to China with these considerations in mind, one would need to consider, first, the problematic status of cosmogonic myths in classical China. If one cannot argue that cosmogonies are efficaciously present in China, then the expectation of interest in the coherence understandings of truth will be rendered less plausible. The reason for this lies in the fact that the overcoming of chaos (as nonbeing, as a separating gap, or as disorder) involves the grounding, shaping, informing activities later characterized as functions of reason.[5] The aim of reasoning, given the importance of cosmogonic speculation, comes to be understood as that of seeking the order of things in or through the chaos of appearances. This is one dynamic of the search for truth.

REALITY AND APPEARANCE

Theories defining truth in terms of a conformation of appearance with reality, or in more contemporary terms, between "language" and "world," or "propositions" and "facts" ("states of affairs") presuppose a distinction between things as they are and as they appear, or are asserted to be. In Western philosophy this distinction has been implicit from its beginnings in classical Greece. When Thales claimed, "Everything is water," a natural response on the part of his communicants would have been, "Well, not everything *appears* to be water. What about mountains and olive trees?"

With Parmenides, this distinction became most explicit. "Only Being is; Not-Being is not." The first half of this proposition conflicts wildly with the way things appear to be for most individuals. Parmenides had to write a sequel to his "The Way of Truth" entitled "The Way of Opinion" in order to provide some characterization of the familiar world of appearance. Being able to connect the way things are or must be, with the way they appear, is a function of our ability to think and speak rationally. This ability involves us in drawing out the consistent and formal (logical) implications of the proposition that states the being of Being and the not-being of Not-Being.

Zeno's challenge to the rational understanding of motion and change, expressed in the form of a set of logical paradoxes, had incalulatable influence on subsequent cosmological speculations. The disjunction between our experience of the world and our rational understaning of it, the disjunction that those inclined toward the rational understanding of things soon saw as the separation of reality and appearance, became a fundamental characteristic of our cultural self-understanding.[6]

Correspondence theories of truth require that a proposition must be independent from the state of affairs it characterizes. On the one hand, this argues for the transcendence of principles and, on the other hand, for the dualistic relations of propositions and states of affairs. Without such independence, both in the sense of dualism and transcendence, nothing like logical truth may be formulated.

The presence of transcendent beings and principles in the formation of Western culture is uncontroversial. The dualism entailed by this transcendence, though discomforting to the theologically doctrinaire, is also a widely accepted characteristic of the rational interests of Anglo-European societies. The polar, interdependent, *yin/yang* 陰/陽, relations of terms and concepts within the Chinese tradition is unquestioned. Correlative terms such as "heaven" and humanity *tian/ren* 天/人, knowing and doing *zhi/xing* 知/行, change and continuity *bian/tong* 變/通, speaking and doing *yan/xing* 言/行, fullness and emptiness *shi/xu* 實/虛, performance and name *xing/ming* 形/名, stuff and function *ti/yong* 體/用, heart-mind and body *xin/shen* 心/身, and so on, constitute a vocabulary which in one form or another, pervades the classical Chinese corpus, insuring a correlation among these complementary terms and a vision of things.

For a proposition to have a univocal sense, terms must be strictly delimitable. This is a familiar condition of a dualistic worldview. The Chinese polar sensibility, on the other hand, renders the defining vocabulary porous and interdependent, precluding such delimitation in any but the grossest terms. "As different as night and day" in this world becomes "as different as night-becoming-day from day-becoming-night." Precisely where does the difference lie? In a polar sensibility terms are clustered in such a way as to be essentially incomplete unless paired with opposing or complementary alter-terms. Classical Chinese may be uncongenial to the development of univocal propositions for this reason. And without such propositions, theories of truth which presume, however tacitly, a distinction between propositions and states of affairs are ultimately untenable.

THEORY AND PRACTICE

A strict distinction between theory and practice generally underlies correspondence and coherence theories of truth. Correspondence theories distinguish representations from that which is represented, thus allowing the entertainment of the propositions about the world in relative separation from the rigors of practical engagement with the real. And coherence theories rationalize our representations in such a manner as to promote idealisms rather far removed from the realm of praxis.

This is no more than to say that there are important senses in which propositions deemed candidates for truth-claims in either the correspondence or coherence views need be held apart from the sphere of praxis. What this means is (1) assent may be withheld until truth is established, and/or (2) even in the presence of assent, no action may be enjoined.

A proposition such as "9 + 5 = 14" must be entertainable apart from the sensuous intuition of any collection of nine and five entities. Likewise the judgment, "The ball is red," expressed as a formal proposition, requires the assessment of "truth conditions" permitting the judgment. These conditions may be expressed summarily as "'The ball is red' is true if and only if the ball is red." This ability to hold a proposition apart from the state of affairs that justifies or disqualifies it can seriously affect the stance taken with respect to the sphere of practice.

Our ability to avoid the participatory knowledge required by the entertainment of at least some propositions is what makes the Platonic dictum, "To know the truth is to do the truth" sound so hollow. That "telling the truth is right" need not involve an intention to tell the truth and that the truthfulness of that proposition (if such a term is made to apply) need not enjoin future truth-telling, are due to the fact that we are accustomed to hold propositions apart from the states of affairs they are meant to express or describe.

Pragmatic understandings of truth attempt to avoid presupposing any disjunction between theoretical and practical activity, but the fact that we can assert the truth of a proposition such as "Diamond is harder than brass," believing that the scratching operations that constitute that truth have been performed, relieving ourselves of having to perform them, means that even on certain pragmatic theories, the truth of a proposition may be entertained apart from any specific operation that establishes it. This having been said, by comparison with correspondence and coherence theories of truth, the various pragmatic understandings certainly appear to resonate more closely with the "way" metaphors in terms of which truth is characterized in classical China.

Some existential notions of truth, however, may have more stringent requirements than the pragmatic. True might have to be "true for me." Such a requirement may, of course, subjectify the notion of truth so excessively as to make it irrelevant to public discourse. Other existential understandings may stress the intersubjective, communal, participatory, vision of truth, thus opening the way for its public viability.

One of the principal manners of discovering the character of formal discussions of truth in Chinese intellectual culture is to assess the importance, if any, of beliefs in the separation of idea and action. One must ask if, and to what extent, does such a separation exist and, if there is one, how important is it in articulating significant elements of Chinese culture? One may further ask, if the separation of theory and practice is broadly absent among the classical Chinese, has this led them toward pragmatic or existential understandings of truth?

An important clue regarding the response to these questions might be contained in the fact that for the classical Chinese, influenced as they are by the interpenetration of idea and affect expressed in notions such as "heart-and-mind" (xin 心), ideas tend to be experienced as "e-motivated" *dispositions to act*. To the extent that this is the case, it would be difficult to find contexts within which the separation of theoretical and practical activities may be efficaciously instantiated.

RATIONAL ARGUMENTS

In our discussion of the rise of second-problematic thinking in *Anticipating China*,[7] we noted how "rationalism" emerged in some measure as a consequence of the coexistence of distinct languages, ethnicities, and customs that required a movement toward general concepts and principles, and, also, due to a sharpening of logical and rational tools consequent upon the dialectical engagements of the various theoretical visions that developed after Parmenides and Zeno. It is not surprising that it was during a period that saw the rise of a number of contending schools of thought that the Chinese experimental forms of rational argumentation developed. This was, of course, the period of the "Hundred Schools," which lasted from approximately the fourth to the second centuries B.C.E. What *is* surprising is that, after 200 B.C.E., these modes of argumentation began to fade, becoming increasingly marginal and unimportant.

Why should rationality, once born, not have continued to develop throughout the history of the Chinese culture? Many explanations have been proffered. The Later Mohist canons, a principal source for the investigation of rational argumentation, along with the writings of the School of Names, were effectively lost in the third and fourth centuries of the common era. But this loss appears to have been more the result of a preemptive rejection by the ruling Confucians than of some indeterminate historical accident. An imported Buddhist logic, which had a brief influence in the seventh century, met essentially the same fate as had the quasi-rationalistic thinkers among the Mohists and the School of Names.

It would seem that rationality in its stricter senses did not survive in China for at least two closely related reasons. First, the seeds of logical and rational discourse in China were to yield a distinctive fruit, appreciably different from that we in the West might recognize as strictly rational thinking. Second, the more formal modes of reflection and debate associated with the Mohists and the School of Names were found, after the growing dominance of a syncretic Confucianism during the Han dynasty, to be inconsistent with social harmony. Such contentiousness was a threat to social order and was, therefore, not encouraged as a mode of engagement.

With regard to the discouragement of contentious arguments, we may simply recall a familar narrative strand of classical Chinese history. After the Warring States period, a period of debate among a variety of schools, the classical tradition settled into an eclectic synthesis dominated by Confucianism. The presence within this synthesis of a variety of strands such as Daoist, Legalist, Yin-Yang cosmologists, and so forth, would have prevented any long-term synthesis had the notion of contentious argument been considered acceptable. Indeed, the third century B.C.E. Confucian, Xunzi, one of the presumably more "rationalistic" of the Confucians whose Legalist-leaning doctrines would become extremely influential in various phases of the emerging Confucianism, is quite specific in his claim that argumentation must be a co-operative affair, and therefore that contentiousness is to be avoided.[8]

Thus even if quasi-rationalists such as the Mohists proceeded in the direction of logical experimentation of the sort recognizable in the West, their influence faded after the Han synthesis, and the ultimate victory of Confucianism effectively absented this philosophy from the tradition.

With the rediscovery of Later Mohism in the sixteenth century, there was little chance for that form of rationality to gain any serious foothold. Indeed, it was primarily in the nineteenth and twentieth centuries, and then only in response to the challenge of the West, that Mohism began to be studied once more with any seriousness.

A more philosophical argument concerning the absence of concern with strictly rational modes of argumentation is that the protorational thinking in China was itself quite different from the nascent forms of rationality in the West—so much so that even the fully developed forms supplied by later Mohism bore no strict resemblance to Western rationality.

To expect discussions of truth sustained by rational arguments we would have to find among the Chinese at least the beginnings of truth functional logic. Mozi himself subordinated logical and rational argumentation to what we would term ethical considerations. He sought principles of ethical utility in a manner that would align him with certain rather broadly conceived forms of pragmatism. There is little by way of dispassionate rationalism to be found in the early Mohist doctrines.

Many of the discussions found in later Mohist thought, expressed in the work *Names and Objects*, recovered in the sixteenth century, comes closer to what we in the West would recognize as rationalism. But, even here, there is a crucial difference. The paradigm of Western rationality is the employment of logic in the search for necessary truths. Leibniz begins his philosophical reflections from the logical form we call the principle of identity. Hegel may be said to begin his dialectical arguments from an interpretation of the principle of noncontradiction. Updated forms of the Anselm's ontological argument for the existence of God employ modal logic to demonstrate that "perfection (God) exists." The point here is that Western modes of rationality have elided rational and logical discourse.[9]

In Later Mohist philosophy, discourse and logical argumentation remained distinct. Neither in the part of *Names and Objects* dedicated to discourse nor in that concerned with argumentation, is the Mohist interested in establishing logical forms. Chinese reflections and conversations were conducted without the benefit of those sorts of distinctions that identify logical or grammatical relations. The principal aim was to produce a discourse shaped in such a manner as to guard against the expression of incoherent or unproductive analogies. Though the Mohists were able to develop procedures for testing the viability of descriptive expressions, they did not see the relations of such discourse shaped by the criteria of logical necessity. As a consequence, whatever development of logical forms took place, it did not contribute to the construction of more rigorous modes of discourse.[10]

Questions of truth and falsity in the strict sense depend upon notions of the *necessity* of the conclusions of arguments and forms, such as the syllogism, by which this necessity may be expressed. Without an attempt to render explicit the logical forms of argumentation, discourse establishing the truth of this or that, would not be possible. To the extent that there is a split between discourse and argumentation, as in later Mohism, there can be no efficacious concern with strictly necessary truth as formal coherence or correspondence.

If we turn from the subject of general logical forms of argumentation to the topic of strictly *dialectical* argument, we find our previous claims corroborated by appeal to a modern example. When Mao Zedong and his comrades imported dialectical materialism from the West, they followed Lenin in distinguishing "metaphysical" and "dialectical" modes of thought. This being the case, one might think that the Chinese Marxist uses of dialectical methods would be familiar to those found among Western Marxists. That would be a misplaced expectation, however, for the meaning of "dialectics" in contemporary China bears little if any strict relationship with the usual forms of Western Marxism.

To realize this, one might compare the 1937 and 1946 versions of Mao's "On Contradiction" with the 1952 official revision. The original version requires both an imaginative and heavy-handed English translation to make its arguments appear to conform to Lenin's definition cited at the beginning of the essay: "Dialectics is the study of the con-tradiction within the very essence of things."[11] The 1952 version, in which the section "On Formal and Dialectical Logic" was deleted, presents even greater difficulty.

The expression translated as "essence" in the definition above means more literally, "the basic stuff in itself (*benzhi zishenzhong* 本質自身中)" where "stuff" refers to a thing in its entirety, standing in interdependent correlation with its equally real refinement or articulation (*wen* 文). The meaning of this Chinese expression does not resonate well with any sense of "essence/attribute" in our own tradition.[12]

Concerning the term translated "contradiction," one can see that the eliding of "not-p" and "non-p" characteristic of even the most sophisticated of Chinese logical texts, allows us to infer much about the character of "Chinese dialectics." The meaning of *maodun* 矛盾 (literally, "spear-shield") derives from the story of an arms merchant in the state of Chu who claimed that there is nothing in the world his spears cannot pierce, and that there is nothing in the world that can pierce his shields.[13] While to a mind oriented by formal logic, this would seem a perfect illustration of a set of contradictory propositions and to suggest, therefore, the simultaneous assertion of "x" and "not-x." The oft-celebrated absence of the existential uses of *you* and *wu* means that "argumentation," (*bian* 辯) does not involve the contradictories "x" and "not-x," but the contrast of some particular "x" and everything else as "*non-x*."

Given the irreducibly social nature of person in the Chinese canons, "thinking" is invariably a cooperative enterprise that sets it apart from strictly rational discourse. The model of rationality in the West has been predominately the solitary thinker: Platonic dialogue to the contrary notwithstanding, the intuition of the Good is a solitary activity that leads the enlightened individual to return to the cave to rescue others. Aristotle's "thinking on thinking" is itself a solitary affair. Consider the brooding Augustine, the closeted Descartes, Kant in his study, interrupted only by his daily walks, Hegel communing solely with the Absolute.

In the West thinking, insofar as it is patterned by rationality, is taken to be the act of an individual. It is not until after the theory is constructed and the system is formulated, that engagement aimed at establishing one's viewpoint begins. But this engagement is one of two solitary thinkers, each encapsulated within his own system, and requiring that conversation take place in the vocabulary each has constructed.

It is not until the twentieth century that pragmatists such as Charles Sanders Peirce, idealizing the methods of the scientists, will speak of a community of enquirers. But, of course, even in science it has been the celebration of the solitary thinkers such as Kepler, Galileo, Newton, Darwin, Einstein, that has set the tone for our understanding of real genius.

Among Chinese thinkers after the Han synthesis, ideas are formed and visions are entertained against the background of *li* 禮 (ritual practices). Appeals to *li* 理 (often translated "reason") always presupposes the communal context of ritual action and the world more broadly construed. Thus, there are good reasons to expect that the Chinese context would not be so congenial to the strict *logos* style of accounting. This is not to say that ideas and actions could not be assessed in terms of some form of reasonableness, but only that the culture within which it is deemed reasonable to behave in this or that manner is itself a product of human conventions.

Discussions of classical Chinese methods of argument, explanation, and interpretation must not employ analytical, dialectical, or analogical procedures in an uncritical manner. For example, the analogical style of argumentation dominates most classical Chinese texts. We must be cautious, however, in presuming that analogical operations found in Chinese speculations and reflections are identical with analogical operations familiar within the Western context. More often than not, analogical thinking in the Western tradition presumes a primary analogate operative in the important texts that permits the elaboration of explicit or implicit truth-claims. That is to say, arguments are made by analogical appeals that presume the existence of a standard such as Being, God, laws of nature, logical necessity, the principle of identity (or of noncontradiction), or the principle or principles grounding a particular systematic theory or logical argument.

In China, arguments are ultimately aimed at demonstrating conformity with the acknowledged excellences of tradition. Critical sorts of arguments aimed at demonstrating an opponent's lack of such conformity may appear to have dialectical form, but, as we have indicated, this is in itself quite misleading. Certainly analytical argumentation of a sort is employed in the philological work (which seems to become, at least for a time, more rigorously analytic after the incursion of Buddhism into China). But the same is true for quasi-dialectical and analytical argumentation as is so for analogical thinking. The arguments are, strictly speaking, "groundless." There is nothing ontologically final that serves either as the capstone of synthetic dialectics, or as the analysandum open to no further analysis. Neither a "final principle" nor "atomic facts" are discoverable at the end of the arguments.

The historical rejection of the Mohists and Logicians as contributors to cultural orthodoxy of classical China, along with the gradual submergence of Buddhist speculations in the Confucian synthesis of the post-Han period, are instances of the general rejection of the cultural requisites for a concept or theory of truth. And the recent interest in these schools of thought under the pressure of both Western and Chinese scholars who wish to discover truth functional logic in China well illustrates that cultures are inexhaustibly rich resources for ideas and values, and that notions of little interest to previous epochs can become important to later thinkers. Yet, as we have have seen with regard to the translation of Marxist dialectics into the Chinese tradition, the Mohist logical canons provide something less than an ideal language for this task.

LOGIC AND RHETORIC

In his *Rhetoric* and *Prior* and *Posterior Analytics*, Aristotle codified the methods of logical and rhetorical argumentations that had already been subjects of the speculations of the Sophists and Plato. We have since come to take for granted something like the triadic classification of arguments contained in the first pages of Aristotle's *Rhetoric*: There are arguments that persuade by virtue of an appeal (1) to *ethos*, or the authority, character, or personality of the speaker, (2) to *pathos*, or the emotions of the audience, and (3) to *logos*, or the subject matter under consideration. The separation of arguments grounded in appeals to *logos* from the *ethos*- and *pathos*-based arguments, reflects the standard contrast of rhetorical and logical argumentation, so familar in our culture.

A claim implicit in our discussion thus far has been that the divergence of rhetoric and logic in the classical Western tradition is not importantly present in classical China. It is true that later Mohist speculations, perhaps the the most sophisticated approach by the Chinese to the development of rational argumentation, kept logical forms distinct from practical discourse, and so may be said to argue for something like a logic/rhetoric distinction. In the case of these Mohists, however, logical forms were not employed to discipline discourse, and so did not contribute as a resource for the construction of rigorous discursive arguments. Quite the contrary, to the extent that a rhetoric/logic distinction was construed by the Mohists, it was not logic, but *rhetoric*—that is, ethical reasonings overriding the discipline of logical forms—that was the privileged mode of communication.

Such speculations aside, throughout their history the Chinese have been more apt to argue along *pathos*- and *ethos*-based lines than to employ objective *logos*-style argumentation. This does not mean that the Chinese do not speak and write in ways that presume the facticity of assertions. It is only that there is little interest in raising the issue of facticity or literalness to the level of speculation and theory. The primary consequence of the Western interest in the literalness of language has been the development of truth-functional logics.

The priority of logical over metaphorical or imagistic language in the Anglo-European tradition is guaranteed by the historically assessable transition from *mythopoetikos* to *logistikos* as the privileged form of discourse. This was determined in part by an alliance at their very origins of what will come to be known as the disciplines of philosophy and history.

Both philosophy and history are shaped by the cultural dominance of the *logos* style of argumentation. Philosophers ask "What kinds of things are there?," seeking some understanding of the natural world. In the beginning, historians offered *logoi*: "accounts." These narratives articulated the sense of present public actions in the light of the past or one's own, or an alternative, society. The concern for *truth* as a quality of propositions housed in either sort of accounting is a not unpeculiar characteristic of cultural development motored by these Hellenic resources.

Both correspondence and coherence theories of truth require some means of characterizing propositional forms as univocal or unambiguous. This would be possible only if there were an unambiguous way of indicating the literalness of a proposition. For this to be so, literal language must have precedence over figurative or metaphorical language. This means that, in addition to richly vague sorts of language associated with images and metaphors, there must be concepts as candidates for univocal meaning.

The distinction between rhetorical and logical uses of language is reflected in the distinction between objective and subjective connotation. In logic, connotation refers to those properties held in common by all members of a class. In rhetoric, connotation means the emotional associations evoked by a word. Literal language depends upon only objective modes of connotation.

The press toward literalness and univocity finds its most refined expression in the emergence of abstract nouns. Such nouns serve to characterize the sense of a term at which one arrives through the process of objective connotation. This issue is made most complex by the question as to how the sense of a term, specifically an abstract noun, becomes fixed. Platonists hold that there are real essences, and that understanding a term requires the construction of a connotative definition that identifies the properties forming those essential characteristics. Denotative definition, properly speaking, would follow. One would be able to identify an object after having recognized that it possesses the essential properties connotatively grasped.

In its formal sense, a concept is a general notion owning the properties common to the particulars belonging to an ostensive or denotatively defined class. These connotative qualities or properties may be unpacked through analysis. In slightly less systematic form, a concept is that which is understood by a predicative term. One may be said to possess a concept when one can use the term designating that concept meaningfully in a judgment. Indeed, having a concept may be thought to mean nothing more than being able to use a word correctly in acts of communication. What is at issue, however, is the Western tendency, whatever the meaning of concepts presupposed, to develop a very sophisticated logical apparatus to specify the manner in which concepts are employed. For example, concepts, as abstract nouns, are primary ingredients in counterfactual locutions. Such locutions are essential to a semantic theory of truth, since the hypothetical assertion of truth or falsehood is required to test the truth-value of a given proposition.

In the absence of a rhetoric/logic distinction that allows for the privileging of logical discourse, the Chinese may be said to employ language in ways that recall the languges of *ethos* and *pathos*. We must not assume that rhetorical language, as employed by the Chinese, simply means "persuasive communication." And, clearly, the importance given to canonical texts and ritual forms is meant to militate against communicative acts serving as tools of individual demogoguery.

The safest generalization concerning the rhetorical uses of language found in classical Chinese texts is that they involve "analogical reasoning." Analogical argumentation of the sort employed must be understood as a mode of "correlative thinking." A significant portion of our *Anticipating China* is given over to the explication of this mode of thinking. We refer the reader to that work for an elaboration of the following remarks.[14]

As employed by the majority of Chinese philosophers, analogical procedures are rhetorical in the senses of the term discussed above. They appeal to the authority of tradition and to the exemplars (the sages and cultural heroes) of that tradition. And though this appeal to authoritativeness might seem to shape the arguments into those of the *ethos* variety, the institution of ritual behavior insures that *pathos* is involved as well.

It is an interpretative misstep to understand the "rectification of names" (*zhengming* 正名) as a search for univocity, as it so often is. For the attempt to properly order names is a functional and pragmatic, rather than a logical or strictly semantic, procedure. This means that ordering names involves establishing coherence between roles already spelled out by tradition (*li* 禮), and the specific actions of individuals (husbands, fathers, ministers, sons) whose ostensive identity as functionaries within the society is not in question.

In China, tradition is comprised by language, music, rites, the narratives of sage-kings and cultural heroes (as well as the negative models), the authoritative texts—both originary and commentarial. Arguments that seek to harmonize an element with the tradition without appealing beyond the tradition to some transcendent source, or that do not claim a necessity to break with the tradition in some radical manner, must be primarily analogical in intent. This is so even if they include analytical or dialectical procedures as subroutines. After all, if the tradition serves as context, and if the exemplars of that tradition are essentially known in advance (as are the sage-kings), then arguments will be of the sort that seek to establish similarities and differences among paradigmatic situations such that the historical models of appropriate and productive action can serve as resources for positive, practical proposals. Further, these "practical proposals" will not be of the sort that may be presumed independent of the dispositions of the individuals to whom the proposals are addressed.

The Sea of Communal Dispositions possessed by and possessing the individuals in a society is a crucial factor in determining the pragmatic viability of a proposal. We have argued elsewhere,[15] in consonance with Donald Munro, Chad Hansen, and others, that in China an idea is a proposal for feeling and action. Thus, an idea is *dispositional* in the strict sense that it disposes individuals to implement it.

Here we find a clear means of contrasting Truth-seekers and Way-seekers. "Truth" construed in terms of Way metaphors is a function of the efficacy of ideas in evoking those dispositions leading to the achievement of an approriate harmony of social interactions. When Willaim James claimed that "truth" is the expedient in the way of thinking and "right" is the expedient in the way of acting, he characterized truth in something like the same *way* as the Chinese. The difference is there is no reflection of a thinking/acting dichotomy in the Chinese formulation.

Parenthetically, the dispositional character of ideas suggests the rationale for the State serving as mediator and moderator of both norms and information in Chinese society. Censorship is legitimated on the assumption (contrary to most Western understandings) that ideas are known to be the sorts of things that dispose an individual to act.

There is every reason to believe that what we call metaphors, images, and concepts are more on a par in classical China, and that, as a consequence, the concern for the establishment of univocal sentence forms is much less emphasized. In the absence of a preference for strictly logical discourse as a means of determining the truth or falsity of propositions, classical Chinese modes of expression may be thought to function imagistically and metaphorically, though even the meanings of these terms must be adjusted if we are to most closely approximate Chinese understandings.

In English, the word "image" is used with appropriately different connotations in psychology, epistemology, and literary criticism. In the sense in which we shall be using the term, an image is a sensory (that is, visual, auditory, tactile, olfactory) presentation of a perceptual, imaginative, or recollected experience. The form of the perception, memory, or imagination may be distinct from the mode of its presentation. That is to say, the olfactory or visual experience of a rose may be imaged in the words of the poet. It is the word-picture as experienced by the celebrant of the poem, and not (necessarily) the private experience of the poet, that constitutes the image. In fact, the most productive manner of discussing images is in terms of their communally experienceable character. Only such images are directly efficacious.

The images associated with the hexagrams of the *Yijing* (*Book of Changes*) are good examples since they are particularistic. That is, the image "fire" may be said to represent particular experiences of the phenomenon of fire that are housed in the individual consulting the *Yijing* by virtue of his or her recourse to social memory and communal experiences such as traditions, institutions, ritual practices, music, and literature.

In the Chinese context it is common for images to be invested with their associations through a distinctly communal process. Images so constructed, are ritually protected.[16] This is but to say that individual creativity and originality has been valued less in China than in the West. We have only to allude to the commentarial tradition on a fixed canon, the intertextuality of most Chinese works, the attribution of one's own work to another more celebrated cultural hero, and so on, to make this point.

One other troubling term must be introduced—namely, "metaphor." Metaphor functions in a slightly different manner than do images or symbols. But, depending upon the stipulation, metaphors can be confused with one or more of these. In the West literal language has been privileged over figurative language. And though to say this seems truistic and almost trivial, it is likely not the case that the origins of language has that preference built in. Did we first speak in order to name, to *denote*? And even if this were so, was this desire to denote simply the desire to denote something that is physically or otherwise objectively referable?

In Western cultures, metaphors have been perceived as parasitical upon literal significances. Thus rhetoric, insofar as it employs this trope called metaphor, is ultimately tied to logic as ground. This serves to discipline intellectual and aesthetic culture, precluding untrammeled flights of the imagination. If we are to provide the term "metaphor" with enough weight to help us to understand Chinese modes of communication, "expressive metaphor" (metaphors expressing in some extended or alternate context the literal sense of a term) must be supplemented by more radical tropes that we shall term "allusive metaphors." Expressive metaphors extend the sense of terms that could be understood "literally" in terms of (objective) connotative properties. Allusive metaphors are interestingly different since they are groundless. They are free-floating hints and suggestions. They *allude*; they do not *express*. Their "referents" are other allusive metaphors, other things that hint or suggest. Language at one level is all allusive, functioning primarily as an undulating sea of suggestiveness.

Perhaps the closest approximation to what we are calling allusive metaphors is to be found in the notion of "signs" as utilized in the semiotics associated with Ferdinand Saussure, and in the deconstructive analyses of Derrida and others influenced by Saussure. Normally, signs are thought to be conventional indicators. Traffic signs, street signs, and so on, are simple examples. Economic indicators may be "signs of the times." Semiology, originally developed by C. S. Peirce along realist lines and independently announced in a more idealist version by Ferdinand Saussure, formalizes the understanding of signs by defining them as the resultant of the signifier-signified relationship. Linguistic signs are the most important units for the discussion of language and language-use (*langue* and *parole*).

The reflections of Saussure help us to understand that a principal difference between Chinese and Western language systems is analogous to the distinction Derrida has drawn between a logocentric and a "deconstructed" language. As Angus Graham notes:

The Chinese opposition *ming/shih* [*ming/shi* 名/實] 'name/object' is very unlike the Saussurian 'signifier/signified' which Derrida takes to be implicit in Western thought from the beginning. A name is used to 'point out' (*chih* [*zhi* 指]) an object, and if appropriate to it 'fits' (*tang* [*dang* 當]). Nominalized *chih* is sometimes conveniently translated by 'meaning' [but] there is...no tendency (as I at one time supposed myself) for the *chih* of names to turn, like 'meanings' or the 'signified,' into third entities on the same level as the objects and the sounds of names. In the hypostatising terminology of Saussurian linguistics signifier and signified are two entities combined in the sign, specifically compared to the two sides of a sheet of paper; signifying has somehow disappeared, and for Derrida the object too has dissolved into the signified ("There is nothing outside the text"). For a Chinese thinker, on the other hand, there would be nothing, except the present or absent oxen to which the use of 'ox' points, which could be credited with existence or reality in detachment from the phonic exterior of the sign.[17]

An implication of the above is that (*pace* Derrida), classical Chinese is an already deconstructed language.

The Chinese tradition is...not logocentric in Derrida's sense, centred on living speech and the full presence of the signified. Reversals in *Lao-tzu* [*Laozi*] are merely of relative superiority, they are not experiments in abolishing A in revenge against the traditional effort to abolish B.[18]

According to Graham, Laozi's reversals are analogous to those expressed in Derrida's project of deconstructing the chains of oppositions underlying Western logocentricism. But there are clear differences, as Graham also understands.

Laozi certainly wouldn't share the background of Derrida's very Western conclusion that philosophy losing hope of discovering reality as the full presence of A has to be satisfied with the *trace* of it, which on inspection turns out to be only the trace of a trace of a . . . . Perhaps *Lao-tzu*'s Way is how the Trace will look to us when we are no longer haunted by the ghost of that tran-scendent Reality the death of which Derrida proclaims.[19]

Saussurean linguists and some semiologists influenced by Saussure, as well as the poststructuralists who would expunge from language such notions as "authorial intent," "textual coherence," or "univocity," might be attracted to the concept of allusive interpretations. Language as a system of differences—as a "structure" or "context" within which meaning is indefinitely deferred—may be nothing more or less than an allusive system. The importance of context to meaning in Chinese language and culture argues for the play of differences establishing meaning. As Chang Tung-sun observes,

> The Chinese are merely interested in the inter-relations be-tween the different signs, without being bothered by the sub-stance underlying them.[20]

Said another way, the classical Chinese commentators focus their interest in *how* a living term discloses its meaning within its various contexts, rather than assuming that terms have some univocal, essential meaning independent of how they are used.

We may summarize the relevance of this discussion for our under-standing of the character of Chinese discourse in the following manner: In China, "images," particularly in the sense illustrated by the *Yijing*, serve as allusive metaphors. But, as we have noted before, the Chinese tradi-tion disciplines and stabilizes the indefinite allusiveness of the language through authoritative texts and ritualized activities.

Realist understandings of truth, and the semantic theories that justify those understandings, depend upon a subordination of images, signs, metaphors, and affective symbols to at least some concepts defined as class terms or universals that may in principle achieve univocal definition. Much could be gained by continued research into the relevance of such understandings in classical Chinese culture. It would, we believe, reveal striking differences in the character and shape of Chinese notions serving as functional equivalents of concepts, images, and metaphors. It would require the translation of such terms from a logical to a rhetorical context, and thus a tranformation of these terms into allusive metaphors.

SENSIBILITY MATRICES: CHINA AND THE WEST

n valism

Thus far we have attempted to highlight the importance of the *logical* mode of discourse in the origins and development of Western culture and the essential connections of that mode of discourse to the concern for truth and falsity of propositions.

Translation of Western ideas into a Chinese context requires appreciation of the distinctive character of the tacit and explicit assumptions advertised by each. These uncommon assumptions provide the basis for constructing "sensibility matrices" that permit the transvaluation and translation of our Western philosophical or interpretative vocabularies into terms with Chinese meanings.

For there truly to be a priority of literal over metaphorical or imagistic language, something like a *mythos/logos* transition as experienced in the beginnings of Western culture must be present. This involves the assumption that progress in understanding requires the interpretation, articulation, and critique of mythopoetic forms of expression by recourse to more principled discourse.

Just as the dominance of literal language presupposes something like a *mythos/logos* contrast, so this contrast itself presupposes the assumption of a single-ordered world. This assumption was alluded to with respect to coherence theories of truth that depend upon a generalized structure for coherence. This structure is ultimately presumed to be a cosmic or world order. And as univocity depends upon the priority of literal language and that priority depends upon the *mythos/logos* contrast, which in turn depends upon the assumption of a single-ordered world, so the assumption of a single world-order may be said to undergird all types of *logos*-based argumentation.

We suggest that this sensibility matrix could be found in China only if, as has too often been the case, it is first impressed upon the data by an exoteric observer. The classical Chinese (1) tended to think within a context that requires interdependent notions, (2) had little *logos*-dominant discourse, (3) did not employ cosmogonic myths in any important manner in their formative stages, (4) had no viable sense of radical transcendence, and (5) possessed no important sense of a world or cosmos as a coherent, single-ordered whole.

We certainly do not wish to deny that something like the idea or concept of truth as correspondence or coherence may be constructed in the Chinese language. There is certainly no insurmountable impediment, linguistic or otherwise, to the development of such theories. On pragmatic assumptions of the sort with which we are operating, there are very good arguments for the conclusion that the language of any major culture could be made speak the texts of any other. Cultures are, we believe, indefinitely pliable. China could become France. But then China would no longer be China. It would be France. One essential entailment of the question whether or not there are important concepts or theories of truth (or, indeed, any important objectivist or realist concepts or theories at all) in China is this: Can such theories or concepts be effectively present without China becoming something other than China?

This question is not asked in order to suggest that China should necessarily maintain its present identity. We are not romanticizing Chinese culture. The evolution of institutions as surely as that of biological species is ruthlessly neutral with respect to issues of survival. Our point is merely that if we wish to understand Chinese cultural sensibilities circa 200 B.C.E., or 200 C.E., or 2000 C.E. for that matter, we must avoid importing irrelevant interpretative categories into our comparative discussions.

From Plato's discussion of the analogy of the Sun and the Good, and Aristotle's privileging of the sense of sight as the ground of wonder, to the medieval constructions of the *speculum mentis*, on to Jacques Derrida's analysis of the dominance of the heliotropic metaphor in *White Mythology*[21] and Rorty's critique of the "mirroring mind" in *Philosophy and the Mirror of Nature*,[22] Western philosophy has focused its epistemological interests by an appeal to two sorts of *seeing*. One sort entertains what appears to the senses, primarily the sense of sight; the other which envisions a reality lying behind appearances.

Reflections on the metaphysical tradition in terms of notions such as "logocentrism" and "the language of presence" carry the message that the effort of understanding knowledge, reason, and truth in *representational* terms is under assault. Though we cannot enter into the debates surrounding this critique of the Western tradition in any direct manner here, the movement from representational to nonrepresentational understandings of knowledge and truth might well provide an appropriate bridge to the consideration of classical Chinese sensibilities on these topics.

The replacement of nonrepresentational for representational understandings is familiar in contemporary American pragmatism, and we believe that a viable bridge to China can be constructed from elements of the pragmatic tradition. In this task, however, we are not seeking to impose upon Chinese thinking the streamlined sort of neopragmatism associated with some contemporary American thinkers. Our claim is merely that, of all the theoretical baggage with which we might approach Chinese culture (and it is, of course, irresponsible to think that we can approach an exoteric culture without *some* predispositions), pragmatism interferes least with our appropriation of Chinese understandings of the notions allied to what we think of as "knowldege," "reason," and "truth."

There are three aspects of pragmatism that prepare us to access Chinese modes of thinking. First, the pragmatist's rejection of both realist and idealist ontologies (which is effectively an abandonment of the Western metaphysical tradition); second, the consequent rejection of representational understandings of knowing (which is in effect an abandonment of the epistemological tradition in the West); and, third, the substitution (by some contemporary pragmatists) of "language" for "mind" and "experience" as the central metaphor in terms of which to couch philosophical discussion.[23]

The functional equivalent of reflections concerning truth in the Chinese tradition is closely related to what we term pragmatism. But, if we say that the Chinese have a pragmatic understanding of truth, are we not denying our claim that there is effectively no concept or theory of truth in China? We avoid this inference by noting that the pragmatic "theory" of truth drawn from Charles Sanders Peirce, William James, and John Dewey is itself less a theory of Truth than a vision of the Way. Further, the sort of instrumentalism associated with pragmatism so alters the grounds of discussion of notions of truth and falsity as to constitute a revolutionary departure from traditional epistemologies.

In the first place the pragmatic theory of truth is not a theory. As James says, pragmatism is "a method only." As a *methodos*, pragmatism is merely a *way*, a set of means or instruments that permits the accomplishment of certain practical actions involved in "getting on with it." In the second place, the pragmatic understanding of truth is not strictly conformable with either correspondence or coherence theories. According to James, "Truth is the expedient in the way of thinking." For the pragmatist, a belief is a habit that guides action. If the belief brings the individual into productive harmony with his or her community, it functions expediently, and it is true insofar as it so serves.

It is doubtful that we should call this an understanding of truth in the more classical senses of the term. For the pragmatist surely shares with the Chinese thinker a disinterest in the cultural requisites that underlie classical theories of truth. The Jamesian pragmatist explicitly denies a reality/appearance contrast and the notion of a single-ordered world, rejects any theory/practice dichotomy that would enable one to hold propositions apart from states of affairs, treats concepts not in terms of essences, but as tools for action, and accedes to the dominance of metaphor in language, thus denying the value of the quest for univocal discourse.

CHAPTER SEVEN

A Pragmatic Understanding
of the Way (*Dao* 道)

adaptive shr

As we have stated, our purpose is not to search out some presumed equivalent term for "truth" in any of the Western senses. Instead, we intend to focus our following discussion upon the Chinese question, "Where is the Way?" In so doing we shall be supplementing our discussions of "Han thinking" contained in *Anticipating China*.[1] In that work we considered the central role of notions such as "pattern" (*li* 理) and "image" (*xiang* 象) in understanding "thinking" and "reasoning" in the Chinese tradition. This approach led us to substitute "mapping" and "modeling" for "mirroring" as a means of characterizing nonrepresentational understandings. In the first part of the present work, we discussed the altered sense of the mirroring activity in the Daoist tradition.

In a representationalist culture, a model is a scaled down (or up) version of a reality (terrain, atomic structure) that the model is meant to re-present. In Chinese discussions of thinking, however, mapping and modeling are ways of coping directly with the inherent order of one's ambiance. Such a map does not represent terrain; it *realizes* it. A model does not render an antecedently existing state of affairs to scale, but brings a state of affairs into being. Existing maps and models are utilized as models in accordance with which one may proceed, always with regard to the novel demands of one's circumstances, to map and model another ambiance.[2]

We shall now proceed to supplement the discussion of thinking and reasoning in *Anticipating China* by dealing with a cluster of terms, including *dao* 道, *jun* 君 "nobility," *yi* 義 "appropriateness," *zhen* 真 "genuineness," *he* 和 "elegance, harmony," *xin* 信 "living up to one's word," *cheng* 誠 "integrity," and *shu* 恕 "deference." It is through the exposition of the sense

147

of these terms that we shall gain some understanding of the Chinese way, and thereby find access to the meanings of "truth" in the Chinese tradition.

PLOTTING A COURSE (DAO 道)

One way of focusing the difference between the search for truth and the mapping of an appropriate and productive way (*dao*) is to examine the different interpretations that a story in the Pali canon has provoked within the traditions of Indo-European and Chinese cultures respectively.[3] The story is of one Kīsagotamī, whose suffering as a Buddhist "Job" seems to know no bounds:

> Going along, about to bring forth, I saw my husband dead; having given birth on the path, [I had] not yet arrived at my own house. Two sons dead and a husband dead upon the path for miserable [me]; mother and father and brother were burning upon one pyre.... Then I saw the flesh of my sons eaten in the midst of the cemetery; with my family destroyed, despised by all, with husband dead, I attained the undying.[4]

As the story is recounted, Kīsagotamī "attained the undying" with the help of the Buddha. As a strategy for relieving her plight, Buddha instructed her to go around to the various houses in her village and return to him with a mustard seed from that residence that had not been visited by death.

A familiar Indo-European interpretation of this story is that Kīsagotamī, in pursuing the mustard seed from house to house, came to the realization that death always attends life. Death is a universal and inescapable truth, and the knowledge of this truth has set her free.

Peter Hershock, in his *Liberating Intimacy*, retells this story and characterizes this kind of response in the following terms:

> According to our usual set of presuppositions, the point of this story is that suffering is universal. Kīsagotamī learns that grief is an experience common to all of us, one that is perhaps inevitable given the nature of sentient being. Among these presuppositions ... is a more or less well-articulated belief in the objectivity of identity and hence in the reality of essences or universals.[5]

Within the Chinese tradition, on the other hand, there is a narrative rather than a conceptual reading of Kīsagotamī's plight and her return to health. The basic unit of humanity and the pervasive cultural metaphor in China is family. Kīsagotamī's predicament is that the traumatic serial deaths of her family members has led to her gradual disintegration from the village community. In the course of this growing isolation, there has arisen a challenge to her own life, constituted as her life is, by these relationships. The fading of the roles and relationships out of which a person is constituted is indeed a life-threatening situation.

The Buddha's wisdom is to send Kīsagotamī back into her community, constituted by those specific family members, neighbors, and friends from which her life narrative has been constructed. By rekindling and renewing these relationships, she is able to reestablish her continuity within her community and to restore her sense of person/Far from attaining some universal insight, Kīsagotamī who has wandered from her own path and lost her direction, has simply found her way back and relocated herself. In reconstituting herself, she has regained a sense of continuity: a trust in the community, and a feeling of belonging. This smaller sense of truth, which involves Kīsagotamī's trust in the shared narrative of her in community, is a realization that restores her life's path.

Here we see the importance of the "how-prority" thinking of the classical Chinese cited by Chang Tung-sun above. This peculiar orientation to the "how?" question has the broadest of possible effects on the Chinese manner of thinking. Again we cite Chang Tung-sun:

> *(values)*
>
> The Chinese are only interested in knowing the will of Heaven in order to seek good fortune and to avoid misfortune. As to the nature of Heaven, they are indifferent. This fact shows that the Chinese have not applied the category of substance to the idea of Heaven and have not taken Heaven as the ultimate stuff of the universe.[6]

It is certainly the case that notions such as *tian* 天 and *dao* 道 are profoundly recondite in the Chinese classics, with language such as "distant" (*yuan* 遠) and "dark" (*xuan* 玄) being frequently invoked to describe them. This is because the project in a text such as the *Analects* is not to speculate on *what* the ultimate source of value in the world might be, but to recount *how* one sensitive man—Confucius—made his way in the world as a possible model for others. The *Daodejing* does not purport to provide an adequate

adaptive shr

and compelling description of *what dao* and *de* might mean as an ontological explanation for the world around us; rather, it seeks to engage us
and to provide guidance in *how* we *ought* to interact with the phenomena,
human and otherwise, that give us context in the world. And the *Yijing*
is not a systematic cosmology that seeks to explain the sum of all possible
situations we might encounter in order to provide revelatory insight into
what to do, but is a resource providing a vocabulary of images that enable
us to think through and articulate an appropriate response to the changing
conditions of our lives.

"Knowing," then, in classical China is not a knowing *what* that provides some understanding of the environing conditions of the natural
world, but is rather a knowing *how* to be adept in relationships, and *how*,
in optimizing the possibilities that these relations provide, to develop trust
in their viability. The cluster of terms that define knowing are thus
programmatic and exhorative, encouraging as they do the quality of the
roles and associations that define us. The concern is not so much that
propositions be true, but that ministers and friends be so.

Rather than a vocabulary of truth and falsity, we find the language
of harmony and disorder, genuineness and hypocrisy, trust and dissimulation, adeptness and ineptness. Such terms reflect the priority of the
continuity that obtains among things and tell how well things hang together.

A by-product of our reflection on the Way (*dao*) as a Chinese functional analog to truth in the classical Western tradition, is to advance the
claim implicit in our interpretative efforts that there is an unadvertised
commonality between the teachings of Confucius and the Daoists even
more fundamental than their differences, a set of unannounced presuppositions that has not only made communication and even disagreement
between them possible, but that has further made the syncretism so
characteristic of their interaction an historical fact. Until this commonality
is identified and articulated in a clear way, we shall not be able to isolate
and explain those important divergences that do legitimately constitute
the contrast between the two philosophies.

ONE WAY OR MANY?

The argument in this chapter lies with the claim that truth and knowledge
in the classical Chinese world lies in the quality of the relationships that
define one. Knowledge of how to be a father is not a correspondence

between one's conduct and an available ideal that defines what a father is, but rather the capacity for the genuineness of one's specific relationships to generate trust and deference. A true father is defined in the uninhibited responsibility to, and responsiveness of, his children. To be consistent with this premiss, we must understand the *relationship* that has obtained historically between Confucianism and Daoism. Just as persons are to be known through their relationships, so a tradition of thought is to be known by its relationship with those other traditions of thought that give it context. (In other words, Confucianism and Daoism can perhaps be better understood by asking how they responded to their respective circumstances and to each other, rather than by analyzing their specific doctrines.)

In describing the "infancy" of Chinese civilization, scholars have often represented classical Daoism and Confucianism as a *yin-yang* 陰陽 contrast. Daoism has frequently been characterized in terms of passivity, femininity, quietism, spirituality. It is said to be a vision embraced by artists, recluses, and religious mystics.[7] Confucianism, on the other hand, has been construed in the language of moral precepts, virtues, imperial edicts, and regulative measures. Its doctrines are embodied in and administered by the state official. This distinction has been registered through a plethora of distinctions, such as femininity versus masculinity, heterodoxy versus orthodoxy, mysticism versus mundaneness, chaos versus order, anarchy versus regulative government, other-worldliness versus this-worldliness, discontinuity versus continuity, rebellion versus political order, spontaneity versus conservatism. There has been a long standing tendency to associate Confucianism with a reasoned orderliness and a conservative morality, and to link Daoism to the more radical, and certainly more creative, aesthetic and religious dimensions of human experience.

Joseph Needham is a fair representative of this willingness to read the Daoist-Confucian distinction in such severe terms:

> The Confucian and Legalist social-ethical thought-complex was masculine, managing, hard, dominating, aggressive, rational and donative—the Taoists broke with it radically and completely by emphasising all that was feminine, tolerant, yielding, permissive, withdrawing, mystical and receptive.... If it were not unthinkable (from the Chinese point of view) that the Yin and the Yang could ever be separated, one might say that Taoism was a Yin thought-system and Confucianism a Yang one.[8]

Richard J. Smith, in his study on *China's Cultural Heritage*, echoes this language in describing attitudes prevalent during the Qing dynasty:

> For the elite, at least, the *yang* of Confucian social responsibility was balanced by the *yin* of Taoist 'escape' into nature.... It provided an emotional and intellectual 'escape valve' for world-weary Confucians, trammeled by social responsibility.... The Taoist impulse was to defy authority, question conventional wisdom, admire the weak, and accept the relativity of things.... Taoism was preeminently a philosophy of individual liberation. Where Confucianism stressed others, Taoism stressed self. Where Confucians sought wisdom, Taoists sought blissful ignorance. Where Confucians esteemed ritual and self-control, Taoists valued spontaneity and naturalness (*tzu-jan* [*ziran*]). Where Confucianism stressed hierarchy, Taoists emphasized equality, and where Confucians valued refinement (*wen*), Taoists prized primitivity. What to Confucians were cosmic virtues were to Taoists simply arbitrary labels.... The former gave Chinese life structure and purpose, while the latter encouraged freedom of expression and artistic creativity. Most Ch'ing [Qing] scholars had a healthy schizophrenia.[9]

Other scholars use very different distinctions to promote an equally radical disjunction between Daoism and Confucianism. Yü Ying-shih, for example, substitutes an "other-world"/"this-worldly" distinction for the bipolar *yin-yang* contrast, and in the process of doing so attributes a specifically two-world theory to the *Zhuangzi*:

> I agree with most observers that since the time of the classical antiquity one of the dominant tendencies in the Chinese intellectual tradition has been "this worldliness." However, I would propose that due recognition be also given to Chuang Tzu's [Zhuangzi] "other-worldly" *Tao* [*dao*] as an important undercurrent in that tradition.... I wish to stress that a central historical significance of the Taoist breakthrough lies in the fact that with its "realm beyond" in which the metaphysical *Tao* resides, philosophical Taoism has provided Chinese spirituality with a "real" world characterized, among other things, by freedom and

self-sufficiency. As such it has served admirably well as a counterbalance to the essentially this-worldly moral teachings of the Confucians.[10]

In this reflection, Yü Ying-shih compares *Zhuangzi* explicitly with a Platonic two-world theory:

> If the "Idea of the Good" has made Plato the father of "otherworldliness in the west," then Chuang-tzu on account of his conception of *Tao* in the "realm beyond" also deserves to be called "the father of otherworldliness in China."[11]

Vitaly Rubin was convinced that the Daoist and Confucians parted company along the lines of "individual" as opposed to "society," and "nature" as opposed to "culture":

> The idea of man setting himself up against society and rejecting it is one of Chuang Tzu's basic themes.... According to Chuang Tzu, merging with nature means forgetting about men.... In Chuang Tzu's eyes, culture is the embodiment of artificiality and the direct antithesis of natural simplicity.[12]

A general willingness to accept the strict terms of this Daoist/Confucian contrast to explain the dynamics of the Chinese tradition is reinforced by several factors. First, the earliest representatives of these two philosophies seem to have characterized each other in precisely such terms. Confucius himself criticizes some recluses as ignoring the demands of humanity that require their responsible participation in the social and political order.[13] This is generally interpreted as a commentary on the proto-Daoists. And then there are the numerous passages in the Daoist classics that dismiss Confucian moralizing as an egregious assault on our natural human proclivities.[14] The strictness of this separation seems to go back to the earliest proponents of these doctrines.

A second factor that reinforces a *yin-yang* contrast between Daoism and Confucianism is the actual way in which these two traditions have served the development of Chinese civilization. After all, Confucianism did become the official state doctrine during the Han dynasty, and Confucian classics were the curriculum that traditionally led to political office. By way of contrast, Buddhism was introduced into China largely through

Daoist categories (*geyi* 格義), and many popular uprisings were justified under the banners of rebellious Daoists.

The tendency to read the relationship between Confucians and Daoists in such a sharply contrastive manner derives in large measure from the use of dialectical analyses. Both Western scholars, and some Chinese scholars who imitate dialectical modes of historiography, set up the Daoist/Confucian contrast in an oppositonal manner. There is a danger in this, however, since the *yin-yang* contrast is a comparison of "thises" and "thats," and not a radical opposition. Daoism and Confucianism should certainly be contrasted, but not in the sense that they consititute oppositional modes of thinking that together "sum up" the Chinese way of thinking.

One factor contributing to an exaggeration of this contrast between the Daoists and the Confucians is the failure to distinguish the teachings themselves from their historical interpretations. The criticisms that we find in the Daoist texts, directed as they are against what they take to be the unnatural and ossified rules for living advocated by Confucius, might have, in fact, a fair target in historical Confucianism. It would be unfair of the *Zhuangzi*, however, to represent a Confucius who himself claims that "it is the human being who is able to broaden the way"[15] as one who cannot distinguish between the mere "footprints" on the way and the feet that made them.[16] Similarly, it is unfair of Xunzi to criticize Zhuangzi, a philosopher with profound insights into the most fundamental human questions, as being so "blinded by nature (*tian* 天) he did not understand the human experience."[17] Neither is it fair of us as commentators to describe a Confucius who was adamant that "a person born into the present age who attempts to return to the ways of the past is disaster's prey"[18] as advocating "a return to the Zhou" in the sense of a simple readjustment of the "powers and duties of ruler and minister, superior and inferior, according to the institutions of the Chou [Zhou] feudal world's most flourishing period."[19] And, again, it would not be fair to suggest that a Laozi who advocated that "one who knows masculinity and yet preserves femininity becomes the river gorge of the world"[20] at the same time "sought after a feminine and receptive knowledge which could arise only as the fruit of a passive and yielding attitude in the observation of Nature."[21]

The *yin-yang* contrast, properly understood as a correlative distinction rather than as an dichotomizing principle, can be an appropriate and illuminating way of characterizing the relationship between the teachings of Confucius and Lao-Zhuang. The real problem with this contrast is not that it is wholly false, but rather than it is overstated and simplistic. Without due attention to the fact that, unlike *independent* dualistic categories, *interdependent* correlative categories are registered on a shared continuum, this kind of *yin-yang* characterization can focus on differences alone without illuminating the common presuppositions that underlie them. Instead of serving to clarify legitimate distinctions against an even more fundamental commonality, it can obscure these differences by prompting simple answers. Used in a heavy-handed way, this failure to appreciate the nature of the relationship between Confucianism and Daoism, has the potential to obfuscate the robust *yin-yang* character of both the Confucian and Daoist visions of a meaningful human existence by separating them, and by then imposing an unwarranted conservatism on Confucius and an unjustified radicalism on Lao-Zhuang.

"Self-cultivation" is referred to variously with terms such as *xiushen* 修身 and *zuowang* 坐忘 in the Confucian and Daoist traditions respectively. Both Confucians and Daoists express a commitment to deepening and refining those relationships that constitute a person in his or her environments. By examining the comparable goals of self-cultivation in the tradition, we shall be able to understand the *way* one becomes an elegant human being. It is this way of self-cultivation that does the work of "truth" in the classical Chinese tradition.

BECOMING AN EXEMPLARY PERSON (JUNZI 君子)

One important model of self-cultivation is that which leads along the path to becoming a *junzi*, an "exemplary person." The *Shuowen* 說文 lexicon defines *jun* 君 with the rhyming *zun* 尊, meaning "a kind of vase," "of high rank," and then derivatively, "to honor," "to defer to."[22]

The etymological data on *jun* 君 provides the following associations:

1. Nobility, with an equivocation between rank and character
2. A term of respect
3. A "model" of order, cultivation, and refinement, attracting the emulation of those below, and
4. An exemplary person whose influence is extended through political responsibility and effective communication

Importantly, *jun* 君 is a source of order in a decidedly communal frame of reference.[23] The question arises whether this order is a preassigned pattern that the *jun* instantiates, or is it, at least ideally, an order that derives from the particular person as that person is engaged in a sociopolitical context?

In the literature prior to Confucius, the expression *junzi* 君子, a diminutive form of *jun* 君 meaning "son of *jun*," had a strictly political reference. That is, *junzi* was a term that specifically denoted nobility of birth and rank, and had no application as a category of personal achievement.[24] Confucius then appropriated this political category and redefined it for his own purposes so that political participation became a necessary component in the process of personal cultivation, and personal cultivation became a necessary qualification for political office and influence. This correlative relationship between personal achievement and political responsibility has frequently been described in the not wholly appropriate terms of "means" and "end." The contemporary sinologist Hsiao Kung-chuan observes:

> The old meaning of the word [*junzi*] contains the general im-
> plication that the man who possessed rank should cultivate his
> virtue, while Confucius tended toward an emphasis on the culti-
> vation of virtue in order to acquire rank.[25]

H. G. Creel discounts the political connotations of the revised notion of *junzi* altogether:

> *Chun tzu* [*junzi*] has been used, especially by Confucius, to mean
> "gentleman" (or in Legge's well-known rendering, "superior
> man") in a moral sense, without any other connotation.[26]

These descriptions obscure the presumption that personal cultivation and communal responsibility are interdependent and mutually entailing. A person is refined in the kiln of bureaucratic office, and such an office is an essential element in the education of the person who would be refined. Confucius did not replace the bureaucratic and political qualifications previously defining of *junzi* with new moral ones. What he did do was to insist that political responsibility and moral development are inseparable correlates. Self-cultivation necessarily entails active participation in the family and the extended order of the community as a means of evoking the compassion and concern that leads to one's own personal growth. It is inconceivable that full personal growth and disclosure could be achieved in the absence of social and political responsibility.[27]

Now there can be at least two objections to this claim that, for Confucius, personal cultivation and communal responsibility are mutually implicative/First, Confucius states on any number of occasions that when *dao* does not prevail, the *junzi* should withdraw from involvement in administration:

> Be known when the way prevails in the world, but remain hidden away when it does not.[28]

But withdrawal from formal participation in the administration of bad government does not mean the abandonment of responsibility for the community. On the contrary, it is precisely to serve this wider order *at its most fundamental level* of family that the *junzi* withdraws from office:

> Someone asked Confucius, "Why do you not take up office in government?" The Master replied, "The *Book of Documents* says: 'Filiality (*xiao* 孝)! Simply being filial and being a friend to your brothers extends into exercising governance.' These family virtues are also the stuff of government. Why must one 'take up office in government?'"[29]

Communal order is proximate; it is derived from the most concrete and particular level and is grounded in specific familial relationships.

A second objection that might be raised is that Confucius' own limited political experience is a rather compelling argument against the correlativity of his rather modest political career and his personal achievement. However, Confucius was significantly "revisioned" by subsequent biographers who accorded him increasingly important political positions, from minister of justice to prime minister, culminating in the status of "uncrowned king (*su wang* 素王)" during the Han dynasty.[30] Thus, it seems that growing recognition of his personal worth required a concomitant attribution of political stature. Or said in the opposite way, it was more likely for his followers that the historical records were incomplete than it was to allow that Confucius could have become the person he was without having served in political office.

In the *Analects*, *junzi* stands in contrast with a list of alternative designations for personal achievement such as *shengren* 聖人, *renzhe* 仁者,

shanren 善人, *xianren* 賢人, *chengren* 成人, and *daren* 大人. To understand the semantic content of *junzi*, we must take advantage of these alternative designations as a source of focus and discrimination. What are Confucius' grounds for establishing such distinctions? D. C. Lau observes:

> For Confucius there is not one single ideal character but quite
> a variety. The highest is the sage (*sheng jen* [*shengren*]). This ideal
> is so high that it is hardly ever realized.... Lower down the scale
> there are the good man (*shan jen* [*shanren*]) and the complete
> man (*ch'eng jen* [*chengren*]).... There is no doubt, however, that
> the ideal moral character for Confucius is the *chun tzu* [*junzi*]
> (gentleman).[31]

Chen Daqi 陳大齊 identifies these several categories of personal achievement in the *Analects*, and, by a close scrutiny of the text in which they occur, argues that they express various degrees of achievement which can be ranked in a specific relative hierarchy.[32] He suggests that, for the most part, there is a difference in level that clearly distinguishes the three most prominent designations, *shengren*, *renzhe*, and *junzi*. *Shengren* is higher than either *renzhe* or *junzi*:

> The Master said, "I will never get to meet a sage—I would be
> content to meet an exemplary person (*junzi*)."[33]

> Zigong said, "What about someone who is broadly generous with
> the people and is able to help the multitude—could we call such
> a person *ren*?" The Master replied, "Why stop at *ren*? This by all
> means is a sage (*shengren*)...."[34]

And according to Chen Daqi, it is equally clear that the *renzhe* ranks second as higher than the *junzi*:

> The Master said, "There have been instances of an exemplary
> person (*junzi*) acting perversely (*buren* 不仁), but there has never
> been a case of a small person acting *ren*."[35]

Confucius is unwilling to allow that he is either a *shengren* or a *renzhe*.[36] However, in spite of the fact that he explicitly denies he is a *junzi*,[37] the text implies repeatedly that he can be appropriately called a *junzi*.[38] Also, where he is most reluctant to identify any of his protégés as *renzhe*,[39] he does designate even some of his lower-order disciples as *junzi*.[40]

Of course, the real problem with Chen Daqi's analytical approach to these categories of the achieving person is that it provides us with little more than a bald ranking without being specific as to the content and criteria that justify them. Further, and more dangerously, it obscures the intrinsic relatedness of these categories to the point of suggesting that we are dealing with different models of personal achievement.[41]

An alternative, perhaps more profitable, way of explaining the several categories of personal realization is to begin by allowing that Confucius is using them as ways of focusing different dimensions in the process of becoming a sage. There is no attempt to essentialize this process, and these categories of personal realization are certainly not fixed or final in meaning and function. Reflection upon them has some pragmatic value, however, in helping to articulate the nuances of the steps one takes on the road to sagehood.

A concentric circle model of understanding these terms may be helpful. In such a model, *ren* is at the center as interpersonal relatedness, *junzi* is at the next circle as communal relatedness, and *shengren* is at the next circle with more cosmic implications. The furthest circle is broken to represent the inexhaustibility of sageliness. *Shengren* is the broadest category because it describes the whole process at its most comprehensive level. The other categories can be differentiated inasmuch as each of them represents a distinctive emphasis in this project. At the same time, these categories are fundamentally correlative in that they are all contributions to the achievement of sagehood.

As we have seen, even though *junzi* is a category with important communal reference, it necessarily entails the strongly interpersonal category of *ren*. The overlapping of *ren* and *junzi* as two foci in the project of becoming a sage accounts for the fact that many characteristics of the *renzhe* are also distinguishing features of the *junzi*. Further, to the extent that both refer to specific areas in the general project of personal growth, the characteristics of commitment to learning, cultivation, and refinement are held in common.[42] Sagehood as a category is strongly associated with political influence as well as personal worth. What is distinctive about sagehood is that the quality of one's achievement is a source of meaning, value, and purpose to the extent that one becomes godlike, a person of cosmic proportions and influence. The notion of sage has a profoundly religious dimension. As Mencius observes:

That which is desirable is called being adept (*shan* 善); having it in oneself is called being trustworthy (*xin* 信); and manifesting it fully is called elegance (*mei* 美). Manifesting it fully and being radiant with it is called being great (*da* 大); being great and being transformed by this greatness is called sageliness (*sheng* 聖); being sagely and going beyond the understanding of others, is called being godly (*shen* 神).[43]

This passage in the *Mencius* begins from the idea of being adept or good at forging relationships. Viewed from one's own perspective, forging such relationships makes one trustworthy. Viewed from the perspective of others, it makes one "elegant." The extension of this adeptness at forging relationships makes one in turn a great person, a sage, and ultimately, a god. Gods are cultural heroes and ancestors, revered as models of desirable conduct, who become corporate by attracting the deference of their tradition.

For Confucius, the *junzi* is a qualitative term denoting someone who has an ongoing commitment to personal growth as it is cultivated and expressed through political leadership. "The *junzi* is not a functionary 君子不器" means that such growth is not describable in terms of specific skills or expertise, but rather is a measure of character, and of the quality of one's interactions with others. As a device for underscoring the qualitative nature of this designation, Confucius repeatedly draws a contrast between the socially expansive and inclusive *junzi*, and the disintegrative and retarding characteristics of what he terms "the small person (*xiaoren* 小人)."[44] This "small person," far from making a social or political contribution, is motivated by selfishness, and thus detracts from the effective coordination of community. Where the conduct of the small person is least obstructive, it simply reduplicates what is already there (*tong* 同) rather than contributing any qualitative enhancement to the situation (*he* 和).[45] The signature of the qualitatively achieved person is found in the creativity, imagination, and influence to make community not only different, but better. Throughout the classical corpus, the sage (*shengren* 聖人) is frequently associated with innovative activity (*zuo* 作). When Confucius says of himself, "Following the proper way, I do not forge new paths (述而不作)," he is in fact with modesty saying, "I am not a sage."[46]

Because of the fundamentally social and political frame of reference of the *junzi* aspect of personal realization, this innovative activity entails effective communication. Effective communication has a central role both as the medium through which one articulates oneself, and in attracting participation in the kind of order that the *junzi* models for community.

Language shapes and valorizes the world. Thus, throughout the *Analects*, enormous emphasis is placed upon both the danger and the opportunity that language represents.[47] The *junzi* is what he says, and where he is exemplary, the world is as he speaks it. It is the *junzi*'s speaking that brings the world into being. Hence, he speaks slowly and with some hesitation: "The exemplary person (*junzi* 君子)... is a person of action yet is cautious in what he says (*shen* 慎)."[48] As will be noted below in the discussion of being "genuine (*zhen* 真)," the term "cautious (*shen* 慎)" is cognate with "genuine (*zhen* 真)," meaning that one is circumspect, every detail being taken into account.

One final point should be underscored with respect to the correlative relationship between becoming a truly viable person (*renzhe*) and becoming socially and politically effective (*junzi*). The private/public distinction that has been so basic to Western political theories is largely absent. The Confucian model of personal realization does not permit severe distinctions between ethics and politics, between the personal and social, between the private and public.

LIVING UP TO ONE'S WORD (*XIN* 信) AND HAVING INTEGRITY (*CHENG* 誠)

The classical Confucian texts are replete with a vocabulary that speaks of forging harmonious relationships. Interestingly, most of this vocabulary entails some etymological indication that these relationships are accomplished through effective communication. For example, in our review of the *Analects* in *Thinking Through Confucius*, we have an extended discussion of "living up to one's word (*xin* 信)," which is etymologically constituted by "persons (*ren* 人)" and "to speak (*yan* 言)"— standing by one's word.[49] In the present discussion, we shall emphasize the pragmatic import of *xin*, which means not only being "trustworthy" in the sense of being well-intended, but also entails having the actual resources to follow through and make good on what has been promised.

"*Cheng* 誠," conventionally translated as "sincerity" or perhaps better, "integrity," is another example of a term that expresses the effecting of "true relations" through communication, being etymologically constituted by "to speak (*yan* 言)" and "to consummate, to realize (*cheng* 成)"[50] There is a close association in the literature between *dao* 道 and *cheng* 誠:

> Integrity (*cheng*) means self-consummating; *dao* means self-articulating (literally, self-"*dao*-ing"). For something to have integrity is the full substance of that thing from its beginning to its end; for it to be lacking in integrity is for it to be nothing. For this reason, the exemplary person (*junzi*) prizes integrity. Integrity is not simply the means to consummate oneself, but also the way to consummate other things. To consummate oneself is to distinguish oneself as a person (*ren* 仁); to consummate other things is to realize them (*zhi* 知). The persistent focus (*de* 德) of one's natural proclivities (*xing* 性) is the way to coordinate self in context. Thus, integrity is being appropriate anytime and anywhere.[51]

Integrity is more than being true to oneself. Since all selves are constituted by relationships, integrity means being trustworthy and true in one's associations. It is effectively integrating oneself in one's social, natural, and cultural contexts. At a cosmological level, integrity is the ground from which self and other arise together to maximum benefit. It is not *what* things are, but *how well* and *how productively* they are able to fare in their synergistic alliances. This sense of "abundance" or "plenty" is evident in *cheng*'s cognate, *sheng* 盛, which means "to prosper," "to flourish."

There is a passage in the *Mencius* that brings both "living up to one's word (*xin* 信)" and "integrity (*cheng* 誠)" together as a kind of communal syntax that makes the human community meaningful:

> If, serving in a subordinate office, a person is unable to gain the support of his superiors, he will not be able to win the people over to proper order. There is a way of gaining the support of one's superiors: One who does not live up to his word in dealing with his friends will not gain the support of his superiors. There is a way of a living up to one's word in dealing with one's friends: One who in serving his relatives does not bring them pleasure, will not live up to his word in dealing with his friends. There is a way of bringing one's relatives pleasure: One who on introspection finds that he lacks integrity will not bring pleasure to

his relatives. There is a way of having integrity in one's person: One who is not sure that he is acting well will not have integrity in his person. It is for this reason that integrity is the way of nature, and to reflect on integrity is the way of being a person. There has never been a person of the utmost integrity who has not affected others, just as there has never been a person lacking in integrity who has been able to affect anyone at all.[52]

BECOMING A GENUINE PERSON (*ZHENREN* 真人)

While the *Shuowen* 説文 lexicon can be of considerable service in defining central terminologies of the pre-Qin philosophers, on occasion, because of the changing face of some of these ideas during the Han dynasty in which it was compiled, it can instead be anachronistic, and hence, a source of some confusion. Such is the case in the attempt to explain the rather mysterious character, *zhen* 真, glossed in the *Shuowen* as "the immortals undergoing physical transformation and ascending to the heavens 仙人變形而登天也." *Zhen* is mysterious because, although the earlier classics contain the various cognates derived from it, this character itself is nowhere to be found. The earliest occurrence of *zhen* would seem to be in the *Daodejing* and *Zhuangzi* texts from which it was popularized as a special Daoist term.[53]

Where then is the anachronism? Many commentators believe that *zhen* was altered by the emergence of institutionalized religious Daoism in the last century of the Han dynasty, and are unconvinced that it had such implications for the *Zhuangzi*. While the several references to *zhenren* 真人 in the *Huainanzi* and *Lüshi chunqiu* are ambiguous, and might be construed as denoting immortals, *Zhuangzi* defines *zhen* as "the highest degree of purity and integrity."[54]

In the *Shuowen* lexicon, *zhen* is classified under the radical *bi* 匕, the original form of *hua* 化, "to transform, to change to," so whatever "genuine" might mean, it does entail a process of transformation. At the same time, the pursuit of personal immortality through elixirs and breathing exercises conflicts with the *Zhuangzi*'s notion of comprehending the synergistic continuity of the human experience, thereby overcoming any severe distinction between life and death. Similarly, escape from the world and ascent to the heavens as an immortal is anathema to *Zhuangzi*'s notion of total integration in the process of the "transformation of things (*wuhua* 物化)."

The *Zhuangzi*'s "Paring Down Intentions (*Keyi* 刻意)" chapter, frequently considered as an elaboration on the text's *locus classicus* for *zhenren*, "The Great Ancestral Teacher (*Dazongshi* 大宗師)," specifically condemns the life directed at a purposeful pursuit of physical immortality (together with the careers of the moralist, the scholar, the politician, and the recluse) as being inconsistent with the purity and integrity of the *zhenren*.

If the *Shuowen* is anachronistic, and *zhenren* in the *Zhuangzi* does *not* refer to the transformation of the immortal and his assent to the heavens, what does it mean? The *Zhuangzi* develops a rather clear definition of *zhen* while causing Confucius some discomfiture—because he too does not grasp its meaning:

> Confucius, changing his composure, inquired, "Could you please tell me what 'genuineness (*zhen* 真)' means?"
>
> The fisherman replied, "Genuineness (*zhen*) is the highest degree of purity and integrity. Without purity and integrity, one cannot affect others. Thus, the person who forces his tears, although pathetic, does not arouse grief; one who forces his anger, although severe, does not inspire awe; one who forces his affections, although cordial, does not effect harmony. Genuine pathos arouses grief even without tears; genuine anger inspires awe even without rising to the surface; genuine affection effects harmony even without cordiality. It is because the spirit of one who is genuine within affects those around him that genuineness is to be prized."
>
> "When genuineness is applied to human relations, in the service of family, it is compassion and filiality; in the service of the state, it is loyalty and justice; in feasting and drinking, it is pleasure and enjoyment; in mourning, it is pathos and grief. Most important in loyalty and justice is effort, in feasting it is enjoyment, in mourning it is grief, and in service of the family it is accommodation. And there is certainly more than one path to follow to arrive at these. One serves the family to accommodate its members, and is not concerned with how this is done; one feasts to enjoy and is not concerned with the choice of dishes; one mourns to grieve and does not ask after the rituals. Rituals are laid down by convention; genuineness is received

from nature. What is so-of-itself (*ziran* 自 然) cannot be sup-
planted. Thus, the sage emulates nature and prizes genuineness
without being caught up in conventions. The fool is the opposite. Unable to emulate nature, he frets over what human
beings have established, and not having the good sense to prize
genuineness, he goes along altering himself to suit the world,
never himself knowing contentment. It is indeed a pity that
you were so early in being steeped in human devices and have
come so late to hear the great way!"[55]

There are several points to be highlighted in this passage. What is genuine
(*zhen*) arises as a natural expression as opposed to being dictated by convention. It is the disclosure of one's own significance and value, personalizing
the institutions and rituals that structure one's world and rendering them
meaningful.

    Zhen is the ground of personal, social, and political integration that
makes one continuous with one's natural and cultural environments.
Institutions and conventions are nothing more than artificial structures
established by the human being as an apparatus for giving expression to
the accommodation, enjoyment, and harmony, that constitute the fabric
of an integrated human existence. The quarrel is not with the conventions
per se; which have their place. Rather, there is suspicion of an overriding
concern for and attachment to these conventions at the expense of the
disclosure of one's own distinct genuineness, one's self-so-ness. The
argument here is against misplaced concreteness.

    There is a passage in the *Huainanzi* that provides us with further
clarification of the meaning of a "genuine person":

> He "has" and yet seems "not to have;"
> He is solid yet seems empty.
> Dwelling in continuity,
> He does not know duality;
> Managing himself within,
> He is not cognizant of things external to him.
> Bright and supremely simple,
> He returns through non-coercive activity to the unhewn
>   block.
> Embodying the roots and embracing the spiritual,

He thus rambles about in the enclosure of the cosmos.
He soars, unconstrained, beyond the mundane world,
And moves freely in the enterprise of being free from work.
So vast and expansive,
There is no freight of cleverness or craftiness carried in his heart-
and-mind.
Hence, even though dying is certainly a matter of great
     import,
     He will not change in the face of it.
     Even when heaven and earth collapse,
     He will not get entangled with them.
     Conversant about what is flawless,
     He does not mix with other things.
     Seeing the confused state of things,
     He is yet able to hold onto what begot him....
     He regards life and death as making up a single
        transformation,
     And considers the myriad things as of one kind.[56]

This account of the cosmic wanderings of the genuine person centers
on the repeated themes, "dwelling in continuity, he does not know duality,"
and regarding "life and death as making up a simple transformation," he
"considers the myriad things of one kind." The life of the genuine person
is one of integration in which all dichotomies find reconciliation. As such,
he is unattached, and unperturbed at the course which circumstances
take.

Throughout the Daoist corpus, the expression "bright (*ming* 明)" is
used repeatedly to characterize the quality of the genuine person's understanding. This expression is important because it gives us the opportunity
to take a further step away from a representational understanding of what
it means to know. *Ming* is frequently glossed in commentaries as *zhu* 著,
which means "to make manifest." This explains its cognate relationship
with *meng* 萌, which means "to sprout forth." In this sense, the writings of
worthy persons are called *ming* because they make the world brighter and
make it easier to find our way. A second gloss on *ming* 明 is "to connect,
penetrate (*tong* 通)" and "pattern, coherence (*li* 理)," explaining the
cognate relationship between *ming* and "covenant (*meng* 盟)." That is,
making the world brighter entails forging fiduciary relationships and
strengthening connections. It is not surprising that *ming* is used in
expressions such as *shenming* 神明, meaning gods and spirits. After all, to

be a seen luminary, a cultural beacon, is what it means to be a god in this culture.

In this characterization of the genuine person, we cannot but recall the "*wu*-forms" of the *Daodejing* discussed in part I. Throughout the early Daoist literature, there is considerable discussion of a series of integrative processes: *Wuwei* 無為 is nonassertive activity; *wuzhi* 無知 is unprincipled knowing; *wuyu* 無欲 is objectless desiring. Such activities are described figuratively in *Zhuangzi* as "breaking up one's body (*duo zhi ti* 墮肢體)" and thus dissolving the dichotomy of self and other to integrate fully into the continuity of existence (*tong yu da tong* 同於大通).[54]

This integration has the effect of making the genuine person different from others in the quality of his existence. The activity of the genuine person is characterized by flexibility, efficacy, and noncontention, collaborating with the social and natural environments in mutual disclosure, and serving as frictionless ground for their "self-so-ing," and they for his own.

The transforming person has an uninterrupted continuity with the whole process of existence, and a calmness and imperturbability that comes with nonattachment. Existing beyond the plethora of disintegrative dualisms of self and other, creator and creature, reality and appearance, life and death, the genuine person achieves a kind of immortality—not by escaping to some purer realm, but by realizing himself in the concrete and persistent here and now.

The choice of the word "genuine" to translate *zhen* is calculated. The root, *gen-*, meaning "to beget, produce," captures the primacy given to the creative contribution of the particular person. It further registers this contribution as what is most fundamentally true in the sense of being consonant with its environing conditions, being "just so," "exactly," "on the mark."

The importance of the "*auth*orship" of the *auth*entic person, the self-*generating* character of the *gen*uine person, is precisely why

> there must be the genuine person (*zhenren* 真人) before there can be genuine knowledge (*zhenzhi* 真知).[58]

Here the *Zhuangzi* rejects any representational or correspondence theory of knowledge that demands a fixed reality to which an idea can correspond:

> Knowledge depends on something to which it can correspond, but what it depends upon is never fixed.[59]

The knower does not cognize a preexisting reality, but participates actively in the realization of the world through self-disclosure. Knowing certainly entails cognition, but it is also profoundly experiential and performative, involving the making of one's own world. The genuine person must "realize" the world in order to "know" it. This integration of *zhen* cancels the familiar dichotomies of knower and known, and knowledge and experience. *Zhen* is *how* the world is experienced, and only derivitively *what* the world is. *Zhen* describes the *true* accommodation one makes to one's environing community. A cognate of *zhen* 真 that suggests care and sensitivity in the posture one strikes is *shen* 慎 "to be cautious and circumspect." Other cognates of *zhen* such as 鎮 and 縝 mean "dense, compact." Yet others such as *tian* 填 mean "to stop up, to plug." Broadly, the underlying idea would seem to suggest a kind of fullness that can neither be added to nor diminished, a fullness that in itself is ample.

However, there is need for even further refinement. When we say *ziran* 自然, meaning "self-so-ing" or "self-disclosing," we must bear in mind that self is always in context, a particular focus in a dynamic field of existence that is continuous with and ultimately reflects in itself the full consequence of existence. As a particular current in an ongoing fluid process, the genuine person has an synergistic interdependence with all of his environing conditions. Disclosure for self and context is mutually entailing.

Full disclosure of a particular person in coordination with his environing others is the ground for optimum creativity. This creativity can be compromised, however, by attempting to express one's individuality in disintegrative ways. One must not fail to accommodate the interdependence of things. This limitation on creativity can emerge either by forcing one's environment into fixed conceptual structures, thereby impoverishing context in service to self, or by allowing oneself to be shaped wholly by context without contributing one's own uniqueness, thereby impoverishing self in service to context. In order to be fully integrative, one must cultivate an optimum continuity with one's context by contributing personally and creatively to the emerging order of existence. While maintaining one's full integrity as an insistent particular, any sense of discreteness or disjunction needs to be overcome.

As we have seen above, in the classical Confucian tradition, we can isolate a range of terms that identify different dimensions in the project of becoming a sage, all of which refer to different aspects of extending oneself outward from the "small person (*xiaoren* 小人)" to the "interpersonally achieved person (*renzhe* 仁者)" to the "sociopolitically exemplary person (*junzi* 君子)," and ultimately to the "cosmically sagacious person (*shengren* 聖人)." A comparable situation obtains in the Daoist texts, where the genuine person (*zhenren* 真人) is alternatively described as "the superlative person (*zhiren* 至人)," "the spiritual person (*shenren* 神人)," "the great person (*daren* 大人)," or "the intact person (*quanren* 全人)." As with the Confucian terminology, we find that these Daoist expressions converge in the meaning of "extension" and "integration." Such integration is effected largely through modes of communication such as language and ritual for the Confucian, and natural communion for the Daoist.

For both Confucian and Daoist alike, there is a primacy given particular modes of self-realization. The insistent particularity of any person or thing is most fully disclosed under the conditions provided by integration. Energies are not diffused through attachment and contentiousness, but are fully focused in self-expression. The emergent pattern of existence returns to and is derived from the collaboration of harmoniously integrated particularity. Hence, we read in the *Daodejing* that political organization is best when it emerges from the bottom:

> Thus, in the words of the sage:
>   I am free of coercive activity
>   And the people transform of their own accord.
>   I cherish tranquility
>   And the people are ordered of their own accord.
>   I have no agenda
>   And the people prosper of their own accord.
>   I desire without attachment
>   And the people are like unhewn wood of their own accord.[60]

Again, in the *Zhuangzi*, exercising impositional authority is anathema to effecting social order:

> Shoulder-Us went to see the madman, Came-into-Contact-with-a-Carriage. The mad Came-into-Contact-with-a-Carriage asked him, "What has Beginning-Midday been telling you?"
> Shoulder-Us replied, "He told me that when a ruler on his own initiative lays down the formal instruments of government, who would dare disobey or remain unreformed by them!"

The mad Came-into-Contact-with-a-Carriage observed, "This is a ruffian's kind of virtue. As far as its bringing proper order to the world is concerned, it would be like trying to walk across the ocean, or trying to drill one's way through a river, or trying to make a mosquito carry a mountain on its back. When the sage governs, does he govern the external? He straightens himself out before he does anything, and is concerned precisely with being able to go about his own business—no more, no less."[61]

The way in which the Daoist seeks to pursue personal realization is to coordinate his conduct with the emergent cadence and regularity of the world around him, overcoming any tendencies he might have toward independence and self-sufficiency (wu sang wo 吾喪我),[62] and loosing himself from any attachments that establish this discrete identity:

> Because the sage does not grab hold of anything,
> He does not lose anything.[63]

But the absence of a discrete and individuated self and the attachments that define it, does not discount the importance given to the particular and the uniqueness of its perspective. In chapter 3 we rehearsed the anecdote of Zhuangzi and Hui Shi standing on a bridge over the Hao river in which Zhuangzi claims that he knows that the fish are happy *from here* on the bridge. His point is that knowledge is always proximate, situational, participatory, and interpretative. It is because Zhuangzi is continuous with his surrounds that knowledge of the situation emerges, where the fishes are no less entailed in the realization of the happy experience than Zhuangzi himself. It is the situation rather than some discrete agent that is happy. The reflexivity of Zhuangzi is himself-in-context, where the membrane between Zhuangzi and context is porous and fluid. The event is realized in the doing of it. And language both articulates (ming 名) and commands (ming 命) the relationship between Zhuangzi and his world. As the *Zhuangzi* observes,

> A path (dao) is made in the walking of it.
> A thing being called something becomes it.
> Why is it so?
> It is so because it is so.
> Why is it not something other than what it is?
> It is not because it is not.[64]

There is a recurrent expression in the *Daodejing* that makes a similar point in a refrain that ends several of the passages: "From this (*yici* 以此)." For example, posing the question: "How do I know that the world is so?" the text answers, "From this."[65] The question rephrased is: What is your perspective? Hence, the question "how?" also means ""whence?" And the answer is "from here." Knowing can only be "here" and thus can only be "this," which is inclusive of one's perspective, as opposed to "that," which would exclude it. The focus, then, is not upon the external environs as an object of knowledge, but upon the site at which the act of knowing takes place.

Also implicit in this question, "how?" is "how well?" That is, how much influence do you have in the shaping of this world? The expression "this (*shi* 是)" certainly functions locatively and demonstratively, pointing at a particular event. A familiar pattern is for a passage in the *Daodejing* to end with "this is what is meant by..." (*shi wei*...是謂...). But this refrain is not simply a descriptive claim; it is prescriptive and affirming. This is how things are; this is desirably so. The dictionary tells us that *shi* 是 sometimes means "this" as in the phrase, "that (*bi* 彼) comes from this (*shi* 是),"[66] and sometimes means "right" as in "what is right (*shi* 是) for one is wrong (*fei* 非) for the other."[67] In fact, *shi* is an affirmation of what is so. And since affirming something commands it to be so, it is an effort to construe the world in a particular way with the authority that, from one's perspective, this is the way it ought to be: "This is so (and that is not), and I affirm it so."

CONFUCIANISM AND DAOISM: CONVERGENCES AND DIVERGENCES

In our comparison between the Confucian *junzi* 君子 and the Daoist *zhenren* 真人 as their respective embodiments of "the way," we have been able to trace order for both of them back to the primacy of those proximate relationships that constitute the concrete particular. Confucius advocates the disciplining of any disintegrative discreteness (*keji* 克己) and the forestalling of any selfish attachments that such individuation might generate (*li* 利) as a precondition for the disclosure of one's own personal significance (*yi* 義) through the performance of socially integrating ritual roles and practices (*li* 禮).[68] But this does not entail the assumption that one begins as a fixed "ego-self," which one must then seek to overcome. In fact, one is born into and constituted by an incipient nexus of relationships that must then be cultivated and extended. Although these inchoate relationships, and the ritual structures through which they are extended, are immediately interpersonal, their greater significance lies in their character of locating and integrating the particular human being in the larger world most broadly construed.

We would claim that the basic outline of this Confucian program is also Daoist. As we have seen, personal realization requires the overcoming of any tendency toward disintegrative discreteness (*wu sang wo* 吾喪我) and the attachments attendant upon it (*shengren . . . wuzhi gu wushi* 聖人 . . . 無執故無失) as a condition for full personal disclosure (*zhen* 真) in coordination with the emergent regularity of the world around one (*dao* 道/*li* 理). In both the Confucian and the Daoist cases, there is a commitment to the uniqueness and the integrity of the particular, and in both cases, the definition of the particular emerges out of a collaboration with its environing conditions.

Another important point of congruence lies in the use, by both Confucians and Daoists, of analogy to determine the appropriate relationship among things. In this respect, Confucius's notion of *shu* 恕, "putting oneself in the place of others," is analogous to the Daoist's *wuwei* 無為, "acting nonassertively." Where Confucius appeals to the repository of formal conducts (*li*) that constitute the cultural tradition as his resource for drawing analogies to inform and refine human conduct in the present moment, the Daoist appeals to the regularity and constancy of nature around us (*tiandao*) as an appropriate analogical order. Both traditions rely upon analogy in taking model emulation as a means of discipline and education. While, for Confucius, the focus of model emulation lies within the parameters of human community, the Daoist establishes what we might term "the grand analogy," describing the appropriate attitude of the sage in precisely those terms used to characterize *dao*. The sage, in becoming *dao*-like, functions as a model for all humanity:

> Therefore, the sage embracing continuity becomes the model of the world.[69]

Finally, both the *junzi* and the *zhenren* are authoritative. They evoke deference from those around them. They are achieved models whose own efficacious, integrative activity conduces to the genuine expression of others. In both the *Daodejing* and the *Zhuangzi*, position and responsibility pursue the "genuine person." For example, the "Potency Satisfies the Tally" chapter of *Zhuangzi* appeals to a congeries of unfortunates who have been crippled and grotesquely deformed both by nature and the executioner's axe. But in spite of their deformities, the world flocks to them. Typical among them is Ugly Hunchback:

> Duke Ai of Lu asked Confucius, "In Wei there was this grotesque fellow called 'Ugly Hunchback.' Young men who lived together with him were overwhelmed and could not leave his company, and young women on meeting him would implore their parents, 'I would rather be this man's concubine than another man's wife.' There were innumerable such cases. No one ever heard him take the lead; he always just joined the chorus. He had no ruler's throne from which he could rescue others from death and had no stash of wealth from which to fill the stomachs of others. Moreover, he was ugly enough to put the whole world in shock. He joined the chorus and did not lead, and he knew no more than his immediate circumstances. Still, men and women rushed to where he stood. This was certainly a man with a difference. I summoned him to get a better look, and he certainly was ugly enough to put the whole world in shock. He lived with me, and before a month had passed, I had some insight into what kind of a person he was. And before a year was done, I was sure about him. The nation was without a prime minister, and so I turned the nation over to him. He responded only after becoming depressed, and then gushed forth as though he wanted to decline. I was ashamed, but in the end, he accepted the commission. Not long after, when he left me and went away, it was as though I had lost a loved one and had no one left with whom to enjoy this nation. What kind of person was this?"[70]

If there is a reluctance on the part of the genuine person to assume political responsibility, it is because the social and political worlds are only one dimension of his environment, and it might not be the one that *this* particular genuine person finds most congenial to self-expression. Again, we must bear in mind that political organization in the classical Chinese world is perceived as a natural and inevitable condition, like the institution of family, and much of the polemic directed against it is compensatory. It is a rejection of the disingenuous in its most obvious and common form, where one's authentic expression is subordinated to and disciplined by abstract regulations. Government so defined distracts the rulers from their natural inclinations through unhealthy attachments to wealth and fortune, and prevents the flourishing of the ruled through oppressive, dehumanizing laws and regulations.

These, then, are some of the fundamental similarities between the Daoist and the Confucian models of personal cultivation. How may they be said to diverge?

With respect to the issue of communal responsibility, it is clear that the Confucian and Daoist frames of reference are different. Confucius' concern to pursue personal realization within the human community gives him his practical orientation. But, for the Daoist, personal extension and integration means more than extending the limits of one's concerns to accommodate the human community. For the Daoist, the Confucian exaggerated emphasis on humanity simply sets up a "human/nonhuman" dichotomy, thereby disintegrating the human being and human culture from the natural world.

As we have seen above, there are scholars who, in service to a yin-yang distinction between Daoism and Confucianism, would read this differently. They would balance the communal orientation of Confucius by defining the Daoists as being radically individualistic and antisocial. Vitaly Rubin, for example, suggests that:

> Taoist teaching, which rejects the notion of man as a social being, clearly has no room for the categories of human personality.... In his [Zhuangzi's] view, man—far from being the crowning achievement of nature—is simply a dismal exception to nature, a feeble degenerate who, forgetful of the calm grandeur of nature, has plunged into the vortex of his own senseless affairs.... Unlike the *chun tzu* [*junzi*], the Taoist must forget people and their affairs, cares and sufferings.[71]

This characterization of the Daoist is difficult to square with the seemingly political *Daodejing*, which appears to accord quite closely with the classical Confucian view in describing social and political organization as a natural condition, and political responsibility as a consequence of personal achievement. *Zhuangzi*, as well, contains chapters entitled "In the Human World 人間世" and "Responding to Emperors and Kings 應帝王."

The Daoists do not reject society. Rather they reject the notion that human society exists in a vacuum, and that the whole process of existence can be reduced to human values and purposes. They reject the anthro-pocentrism they take to be implicit in Confucian religio-humanism because it gives the human being special status in the world, a status that ultimately decontextualizes the human experience from nature as a whole. The *Zhuangzi* contrasts the Confucian sage, Youyu (the legendary Shun), who is preoccupied with the human world, and the Daoist Tai (the patriarch of the "Ultimate" clan), who roams freely throughout the natural world unfettered by the limitations of purely human values and concerns:

> The House of Youyu is no match for the House of Tai. As for Youyu, he is still hangs onto his "humanity (*ren* 仁)" in order to intercept others, and he does indeed win them over, but he has never begun to venture out into what is not-human (*feiren* 非仁). As for Tai, he sleeps deeply and contentedly, and wakes up vacant, this time taking himself as a horse, and another taking himself as an ox. His awareness is sensitive and credible, and his potency (*de* 德) is utterly genuine (*zhen* 真). And he has never begun to entertain the idea of "the non-human."[72]

In this passage, the Confucian sage does not venture out into what is non-human because of his exclusive commitment to the human world. For the Daoist, existence is impoverished when one limits the focus of one's concerns to purely human matters. The Daoist patriarch moves freely throughout a world without such human and nonhuman boundaries. If one reads "constant *dao*" (*changdao* 常道) myopically as "the human *dao*" (*rendao* 人道), one is bound to experience the world through a welter of delimiting presuppositions. As the *Zhuangzi* enjoins,

> The genuine persons (*zhenren* 真人) of antiquity did not know to be pleased at being alive nor to dislike the prospect of dying. They embarked on life without rejoicing, and passed on without resistance. In a flash they came, in a flash they went, and that was all. They did not forget where it began nor seek after where it would end. On receiving life they were glad; forgetting about it, they gave it back. This is what is meant by: "Neither harm *dao* with the heart-and-mind nor help nature (*tian* 天) with what is human."[73]

On the basis of this passage and others like it, one might want to argue that the Daoist does in fact allow for the distinction between the human and the nonhuman by siding with the natural against the human. This is certainly Xunzi's criticism of Zhuangzi: "Being blinded by nature (*tian*), he does not know the human experience."[74] This would also seem to be the message in the "Autumn Floods " chapter of *Zhuangzi*:

> The natural (*tian*) resides within, the human resides without, and potency (*de* 德) resides in what is natural. Being aware of the workings of nature and the human, root yourself in the natural and take up a place with potency . . . . Don't destroy the natural with the human; don't destroy possibilities (*ming* 命) with preconceived ideas; don't chase after fame with your potency. Guarding it carefully, don't lose it—this is what is meant by "returning to the genuine (*zhen* 真)."[75]

But if we want to give the *Zhuangzi* its best argument, we have to allow that the text acknowledges the problematic status of this "human/ nonhuman" distinction, and that its compensatory efforts to reinstate the natural should not be read as an advocacy of the natural at the expense of the human. The text says flatly:

> How do we know that what we call "natural" is not in fact human, and vice versa?[76]

A resolution to this problem is provided in *Zhuangzi*'s definition of the Daoist "complete person (*quanren* 全人);"

> Yi the archer was skilled at hitting minute targets, but clumsy at preventing others from making him celebrated because of it. The sage is skilled at what is natural (*tian* 天) but clumsy at what is human. To be skilled at what is natural and to be equally good at what is human—only the complete person (*quanren*) can do this! Only critters can be critters and at the same time, be natural. The complete person hates what is natural, and hates what is natural about what is human. How much more does he hate this flip-flopping between "am I natural?" or "am I human?"[77]

In this passage, the *Zhuangzi* rejects the dichotomy between the natural and the human by positing the complete person who, like other living things, is defined as being what they are and natural at the same time.

Wherein, then, do the Daoist and Confucian ways diverge? They are agreed that personal realization comes with cultivating one's relationships. But the Daoist accuses the Confucian of throwing the net too narrowly in determining *which* environments and *which* range of relationships defining the human experience are relevant to the project of personal realization. This criticism does not go unjoined by Confucius, who is rather explicit on this issue. Confucius and Zilu, his oldest and one of his closest disciples, were traveling together. They stopped to ask two farmers for directions. One of the farmers challenged his relationship with Confucius in the following terms:

> "A veritable deluge—and the whole empire is like this. Who then is going to change it into a new world? You follow after a teacher who avoids people selectively. Wouldn't you be better off following a teacher who avoids the world altogether?" As he spoke he continued to tend his field.
>
> Zilu left to inform Confucius. Confucius absently replied, "We cannot run with the birds and beasts. Am I not one among the people of this world? If not them, with whom should I associate? If the way prevailed in the empire, I wouldn't need to change it."[78]

For Confucius, the farmers in failing to take responsibility for order within the human realm, are violating the premise that order be *proximate*, starting here and extending there. For the same reason that communal order broadly construed is no more or less than an extension of familial order, so order within the human world must begin by prioritizing those with whom we most closely associate.

Although Confucius does not invoke the notion of "appropriateness (*yi* 義)" in this particular discussion, he does so implicitly in the context of commenting on the conduct of cultural heroes such as Bo Yi and Shu Qi who have become recluses as a matter of principle. These heroes, unwilling to lower their standards or to accept indignity, turn away from the human community. Although appreciative of their highmindedness, Confucius' response is to distance himself from them:

> I am different from these people. I do not have fixed rights and wrongs.[79]

Elsewhere, Confucius uses a similar formula that makes this previous passage clear by explicitly positing "appropriateness (yi 義)" as the alternative to preconceptions about what is right and what is wrong:

> The exemplary person (junzi 君子) in making his way in the world is neither bent on nor against anything; rather, he accords with what is appropriate (yi).[80]

There is a related allusion to the "recluses" in the *Analects* in which "appropriateness" is again offered as the alternative to abandoning community to avoid tarnishing one's own character:

> To refuse office is to withhold one's contribution of what is appropriate (yi 義). If the differentiation between young and old cannot be abandoned, how could one think of abandoning what is appropriate between ruler and subject? This is to throw the most important relationships into turmoil in one's efforts to remain personally untarnished. The exemplary person's opportunity to serve in office is the occasion to carry into practice what is appropriate. That the *dao* does not prevail—this is known already.[81]

Here Confucius naturalizes the political relationship between ruler and subject by comparing it to those familial ties between young and old that function as the ground of filial piety and commiseration. "Appropriateness (yi 義)" is Confucius' answer to the Daoist recluse—to do what is natural and proper, given who you are.

Ironically, Confucius' best defense against the Daoist charge that he is promoting unnatural institutions and artificial sentiments comes from a popular misreading of the *Zhuangzi* itself, where Confucius becomes the spokesperson for a Daoism that wants to distinguish itself from the life of the recluse. Zigong, another disciple of Confucius, travels south to the state of Chu where he encounters an old farmer using a pitcher to irrigate his fields. This farmer, huffing and puffing, is using a great deal of effort with little result. The considerate Zigong explains the principle of the well-sweep to the farmer, suggesting to him that he could save a lot of trouble by employing this new technology for irrigation.

The old farmer is incensed, and draws a straight line between the use of such contrivances and a contriving heart-and-mind. The cost, for him, is far too great:

> If one has a contriving heart-and-mind lodged in his breast, he
> will be impure, and if he is impure, his spirit will be agitated, and
> the way (*dao*) will not carry someone whose spirit is agitated.[82]

On learning that Zigong is a disciple of Confucius, the old farmer scolds
him for talking a bunch of nonsense to win a reputation from the world,
and then sends him packing. Zigong is stunned, and confides in a disciple
that he used to think Confucius had the best strategy: To get the greatest
results for the least effort is the way of the sage. But it is in fact this old
farmer who is able to keep his spirit whole that has the way of the sage.
Nothing phases him; he is totally indifferent to the opinions of the world.

On returning to Lu, Zigong confronts Confucius with this incident.
In the popular misreading, Burton Watson, following Fukunaga Mitsuji
and a host of commentaries, has Confucius respond to the reclusive old
farmer in the following terms:

> Confucius said, "He is one of those bogus practitioners of the
> arts of Mr. Chaos. He knows the first thing but doesn't understand
> the second. He looks after what is on the inside but doesn't look
> after what is on the outside. A man of true brightness and purity
> who can enter into simplicity, who can return to the primitive
> through inaction, give body to his inborn nature and embrace
> his spirit, and in this way wander through the everyday world.
> If you had met one like that, you would have real cause for
> astonishment. As for the arts of Mr. Chaos, you and I need not
> bother to find out about them."[83]

This *Zhuangzi* passage was unmistakably written as a direct response
to the Confucian challenge outlined in the *Analects* passages cited above.
According to Fukunaga, Confucius here as in the *Analects* is defending the
position that the sage, far from being an escapist, lives comfortably in the
world. We can be reasonably sure that this is a misreading of *Zhuangzi*
because Fukunaga and colleagues are clearly forcing the text, and because
of corroboration for our alternative reading found in a *Huainanzi* passage
describing the genuine person (*zhenren* 真人) that was cited above.[84] We
read the Confucius in this *Zhuangzi* passage as being a somewhat more
contrite spokesperson for his Daoist appropriators:

> Confucius said, "He has borrowed the arts of the Chaos clan.
> Knowing continuity, he does not know duality; bringing proper

order on the inside, he does not order it as something external. This is a person who with clarity enters into the unadorned and through noncoercive activity returns to the unhewn block, who realizes his natural inclinations and keeps his arms around his spirit to roam through the common world. Does he really cause you such alarm! As for the arts of the Chaos clan, how could the likes of you and I have any understanding of them!"

Zhuangzi's "Confucius" (and there are many) here allows that his own human-centered position entails a duality between the human and natural worlds, and so is no match for the Daoist. However, this *Zhuangzi* passage is really not as devastating for the Confucian rejection of what it takes to be Daoist escapism as it might first appear. There are in fact several thick strains of Daoism that are on Confucius' side. Within the pages of the *Zhuangzi*, there are other Daoists who, like Confucius, want to distinguish themselves from those who would look back fondly to some utopian past and who would abandon this world for a life of simplicity, primitivity, and seclusion.[85]

The principal point is that Confuciansim and Daoism may be thought to exist on a continuum, or a set of continua really, with respect to any number of variables. The Chinese penchant for seeing things in terms of interdependent categories rather than dualistic or dialectically paired distinctions means that, however anyone else might view the relations of Daoism and Confucianism, the goal of the tradition is to construe them in a harmonious fashion. For it is, ultimately, not in noting the competition between the Daoist and Confucian "ways," but in celebrating the various harmonious relationships between the two sensibilities, that one best understands the classical Chinese seekers of the Way.

TRUTH AND THE HARMONY OF THE WAY

The final notion helpful in promoting an understanding of the differences between Truth-seekers and Way-seekers is that of *he* 和, conventionally translated "harmony." The *Shuowen* defines *he* as "mutual responsiveness" *xiang ying* 相應. The etymology of this term is culinary, taking us back to *geng* 羹, a gruel-like staple of the early diet, comparable probably with the contemporary congee or *zhou* 粥. Geng was made by combining *he* 禾, the widely cultivated fox-millet, and other locally available ingredients, in service to the palate, *kou* 口.[86] Harmony is the art of combining and blending two or more foodstuffs so they come together with mutual benefit and enhancement without losing their separate and particular identities, and yet with the effect of constituting a frictionless whole. An important characteristic of this harmony is the endurance of the particular ingredients and the cosmetic nature of the harmony. It is an order that emerges out of the collaboration of intrinsically related details to embellish the contribution of each one. Throughout the early corpus, the preparation of food is appealed to as a gloss on this sense of elegant harmony. In the *Lüshi chunqiu*, the art of achieving harmony is defined in the following terms:

> In the business of flavoring and harmonizing ingredients, you must use sweet, sour, bitter, acrid, and salty, and you must have a sequence for mixing them and a sense of proportion. Blending the ingredients in proper balance is very subtle; all of them are self-awakening. The variations within the cooking pot are so delicate and subtle that they defy words and conceptualization.[87]

Important in this description of cooking is the respect for each of the "self-awakening" (*ziqi* 自起) ingredients and the need to find a proper balance by acknowledging the parity that obtains among them (*qi* 齊).

In the *Analects*, this sense of harmony is celebrated as the highest cultural achievement. Here, harmony is distinguished from mere agreement by again invoking the central role of particularity. The family metaphor pervades this text, encouraged by the intuition that this is the institution in which members typically give themselves most fully and unreservedly to the group. "Propriety" or full participation in ritualized roles and relationships (*li* 禮), is the pursuit of a flourishing community through the personalization of overlapping familial roles and relationships:

> The achievement of harmony is the most valuable function of propriety (*li* 禮). In the ways of the Former Kings, this achievement of harmony through ritual was elegant, and was a guiding standard in all things large and small. But where there are situations which are not harmonious, to realize harmony just for the sake of harmony without regulating the situation on the basis of propriety, will not work.[88]

In the *Daodejing*, harmony is defined explicitly in terms of "being adept" (*shan* 善) in one's relationships:

> In bringing harmony to a situation of intense enmity,
> There is sure to be some animosity remaining.
> How can this be considered adeptness?
> [Respond to enmity with potency (*de* 德).][89]
> The sage, holding onto the left half of the tally,
> Does not demand payment from others.
> The person who has potency (*de*) takes charge of the tally
> The person without potency looks to collect on it.
> The way of nature (*tian dao* 天道) shows no partiality;
> It is constantly on the side of the adept person.[90]

Relationships are like tallies shared between persons, and those with potency are able to make the most of them. As discussed in part I above, "Potency Satisfies the Tally" is the title of book 5 of the *Zhuangzi*, *de chong fu* 德充符.

At this point we would like to introduce a few technical terms of aesthetic analysis that might help us make the argument that the tensions qualifying the relations of the classical Confucians and their Daoist interlocutors are a function of complementary modes of attaining aesthetic harmony. The vocabulary is drawn from A. N. Whitehead's *Process and Reality*, a work grounded in aesthetic principles of order.[91]

According to Whitehead, there are four fundamental variables that contribute to the achievement of that harmony deriving from a balance of simplicity and complexity. These are *triviality*, *vagueness*, *narrowness*, and *width*.

Triviality involves an excess of differentiation. An order is trivial when characterized by an excess of differentiation among its elements, all of which are given equal importance. It is what systems theory would call an excess of information leading to the production of mere "noise." It is chaos. A trivial order has no organizing strategy, no hierarchy, no differential importance. Viewed as a whole, Wall Street traders on the floor of the Stock Exchange on a busy day constitute a trivial order.

Vagueness, as Whitehead uses the term, is an excess of identification. In a vague order, the differences among items are irrelevant factors in constituting the order. The order expresses an undifferentiated commonality of character. A faceless crowd of pedestrians walking along Fifth Avenue comprises a vague order.

Narrowness is the emphasis upon certain components at the expense of others. An order dominated by narrowness has an intensity of focus that backgrounds strongly differentiated factors. A pep rally and a lynch mob are examples of a narrow order.

Finally, *width* involves the coordination of differentiated elements, each with its own unique contribution to an order. The kind of discussion one might expect in an interdisciplinary university seminar would likely contribute to an order characterized by width. Width involves the balancing of narrowness and vagueness.

A productive order has all four characteristics in various forms of background/foreground combinations. Vagueness focused by narrowness, produces the contrasts appropriate to the production of harmony. Contrast involves the interweaving of triviality and vagueness through a shifting foreground/background gestalt. Depth of contrast is a function of its degree of complexity.

With this relatively simple vocabulary we shall be able to better understand, first, the relations between Western Truth-seekers and Chinese Way-seekers, and, second, the Daoist and Confucian contributions to the realization of truth as the harmony of the Way.

In the first place, Truth-seekers following the Whiteheadian prescription would look for propositional truth owning a high degree of harmony or balanced complexity. The prescription of metaphysical Truth-seekers from Plato through Hegel to Whitehead has involved the construction of general theories capable of interpreting the whole of experience. The highest level of Plato's Four Levels of the Clarity of Knowledge is that of *noesis*, or "Reason," which requires that claims to true knowledge be contextualized within a general theory accounting for the nature of things. Hegel thinks that truth in its most general sense can only be found once the historical unfolding of the Absolute has been expressed in a complete metaphysical system. Whitehead sees the aim of speculative philosophy to be the construction of "a coherent, logical, necessary system of general ideas in terms of which every element of our experience can be interpreted."[92]

Normatively, the propositional truths sustained and interpreted by recourse to such systematic contexts are meant to characterize an order of intellectual culture possessing harmony in the aesthetic sense just rehearsed. The various cultural interests of art, science, ethics, religion, philosophy, and so on, together provide the width of diversity conducive to such harmony. The specialized interests individually conceived contribute the narrowness. The massiveness of the "known" as a cultural repository provides the possibilities of the appropriate degrees of triviality and vagueness from which a balanced complexity arises.

The same categories that allow us to interpret a Truth-seeking culture may be employed to illumine a culture of Way-seekers. The difference is that, in place of propositional truth, we are after the truth of integral action.

The *Daodejing* centers its discussion in the relationship between vagueness (*dao*) and narrowness (*de*), pointing out along the way that coercive, contentious activity diminishes the balance between them. Noncoercive relatedness provides width, while the alternation between vagueness and triviality provides contrast. The abstractness of the text and the absence of concrete examples trades complexity and intensity for an accommodating width that allows it to be broad in its relevance and applications. The demand on the reader is to supply the narrowness with which to create the intensity and to deepen the degree of contrast.

The *Zhuangzi* emphasizes the tension between that narrowness entailing the integrity of the particular, and the unfathomable vague width of the unarticulated field of experience. The specificity of the examples and the ironic humor provide the narrowness that saves the text from triviality. Intensity and depth of contrast are achieved by its shifting perspectives and the disjunctions that follow from these changes. Still, given the degree of emphasis on both narrowness and width, the danger lies in that triviality involving an excess of differentiation where nothing relates to anything else, and everything is on a par.

The *Analects*, likewise, with its stress upon ritualized roles and relationships (*li*), is preoccupied with the tension between narrowness and width. The text depends upon "appropriateness" (*yi*) to guarantee a certain narrowness of focus. The coterminous relationship between *ren*, *jun*, and *sheng* allow for degrees of width. One concern here is with the possibility that formal roles and relationships will cancel the possibilities of intense contrast by overdetermining the person who performs them. The narrowness of a given ritual focus might preclude the possibility of appropriate degrees of width.

This language of aesthetic analysis may be seen germane to the disputes between the Confucians and the reclusive strain of Daoists. For the Confucians, the vagueness of human relatedness is focused through the performance of hierarchical roles and formal practices (*li*). These institutions enable all human beings to take a stand, to find a place with a value relative to other members of their community. Ritual performance is an instrument for registering the narrowness of each human perspective, while allowing for enough width to promote effective tolerance. The narrowness of human concerns provides a necessary intensity. Being overly inclusive would move humanity beyond width in the direction of a nonproductive vagueness.

The central complaint of the Confucian against the Daoist concerns the triviality of the latter. In fact, the Confucians accuse the reclusive Daoist of sacrificing the intensity that comes with narrow focus for an inclusiveness that is too diffuse and trivial. The Daoist recluse, as a student of the arts of the Chaos clan, would insist that the Confucian claim to narrowness is bogus. In fact, the various *de* of human beings are rendered vague by recourse to contrived rules and relationships, and by strategies for social regulation that privilege an ordered uniformity over spontaneity. Further, the exclusion of the natural environment transforms Confucian narrowness into a kind of intolerance that jeopardizes the depth of contrast and the intensity of one's experience.

The aesthetic categories of triviality, vagueness, narrowness, and width help us to understand the mutual criticisms of the Daoists and the Confucians. They are also of value in helping us understand the way each school attempts to avoid the lapses leveled against them by their critics.

The Daoist guarantee against triviality lies in the appropriate exercise of the *wu*-forms. The various forms of deference associated with unprincipled knowing, nonassertive action, and objectless desire, permit the maintenance of width as a combination of triviality and vagueness while maintaining the narrowness of particular focus.

The Confucian guarantee against vagueness of unrelieved conformity lies in the maintenance of sharp distinctions among the roles of father, son, brother, and so on, while affirming the need to practice the *li* associated with these roles with *yi*—that is, in the manner that renders ritual activity particular and specific. Thus, the guarantee of a viable narrowness and width lies in allowing for the celebration of a variety of roles and ritual functions, each of which is rendered specific to the individuals involved in the ritual acts.

The "truth" of the distinct Daoist and Confucian Ways is enlarged, and achieves a greater degree of complexity and balance, by virtue of the heightened contrast attained when both sensibilities are allowed to contribute to the overall order of Chinese society. This was the ideal of classical Chinese culture and, *mutatis mutandis*, remains the goal of contemporary China.

The point of this technical aside, however, is a simple enough one: The interfusion of the variables leading to a balanced complexity of experience involves recourse to distinctly nonlogical criteria. There is no means of establishing the superiority of vagueness, or narrowness, or triviality, or width. These are all presuppositions of realized order. Nor is there any final science that could advise one as to the correct intermixing of these forms of order.

One cannot say that either Confucianism or Daoism is finally superior to the other. Nor is there any means of separating the two movements into distinctive schools in terms of orthodoxies of belief or practice. There is no final truth either about the nature of things, nor about the means whereby that nature is sought. The realization of *dao* through the achievement of order and harmony in nature and society is a multifaceted effort dependent less upon uncovering true principles or right forms of conduct than on the exercise of creativity and imagination within the most deferential of contexts. The broadest context, the one leading to the richest resources for seekers of the Way, is built from the contributions of both the Confucian and Daoist sensibilities.

PART III

Transcendence and Immanence as Cultural Clues

CHAPTER EIGHT

The Decline of Transcendence in the West

WHAT IS 'TRANSCENDENCE'?

We have been arguing throughout this work for a historicist reading of both the Chinese and Western cultural narratives. Such an argument requires that we explain the presence of ideas and institutions by appeal to specific social and historical circumstances. With respect to the subject of this part—the notion of transcendence—the story of the development of rational thinking from out of the linguistic and ethnic diversity of the West, alluded to in the last part, is pertinent. For the appeal to transcendence itself seems in large measure to be grounded in attempts to meet the challenge of the pluralism of beliefs and practices by recourse to objective, unassailable norms.

We shall continue to argue here, as we have in the past,[1] that one of the most striking features of Chinese intellectual culture from the perspective of the Western interpreter is the absence in any important sense of transcendence in the articulation of its spiritual, moral, and political sensibilities. Specifically, we shall be examining the development of theological, scientific, and social appeals to transcendent principles in the West, and contrasting these with the sort of interpretation one would give of Chinese spiritual and social practices in the absence of such appeals.

Before we take up the substantive issues of this part, it is essential that we discuss the various understandings of transcendence in our own tradition as a means of isolating the senses of that term that we hold to be decidedly irrelevant to the classical Chinese cultural milieu.

Our argument will proceed in this manner: We shall consider the meaning of "strict transcendence" isolated from other, less formal, senses

189

of the term. In this chapter we shall briefly trace the importance of strict transcendence in helping to shape the beliefs and values of the dominant strains of the Western sensibility. In the course of this argument we shall insist that informal or casual uses of the concept of transcendence to articulate the Chinese sensibility more often than not lead to serious confusion by permitting the uncriticized importation of the stricter senses of the term into one's arguments. This is precisely what has happened in familiar interpretations of Chinese Confucianism and Daoism. Thus, in addition to those who would insist that the stricter sense of transcendence does in fact apply to the Chinese sensibility, there are those whose more modest interpretative claims with respect to this topic are misinterpreted by nonspecialists who unwittingly understand these claims by appeal to the stronger sense of the term.

In *Thinking Through Confucius*, we characterized strict transcendence in the following way: A is transcendent with respect to B if the existence, meaning, or import of B cannot be fully accounted for without recourse to A, but the reverse is not true.[2]

A coherent notion of strict transcendence requires a doctrine of external relations.[3] And this has been more difficult to express than one might think. The moment one begins to articulate the consequences of epistemological or ontological independence, incoherences and inconsistencies begin to multiply. How might one characterize a being externally related to oneself? Surely independence in this sense suggests complete ignorance of the object or entity. Whether Kant's noumenal realm, externally related to the phenomenal at the epistemological level, is populated by things-in-themselves, or is one giant *Thing*-in-Itself, or whether "thing" language even applies in that realm is, of course, unknowable.

It is possible, of course, to use the term transcendence simply to mean "surpassing," "going beyond." Something may be said to be transcendent, then, when it serves as a preeminent model or ideal for possible emulation. In another context, "transcendent" language refers to the abstract and abstruse, something incomprehensible. In a more formal sense, the scholastics used the term to refer to anything that could not be classified under the Aristotelian categories. This comes close to the later Kantian sense of the term as meaning that which is "beyond experience."

As applied to the Deity, transcendence usually indicates "independence from the created order." In its earliest uses such transcendence entailed a denial of Divine intervention with respect to the world. This suggested a bilateral transcendence in which, at least after the creative act, the world and God remained independent of the one another. Later references, however, almost always referred to an asymmetrical relationship in which God transcended the world, but not vice versa.

The contrast of "transcendence" and "immanence" is rooted in the theological tradition. Most theological and philosophical understandings of God relative to the Judeo-Christian tradition employed these binary concepts in the attempt to characterize the independence of God from the world while also affirming God's providential relatedness to it.

The point of the above paragraphs is simply to isolate the more radical sense of transcendence from the more informal uses of the term. Our argument will be that the sense of transcendence expressing effective independence and self-sufficiency has been most influential in shaping the character of Western culture in terms of aesthetic, religious, scientific, and philosophic values and beliefs.

The strict sense of transcendence was perhaps most effectively used by theologians as a concept guaranteeing the *aseity* or self-sufficiency of God. Theological disputes of the early patristic period—particularly those centering in the trinitarian doctrines and the divine and human natures of Christ—led to the notion of God's unqualified independence of the created order.[4] God affects the world but is in no way affected by it. Thus God transcends the world (that is, is independent of it, unaffected by it), but the world does not transcend God (since it is dependent upon God, affected by Him).

This sense of transcendence did not begin with Judeo-Christian theology. The Greek philosophical tradition implicitly appealed in various ways to transcendence as a means of developing various world-views. Parmenides' claim, "Only Being is; not-Being is not," which entailed a radical distinction between the ways things appear and the world as it truly is, sets the pattern for the notion that Being, as ground, *transcends* (is independent of, unaffected by) the beings of the world.

Leucippus and Democritus developed the notion of "atoms" as the basic building blocks of the world. These were eternal unchanging bits of matter that were independent of, and unaffected by, both that which they comprised, and one another as well. At the opposite end of the theoretical spectrum, Plato proposed a world of unchanging forms that were independent of and unaffected by the things that they in-formed.

Both philosophical and theological understandings gave rise to the idea of "Laws of Nature," which, as unchanging rules defining the operation of the natural world, were strictly transcendent of that world. Such laws were often thought to be *logically necessary*. Necessity, as Leibniz conceived it, simply meant "present in all possible worlds." Such trans-world identity and existence carries the notion of transcendence to its furthest extreme, incorporating the realms of both possibility and actuality.

The strictest senses of transcendence are operative in Leibniz's Principle of Sufficient Reason, which simply means that nothing occurs without there being a reason for its occurrence. This principle, applying without exception to all events in the world and the world itself, transcends the world and its events. Implicated in this and similar principles is the notion of *transcendent rationality*. To the extent that impersonal reason is guided by necessary rules or laws associated with logic, and to the extent that it discovers the permanent, unchanging laws or essences, which serve as guides and models of the world, reason itself is strictly transcendent.

We could continue this instancing of the uses of transcendence in the Western tradition indefinitely. The point should be obvious: The notion of *strict transcendence* is a profoundly important notion in the Western intellectual tradition. In logical, scientific, philosophical, and theological discourses, the concept of transcendence has usually been stipulated in the strictest of terms.

We stress this claim, perhaps to the point of tediousness, for two reasons: First, as we shall see in our discussion of the fate of the concept of transcendence in contemporary Western culture, the assault upon the notions of transcendent beings and principles has become well-nigh wholesale, affecting our theological, philosophical, aesthetic, socio-political, and scientific understandings. Second, when we come to discuss the applicability of the notion of transcendence to the Chinese context, we shall find that the incautious use of the term, and perhaps more frequently, the inadvertent assumption of the relevance of this idea, by modern Chinese and Western interpreters alike, has led to fundamental misunderstandings and misappropriations of the classical Chinese tradition.

Sinologists, translators, native interpreters, and so on, not fully aware of the efficacious sense of the terms within the Western tradition, have argued for the importance of a notion of transcendence among the Chinese that in the beginning appears to be a vague and informal one, but that ends by being interpreted as carrying the semantic content of the strictest senses of the term.

Of course, the importation of notions of transcendence into China does not always, or even usually, involve direct uses of the term "transcendence" and its cognates. The most serious examples of distortion have involved translation of Chinese terms by the use of Western concepts that themselves entail strict transcendence. Interpretations of terms such as the Confucian *tian* 天 and the Daoist *dao* 道 in theological terms are important instances of this. *Tian* translated as "Heaven" and *dao* interpreted as "*the* Way" or even "God," have imported notions of transcendence into the Chinese tradition. These renderings and the confusion they have promoted have, we believe, been most unfortunate.

When the secular analogies of theistic metaphors have been employed ("Absoluteness" or "Reason" or "Natural Law" for *dao*, for example), perhaps even greater harm has been done, for in these instances, we have effectively secularized a culture that, in fact, is profoundly religious. We have victimized classical Chinese thinking, therefore, first by giving it an inappropriate *theistic* interpretation and, secondly, by giving it an inappropriate *secular* interpretation—both interpretations attributing to Chinese philosophy a sense of transcendence that has not been a part of the cultural narrative in its classical tradition.

The irony of this situation should not be missed. At the very moment when, in the West, there is a broad, significant, and apparently decisive turn away from cultural self-understandings that appeal to the notion of transcendence, many Chinese intellectuals seem anxious to claim the importance of such a notion for their own culture. Such a situation could lead finally to the development of a second barrier to mutual understanding, at least as formidable as that which three generations of effort on behalf of Chinese and Western scholars was supposed to remove.[5]

THE COLLAPSE OF THE WESTERN GODS

In the first chapter of *Anticipating China*, we considered in the broadest manner how the confluence of the Hebraic and Hellenic sensibilities in due course gave rise to the Augustinian notion of the trinitarian God. At that point we were attempting to show how the elements of the Platonic *psyche* had come to be analogized from person to society to the Creator of the cosmos. We also called attention to the development of four semantic contexts or root metaphors—materialism, formalism, organicism, and volitionalism—that were themselves drawn broadly from the perspectives constituted by Platonic and Aristotelian taxonomies. In the first part of this present work, we employed these contexts in order to articulate various models of the self. In the following paragraphs we shall see how these semantic contexts were employed to provide variant meanings of the concept of God as transcendent Being.

The concept of God as Divine Mind—the repository of the eternal possibilities and values associated with the notions of the intellectual and moral virtues—has been one of the most prominent of the theological understandings in our culture. It is the one to which rationalist philosophers such as Descartes, Leibniz, and Hegel appealed in the construction of their philosophical systems. It was to such a God that scientists from Kepler to Einstein appealed in searching for an analogical ground for their understandings of the cosmos.

> For in the sphere, which is the image of God the Creator and the Archetype of the World . . . there are three regions, symbols of the three persons of the Holy Trinity—the centre, a symbol of the Father; the surface of the Son; and the intermediate space, of the Holy Ghost.[6]

> For the Creator, who is the very source of geometry and, as Plato wrote, "practices eternal geometry."[7]

> For in geometrical things, which are subject to free choice, God chose nothing without a geometrical cause of some sort, as is apparent in the edges of leaves, in the scales of fishes, in the skins of beasts and their spots and the order of the spots, and similar things.[8]

Allied with the development of the scientific mentality that could appeal to Platonic perfection as the grounding of the mundane realm, there was the notion of God undergirding the mechanistic and materialistic thrust of modern science. The Deistic God, most notably forwarded by the work of Newton, functioned as a Great Mechanic whose creative powers were suspended once the world system had been constructed.

God in the beginning formed matter in solid, massy, hard im-
penetrable, moveable particles, of such sizes and figures, and
with such other properties, and in such proportion to space, as
most conduced to the end for which he formed them.[9]

Thus all material things seem to have been composed of the
hard and solid particles...variously associated in the first
creation by the counsel of an intelligent entity. For it became
Him who created them to set them in order.[10]

It is unphilosophical to seek for any other origin of the world,
or to pretend that it might arise out of chaos by the mere laws
of Nature; though, being once formed, it may continue by these
laws for many ages.[11]

This understanding of God appealed to moral as well as to scientific
sensibilities. An entire movement of secular humanism was developed
from this notion of Deity where, in America, of course, it came to be
associated with names such as Benjamin Franklin and Thomas Jefferson.
The Great Mechanic metaphor justified the most enthusiastic support of
the goals of scientific rationality as defined by the eighteenth and
nineteenth centuries while providing a transcendent ground for ethical
beliefs.

A third understanding of God appeals to the notion of "Arbitrary
Will." This model has reinforced both the Sophistic Greek understanding
of the importance of "action" and "power," and the Hebraic vision of the
Divine as Creator and Sustainer of the world. This volitional strain of
theology begins with Augustine and continues through the nominalist
tradition of John Duns Scotus and William of Occam, and culminates in
the Calvinist vision of the free spontaneity of God's Will as the source
of the election of souls for salvation or damnation. According to Calvin,

the Will of God is so much the supreme and sovereign rule of
justice that whatever he wills must be held to be just in so far
as he wills it.[12]

The credibility of this proposition receives its greatest test with regard to
the notion of "predestination."

We call predestination God's eternal decree, by which he determined within himself what he willed to become of each man. For all are not created in equal condition; rather, eternal life is foreordained in some, eternal damnation in others.[13]

Calvin's understanding of God's Power is usually not interpreted as being as severe as that of the Occamists. And occasionally Calvin seeks to qualify the most stringent claims about the arbitrariness of God's Will. For example, he claims that we should understand God's providence as

that determinative principle of all things, from which flows nothing but right, *although the reasons have been hidden from us.*[14]

But even on the somewhat more charitable reading, the essential effect of our inability to discern the justice or rightness in God's foreordinations is, as Max Weber's analysis in *The Protestant Ethic and the Spirit of Capitalism* suggests, to create a sense of arbitrariness and contingency relative to the conditions of human existence.[15]

A final source of objectivist appeals has been the notion of God interpreted as the Telos of Nature. Here we have Tennyson's "far off divine event." Along with the Platonic notion of Divine Mind, this is the oldest of our understandings of divinity. Aristotle's Unmoved Mover is one of the first expressions of this interpretation. God is identified with the Unmoved Mover, the supreme final cause Who "produces motion by being loved."[16] Since "all other things move by being moved,"[17] their most beneficial movements, and ultimately those that coordinate all the ends in Nature, are movements occasioned by the love for the Unmoved Mover.

Later versions of this interpretation are to be found in the works of thinkers such as Teilhard de Chardin, and the emergent evolutionists, who seek to explain evolutionary developments both in the biological and physical spheres in terms of teleological convergence. Also, ideas of human progress have often been implicitly associated with teleological understandings of God.

What are we to make of this variety of interpretations of God in the Western tradition? The most important thing to be said in this context is that theistic beliefs serve to undergird the sort of objectivism that guarantees a certain kind of meaningfulness to the world. The world conceived as a rational pattern, paradigmatically expressible in formal mathematical terms, receives its warrant from the metaphor of God as Divine Mind. This metaphor in due course became secularized into the notion of Absolute Spirit or Principle of Sufficient Reason, or simply as the Laws of Nature construed in mathematical terms. In fact "Reason" with a capital "R" is little more than a translation of this theistic metaphor. Alternatively, the world understood as a set of causal interactions ultimately reducible to matter and motion does not have to be thought to "blindly run," but can receive the benefit of a perfectly mechanical explanation. The metaphor of God as "Great Mechanic" served that function.

The metaphor of "Arbitrary Will" is one that best accounts for the sense of radical contingency to which many perforce must appeal in order to make some sense of their circumstances. There is of course a certain wildness admixed with the conditions of human experience that must be accounted for. Individuals characterized by psychological dependency, function best when they are able to organize their lives in terms of authority and obedience.

The metaphor of God as Telos of Nature has been one of the most influential tropes in our culture. The strictest interpretations of evolutionary theory require no resort to ideas of progress or movement from "lower" to "higher" organisms. Biological evolutionary theory merely seeks to describe and account for changes in animal populations, without importing notions of progressiveness. Teleological interpretations of evolution, even when these are presented in wholly secular language, are clearly freighted with theological meanings of the sort that entail appeals to a Telos of Nature.

It would be vain were one to seek a means of rendering rational, mechanistic, volitional, and teleological understandings coherent; it is sufficient to note that each has played a role in underwriting the objectivist interpretations of the values and beliefs of an important segment of the culture at various times throughout our history. And it is a significant comment upon our recent past to note that these objectivist interpretations have often taken a theological guise.

Beginning with Dostoevski and Nietzsche and moving well past the middle of the twentieth century, Anglo-European intellectual culture experienced the "Death of God" movement, in which theological interpretations of God were assaulted in such a manner as to lay to rest among large segments of the intellectual community the notion of God as source or ground of rational or objectivist appeals. No more dramatic evidence of the intransigent co-presence of these four models of Deity may be found than that the so-called "Death of God" movement occasioned *four* announcements of God's demise. Each of the characterizations of the death of God is an expression of some aspect of the generalized assault upon the notion of transcendence that has come to characterize our late modern period.

Some champions of the Death of God movement took as their theme the notion of the disenchantment of the world through processes of secularization. Harvey Cox's *Secular City*[18] addressed a "world come of age" in which many of the forms and functions associated with religious belief and ritual had been reconstituted in the nurturing and mediating activities of the modern city.[19] Technology has the potential to fulfill promises associated with spiritual hope. The Great Mechanic who disposed the apparatus of our world in beneficent ways is dead; He has been replaced by the technicians who have at their disposal the resources that can reshape the world in humane terms.

Likewise with the Telos of Nature. There is no longer a need for a far-off divine event; rather, as the "kenotic" theologians testified, the transcendent God has poured himself into the world and we are now served by immanent modes of spirituality. "New Age" religions, eclectic combinations of Christian, Buddhist, Hindu, and Sufi beliefs and practices, filtered through quasi-scientific worldviews, have become an expression of the spiritual activity of a large number of so-called religious individuals. There being no longer any single line of development, no single communal, millennial period for which to look forward, we realize the ends of nature and spirit through the individualized techniques of meditative practices.

Nietzsche's proclamation was perhaps the most dramatic announcement of the death of God. The existential strain of theology associated with the Dionysian side of Nietzsche defined human existence as a project of individual will, rendering the notion of Divine Will inimical to human authenticity. God as Arbitrary Will must die that human beings might achieve authenticity. This is the message of Ivan in Dostoevski's *The Brothers Karamazov*; it is Nietzsche's message; it is also the message of Jean-Paul Sartre and the atheistic existentialists.

Finally, the notion of Divine Mind that had served those who defined their lives in terms of a search for truth has been dissolved by the acids of pluralism and relativism, leading to a situation in which the notion of a capital "T" Truth has been relegated to the status of naive mythology. Most philosophers have given up the search for a final systematic statement of the important truths; many, if not most, scientists have given up Einstein's hope for a unified theoretical understanding of the worlds of relativity and quantum theory. "Chaos theory" has forced us to think of order and unpredictability as companionate terms. If there is, in no operative sense, Absolute Truth, there is no need for a Mind that is believed to house it. God as Divine Mind is dead.

As abstract as has been the foregoing discussion, it will have served at least to indicate the manner in which four models of transcendence drawn from classical Western theism have served to ground elements of our cultural tradition.

Classical theism suffers from the adherence to two incoherent claims. The first defines God in terms of a specific notion of perfection. God is *a se*, complete in himself, and is not subject to alteration in any manner, since any alteration would count as a defect. This view simply asserts that God is a perfect being, possessing all positive attributes in the highest degree. The cash-value of the notion of God's transcendence of the world is simply that he is thereby protected from alteration. In the back of this understanding of God is the Greek identification of perfection with the eternal and immutable.

The second claim is that God is related to the world through his providential care. God, the noncontingent, knows, loves, and judges his contingent creation. He acts through history, yet he is said to remain unchanged. In the absence of any meaningful sense of knowing, loving, and acting that does not alter the knower, lover, and actor, devotees, and the theologians who purport to guide their understanding of the faith, have suffered continual disquiet.

The attempt to reconcile the God of Athens with that of Jerusalem has been a besetting problem of apologetics and constructive theology from the early period of Judeo-Christian speculation and reflection. As we shall see when we discuss next the subject of mystical experience, the attempt to give some content to the phenomenological descriptions of God's love, or of the intimate relationship with Him that emerges from spiritual union has been resisted by the defenders of orthodoxy precisely because such accounts challenge the aseity of God.

Spinoza resolved the problem of how a noncontingent God might relate to a contingent world by denying the contingency of the world. Once he had done that, he recognized that there was no longer any coherent means of distinguishing God and the world. How, after all, are we to explain the existence of two independent necessary beings? Spinoza's pantheism identifies the world as a complex set of modifications of God. Just as the relation of diameter to circumference in a circle is a necessary fact about the circle, so the elements and relationships that constitute the world are necessary modifications or qualifications of God.

This resolution to the paradox involved in the affirmation of the strict transcendence of God errs at the opposite extreme. How are we to make sense of our world without a distinction between contingent and noncontingent, between necessity and possibility? If God, as necessary and immutable Being is the Whole *and His parts*, the parts (the world) are also necessary. Nothing could be otherwise than it has been, is, and will be. If one attempts to free Spinoza from such a dilemma, it can only be by reintroducing the distinction between contingent and noncontingent (this time *within* God) that Spinoza's philosophy was designed to overcome.[20]

In the wake of the challenge to the doctrine of radical transcendence evidenced by the "death of God" movement rehearsed above, two theological movements have emerged with some prominence. The first is constructive; the second deconstructive. The deconstructive approach in theology follows directly upon the recognition of the collapse of transcendence expressed in the poststructuralist and deconstructionist critiques of logocentrism and the language of presence, the Transcendental Signifier, and so on.[21]

Constructive theology continues among process philosophers who trace their lineage through Charles Sanders Peirce, Henri Bergson, William James, A. N. Whitehead, and Charles Hartshorne. It would not be an exaggeration to say that, within the Western tradition, it is Spinoza who is the true spiritual father of the process movement. For, in one sense, what the process theologians have done is to attempt to render coherent the sort of theistic understanding Spinoza affirmed by taking the step Spinoza himself refused to take—namely, that of rendering God contingent.

Whitehead is perhaps the best-known figure in the process tradition. He criticized orthodox theism for its belief in "an entirely static God, with eminent reality in relation to an entirely fluent world with deficient reality."[22] This is the consequence of radical transcendence. Whitehead points out one of the many incoherent implications of the Christian worldview based upon such transcendence:

> In some schools of thought the fluency of the world is mitigated
> by the assumption that certain components in the world are

exempt from this final fluency and achieve a static survival. Such components are not separated by any decisive line from analogous components for which the assumption is not made. Further, the survival is construed in terms of a final pair of opposites, happiness for some, torture for others.[23]

Whitehead's philosophy seeks to overcome the incoherence of such a vision by offering a model of God and his relationship to the world that allows real contingency to be introduced into the Divine Nature. His strategy is to characterize God in terms of dual natures, the primordial and consequent. The primordial nature of God is constituted by his enter-tainment of eternal ideas, pure possibilities, as candidates for actualization by the temporal events (the "actual occasions") that comprise the world. The consequent nature of God is constituted by God's reception into himself of the realized actualities of the world. Thus, in one sense God transcends the world; in another the world is immanent within God. In this later sense, God is contingent upon the world, just as in the former sense the world is contingent upon God.

In Whitehead's process philosophy, the interactions of God and the world proceed in this fashion: In his primordial nature God functions as a lure for actual occasions of the world by providing optimal ordering of possibilities that could serve as the "subjective aims" that shape the actualization of the occasions in their acts of becoming. In accordance with their subjective aims, actual occasions in the process of becoming prehend past, objectified, actual occasions as data permitting their own actualizations. After coming into being, these momentary occasions which comprise the things of the world realize objectivity and "perish." The perishing occasions are received into the consequent nature of God and achieve "objective immortality."

Whitehead summarizes his understanding of the relations of God and the World in this manner:

> It is as true to say that God is permanent and the World fluent, as to say that the World is permanent and God fluent.
>
> It is as true to say that God is one and the World many, as to say that the World is one and God many.
>
> It is as true to say that, in comparison with the World, God is actual eminently, as that, in comparison with God, the World is actual eminently.

It is as true to say that the World is immanent in God, as that God is immanent in the World.

It is as true to say that God transcends the World, as that the World transcends God.

It is as true to say that God creates the World, as to say that the World creates God.[24]

Despite its obvious conflict with Judeo-Christian orthodoxy, this understanding of God seems to resolve the Athens-Jerusalem conflict better than its predecessors. Philosophically, the problems associated with this notion lie in the possible incoherence of the dual natures of God.

These problems are not, of course, any greater than those beset-ting classical theism on other grounds. Indeed, the early attempts by the Fathers of the Christian church to reconcile the two natures of Jesus Christ by appeal to the formula "Very God and Very Man" are reflected in Whitehead's formulation of the primordial and consequent natures of God. Whitehead may be said to have employed a distinctly Christological model for his doctrine of God.

From the perspective of our present discussion it is worth noting that Whitehead is far from giving up transcendence in its radical form. Eternal Ideas, as pure possibilities, are independent of and unaffected by either God or the world. Likewise, the primordial nature of God transcends the world absolutely. Further, the world *as this actual world* transcends God in a rather Pickwickian sense since it needs God for its actualization, while God needs only some actual world, not necessarily this one. Yet further, there is an ultimate that altogether transcends God:

In all philosophic theory there is an ultimate which is actual in virtue of its accidents. It is only then capable of characterization through its accidental embodiments, and apart from these acci-dents is devoid of actuality. In the philosophy of organism this ultimate is termed 'creativity'; and God is its primordial non-temporal accident.[25]

We seem to be back to many of the same problems associated with transcendence in classical theism, except that the difficulties have been shifted away from God's relationship to the world and toward the mu-tual relations of God's dual natures, and of the relations of the ultimate, represented by the creative process, to God. From the theoretical perspective, the culprit causing the problem for rational explanation is not that of transcendence or immanence per se, but is rather the polar principle of transcendence and immanence.

Our primary purpose in this section has been to highlight the various uses of transcendence within the philosophical and theological spheres of Western culture, and to note some of the transformations of the theistic understandings entailed by these uses. Again, in the light of our distinctly pragmatic aims, we believe it helpful to discuss as we have, the issues that give rise to the need for doctrines of transcendence as well as the problems that emerge from the uses of such a concept. For the relevance of this notion to the interpretation of classical and modern Chinese thought can best be assayed if we ask, much as we did in the last part concerning "Truth," whether the "cultural requisites" for theories of transcendence are importantly present within the Chinese cultural milieu.

THEOLOGY AND MYSTICISM

The "death of God" movement in the West served as a symptom and metaphor both for the radical turn away from objectivist modes of explanation, and toward nominalist and historicist alternatives such as poststructuralism and deconstruction, as well as the more moderate reconstructive turn associated with process theology. In addition to these novel responses to our religious situation, there is long-standing and still viable strand of spirituality that has, for the most part, received insufficient stress in our rationalist culture. Moreover, it is this strain, perhaps, that will provide us with the appropriate language with which to consider the topic of classical Chinese spirituality. We are referring to the mystical sensibility.

Recently, while visiting a New England university to present ideas deriving from the preparation of this book, we were asked to highlight some of the implications of our immanental understanding of Chinese culture by addressing a class in religious studies on the topic "Can there be mysticism without transcendence?" Our response was to reverse the question and attend to it in the form, "Can there be mysticism *with* transcendence?" Our version of the question highlights one of the great unrecognized scandals associated with the development of the religious sensibility within our own culture.

From the Greek mantic traditions through the Cabalistic mysticisms of Judaism and the Christian mystical literature, there has been a strong empirical side to the practice of spirituality. On the other hand, the apologetic context of Christianity led quickly to the necessity of doctrinal constructions that would justify the nascent religion within the broader context of the intellectual world. The early Christian Fathers warred among themselves to settle upon a firm doctrinal consensus that would ground the Christian faith. St. Augustine extended that battle to the broader Roman world to justify the viability of Christianity as an intellectual and moral force capable of serving as the primary matrix of beliefs and values for its own and future times.

The diverse motives associated with these diverse religious sensibilities led to a situation in which there were effectively two contradictory strains of spirituality developing alongside one another. In an ironic turn on Augustine's contrast of the City of God and the City of Man, we might see the heavenly metropolis further divided into the Mystical and Doctrinal Cities. For there is something like a conspiracy of silence that has effectively suppressed the fact that doctrinal and mystical interpretations of Christianity conflict with one another to the extent that they might as well be dealing with distinct phenomena, a fact that was not lost to William Blake on the side of the Dissenting Sects, and the principals of the Inquisition on the side of orthodoxy.

The issue is the relationship between religion and transcendence. By highlighting the contrast between the mystical and the doctrinal forms of religious sensibility, we hope to show that there is a strong immanentalist tradition of spirituality in the Western world, expressed in its mystical literature and practice. This discussion will be helpful since interpretations of Chinese religion require resort to nontranscendent categories. Indeed, we would claim that much havoc has been wrought upon the Chinese culture by those, from Voltaire forward (some of whom, like Voltaire, thought this a virtue) who would, in the absence of any recognized transcendent Deity, claim that the Chinese are wholly without religion. This havoc was further compounded by those, from Leibniz and the Jesuits to the later Protestant missionaries, who have been able to find a religion among the Chinese, but only by foisting upon them extraneous transcendent interpretations.

The shape of a religious tradition both determines and is determined by the general character of its culture. Second-problematic cultures are given to the development of a distinction between the rational and practical dimensions of spirituality, a phenomenon that is not so evident in first-problematic cultures.[26] The shape this distinction takes in the Hellenic-Hebraic tradition underlying Western societies is one that can be discussed in terms of the difference between theological and mystical traditions.

We were concerned in the first chapter of *Anticipating China* with the way in which the Hebraic-Christian God came to be co-opted by the Hellenic sensibility in such a manner as to serve, via the trinitarian analysis, as a Primary Analogate to which argumentative appeals might be addressed to justify and legitimate programs of scientific, social, and political understandings and practice. In the following paragraphs we shall concentrate on the alternative strand of the religious sensibility, that associated with the *philosophia perennis*, as a means of highlighting a contrast in Western religion which parallels the contrast of "rational" and "aesthetic" understandings discussed throughout our comparative writings.

In Augustine's description of "the Beatific vision," the most profound experience vouchsafed those who win eternal life, he tells of how the

> saints shall be employed when they are clothed in immortal and spiritual bodies, and when the flesh shall live no longer in a fleshly but a spiritual fashion. They shall in the body see God.[27]

References to seeing God while *in the body* make it clear that the beatific vision is one that in no wise suggests mystical union. This places the beatific vision, an experience supported by the doctrines of the Christian church concerning the "afterlife," in serious conflict with accounts from the literature of the Christian mystics.

In the phenomenological descriptions of the mystics, we are often told of an encounter with God in which "all uplifted spirits are melted and naughted in the Essence of God"[28] and "the mind, drunk with divine love and forgetting itself, making itself like a broken vessel, throws itself wholly on God and clinging to God, becomes one with him in spirit."[29] The God-soul identity is characterized by John of the Cross as one in which "all things of God and the soul are in participant transformation; and the soul seems to be God rather than a soul, and is indeed God by participation."[30]

One usually finds some equivocation in the mystical reports. Partly this is due to emendations made by later editors seeking to avoid conflict with the "learned theologians." This was particularly so in the case of

Teresa of Avila and John of the Cross, her younger contemporary. When they wrote, the Inquisition was actively interested in maintaining the doctrinal purity of the mystical reports.

The mystics are certainly capable of some doctrinally questionable statements. These words, for example, are from Teresa's *Interior Castle*:

> God so places himself in the interior of the Soul that when it returns to itself it can in no way doubt that it was in God and God was in it. This truth remains with it so firmly that even though years go by without God's granting that favor again, the soul can neither forget nor doubt that it was in God and God was in it.[31]

But as preface to the statement just cited we read:

> In difficult matters, even though it seems to me I understand and that I speak the truth, I always use the expression "it seems to me." For if I am mistaken, I am very much prepared to believe what those who have a great deal of learning say. Even though they have not experienced these things, learned men have a certain I don't know what.... I have a great deal of experience with learned men, and have also had experience with half-learned, fearful ones, and these latter cost me dearly. At least I think that anyone who refuses to believe that God can do much more or that he has considered and continues to consider it good sometimes to communicate favors to His creatures has indeed closed the doors to receiving them.[32]

This qualification, by virtue of its obvious irony, hardly serves to qualify any report in any serious manner.

Phenomenological accounts of this sort led individuals such as William James and W. T. Stace to take the reports of the mystics in a literal fashion and to broaden their understanding of religious experience as a consequence. Christian mysticism is plausibly consonant with the *philosophia perennis* at the phenomenological level; but, were we to take the theological interpretations upon which the Church insists, we should hardly find much that is perennial in the Christian mystics.

One of the true ironies of the present scholarship on the phenomenon of Christian mysticism is that it comes from the rather narrow rationalistic perspective of the analytic tradition. Why should this be so? Why have analytic philosophers reached their hands back across the centuries to clasp the bloody hands of the Inquisitors and Learned Doctors of the Church?

The answer is simpler, perhaps, than it should be. Our postmodern period is one defined by assaults upon the concept of reason as an ahistorical category. The deconstructionist movement, along with appeals to alternative cultural sensibilities, leads to a condition in which reason is on the defensive. It so happens that in the West the most effective appeals to nonrational models appear within the mystical literature. Mysticism is institutionalized arationality. Though the full Enlightenment sensibility led to the critique of religion as superstition, that assault was not wholly successful. Even after the deaths of the "Gods" of the West, religion is still with us. Defenders of the faith, where they still may be found, often take the apologetic route of attempting to show that reason and religion are not in conflict.

In Nelson Pike's recent, most careful study of the Christian mystical literature, specifically as it relates to questions of the "unitive experience" reported by mystics, he presents the paradigm instance of the rational interpretation of mystical experience.[33] His chief concern is with the "God-Soul identity state" or "union without distinction," and he cites examples from mystical literature that describe unitive experiences. He then cites, quite rightly, the *disclaimers* usually attached to these descriptions—all variations of St. Teresa's "it seems to me"—which seek to bring the phenomenological description into accord with the doctrines of the Church. Thus, immediately following the claim of John of the Cross cited above, he adds "although it is true that its natural being, though thus transformed, is as distinct from God as it was before." John van Ruysbroek, who described the phenomenon in which "all uplifted spirits are melted and naughted in the Essence of God" adds that, of course, "no created essence can become one with God's essence . . . for the Divine Essence can neither wax nor wane, nor can anything be added to it nor taken from it." There are exceptions, of course, to such qualifications. But these, if prominent, led to condemnation by the keepers of doctrinal orthodoxy. In general, however, the mystics seem to espouse the view, quoted by Pike from St. Teresa's *Life*, that no experience should ever lead the soul to "budge an inch from the Church's teachings."[34]

The controversy over the epistemological status of mystical experiences pivots on the contrasts between phenomenological description, on the one hand, and theological interpretation, on the other. Walter Stace, in his *Mysticism and Philosophy*, argues explicitly that the mystics were so abused and intimidated by their confessors and ecclesiastical inquisitions, and so emended by timid editors and redactors, as to have much of their work threatened with death by qualification. Employing the distinction between "experience" and "interpretation," Stace is able to argue that the evidential weight of the mystical literature is to be found in the naive descriptions rather than in the subsequent doctrinal interpretations, however these interpretations came to be made.[35]

There is much to be said for this argument. There is evidence enough that both friendly and unfriendly editors of mystical works attempted changes in the original texts.[36] The ironic treatment of the advices of "learned men" cited from St. Teresa ("even though they have not experienced these things, learned men have a certain I don't know what...") suggests a strain in the literature between the authority of the Church and that of immediate experience. The inquisitorial bodies of the Church (the most dramatic example, of course, being that of the Spanish Inquisition), armed with threats of imprisonment, excommunication, and ultimately execution, could not but have had some disciplinary effect upon mystical writings.

But we need not take the negative path here. We could say, along with Nelson Pike, that the conflict between phenomenological and doctrinal accounts of the mystical experience is a function of the correction of experience by a more general and dependable worldview. Pike provides an illustration of his point by supposing that were one to attend a magic show at which a magician was observed pulling quarters out of the air, one should judge the perception false. One comes to the show possessed of a world-picture that precludes the possibility of anyone pulling quarters out of the air. There would be nothing artificial or contrived about such judgment; it would not be felt as imposed by the threats of others (even though, as Pike admits, one might be called "stupid" for believing that the quarters came from thin air). According to Pike, the judgment would be a

> "spontaneous" consequence of *my* visual perception judged against *my* basic picture of the way in which the world is put together. Let me add that this kind of spontaneity is one of the things that mark my reaction as *rational*. No thinking person scraps a deeply ingrained and otherwise well-working world picture just to give credence to a single recalcitrant phenomenon.[37]

There are two problems with Pike's appeal to rationality in this context. In the first instance, we are dealing with a rather loose sense of rationality that more or less means making sense of one's world by appeal to generic rather than extraordinary features of one's experience. The difficulty with this was pointed out long ago by William James in his *Varieties of Religious Experience*.

> The existence of mystical states absolutely overthrows the pretension of non-mystical states to be the sole and ultimate dictators of what we may believe.... For there never can be a state of facts to which new meaning may not truthfully be added, provided the mind ascend to a more enveloping point of view. It must always remain an open question whether mystical states may not possibly be such superior points of view, windows through which the mind looks out upon a more extensive and inclusive world.[38]

It is a question-begging enterprise, to say the least, if we exclude *ex hypothesi* the experiences of the few by appeal to the standards of the many. To the extent that experiences help to tell us of our world, there are many areas in which we permit those of greater sensitivity in this or that area to add to the rationality of our world. Great poets and novelists, though not entirely free from censors and inquisitorial bodies are certainly less beset by them, have been able to refine and educate our sensibilities. Mystics might be encouraged to do the same.

Of course, institutionally this was not the case within Christianity. The very doctrines of the Church employed to "correct" the phenomenological descriptions of mystical experiences were forged by the Fathers of the Church, by theologians whose work was then culled, edited, and authorized by ecclesiastical councils, papal conferences, and so forth. If the sources of religious doctrine are so little to be reckoned as experiential, then we can hardly fail to see the questionable nature of the use of the corrective lenses of doctrine to establish the veridicality of experience.

The second difficulty with Pike's analogy is closely related to the first. Pike's sense of rationality can hardly be that of the scientific Enlightenment that would, of course, dismiss *both* the mystical experience and its doctrinal corrective as superstitious nonsense. Many scientists would doubtless paraphrase Pike in this manner: *No thinking scientist scraps a deeply ingrained and otherwise well-working world picture just to give credence to a set of theological doctrines explicitly grounded in faith and the authority of a religious community*. In fact, the scientific rationalist would obviously be far more open to experimental research into "paranormal experiences" than she would to the defense of ecclesiastical doctrines.

We are not considering the truth or falsity of mystical reports, only the degree of relevance they might have in helping us along with the task of comparing classical Chinese and Western understandings of religion. And there is in fact every reason to believe that we might find mystical reports better adapted than are theistic doctrines to the task of such comparison. The basic reason for this is that the naive phenomenological descriptions of the mystics depend far less upon the presumption of transcendence.

Another controversial issue in the discussion of mysticism involves the question of types of the mystical experience. The general idea of a *philosophia perennis* suggests that mystical experiences are essentially the same from one culture to another, and whatever differences there might seem to exist among them really concern questions of interpretation.

W. T. Stace classifies types of mystical experiences as "introvertive" and "extrovertive." The former involves a sense of unitary consciousness, and the latter a sense of the unity of all things. Stace also provides what amounts to a set of defining characteristics of the mystical experience. Characteristics such as "ineffability," "paradoxicality," a sense of "reality," the experience of "blessedness, "peace," a "sense of the holy" are alleged to be common to all mystical experiences in all ages and cultures.[39]

R. C. Zaehner is at pains to make a harder, faster, distinction among types of mystical experience.[40] There are "monistic" and "Theistic" varieties and these must by no means be elided. Stace would criticize Zaehner for failing to make a distinction between experience and interpretation. The appropriate reply to such criticism would then be that such a distinction itself is hardly possible since all experiences are interpreted, no matter how far down the line we might go.

Ninian Smart provides the appropriate mediating response. Granting that there are no uninterpreted experiences,[41] there are, he claims, degrees of interpretation, and it is often advantageous to approach as closely as possible an unfreighted description of our experience. This is useful in comparative religions precisely because of the obvious and unavoidable conclusion that doctrinal beliefs and institutional practices diverge to a far greater extent than do naive accounts of so-called mystical experiences. It may be that Stace is wrong in claiming that there is a "Universal Core" found in all mystical experiencing, but it is certainly true that the mystical literature provides a wider expression of commonality than theological or doctrinal accounts. This should not be surprising, of course. Any experience which is relatively unmediated seems to express commonality. When we claim that the experience of pain is common to all human beings, we are seeking in the relatively unmediated some sense of a common bond.

Mystical experiences are identifiable in the widest variety of cultures. Certainly Jewish, Christian, Hindu, Buddhist, Islamic, and Daoist reports have been classified as mystical. In addition, there are the variety of apparently nonreligious reports collected by William James among others that are not identified with any particular religious tradition and, indeed, seem to have no particular religious import. These are the experiences of the oneness of things or a sense of being one with this or that object in one's environs often reported by particularly sensitive poets and painters, and popularly associated with experiences with hallucinogenic drugs.

We might begin with the rough classification found in many treatments of mysticism that involves a contrast of God, soul, and nature mysticism. But it is obvious that an even more naive classification would have to accept the fact that "God" might be an overly freighted word. A more adequate treatment then would be one that dealt more "phenomenologically" with the experience itself.[42]

Mystical experiences are often associated with three references that are most generally classified in terms of the internal and external (Stace's "introversive" and "extroversive"). The first two are "ec-static"[43] and "enstatic," a standing-out or standing-in experience, respectively. A third type involves a standing-with and may be termed "con-static." If the combination of Latin and Greek roots seems too clumsy, we may call this sense of the standing together of all things "synstasy." The value of this type of classification is that it does not prejudge the object of, for example, ecstatic union to be that of "God" or "Brahman" or "Nirvana." There is an experience in which one's self or soul is felt to be the locus of meaning and value, or an experience in which something outside is referenced at that locus, or, finally, an experience in which all things stand together in a felt relationship.

These experiences in themselves do not have to have an absoluteness about them. One can have an ecstatic experience in which another person or natural object is the reference. Enstasy can likewise be an experience of oneself as focusing some finite part of one's environs. Finally, all things standing together does not have to add up to some undifferentiated

One. Indeed, as we shall see in discussing *tian* 天 and *dao* 道 below, the belief in a cosmic unity is itself a specific *doctrinal belief that* does not enter into the classical Chinese notion of world order.

At this juncture we might indicate more clearly where all these ruminations on the relationship between doctrinal and mystical strains in religion might be leading us. In the first place, we have argued that resort to theistic notions that appeal to any of the four primary metaphors familiar in the Western context clearly involves culture-specific abstractions. These theistic metaphors are associated with particular theoretical contexts. When employed as distinctly theological notions within the context of ecclesiastical institutions, theistic notions are interpretations belonging to the doctrinal side of the mystical/doctrinal spectrum. If this is so, so-called mystical experiences carry less interpretative baggage. This being the case, there is good reason to believe that it is from this spiritual/mystical context, rather than the theistic/doctrinal, that we may derive language capable of characterizing religious experience beyond the Western context.

As we shall see when we come to consider the notions of *tian* and *dao*, our classification of modes of mystical experience as *ecstatic, enstatic*, and *synstatic* may be shown to resonate rather well with the sorts of spirituality found in classical Chinese Daoism and Confucianism. This will be so because, unlike traditional forms of Western theism that require resort to notions of cosmological unity and divine transcendence, the mystical experience at it lowest interpretative level requires neither assumption. And this is fortunate, for neither assumption is in fact made by the dominant strands of the classical Chinese tradition.

THE WANING OF TRANSCENDENCE
IN SCIENCE AND SOCIETY

We have been recounting the story of the rise and initial decline of the notion of transcendence in Western theology. It is essential to our comparative enterprise that we carry this account at least one step farther and illustrate the intrinsic dependence of appeals to transcendence outside the distinctly theological sphere upon primordial myths and theistic beliefs that have shaped that sphere. Specifically, we wish to call attention to the direct relationship between theological senses of transcendence and those employed in classical science and social theory.

With respect to the claim that classical scientific reasonings are intrinsically tied to theological understandings, the following may be said: At least since the publication of Whitehead's *Science and the Modern World* in 1925,[44] the oft-celebrated belief in a real "warfare between science and religion" has been significantly qualified. For example, Whitehead found possible origins of the belief in ironclad laws of nature in the notion of the inexorability of Fate (*moira*) in ancient Greece. Further, he discerned influences contributing to the development of scientific mentality in the methods of argumentation developed in the late Middle Ages. The overall acceptance of the coherence of the cosmos upon which the viability of science depends is largely a function of the belief in a rational Creator who informed the world with logical order. In *Anticipating China*, we argued at some length that the senses of order and rationality upon which objective reasoning depends are grounded in the cosmogonic activities that guaranteed the victory of Order over Chaos.[45]

In this context we only wish to note, briefly, a specific and most fundamental connection that incontrovertibly demonstrates the dependence of scientific appeals to transcendence upon essentially theological senses of that term. This we shall do by characterizing the manner in which the principal theological arguments for the existence of God provide the paradigm instances for the articulation of concepts and principles that led to the emergence of classical science. At the same time, we shall indicate the increasing irrelevance of strict transcendence in contemporary scientific inquiry.

The argument that follows is in many respects an odd one, for the claim that science is rooted in theology is really rather circular since theology as the "*logos*" of "*theos*" is itself a rather rationalistic enterprise. The development of systematic theological treatises that feature logically sound arguments for the existence of God can hardly be called foreign to the scientific impulse in the broadest sense. Indeed, the movement from Chaos to Cosmos, from *mythos* to *logos*, is precisely the movement in the development of Western civilization that gave rise to an articulated conception of reason and rationality. On the grandest of scales, therefore, a case could be easily made that theology is the stepchild of (proto-) science.

There were three primary arguments for the existence of God developed prior to the end of the Middle Ages. These are usually referred to as the cosmological, ontological, and teleological arguments. Each of the arguments assumes the validity of a principle or concept that later became fundamental in the development of classical science.

The cosmological argument assumes what we have come to call the Principle of Sufficient Reason (PSR). The PSR requires that there be an explanation for every contingent state of affairs. This or that event, within the world of events, may be accounted for by appeal to a conditioning event, or a set of events, which constitutes its causal explanation. The explanation "transcends" the event that is explained, as cause transcends (is outside and independent of) effect. If the sum total of states of affairs (the "world") is presumed to have a coherence that distinguishes itself from any more particular state of affairs, then the PSR applies to the totality as well as to any given member of the totality. That is to say, the world requires an explanation by appeal to a causal event or agency that exists independently of the world. The theological presentation of the cosmological argument finds this agency to be God.

The argument reduces to this: If every contingent state of affairs can be accounted for by appeal to another state of affairs, how are we to account for the existence of the sum total of contingent states of affairs? The requirement seems to be a Self-Existent, noncontingent state of affairs. Scientific cosmologies mimic this theological argument by attempting to find in notions such as Big Bang, or, less plausibly, the continuous creation of matter *ex nihilo*, the reason for the existence of the whole of things.

The cosmological argument in this form is closely related to the ontological argument since both appeal to the notion of necessity. According to the ontological argument, a Perfect Being may be proven to exist by analysis of the notion of "perfection." The idea of a perfect being entails the notion of necessary existence since a contingently existing being would fall short of the perfection of a necessarily existing being. To own necessary existence is to have a being superior to one who possesses only contingent existence. In the modern notation of modal logic, the assumptions of the ontological argument are as follows:

$P \supset \square P$
If perfection exists, it exists necessarily.

$\lozenge P \supset \square \lozenge P$ and $\square P \supset \square \square P$
Modal existence is always necessary.

$\sim \square \sim \square P$
Necessary existence is not impossible.

One need not endorse the soundness of the argument grounded upon these assumptions, or the truthfulness of its conclusion, "Perfection exists," to see the apologetic implications of the ontological argument. For, if the argument is said to fail in its theological guise, then *any* argument that made the same assumptions with regard to necessity and necessary existence, would have to fail. But the idea of necessity, applied to the laws of nature or the causal connections, was once a mainstay of classical science.

Both with regard to the Principle of Sufficient Reason and the idea of necessity, theology and science share a common commitment. Both of these categories are transcendent explanatory principles the appeal to which depends upon assumptions that received their articulation first in the context of theology.

The third principal theistic argument makes an assumption that is equally important to the existence and viability of science. This argument, often referred to as the "argument from design," is an analogical argument that proceeds in this fashion: First, one argues from the existence of perceived order in things to the inference that some ordering agent must be responsible. The second move is to analogize from the perceived order to the unperceived, unexperienced elements of the world beyond one's purview. That is to say, the order of this or that part of the world is presumed to illustrate the coherence of the order of things per se. The upshot of the argument, then, is that the order of *the whole of things* requires recourse to an Orderer.

The assumption behind this argument is that *there is one actual world* ordered in its whole as well as its parts. It is this assumption that allows one to extrapolate from local instances of order to the order of the cosmos itself. Without this assumption, the possible incoherence of the world would lead to the incoherence of ad hoc explanations for the order of this or that aspect of it. The dissolution of the world into incoherently related instances of disparate sorts of order would challenge the existence of rationality itself.

The twin ironies entailed by this brief presentation should be obvious. First, both classical science and theology are grounded in assumptions that are held on faith. It is *faith* in the coherence of a single world-order, *faith* in the necessity of laws and causal connections, *faith* in the Principle of Sufficient Reason that permits the traditional scientist to proceed in a rational manner. Secondly, since the turn of this present century, the faith of the scientist has been so sorely challenged and so seriously undermined that it is difficult to find defenders of the traditional, classical meanings of scientific reason.

The incoherence introduced into the order of things by the necessity to appeal to alternate principles of explanation in order to account for the micro- and macro-worlds, challenges the belief in a single-ordered world. For example, some micro-events seem to present a challenge to the necessity of continuous existence through time. Electrons moving through alterations in energy states seem to exist at the beginning and end of the transition, but nowhere in between. Further, the "limiting velocity" of light may be challenged by the accelerations of certain elementary particles. And the arrow of time may now be seen to move in both directions, qualifying the most ironclad law of modern physics—namely, the Second Law of Thermodynamics. Paradoxes generated by these and so many other anomalous events challenge any simpleminded belief in the Principle of Sufficient Reason.[46]

The rhetoric of science, at least as expressed in the popular press, remains essentially intact. And doubtless the run-of-the-mill scientist may still appeal to that traditional rhetoric, but the fact of the matter is that classical science is perpetuated mostly at this rhetorical level. This is not surprising. Even among the reflective breed of scientist, there has been a tendency toward obscurantism from the beginning. While David Hume's famous critiques of the theistic arguments are held by those unsympathetic to religions (principally the scientists) to be devastating to the claims of theologians, his even more famous critique that undermined the rationality of belief in causality was blithely ignored by these same scientists.

The difference today is that science has been for the most part operationalized and instrumentalized. The language of science is that of descriptions of processes or operations which are discovered through, and partially shaped by, the instruments employed. Appeals to necessity, coherence, or to any other transcendent concept or principle, in order to account for scientific data, is recognizably unwarranted in such a setting.

Though it would be foolish to suggest that "the death of God" occasioned the death of classical science, it is sensible enough to claim that the seeds of both events were to be found in the movement toward cultural self-consciousness born with the modern age.

A few paragraphs will suffice to carry this story over into the social realm. For the effective appeals to transcendence made in the social sphere have been explicitly conditioned by theological and, in modern time, scientific beliefs.

Natural law theory, prominently associated with Thomas Aquinas and later scholasticism, and appearing in numerous secular forms down to the present day, is an application of the ideas of strict and necessary laws of nature to the human realm. According to the most prominent version of this theory, human reason is capable of discerning those objective standards of action and conduct that will bring humanity into the most productive and harmonious relationship to nature and society. Natural laws, as objective standards, are independent of, and unaffected by, the beings and circumstances that they legislate.

In the wake of the shift away from Enlightenment values toward late modern sensibilities, transcendent appeals are less in evidence in Anglo-European cultures. For example, the talk of human rights among our secularized politicians and statesmen, has by and large lost its foundation in natural law theory, though it persists quite effectively in mainstream Christianity, and strongly influences the shape of that tradition's social and political commitments. In the secular world there is less intellectual foundation for such discussions. As a consequence, rights talk, in the absence of secure philosophical justifications, is increasingly looked upon as a useful fiction at best, and at its worst as "nonsense on stilts."[47]

Where the appeal to natural rights is to be found today it is either tacitly grounded upon what is to be an international consensus stipulated in certain proclamations and documents formally (Universal Declaration of Human Rights 1948) and sometimes informally agreed to by the "community of nations." More rigorous treatments of rights theory are often tightly argued presentations that, nonetheless, proceed altogether analytically. These treatments argue for those rights that are entailed by the very conception of the reasonably satisfactory existence of an individual within a complex society of the sorts that presently constitute Western democracies. The truth of the conclusions of such arguments is presumed to be a function of their rationality. In the absence of any external, objective standard, however, their "truth" is actually a function of their persuasiveness.

The dominant trend is clearly away from the employment of any recognizably transcendent appeals in the establishment of the standards that are to guide a society. One important consequence of the pragmatic vision of democracy is an historicist understanding of human rights. John

Dewey, for example, believed it a fiction that "the individual is in possession of antecedent political rights."[48] In fact, he maintained that "there are no such things as individual rights until and unless they are supported and maintained by society through law."[49]

This pragmatic, nonobjectivist, theory of society operates without any transcendent standards of rationality, without any final conception of human nature, and without any progressivist or apocalyptic vision. Neither theology, nor science, nor their reflections and shadows in the form of natural laws or universal rights informs such a view. For Dewey, a flourishing community is the best guarantee of human liberty. Traditional assumptions in Confucian thought about the mutuality of personal and communal ends are in some ways comparable to this Deweyian vision, and resonate with the more recent communitarian values of Michael Sandel and Daniel Bell, where certain communal bonds are constitutive of personal identity.[50]

Perhaps it is from this point of departure within our own tradition that we can best move to understand alternative assumptions that undergird the cultural narrative of China.

CHAPTER NINE

Tian 天 and Dao 道 as Nontranscendent Fields

THE "TRANSCENDENCE DEBATE" IN CONTEMPORARY CHINA

One of the most significant discussions ongoing between Chinese and Western thinkers concerns the notion of whether there are important appeals to transcendence in mainstream Chinese tradition. The debate centers on the question of whether one may legitimately appeal to notions of transcendence in interpreting Chinese texts. In the past, Anglo-European translations and interpretations of Chinese materials have wrought a great deal of havoc by blithely, if unwittingly, attempting to transplant Western understandings of "God" or "the Absolute" into Chinese soil. Later critiques of such transplants on the part of both Chinese and Western scholars have occasioned a reaction from some Chinese scholars who wish to defend the legitimacy of transcendent interpretations of notions such as *tian* 天 and *dao* 道. The consequence of this scholarly interchange has been the production of a rather lively debate on the subject of the relevance of the notion of strict transcendence to Chinese intellectual culture.

Our position on this issue was registered in *Thinking Through Confucius* and has been elaborated since in *Anticipating China*: We have argued that the notion of transcendence is irrelevant in interpreting classical texts in China. We have attempted to demonstrate how resort to the concept of strict transcendence has seriously distorted aspects of Confucian and Daoist understandings. In addition, as we have attempted to demonstrate through our discussions of "truth" in the second part of this present book, the cultural accoutrements of a concept are often imported along with the concept, with the result that appeals to notions such as "truth" or "transcendence" in the Western senses of those terms commits one to an inventory of additional concepts and interpretations that may not be so welcome.

The seriousness of this problem is evidenced by the stature of the scholars who perpetuate it, and the influence they have on the way in which China is understood. These otherwise distinguished scholars who continue to use the Western language of transcendence, thereby recasting classical Chinese philosophy in terms familiar to the Western academy, do not seem willing or able to see the world without it. They do not always use the language of transcendence consistently, and seem unaware, or at least unconcerned about, its rather profound philosophical implications. The irony arises when this distortion, occasioned by attributing a kind of foundationalism to classical Chinese philosophy, is being perpetuated by the collaboration of contemporary Chinese philosophers who are willing to risk misunderstanding in order to bring the sophistication of Continental, principally German, philosophy into play.

Benjamin Schwartz, a fair representative of the community of Western scholars, ascribes transcendence to classical China in a way that can only serve to generate a certain degree of confusion among those students of Chinese culture who might want to appreciate it as an alternative to Western theism. In his own words:

> At the apex of the human order is the universal kingship, which is the central locus of communication, as it were, between the king, who is ultimately responsible for the maintenance of the normative human order, and the supreme God or Heaven (*shang ti, t'ien* [*shangdi, tian*]), who maintains harmony and order in the world of the spirits presiding over the forces of nature as well as over the world of ancestral spirits. While the supreme God never diverges from correct behavior in the order of nature, the king—and by extension his clan, as well as the nobles and functionaries beneath him—may stray lamentably far from the *Tao* [*dao*], thus producing all the disharmonies and dislocations of a disordered society. To the extent that the word "rationalism" refers to the primacy of the idea of order, we can already speak here of the emergence of a kind of Chinese rationalism.[1]

Schwartz, seemingly aware of the overlap between this interpretation of the classical Chinese world order and its familiar Western counterparts, attempts to find some distance between the Chinese worldview and the "One-many" reductionism that classical Western theism entails:

> What we have is the image of an all-embracing and inclusive order which neither negates nor reduces to some one ultimate principle that which is presumed to exist.[2]

But can one posit the existence of a "supreme God [who] never diverges from correct behavior" and who thus stands as the one independent and determinative standard of correct order for the human world, and at the same time, claim that this definition of world order is not reductionistic? Schwartz continues:

> While this concept of cosmic order may be inimical to the mythic, one wonders whether it involves any kind of transcendence, since it seems to freeze and encapsulate the existing images of the contents of reality rather than to transcend them. And yet, the supreme god, or heaven, in contradistinction to nature and ancestral spirits who simply perform, as it were, the functions of their office in response to the prescribed sacrificial rituals, is conceived of as a transcendent ruler—a unifying moral will who sustains the correct order of the world. . . . He does not deviate from this order.[3]

This supreme god, so described, seems to count as a supernatural agent who willfully sustains and determines world order.

> [T]he idea of heaven's mandate does give evidence of a sense of tragic abyss between the normative socio-political-cultural order and the way things actually are . . . . [T]he transcendental element is undeniably present in the sense of the yawning abyss between the ideal social order and the actual state of affairs.[4]

The Confucian *tian* 天 so defined fits comfortably within the parameters of the four notions of the Western transcendent God adumbrated above. In fact, "heaven" for Confucius is treated not simply as the immanent *Tao* [*dao*] of nature and society but as a transcendent conscious will interested in Confucius's redeeming mission.[5]

Now, if Schwartz is quite ready to cast the classical Confucian notion of *tian* in the language of transcendence, he finds an even "more radical transcendental trend in the 'philosophic Taoism' of the Lao-tzu (Laozi) and Chuang-tzu (Zhuangzi) books."[6] In fact, he says, "we find a radical dichotomy between the natural order and the social order based on a notion that is already adumbrated in Confucian writings." For the Daoists, then, "a kind of speculative meditation arose on the nature of *Tao* [*dao*] that seems to parallel later Neoplatonic meditations in the West on the nature of the *Logos*."[7]

As some Western sinologists labor to revise reigning Western interpretations of the Chinese tradition in order to free it from the language of transcendence that they argue has been imposed upon it, many of the best minds of contemporary Chinese philosophy seem reluctant to give up "transcendence" as an appropriate category for defining the uniqueness of Chinese thought.

A discussion in the secondary literature has emerged following our criticism of the contemporary "New Confucian" scholar, Mou Zongsan 牟宗三 (Mou Tsung-san), for appealing to the language of Kant to explain what is unique and distinctive about Chinese philosophy. According to Mou Zongsan:

> The way of *tian* being high above connotes transcendence. When the way of *tian* pervades the human person, being immanent in this person, it becomes one's nature. At this time, the way of *tian* is also immanent. This being the case, we can use an expression that Kant was fond of using and say that the way of *tian* on the one hand is transcendent, and on the other hand is immanent (transcendent and immanent are opposites). When the way of *tian* is both transcendent and immanent, it can be said to have both religious and moral import: religion stresses the transcendent meaning and morality stresses the immanent.[8]

Concerned to identify and preserve the difference between those assumptions about transcendence dominant in classical Western philosophy and those being attributed to the Chinese tradition, Mou Zongsan continues:

In Western discourse on "human nature," the first letter of "nature" is written with a small "n," indicating that it belongs to the "natural" as opposed to the "supernatural." When this "supernatural" begins to have a transcendent import, it belongs to the nature of God rather than the natural world. Western philosophy then entifies it to arrive at a personal God, while the Chinese tradition treats it functionally to arrive at *tiandao* 天 道. These are the different routes that the East and West have taken in understanding the existence of the transcendent.[9]

Mou Zongsan makes it clear that whatever might be construed as transcendent in classical Chinese thought, it is not independent of the natural world, nor is it theistic. Far from entailing the dualism entailed by Western models of transcendence, classical China's world order, according to Mou, is altogether "this worldly." By insisting on "function" as the mediating concept, Mou seems to reject "agency" as an appropriate characterization of *tian*. In fact, the human world in which this transcendent aspect is said to reside has the following conditions.[10]

The "transcendence" of the human heart-and-mind (*xin* 心) is expressed in terms of the ongoing active creation of new values rather than the simple reiteration and instantiation of what is theistically given to the human world. The nature and character of the human being is an ongoing creative process that both stimulates and is affected by change. John Berthrong makes much of this human plasticity in his analysis of the contributions of Mou Zongsan to contemporary Confucian-Christian dialogue:

> Human nature can *change* and in fact is human nature because it is not structurally constrained as other animals seem to be bound by their natures. The soul of the Confucian is what the person seeking sagehood decides to become—you are what you will to be, and you become more fully human as you create your own world as moral community.[11]

In fact, when Mou turns to *tiandao* 天道 and *tianming* 天命, and to their relationship with the notion of human creativity, he defines them ultimately as "the true impulse of ceaseless creativity (*chuangsheng buyi zhi zhenji* 創生不已之真機" or unbounded "creativity itself (*chuangzaoxing benshen* 創造性本身)."[12] This creativity is expressed as ongoing transformation of the world at the synergistic interface between uniquely human achievements and the boundlessly fertile natural and cultural context in which humanity resides.

In contrasting the Confucian worldview with the theologically anchored Western model, Mou places human effort at the center, and dismisses explicitly any association one might make with notions of Divine volition. As Berthrong observes in his analysis of Mou Zongsan's commentary on the Confucian tradition, "humanity can participate in the creativity of the universe as a cosmotheandric agent of the highest order."[13]

For Mou Zongsan, then, it is the process of becoming fully human that constitutes the substance of Confucian religion, and it is the absence of real constraints to that process that prompts Mou to describe it as transcendent. Since, however, Confucian spiritual sensibilities are human-centered in the manner Mou characterizes, there must be an explicit rejection of any notion of radical otherness or ontological disparity between what he calls the immanent and transcendent or the moral and religious aspects of that process. Mou affirms both the continuity between, and the interdependence of, humanity and *tian* as it is expressed in the phrase, *tianren heyi* 天人合一—the continuity between *tian* and the human being. In one's attainment of Confucian sagehood, there is a mutual relationship between the profoundly religious human being and *tiandao* 天道.

Berthrong defends Mou's qualified use of transcendence by arguing that, although what Mou actually means by this term is anathema to many of the irrevocable commitments of orthodox Western theology, it does have a close ally in the process theology movement originating with Whitehead and elaborated in the work of scholars such as Hartshorne. But by attempting to align Mou's understanding of transcendence with a radical position within Western philosophical theology, Berthrong only highlights the difficulty of discovering that notion in any strict form within Chinese speculations. Moreover, as we have noted above, process philosophy departs from more orthodox understandings of transcendence, but certainly does not wish to escape the notion altogether.

In Whitehead's understanding, the dualism of God and the World is replaced, in part, by the dualism of God's "primordial" and "consequent" natures. It is this model of the deity, we will recall, that allows for the understanding of relationships between God and the World as entailing both transcendence and immanence. But, as we have claimed, though this model does better satisfy the intuitions of those who would claim that there must be a truly intimate relationship between God and the world, the model does not escape the sorts of incoherence that plague all under-standings that require, as the process model does, a final resort to strict transcendence. Thus, in importing a version of the process model into Mou's thinking, Berthrong illegitimately introduces the language of strict transcendence into his thinking.

There are others in the transcendence debate who would wish to defend a stronger sense of the term than Mou Zongsan seems to do. A case in point would be Li Minghui 李明輝. Li is clear on what is at stake here:

> The question of whether or not there is transcendence in Chinese thought is not simply a matter of defining transcen-dence, but extends to Confucian thinking and the very way of thinking presupposed in the entire Chinese culture and the *Weltanschauung* that it has fostered.[14]

He is also aware of what transcendence cannot entail in describing Chinese culture:

> Perhaps we can roughly say: The basic model of thinking for the Chinese tradition takes continuity as its foundation; the basic model of thinking in Western culture takes disjunction as its foundation. And the worldview that these two cultures have fostered are distinguished on the basis of these unique charac-teristics.[15]

Taken in a strict sense, such a statement as this aptly characterizes in a general fashion our own reason for denying the relevance of strict transcendence to Chinese intellectual culture. For a variety of reasons, many of which have already been rehearsed, the disjunction entailed by strict transcendence has dominated Western philosophical speculations. That God should not be contingent upon the world requires that he be disjoined in some way from the world. In order that Reason have some unsullied realm untouched by the welter of concrete circumstances, and that causes not be implicated in the clutter of passing facts so as to be clearly distinguishable from their consequences, disjunction is essential.

There seems no reason, or any real disposition, for the Chinese to accept the consequences of disjunction as these implications have played themselves out in the Western tradition. The evidence for continuity as

a preferred value is altogether persuasive in Chinese culture. In the Confucian model, the commitment to the processional and transformative
nature of experience renders the "ten thousand things (*wanwu* 萬物 or
wanyou 萬有)" that make up the world, including human beings, at once
continuous with one another and unique.

The primary philosophical problem is how to correlate these unique
particulars in such manner as to achieve the most productive continuity.
Ancestor worship as the defining religious sensibility, family as the primary human unit, consummate humanity (*ren* 仁) and filiality (*xiao* 孝)
as primary human virtues, ritualized roles, relationships, and practices (*li*
禮) as a communal discourse, are all strategies for achieving and sustaining
the continuity of communal harmony (*he* 和).[16]

In spite of this fundamental appreciation of the problem, Li still
seems willing to argue for the appropriateness of Benjamin Schwartz's use
of transcendence quoted above, stating his views in tandem with those of
Mou Zongsan. The continuity between Schwartz and Mou Zongsan,
according to Li, lies in the shared distinction between "the actual" and
"the ideal":

> When New Confucianism takes *tian* and *dao* to be transcendent
> principles and actualities, the concept of transcendence still
> entails the meaning of "beyond the actual" or "the ideal." To
> my knowledge, this is what Schwartz means by the term "tran-
> scendence."[17]

Here Li seems to accept a weaker interpretation of transcendence as
simply meaning the ideal that functions in relation to actual affairs. This
does not necessarily involve strict transcendence, unless there is some
ontological claim to the effect that the ideal is an existent independent
of and unaffected by the actual. If it is the case that the ideal arises out
of the actual as an extension of it, transcendence in any strict sense is not
suggested. But, as we have seen, Schwartz does in fact understand the
"ideal" as an uncompromising standard of conduct that resides in the
"conscious will" of heaven, as an unchanging and unchangeable given.

In Li Minghui's survey of what the term actually signifies within the
purview of Western philosophy, he recognizes that "transcendence" is
freighted with a whole range of different meanings. This being the case,
Li argues that Mou Zongsan, a seasoned scholar who was entirely in
control of the many uses of transcendence in European philosophy, is

justified in retooling this equivocal European notion as an instrument for making Chinese philosophy clear:

> It is difficult for us to imagine that Mou Zongsan, who has studied Kant so thoroughly, is not clear on what transcendence and immanence mean for Kant. Perhaps the most reasonable explanation is that Mou is certainly not relying completely on Kant's meaning in using these concepts.[18]

Having said this, Li Minghui, in language that sounds very much like Schwartz, cites approvingly Mou's description of the transcendent aspect of *tianming* 天命 as

> having imperceptibly within it an immutable and unchanging standard which causes us to feel as though under its sanction we must not err or transgress at all in our conduct.[19]

In classical China the inexorably dynamic process of existence is defined in correlative dyadic pairs such as *you* 有 and *wu* 無, *bian* 變 and *tong* 通, *shi* 實 and *xu* 虛, capturing in this language the inseparability of change and continuity, process and discernable regularity. This being the case, to characterize *tianming* as an "immutable and unchanging standard" without further explanation, does in fact evoke dualistic notions of transcendence, especially when Mou offers a comparison between *tianming* and the classical Greek notion of Justice (*dikaiosyne*). Li Minghui explicitly defends Mou's comparison between Justice and *tian* in the following terms:

> As noted above, the new Confucians are certainly not using the concept of transcendence with the dualistic framework of a contrast between transcendence and immanence. For example, when Mou Zongsan says that *tianming* and *tiandao* are similar to the notion of Justice in Greek philosophy, he is obviously only saying that they are both "unperishing and unchanging standards," and is certainly not suggesting that he wants to understand the Confucian *tianming* and *tiandao* according to the dualistic framework of Greek philosophy. If it were otherwise, Mou would not say: "The meaning of the latter (*tianming* and *tiandao*) are a long way from the richness and remoteness of the former (Justice)."[20]

We could be sophistical, and claim that it must indeed be "otherwise," since Li Minghui has himself reversed Mou's order here: Mou's actual claim is that it is *tianming* and *tiandao* that are much richer and remote than the Greek notion of Justice, not the other way around.[21] But the problem is more serious. For Li, Mou's use of this language finally encourages him to ask:

> But who can deny that the *tian* and *dao* of the Confucians is independent and eternal, and thus on the basis of Hall and Ames's definition, can be regarded as transcendent principles?[22]

Li's ultimate position is that Chinese philosophy can be accommodated within the understanding of strict transcendence first stipulated in *Thinking Through Confucius*[23] and recalled above.

The question here is whether this debate over the use of the language of transcendence brings light or only heat to our understandings of classical Chinese philosophy? Let it be said that reconstructive efforts in philosophy may certainly lead to both novel interpretations and the construction of new concepts and theories that depart radically from the past. We are by no means attempting to advise Chinese scholars as to how they must perform their philosophical activities. Our concerns are threefold: First, the incautious use of a vocabulary of transcendence may unwittingly contribute to familiar Western misreadings of the tradition. Secondly, understandings of Chinese philosophy aside, use of a language of strict transcendence encourages subsequent generations of Chinese scholars to claim the existence of altogether too much common ground between the classical Western and Chinese cultural traditions, and in so doing, to underappreciate the contribution of Chinese philosophy to world culture as a real alternative to dominant Western sensibilities. Finally, a besetting irony of the present state of our conversations between China and the West should not be missed. We have noted above the serious decline in the Western academy of appeals to conceptual structures built upon notions of transcendence in theology, science, and social theory. The common ground sought by Chinese and Western interlocutors by appeal to transcendent categories may be largely slipping away due to the virtual collapse of the concept of transcendence in the West.

What is really at risk in the "transcendence debates" is nothing less than the philosophical modesty of the Chinese tradition. What is this modesty? Below in attempting to come to terms with *tian* and *dao* we will have occasion to discuss in some detail a set of cosmological assumptions first posited as cultural constraints in the early work of Tang Junyi 唐君毅. At this juncture, we might anticipate our later discussion by citing a passage from Mou Zongsan:

> What Confucius and Mencius mean by *xing* 性 [conventionally translated as "nature"] is not the basic abilities of a sentient being or the nature made manifest in one's physiological structure and psychological dispositions, because this kind of "nature" is a manifestation of the structure of a particular thing. The "*xing*" of Confucius and Mencius arises from an understanding of the meaning of what it means to be human, *ren* 人. The basic meaning of *xing* in the relationship between "*xing* and *tian-dao* 天道" is to be understood by grasping the fact that *ren* is "creativity itself." Human beings have this "creativity itself" as their *xing*. This is the most unique aspect of the human being.... Confucianism calls on the human being to exhaust this *xing* (*jin xing* 盡性), for if one fails to do so, one descends into the ranks of brutes and fowl. To "exhaust one's *xing*" means to give full expression to this creativity.[24]

We must caution that, given the shape of Mou's overall arguments, there is no justification in taking the locution here translated as "creativity itself" to have anything like categorial status. What it means to be human is an ongoing historical and cultural narrative. Further, the world-in-process that shapes and is shaped by this human creativity is always open, always provisional, always changeable, always in some degree a unique disclosure. If we appeal to Gilbert Ryle's distinction between "task or process" words on the one hand, and "achievement or success" words on the other—for example, "to study" versus "to learn," "to listen" versus "to hear"—"process" words are more appropriate for describing the human "task" of continuously going beyond one's present conditions. Process words are a language of continuing disclosure and aspiration. "Success" words on the other hand are inappropriate to describe this processional sense of order because they are a vocabulary of closure: "perfection," "completion," "ideal," "absolute," "eternal," "immutable," "universal," and so on.[25]

We made this same point with respect to "cosmology" in *Anticipating China*.[26] In summary, in classical Western metaphysics the equivocation between "unity" and "uniqueness" has largely been resolved in favor of "unity." Thus in any of the various conceptions of a single-ordered universe assumed by the early systematic philosophers, the many phenomena comprising the world are defined in accordance with unifying principles that determine the essential reality of the things of the world.

In taking a stand against the application of the language of transcendence in interpreting classical Chinese philosophy, we must reiterate a caution first stated in *Thinking Through Confucius*[27] to the effect that the use of the concepts "transcendence" and "immanence" as applied to the Chinese world is misleading since the use of either of the terms seems to entail the other. Thus, simply referring to the Chinese sense of order as "immanental" suggests some type of transcendence by contrast. The resolution of this difficulty is to avoid transcendence/immanence language whenever possible and, whenever such language is unavoidable, to make the proper mental adjustments.

The Chinese sense of order entails a thoroughly symbiotic relationship between its formal and fluid aspects. Given that the patterned regularity of *dao* 道 or *wen* 文理 or *li* 理 or *li* 禮 is never decontextualized nor detemporalized, certain conditions ensue. Order is ever site-specific, like grained wood, veined stone, DNA coding, and so on. Further, the uniqueness of any and every situation makes globalizing and essentializing predicates problematic.

Said another way, if we allow for a full consideration of both determinate and indeterminate forces, each site is going to be attended by a certain degree of unpredictability. This sense of dynamic order is reflected in the language. For example, in the notion *shi* 勢, which possesses in its semantic range the seemingly disparate meanings of "force of circumstances," "disposition," "momentum," "strategic advantage," and so on, the determinate and indeterminate aspects are captured in the contrast between "regularity" (*zheng* 正) and "(what is left over =) strange, surprise, unexpected" (*qi* 奇). The point here is that the indeterminate aspect provides the opportunity for manipulating the existing order for one's strategic advantage. The chaotic element, far from inhibiting order, allows for creative transformation. It is because *shi* describes a sense of order unfamiliar in Western cultures that, even more than many other philosophical terms, it resists adequate translation.

Another set of recurrent terms that reflect this ubiquitous indeterminate aspect is *ji* 幾 and its homophonous cognate, *ji* 機, again with a curious semantic range when rendered into a European language: *Ji* 幾 begins with the notion of "first inklings or stirrings," "minute," "imminent," "nearly," and then to "probability," "anticipation," "occasion," and with *ji* 機 extends to "critical point," "turning point," "pivot," "danger," hence to, "impetus," "motive force," "trigger," "clever device," and then to "opportunity" and one who can seize the opportunity, one who is "adroit," "flexible," "ingenious." The indeterminate aspect in this sense of order is "small," a "first stirring," which, as a "motive force" for self-reorganization and reconstual, is a "critical turning point." As a critical juncture—*weiji* 危機, literally, "danger-opportunity"—it can be either a "danger" or an "opportunity" in providing "impetus" for transformation, depending on whether or not one is able to seize the opportunity and make the most of it.[28]

This term, *ji* 幾, occurs in those canonical documents that have defined the classical Chinese worldview. For example, the "Great Treatise" of the *Yijing* (*Book of Changes*) contains the following passage, which typically associates *ji* 幾 with "deep, profound (*shen* 深)" and "spiritual, mysterious, inscrutable (*shen* 神):"

> The *Changes* is how the sage probes utterly what is profound and gets to the very bottom of things (*ji*). It is precisely because of the profundity of the *Changes* that the sage can penetrate thoroughly the purposes of the world; it is precisely because of its pivotal significance (*ji*) that he can be successful in the business of the world; it is precisely because of its mystery that he can be quick without haste and can arrive without going.[29]

Another passage in the same text reports:

> To understand the first inklings (*ji*)—this is spiritual understanding. The exemplary person in his relationship with his superiors is not given to flattery; in his relationship to his subordinates is not given to putting on airs. He understands the first inklings. The first inklings are the suggestion of movement, what is first shown of good fortune. The exemplary person on seeing the first inklings gets underway, and does not wait the duration of a single day.[30]

It is the general indeterminancy presupposed in the classical Chinese conception of the ordering of events that makes the language of transcendence inappropriate, and that returns us to the Chinese world itself in search of a more liberating and friendly vocabulary, one that allows for the emphasis on life and creativity celebrated by New Confucian philosophers such as Tang Junyi and Mou Zongsan.

There is an anecdote in the *Zhuangzi* which speaks directly to this point. Two high ministers are sent by the king of Chu to Zhuangzi who is fishing in the Pu River. On behalf of the king, they invite Zhuangzi to come back with them and govern the kingdom of Chu. Zhuangzi reminds the ministers of a sacred tortoise that has been dead for three thousand years, now wrapped in finery and stored in the ancestral temple of Chu. I ask you, says Zhuangzi, would the tortoise rather be so honored, or would it rather be alive to drag its tail in the mud? Of course, it would rather be alive and in the mud, reply the ministers. Get lost! said Zhuangzi, and leave me to drag my tail in the mud![31]

In interpreting the classical Chinese worldview, our choice then, is either to abandon that world by appeal to a notion of transcendence, or to remain in the world to drag our tails happily in the mud.

TIAN 天

In *The Religious Dimensions of Confucianism*,[32] Rodney Taylor claims that the reluctance of Western scholarship to factor religious sensibilities into its interpretation of Confucianism has skewed our reading of the tradition in the direction of "grey" theory and has, in so doing, impoverished it. However, having discerned that the Western understanding of Confucianism has failed to appreciate fully its religious aspect, Taylor then goes on to apply a decidedly Western vocabulary of religious culture to reconstruct the Chinese experience: absolute Deity, salvation, faith, hope, truth-value, suffering, conscience, scripture, saint, and so on.

In so doing, Taylor is following an esteemed tradition. In Leibniz's *Discours sur la théologie naturelle des Chinois* (1714), he argues confidently that early Confucianism was consistent with Christian doctrine, but that medieval developments in the tradition have hidden the original message.[33] Two and a half centuries later when the structuralist Claude Lévi-Strauss insists that the transformation of high civilization occurred only once these civilizations had discovered "transcendence," Benjamin Schwartz found transcendence in classical China.[34]

When it became rather plain that the pre-Han Chinese tradition had no developed mythology comparable to the classical Greeks and Romans, Derk Bodde proposed a "reverse euhemerization"—a Confucian conspiracy to transform systematic mythology into history—to account for its absence.[35]

From Leibniz down to the present decade, a primary interest of Western interpreters in engaging Chinese civilization has been to use this high culture to corroborate an Enlightenment universalism aspired to in seventeenth- and eighteenth-century European culture. This approach to the Chinese world has entailed assumptions about a universal God, an infallible geometric method grounded upon self-evident truths, an objective science, a universal language, a privileged model of historical development, universal human rights, and so on. From our early-seventeenth-century encounters with Chinese culture down to the present moment, Western sinologists have been vigilant in their efforts to spare the Chinese world its radical difference by recasting its tradition in their own terms. Nowhere is this more evident than in the area of religion, which, in the West, has been both the birthplace and the principal nurturing context of notions of transcendence.

In order to approach the Chinese religious sensibility, we must first undo what we have already done, because having had Judeo-Christian assumptions imposed upon them, even the Chinese have in large numbers become persuaded that they are not a religious culture. Given the relatively unsuccessful assault on Chinese culture by Christian proselytizers, coupled with the recent influence of Marxist sensibilities, many contemporary Chinese scholars recoil from the accusation that China has had a long-standing commitment to religious values and experience.

We want to argue that China has a tradition that is at once nontranscendent and profoundly religious. We shall do so by initially focusing upon *tian* 天, one of the central notions to which any understanding of Chinese spirituality must appeal. We need to get behind the conventional translation of *tian* as "Heaven" since that translation inappropriately conjures forth the notion of transcendence in the minds of both the non-specialist reader and the uncritical specialist as well. While foregrounding our own philosophical importances, this rendering pays the unacceptable penalty of concealing precisely those meanings that are most essential to an appreciation of its differences.

We can use an exchange with Angus Graham to frame the problem. Shortly before his death, Graham chided us by suggesting that we failed to distinguish clearly enough between translation and exposition:

> Granted that there can be different opinions about what counts
> as legitimate translation, it is reasonable to insist that a philo-

sophical translator does his best to approximate to the key
concepts of the original and to their logical relations, to follow
the structure of the thought rather than to reprocess it; full
success is unattainable of course, so to the extent that translation fails one supplements it by exposition.[36]

The particular term that Graham was concerned about in this article is
tianming 天命, conventionally rendered as "Fate" or "Destiny." Because
such language depends upon a notion of strict transcendence familiar in
the Western philosophical tradition, we came up with a paraphrase for
tianming ("the relationship between man and his world") that surrendered
the underlying metaphor of "command" and emphasized the relational
aspect of *tian* and *ming*. Ironically, in Graham's same written response, he
agrees with the rejection of transcendence as a characteristic of Confucian
cosmology, the very point we were trying to make by employing
paraphrase rather than strict translation. Again, citing Graham:

In the Chinese cosmos all things are interdependent, without
transcendent principles by which to explain them or a transcendent origin from which they derive.... A novelty in this
position which greatly impresses me is that it exposes a pre-
conception of Western interpreters that such concepts as *Tian*
"Heaven" and *Dao* "Way" must have the transcendence of our
own ultimate principles; it is hard for us to grasp that even the
Way is interdependent with man.[37]

When Graham insists on the "faithful" rendering of key "concepts"
such as *tian* and *dao*, he means conformity to the fixed definitions provided
by our lexicons. But there is a problem in insisting upon anything like
literal translation in a tradition that cannot appeal to that objectivity that
transcendent norms permit. Even the notion of "concept," to the extent
that it is dependent on univocal meanings, might be problematic. The
history of "concept" effectively begins with Plato's Eternal Forms, which,
though somewhat naturalized by Aristotle, nonetheless persist as essential
logical forms. In rejecting transcendence as a meaningful framework for
understanding the Chinese tradition, Graham is required to eschew the
possibility of objective, and hence univocal, meanings. In fact, he is
effectively eschewing conceptual language in any formal or technical
sense.[38]

As we noted in part II above, an implication of abandoning the language of transcendence, and with it the foundations of objective certainty itself (the Forms of Plato, the Mind of God, the Kantian categories), is that strictly literal discourse is not possible. If this is the case, Graham must allow that in the Chinese worldview, the act of translation is not complete until readers themselves have read the text. This simply means that the coherence of the Chinese order must take full account of context, including the biography of its readers. Translating *tian* as capital-H "Heaven" for an audience residing within a culture constructed upon Judeo-Christian assumptions leads directly to a distorted understanding. If this is so, then translation may require exposition (*exponere*, "a setting forth and displaying") that anticipates a particular audience. Paraphrase and exposition are essential tools of the translator.

Our current dictionaries are often of little help to the translator in seeking the "best" sense of a term. Using Graham's own examples: The standard Chinese-English dictionary translations for *tian* are: (1) the material heavens, the firmament, the sky; (2) the weather; (3) a day; (4) Heaven, Providence, God, Nature; (5) husband; (6) indispensable. In spite of some overlap, these equivalences contrast rather starkly with those provided by the Chinese-Chinese dictionary: (1) the sky; (2) *qi* 氣; (3) the movement and pattern of the heavens; (4) the sun; (5) spirituality/divinity/mystery (*shen* 神); (6) nature, what is so-of-itself (*ziran* 自然); (7) ruler (*jun* 君); (8) father; (9) indispensable; (10) a period of time; (11) a day; (12) *yang* 陽 (as opposed to *yin* 陰); (13) one's lot; (14) one's natural proclivities and character (*xing* 性), one's person (*shen* 身); (15) great.

The most significant gap in these two definitions of *tian* is the clear absence of "Heaven, Providence, God, Nature" in the Chinese dictionary. In fact, the dualism that requires appeal to transcendent deity in the Western tradition has no relevance at all to Chinese culture. What has happened here is that the purveyors of a Judeo-Christian vocabulary first appropriated *tian* to try to communicate a notion of transcendent deity to their Chinese interlocutors, and then subsequently insinuated this definition into the dictionary itself.

Tian is not an isolated example. Western translations that treat *dao* 道 as an entity rather than a modality, attribute, or action; as an object rather than a subject, would make the point equally well, as would the essentialization of *renxing* 人性 as human "nature," where, as Graham himself observes, "the translation of *xing* 性 by 'nature' predisposes us to mistake it for a transcendent origin, which in Mencian doctrine would also be a transcendent end."[39] In fact, our current Chinese-English dictionaries are freighted with a worldview alien to the culture they are supposed to translate.

This, then, is the magnitude of the problem. Our concern here is to identify and lift to the surface those peculiar features of a Confucian *tian* that are in danger of receding in our necessarily parochial reading and interpretation of the text. Testing whether the limits of our language are truly the limits of our world, we may discover that it is necessary to add to our language. That is, just as an understanding of *nous, phusis, nomos, logos,* and so on, requires that we get behind their renderings in Latinized discourse, so we may need to protect classical Chinese terms such as *tian* and *dao* from being too readily filtered though Western language colored with assumptions extraneous to the Chinese worldview.

In reconstructing *tian,* we want to try to recover what has been lost in the conventional translation and interpretation. To do so, the first step is to establish the fullest possible range and depth of meaning encompassed by *tian.* This will entail not only the gathering of an inventory of the connotative meanings available in the dictionary definition, but also the discovery and articulation of those presuppositions that make *tian* fundamentally different from what is understood by "Heaven."

In studying the Chinese corpus, one consults dictionaries that encourage us to believe that many if not most of the characters such as *tian* have multiple alternative meanings from which the translator, informed by the context, is required to select the most appropriate one. This approach to the language, so familiar to the translator, signals precisely the problem that we have worried over in these prefatory comments.

We would suggest that with the appearance of any given character in the text, the full seamless range of meaning is introduced. And our project as interpreters and translators is to negotiate an understanding that is sensitive to the specific context within which the character is employed. *Shen* 神, for example, is a complex notion, meaning as it does both "human spirituality" and "divinity." *Shen* does not *sometimes* mean "human spirituality," and *sometimes* "divinity." It always means *both* of these, and moreover, it is our business to try and understand philosophically how it can mean both. What are the implications of this particular range of meanings where humanity and divinity are continuous?

How does this factor into the familiar formula, *tianren heyi* 天人合一——
the continuity between *tian* and the human world? In fact, it is this effort
to reconstitute the several meanings of any term as an integrated whole
and to fathom how the character in question can carry what for us might
well be a curious, often unexpected, and sometimes even incongruous
combination of meanings, that leads us most directly to a recognition of
difference.

In I. A. Richard's *Mencius on the Mind* published in 1932, the late
Cambridge scholar used the task of understanding the *Mencius* as an
occasion to pioneer a novel technique for comparative studies. In so
doing, he rehearsed the question of cultural translation under scrutiny
here, and offered a remedy. For Richards,

> the problem, put briefly, is this. Can we in attempting to under-
> stand and translate a work which belongs to a very different
> tradition from our own do more than read our own conceptions
> into it? ... To put it more precisely, can we maintain two sys-
> tems of thinking in our minds without reciprocal infection and
> yet in some way mediate between them?[40]

Richards surmises, we think correctly, that if "analysis" is introduced as
the methodology for understanding *Mencius* as a text or any concept in
it, it smuggles in with it a worldview and a way of thinking that is alien
to the tradition itself. We cite him at some length:

> Our Western tradition provides us with an elaborate apparatus
> of universals, particulars, substances, attributes, abstracts, con-
> cretes, generality, specificities, properties, qualities, relations,
> complexes, accidents, essences, organic wholes, sums, classes,
> individuals, concrete universals, objects, events, forms, con-
> tents, etc. Mencius, as we have seen, gets along without any of
> this and with nothing at all definite to take its place. Apart
> entirely from the metaphysics that we are only too likely to
> bring in with this machinery, the practical difficulty arises that
> by applying it we deform his thinking.... The danger to be
> guarded against is our tendency to force a structure, which our
> special kind of Western training (idealist, realist, positivist,
> Marxist, etc.) makes easiest for us to work with, upon modes of

thinking which may very well not have any such structure at all—and which may not be capable of being analysed by means of this kind of logical machinery.[41]

This complex issue may be framed in yet another manner. In one of his most seminal essays ("'Being' in Western Philosophy Compared with *Shi/Fei* 是非 and *You/Wu* 有無 in Chinese Philosophy"), Angus Graham worries over the very possibility of translating Chinese philosophy into English.[42]

> Every Western sinologist knows that there is no exact equiv-alent in his own language for such a word as *jen* [ren] 仁 or *tê* [de] 德, and that as long as he thinks of it as synonymous with "benevolence" or "virtue" he will impose Western precon-ceptions on the thought he is studying. He is bound to suspect that there are also deeper structural differences which mislead him in the same way, and which it is much harder to identify.[43]

These "deeper structural differences" include the enormous disparity in metaphysical and cosmological assumptions between the Indo-European family of cultures on the one hand, and the rich philosophical tradition of China that developed entirely independent of Europe on the other. Such differences are embedded in the very grammar of our languages, and are so overwhelming that Graham concludes his essay with the humbling yet undoubtedly true assertion: "None of us yet knows classical Chinese."

Neither Graham nor Richards before him were the first philosophers to worry over these deep structural differences that frustrate intercultural translation. Nietzsche and Heidegger, attempting to recover alternative philosophical possibilities within the context of European culture itself, return to the conceptual clusters of pre-Socratic Greece. This is their strategy for getting behind the dualistic, essentializing metaphysics dominant in the received Hellenic-Hebraic tradition. Both philosophers, like Graham, are persuaded that a particular worldview is sedimented into the language of a culture and the systematic structure of its concepts, encouraging certain philosophical possibilities while discouraging others.

As Nietzsche speculates,

> The strange family resemblance of all Indian, Greek, and Ger-man philosophizing is explained easily enough. Where there is

an affinity of languages, it cannot fail, owing to the common philosophy of grammar—I mean, owing to the unconscious domination and guidance by similar grammatical functions—that everything is prepared at the outset for a similar development and sequence of philosophical systems; just as the way seems barred against certain other possibilities of world-interpretation.[44]

Richards, in proposing what he calls his "Multiple Definitions" way out of our dilemma, has greater confidence in our ability to use the dictionary effectively than have we. His "technique for comparative studies" is both semantic and syntactical. In moving between the cultures, he recommends that we "fuzzy up" the meanings of key philosophical terms by bringing the full range of possible meanings of any particular term into consideration. At the same time, we need to be critically self-conscious of the entailments of our implicit syntactic apparatus. In Richards's own words:

What is needed, in brief, is greater imaginative resource in a double venture—in imagining other purposes than our own and other structures for the thought that serves them.... [Multiple Definition] is a proposal for a systematic survey of the language we are forced to use in translation, of the ranges of possible meanings which may be carried both by our chief pivotal terms—such as Knowledge, Truth, Order, Nature, Principle, Thought, Feeling, Mind, Datum, Law, Reason, Cause, Good, Beauty, Love, Sincerity...—and of our chief syntactic instruments, 'is,' 'has,' 'can,' 'of,' and the like.[45]

Richards believes that it is acceptance of one definition of key philosophical terms, as opposed to another, that locates us in different philosophical camps. Hence, by surrendering the specificity of our meanings, we surrender our philosophical presuppositions. In fairness to Richards, we think his perception of the problem is on the mark, and his methodology is fully half of the answer. He registers a fundamental insight when, in passing, he asserts that the classical Chinese philosophers are closer to poets than to analysts, and that if we read their key philosophical terms like "concrete images" rather than "concepts," it will take us much closer to the original intent.

Following this same thought, most of the key terms that have defined the Western philosophical dialectic originally had both a rational and an aesthetic aspect: *Logos* means both *ratio* and *oratio*, both a rational account and the "word" itself, both reason and rhetoric; *aletheia* means both closure and disclosure, both agreement with fact and sincerity, both "truth" and "troth"; *kosmos* means both order and ornament, both form and elegance; *phusis* means both the internal organizing principle on the one hand, and the stuff and process of growth on the others; and so on. For Richards, our metaphysical and epistemological preoccupations get in the way of interpreting classical Chinese philosophy. It is metaphysics and epistemology that have skewed our philosophical vocabulary in a rationalistic direction, leaving the more aesthetic aspect of the Western philosophical vocabulary relatively undeveloped.

Richards appears to assume that if we recover the aesthetic aspect of Western philosophical terms by taking the entire range of meanings into account, these terms will be rich and broad enough to accommodate the classical Chinese worldview. There are, however, two potential problems. First, the aesthetic impulse in Western philosophy, so long masked by the dominance of rational thinking, remains relatively undeveloped, and might not have sufficient resources to accommodate the content of a tradition in which aesthetic sensibilities were the cultural dominant. Secondly, the very richness and breadth of the dictionary meanings might ultimately be our undoing by making the Chinese tradition hopelessly vague.

Without further critical assistance, how do we go about selecting and focusing an appropriate rendering from this admittedly broad range of possible meanings? Richards tells us what we have to include. But what can we leave out to bring this vocabulary into manageable focus? How are we to discover responsible syntactical and semantic constraints that preclude us from making the Chinese translation say anything we want it to?

As an extension to the "Multiple Definitions" strategy proposed by Richards, we will expand upon the research of Tang Junyi 唐君毅 in identifying a set of characteristics that define the parameters of Chinese natural cosmology, assuming that the basic characteristics that are generally presupposed in the tradition alert us to what could *not* be meant in classical Chinese.[46] This set of presuppositions will serve as our self-conscious prolepsis in reflecting on a "cosmology" that became increasingly explicit in the Han dynasty, and that has been influential in shaping

"Han thinking."[47] Presumably, these same presuppositions will also set limits on how we are to understand and translate this tradition.

In the *Shuowen* 説文 lexicon, *tian* 天 is defined paronomastically by reference to a character with a similar sound and with some of the same semantic associations. The character is *dian* 顛, meaning "top of the head," "the highest." Etymologically, it is either explained as a "combined-meaning" (*huiyi* 會意) character as "the one great" *yida* 一大, or, from the oracle bones and bronzes, as an image of some bigger-than-life anthropomorphic deity.

On the basis of the contrasting sets of meanings found in the Chinese-English and Chinese-Chinese dictionaries, then, we can make several observations that reinstate aspects of *tian* that tend to be concealed by the translation, "Heaven." First, the association between *tian* and the sky encourages proper notice of the profound temporality and historicity that attends this idea, frustrating any analogy one might want to find between "*tian*" and "sky" on the one hand, and "Heaven" and "the heavens" on the other. *Tian* is inextricably linked to the pervasive processes of change, and is understood often as an abbreviation of *tiandi* 天地, "heaven and earth," or "the autogenerative and self-sustaining world." Where the Judeo-Christian God, often referred to metonymically as "Heaven," *creates* the world, classical Chinese *tian* *is* the world.

Further, *tian* is an articulated and patterned sky: *wen* 文. *Tian* is thus defined as the "day" and the "skies" under which culture accumulates rather than as some ontologically independent order of Being. Significantly, there is a continuity between the articulation of nature generally (*tianwen* 天文 or *tianli* 天理), and the inscription of human culture (*wenhua* 文化 or *wenxue* 文學). The nature/nurture dualism familiar in Greek-based culture is not operative; instead, the natural world and human culture are continuous.

One consequence of this unwillingness to separate time from matter is that there is no need, in Aristotle's language, to distinguish an active, efficient cause from a passive material cause. In fact, expressions such as *ziran* 自然 and *tiandi* 天地, conventionally translated "nature" and "the world" do not simply refer to a world; they refer to an active, ongoing process. A corollary to this notion of an invigorated world is the absence of any final boundary between the sentient and insentient, animate and inanimate, living and lifeless. Given that there is no separation between physical change and life in a tradition that takes *qi* 氣 ("vital energizing field") as a pervasive category, and, thus, where everything is more or less animated, we can fairly describe Chinese natural cosmology as a hylo-zoism.[48]

For classical China, under the sway of a cosmology that assumes that matter is animate, the Western kind of a mind-body problem that begins in classical Greece and continues in a variety of formulations down to the present day, cannot and did not arise. But there is more to this picture. Since spirituality and life go hand in hand, we can assume that spirituality like life pervades all things.[49]

To say that spirituality and life are all-pervasive has two immediate implications. First, human beings achieve their hierarchical roles through cultivation of a complex spirituality, where this spirituality is understood in terms of extension, influence, and inclusion. In fact, as is evident from the connotations of the character, *shen* 神, conventionally translated as both "human spirituality" and "divinity" (derived etymologically from *shen* 伸: "extend, prolong"), and also from entrenched cultural practices such as ancestor worship and the worship of cultural heroes such as Confucius, gods in the Chinese tradition are generally "extended and prolonged human beings." And *tian* itself is the aggregate spirituality generated by a continuous culture.

Tian is both *what* our world is and *how* it is. The myriad things are not the creatures of *tian* or disciplined by a *tian* that is independent of what is ordered; rather, they are constitutive of it. *Tian* is both creator and the field of creatures. There is no apparent distinction between the order itself, and what orders it. This absence of superordination is a condition made familiar in related notions of the Daoist *dao* and the Buddhist *dharma* that references both concrete phenomena and the order that obtains among them. On this basis, then, *tian* can be described as an in-hering, emergent order negotiated out of the dispositioning of the part-iculars that are constitutive of it.

Tian is "self-so-ing" (*ziran* 自然). While it might be argued that it is in some sense cosmological, it is definitely not cosmogonic in any onto-logical sense. As a narrative constituted by cultural heroes, *tian* is genea-logical and biographical.[50] There is nothing antecedent to it; there is no beginning to it or end of it. There is no distinction between nature and its power of organization and generation.

Tian is anthropomorphic, suggesting its intimate relationship with the process of euhemerization that grounds Chinese ancestor worship. It is probably this common foundation in ancestor worship that allowed for the conflation of the Shang dynasty's *di* 帝 with the notion of *tian* imported with the Zhou tribes. There seems to be sufficient reason to assume that *tian* is consistent with the claim of the anthropologists Sarah Allan and Emily Ahern that Chinese gods are, by and large, dead people.[51] Culturally significant human beings, such as the Duke of Zhou and Confucius, ascend to become *tian*, and *tian* is itself made determinate in their persons.

Tian is not only culturally specific, but also geographical. The discovery of a new and sophisticated culture would anticipate the discovery of a *tian* representative of that culture. Just as there are many skies, one would expect other traditions to have accumulated a *tian* out of their own cultural experience.

Finally, *tian* does not speak, but communicates effectively although not always clearly through oracles, through perturbations in the climate, and through alterations in the natural conditions of the human world. *Tian* participates in a discourse shared by the most worthy among the human community. Given the interrelatedness and interdependency of the orders defining the Confucian world, what affects one, affects all. A failure of order in the human world will automatically be reflected in the natural environment. Although *tian* is not a personal deity responsive to individual needs as in the Judeo-Christian worldview, as aggregate ancestor it would seem that *tian* functions impartially on behalf of its progeny to maximize the possibilities of emergent harmony at all levels.

As suggested above, we really must question the appropriateness of using "concept" language to discuss the Confucian notion, *tian*. Given the dependency of the Confucian thinking on the particular image, we might have to allow that the Confucian "person," for example, is precisely that particular and detailed portrait of Confucius found in the middle books of the *Analects*, where each passage is a remembered detail contributed by one of his protégés who participated in the conversation. And this portrait, as it attracts more disciples and plays a role in shaping unique self-images in the tradition, does the work of a concept. Analogously, *tian*, as a cultural narrative, is made determinate and explicit by a tradition of exemplary models:

> The *junzi* 君子 has three things he holds in awe: the order of *tian*, the great man, and the words of the sage.[52]

The notion, *tianren heyi* 天人合一, "the continuity between *tian* and the human world," does not just mean anthropomorphism (god is manshaped), it also means "theomorphism" (the exemplary person is godshaped):

> How great indeed was Yao as ruler! How majestic! Only *tian* is truly great, and only Yao took it as his model.[53]

Repeatedly, worthiness in the human world defines *tian*:

> Confucius was the sun and moon which no one can climb beyond. Even if someone wanted to cut himself off from the sun and moon, what damage could one do to them?[54]

In the *Zhongyong*, Confucius is described explicitly as *tian*:

> So earnest, he is humanity (*ren* 仁);
> So profound, he is an abyss (*yuan* 淵);
> So pervasive, he is *tian* (天).[55]

The Confucian "*tian*" is the experience of meaningful context felt differently by each person in the Confucian fellowship.

We have said enough to render plausible the conclusion that *tian*, a central notion in defining Chinese spirituality, is not to be interpreted as a transcendent category. Thus, English translations such as "Heaven," "Providence," or "God" are decidedly misleading. We shall now proceed to a discussion of *dao* 道, an equally fundamental notion for the understanding of the Chinese sensibility. We shall find that this notion, as well as *tian*, must be interpreted as distinctly nontranscendent. Further, though we shall not elaborate this point in any great detail, a search for Western counterparts to Chinese spirituality would lead to a focus upon the tradition of mysticism in the West. For, as we discussed above, there is good reason to believe that mystical experience is itself fundamentally nontranscendent.

DAO 道

We discussed philosophical Daoism in some detail in Part I above. We shall presuppose the outlines of that discussion in the remarks that follow.

Our aim is to make explicit here what was primarily implicit in that former discussion—namely, the nontranscendent status of *dao*.

Dao is nameless and formless. This is so because *dao* constitutes the noncoherent sum of all names and forms.[56] As such, *dao* engenders both "one" and "many," both continuity and difference.

> *Dao* engenders one,
> One engenders two,
> Two engenders three,
> And three engenders the myriad things.
> The myriad things shoulder *yin* 陰 and embrace *yang* 陽,
> And mix the *qi* 氣 to achieve harmony.[57]

Having said this, since the myriad things are constitutive of *dao*, we could run the process back the other way with equal effect:

> The myriad things engender three,
> Three engenders two,
> Two engenders one,
> And one engenders *dao*.

The natural cosmology of classical China does not entail a single-ordered cosmos, but invokes an understanding of a "world" or *dao* constituted by a myriad of unique particulars, "the ten thousand things." *Dao* is, thus, the process of the world itself.

In Daoism, the relevant contrast is not between the cosmological *whatness* of things and the ontological *thatness* of things, but rather it is a contrast between the cosmos as the sum of all orders (*dao* 道), and the world as construed from some particular perspective; from, that is to say, any particular one of the orders (*de* 德). In these terms the *Daodejing* 道德經 may be understood as the classic of particularity and the field that it constitutes, or the classic of the field as construed by a particular.

Dao is not organic in the sense that a single pattern or *telos* could be said to characterize its processes. It is not *a* whole, but many such wholes. It is not the superordinate One to which the Many reduce. Its order is not rational or logical, but aesthetic, which is but to say that there is no transcending pattern determining the existence or efficacy of the order. The order is a consequence of the particulars comprising the totality of existing things.

This interpretation of *dao* makes of it a totality not in the sense of a single-ordered cosmos, but rather in the sense of the sum of all cosmological orders. Any given order is an existing world that is construed from the perspective of a particular element within the totality. As a single world it is an abstraction from the totality of possible orders. The *being* of this order is not ontological in a foundational sense, but cosmological. Such an abstracted, selected order cannot serve as fundament or ground. In the Daoist sensibility, all differences are *cosmological differences*.

We have argued elsewhere that a philosophically coherent understanding of classical Daoism depends upon a recognition that neither of the two fundamental metaphysical contrasts of the Western tradition (that between "Being" and "Not-being," and between "Being" and "Becoming") is helpful in understanding the Daoist sensibility.[58] In Daoism, the sole fact is that of process or becoming. Being and Nonbeing are explanatory abstractions from that process.

The opening passage of the *Daodejing* may be rendered in this way:

Speakable *dao*—this is not constant *dao*;
Nameable name—this is not constant name.
The unnameable is the fetal beginning of the world;
The nameable is the mother of the myriad things.

In *Daodejing* 25, we read:

There was something heterogeneously formed
Prior to the heavens and the earth.
Soundless, formless,
It stands solitary and is not corrected.
It revolves without pause.
This can be considered the mother of the world.
I do not know its name;
If forced to, I would use the rubric, *dao*,
And if forced to name it, I would call it "great."

In our discussions of *tian* and *dao*, we have suggested that the belief in a cosmic unity does not enter into the classical Chinese notion of world order. The Chinese notions of *tian* and *dao*, alternatively referenced as *wan wu* 萬物 or *wan you* 萬有 ("the ten-thousand things") do not require a sense of the world as a unified whole. Tang Junyi begins his comparative discussion of Chinese and Western "cosmology" under the heading of the Chinese "(self-so-ing =) natural cosmology," where "natural" *ziran* 自然 contrasts with the "supernatural" or "metaphysical" cosmology of classical Greece.[59] In his study, he independently affirms the point of Graham's article cited above: "something *you* 有" and "nothing *wu* 無" (or "emptiness *xu* 虛" and "fullness *shi* 實") are interdependent and mutually entailing categories. As such, they do not have the ontological weight of "Being" and "Not-being," but serve simply as an explanatory vocabulary necessary to describe our world of thises and thats.

The absence of ontological assertions means that for the Chinese there is no "Being" behind the myriad beings (*wanwu* or *wanyou*), no One behind the Many, no Reality behind Appearance. Thus Zhuangzi's belief that there are only thises and thats readily contrasts with Parmenides' "Only Being is." There is only an ever-changing processional regularity that can be discerned within the world itself that makes the world *in some degree* coherent and determinate, and given its inherent indeterminacy, in some degree novel and unpredictable.

For classical India, there are many worlds of which this is one. For a Platonic Greece, there is one best world that, being bounded, self-contained and self-sufficient, is limited and static. For classical China, neither monistic like Greece nor pluralistic like India, there is "world as such" or "worlding" or "world-in-which-I-am-situated" without the definite article "the" or "this" to objectify it. After all, it is this ability to make an object of the world that allows Western philosophers to decontextualize themselves and step out of the world, thereby assuming "a view from nowhere." And it is precisely this "view from nowhere" that guarantees the possibility of objective truth and certainty.

The Chinese "world as such" by contrast is unique and boundless, and the viewer is always embedded within it. Without a standpoint or basis for asserting objective truths, the line between description and prescription blurs because subjects are always reflexively implicated in the way in which they organize the world. To say something about the world is to say something about oneself, one's disposition, and one's values.

A further consequence of having no objective perspective is that saying, even *thinking*, something about the world is *doing* something to the world. The severe separation between theory and practice separates speaking from doing, and thus trivializes such notions as "freedom of speech." What is merely "theoretical" cannot directly change the world.

In the classical Chinese worldview, thinking and speaking are actions that have real consequences in shaping our environments.

When the *Zhuangzi* recommends that we become "one with all things 萬物與我為一," this is not a Vedānta-like call to surrender one's particularity and dissolve into a unitary and perfect whole. Rather, it is a recognition that each and every unique phenomenon is continuous with every other phenomenon within one's field of experience. There is a passage in the *Zhuangzi* that might be instructive here:

> Zhuang Zhou was roaming about in the fenced preserve at Diaoling when he spied a strange magpie that had flown in from the south. Its wingspan measured seven feet across, and its eyes were an inch in diameter. Grazing Zhuang Zhou's forehead, the bird then perched in a grove of chestnut trees. "What kind of bird is this," observed Zhuang Zhou, "with broad wings that don't take it anywhere and huge eyes that don't see anything!" Tucking up his lower garments, he rushed over to it, and with his crossbow drawn and ready, he waited his chance.
>
> He noticed a cicada that, having just then discovered a beautiful bit of shade, forgot the dangers around him. A mantis hiding in the camouflage was about to seize upon it, and being preoccupied with its prey, had also forgotten its own peril. The strange magpie, following up behind and anticipating the mantis as its own, was so preoccupied with its quarry that it too forgot its real danger.
>
> Zhuangzi with alarm, exclaimed, "My! Things are certainly continuous with each other, where one kind of thing calls forth a different kind!" He then cast aside his crossbow and ran out of the preserve, and the groundskeeper, hot on his trail hurled abuses at him.[60]

Is thus being one with all things an an exhaustive claim? Are we talking about *all* phenomena? Because the world is processional and because its creativity is *ab initio* rather than *ex nihilo*, any answer to this question would have to be provisional. Phenomena are never either atomistically discrete nor complete. The *Zhuangzi* recounts:

> With the ancients, understanding had gotten somewhere. Where was that? Its height, its extreme, that to which no more

could be added was this: Some of them thought that there had never begun to be things. The next lot thought that there are things, but that there had never begun to have boundaries among them.[61]

It is at this point that the applicability of the very word "cosmology," at least in its familiar classical Greek sense, becomes problematic. In Presocratic philosophy, the term *kosmos* connotes a clustered range of meanings, including *arche* (originative, material, and efficient cause/ultimate undemonstrable principle), *logos* (underlying organizational principle), *theoria* (contemplation), *nomos* (law), *theios* (divinity), *nous* (intelligibility). In combination, this cluster of terms conjures forth some notion of a single-ordered Divine[62] universe governed by natural and moral laws ultimately intelligible to the human mind.

The Chinese understanding of "cosmos" as the "ten thousand things" means that, in effect, they have no concept of cosmos at all, insofar as that notion entails a coherent, single-ordered world that is any sense enclosed or *defined*. The Chinese are, therefore, primarily, acosmotic thinkers.[63]

One implication of a distinction between a cosmotic and an acosmotic worldview is that, in the absence of some overarching *arche* explaining the creative process, and under conditions that are thus an-archic in the philosophic sense of this term, although "nature" might indeed refer to "kinds," such categories would be no more that generalizations made by analogizing among similar phenomena. Difference is prior to essential similarities.

The Chinese binomial most frequently translated as *kosmos* is *yuzhou* 宇宙, a term that overtly expresses the interdependence between time and space. The "world" is likewise expressed literally as the "boundaries between one's generation or epoch and the tradition" (*shijie* 世界). For China, and again in contrast with the dominant impulse of Greece and India, time pervades everything; it is not dependent upon things, but is a fundamental aspect of them. Unlike traditions that devalue time and change in pursuit of the timeless and eternal, in classical China things are always transforming (*wuhua* 物化). In fact, in the absence of some claim to objectivity that "objectifies" and thus makes "objects" of phenomena, the Chinese tradition does not have the separation between time and entities that would allow for either time without entities, or entities without time. Thus, there is no possibility of either an empty temporal corridor or an eternal anything (in the sense of being timeless).[64]

What encourages us within a Western metaphysical tradition to separate time and space is our inclination inherited from the Greeks to see things in the world as fixed in their formal aspect, and thus, as bounded and limited. If instead of giving ontological privilege to the formal aspect of phenomena, we observe them in light of their ceaseless transformation, we are able to temporalize them and perceive them as "events" rather than "things," where each phenomenon is some current or impulse within a temporal flow. In fact, the pervasive capacity of the world to transform continuously *is* the meaning of time.[65]

It is because things in the world are reproductive, that time is reproductive. Since the world is always entertained from one perspective or another, and since the temporal aspect is never abstract, fictive, or replicated, any perspective is an advancing path that is neither linear nor cyclical, but both. That is, time-space-matter is an advancing spiral.[66] The expression, "advancing path" is particularly appropriate, because it is this image of our passage in the world that is captured in *dao* 道 as a grounding metaphor pervasive in the tradition.

A predominant understanding of the nature of time and space in modern Western philosophy that has shaped our commonsense view is that time is duration while space is extension. In classical China, as the expression "world" *shijie* (literally, "boundary between generations") suggests, time and space are never separable. Secondly, the deep structure of the language tells us that time and space are specific as opposed to abstract, beginning as they do from the perspective of the speaker: *zuo/you* 左右, *qian/hou* 前後, *shang/xia* 上下, *gu/jin* 古今. The inseparability of time and space as divisible "dimensions" becomes explicit in the Han dynasty correlations, where place is time: East is spring, south is summer, west is autumn, and north is winter.[67]

While the articulation and stabilizing regularity of any specific event anticipates the way in which it will continue to unfold, the chaotic aspect within the event itself defeats any notion of necessity or absolute predictability. The combination of pattern and uncertainty challenges the possibility of universal claims and renders precarious any globalizing generalizations. All we can depend upon is the *relative* stability of site-specific and particular expressions of order, with constant attention to stochastic variables at every level that well might amplify into large-scale changes. Order is thus both *local* and *focal*.[68]

The dominant mode of Chinese thinking is acosmotic and oriented toward the actual particulars whose various correlations are construable only in terms of constituent details. Rational thinking is cosmological, and ultimately cosmogonic, in the sense that explanations are referenced to the pattern regularities associated with the overall context defining the order.

There is something like a "cosmogonic" activity associated with aesthetic, strictly "acosmotic," thinking that can be illustrated by reference to certain of the Song dynasty landscape paintings. Most of these paintings, as we know, are meditative constructions painted from memory after the artist had wandered through the ambiance of the landscape. Such paintings often appear to be constructed from flat planes. Typically a painting might contain a foreground, midground, and background, the *sanjing* 三境 or "three vistas." The principal focus of the painting is found at the center. It is a commonplace to observe that the Chinese sense of perspective locates one within the painting itself. That is, one is drawn in to take up one's stance at the center of the painting, and from that point to wander through its landscape. However, the painting is not bounded, and its surround is the world itself from the perspective of the center of the painting. The artist has construed a world from the perspective offered by the painting's central focus. He has created a world. But, of course, he has not created *the* world, for there are as many worlds as there are discernable foci.[69]

We said at the beginning of this chapter that we intended, at its conclusion, to draw upon our earlier discussion of Daoism found in part I. The principal points considered there that reinforce the argument of this chapter are the following: (1) the distinctly nontranscendent character of the deferential activities expressed through the modes of *wuwei* 無為, *wuzhi* 無知, and *wuyu* 無欲, and (2) the distinctive manners in which the "parity of things" (*qiwu* 齊物) and their transformations (*wuhua* 物化) require no transcendent source or ground.

Perhaps we should briefly note, with respect to the first of these points, the way in which the deferential actions associated with the *wu*-forms provide for a distinctly "horizontal" interpretation of Daoist manners of relating to the world of things.

In our considerations of Western mystical experience as an immanental form of religious experiencing, we cited the three principal types of mysticism identified in the mystical literature. These were God-, soul-, and nature-mysticism. The specific modes of experiencing forms associated with these types were characterized, respectively, as ecstasy, enstasy, and synstasy. All three of these forms of experiencing (taking one's stand outside oneself, or inside oneself, or standing together with all other things) constitute deferential activities that depend upon the absence (or cancellation) of transcendence. There is an analogical relationship between these types of mystical experience and the *wu*-forms. Though, in the absence of strictly dialectical modes of argumentation, the Daoist would never be interested in separating these types of experiencing to the degree one would find in Western philosophical discussions, nonetheless, there are fruitful analogical relationships to be discerned between the activities involving *wuwei*, *wuzhi*, and *wuyu* and those patterned by ecstasy, enstasy, and synstasy.[70] This is certainly not to say that there are one-to-one relationships among these sets of activities; we mean to say only that these are variant manners of characterizing deferential operations that depend upon the absence or cancellation of transcendent reference.

CHAPTER TEN

The Chinese Community without Transcendence

The subject of this part is *transcendence*. Our argument has been that there is no effective appeal to transcendence in the mainstream Chinese tradition, neither as a means of shoring up one's spiritual sensibilities, nor of stabilizing the character of one's social relationships. We have presented sufficient evidence with regard to the former topic. We shall now begin to defend our claims with regard to the latter.

Toward the end of our recently published work, *Anticipating China*, we discussed the subjects of ritual, role, and family in the classical Chinese understanding of society.[1] There we endorsed the claim of Ambrose King to the effect that all social relationships in Confucian China are familial. Of the five cardinal relationships, the two nonkinship relations (friend and friend, and ruler and subject) are patterned directly on familial relations of younger and elder brother, and father and son, respectively.

In the following sections we shall provide two illustrations of the absence of transcendent reference in the Chinese conception of community. Since we are currently engaged in writing a sequel to this present work that will deal with issues of "rights," "justice," and "community" in modern perspective, we shall not address these issues in detail here. We shall be primarily dealing with aspects of the ruler-subject relationship. But we must not neglect the role of "friendship" as a fundamental dynamic serving the end of realizing and sustaining a viable community. Thus, we shall begin our broader discussions of social and political issues with a brief consideration of the contrast between a classical Greek and a Confucian understanding of friendship.

COULD SOCRATES AND CONFUCIUS BE FRIENDS?

If we were to consider friendship in its most general sense within the Western tradition, one could hardly omit, as we shall, reference to Aristotle. His division of the types of friendship (in the *Nichomahean Ethics*) in terms of the criteria of pleasure, utility, and mutual goodwill has had an extremely influential role in the development of cultural self-understanding in the West. But if one focuses upon the comparison of Chinese and Western understandings of friendship specifically with respect to the notion of transcendence, the omission is perhaps forgivable. For focusing upon the distinctly Platonic view of friendship will best highlight the distinction between models of that relationship that depend upon transcendent appeals, and those that do not.

Plato's *Phaedrus* is a dialogue whose discussion of the uses of rhetoric and philosophy serves as the basis of the emerging friendship of Socrates and Phaedrus. When we first encounter Phaedrus, he is under the influence of the rhetorician, Lysias, having just heard him speak on the topic of love. There can be no relationship between Phaedrus and Socrates until the former is freed from his attachment to the persuasive power of rhetoric and raised to the level of dialectic. The dialogue tells how Socrates achieves this end. His first move is a lateral one: He seduces Phaedrus away from Lysias by constructing a superior rhetorical discourse on love. Then, in a second, philosophical speech, Socrates illustrates the employment of dialectic and dialogue, encouraging Phaedrus to accept the role of a fellow enquirer.

The dialogue ends with a prayer of Socrates:

> Beloved Pan and all the other gods who dwell here, grant me to be beautiful within.... Let me believe that it is only the wise man who is rich. Let the mass of my gold be only what the temperate man, and no other, can make his own.[2]

to which Phaedrus responds,

> Please include me in your prayer, for friends hold everything in common.[3]

It is Socrates' desire for temperance, wisdom, and inner beauty that qualify him to be a friend. And it is Phaedrus' sharing of this desire for temperance, wisdom, and beauty that guarantees his friendship with Socrates.

The Platonic message, as we understand it, is that the noblest human quality is to be found in none of the stable virtues, but in the erotic motive force that sometimes leads us, sometimes drives us, toward completeness of understanding, and is the presupposition of all the virtues.

This view of friendship, a variant of Platonic love, entails the consequence that the bond of friendship lies beyond the relationship between the two persons in a common desire for the attainment of a transcendent goal such as Truth, Beauty, or the Good. A common purpose, a common end, a shared project, provided that project, end, or aim is a noble one, is the basis of friendship.

But this raises a problem that has vexed the tradition from the beginning, doubly so after the collision of Hellenic and Hebraic sensibilities. The problem is that of distinguishing the kinds of love appropriate to the differing sorts of relationships, human and divine, available to rational creatures, most of which are beset by disqualifying passions that compromise, if they do not cancel, any chances for true relatedness.

At one level we are embarrassed by the notion that friendship is a kind of love. It is an embarrassment born of the suspicion, strengthened since the advent of Freud, that love is always tinctured by sexuality. On the standard Platonic reading, friendship is a kind of love, and on the modern Hebraic-Christian version of Platonism, it is a kind of love from which distinctly sexual feelings must be effectively absent.

Plato's interpretation of Aristophanes' myth of the round men in the *Symposium* will help us sort out the relations between love and sexuality.

> In the beginning the sexes were not as they are now, but originally three in number; there was man, woman and the union of the two.... The primeval man was round, his back and sides forming a circle; and he had four hands, and four feet, one head and two faces, looking opposite ways, set on a round neck and precisely alike; also four ears, two privy members, and the remainder to correspond.... Terrible was their might and strength, and the thoughts of their hearts were great, and they made an attack upon the gods.
>
> After much deliberation, the gods decided—it was Zeus himself who made the decision—to punish them by dividing them in two. In this manner their power was halved while the number of sacrifices they were made to perform was doubled.

Now they were divided beings, each seeking their sundered half. With disastrous results. Once a pair was reunited, they refused to let go, became tangled together. They began to die of starvation and self-neglect. Zeus realized the problem and set about to solve it in a most proactive manner. He invented the sexual orgasm.

Zeus in pity of them invented a new plan: he turned the parts of generation round to the front . . . and they sowed their seed no longer upon the ground like grasshoppers, but in one another; and after the transposition the male generated in the female in order that by mutual embraces of man and woman they might breed, and the race might continue; or if man came to man they might be satisfied, and rest, and go their ways to the business of life.[4]

The message couldn't be clearer, and with proper adjustments that take into account Plato's slightly different use of irony, couldn't be more Platonic. Love (*eros*) promotes union; sexuality allows disunion. Love promotes interdependence. Sexuality promotes autonomy. Love drives toward physical accord. The gift of physical sexuality allows individuals the freedom "to go their ways to the business of life."

The conclusion of the *Phaedrus* is that friends hold all things in common, and when what they hold in common is an eros directed toward the transcendent Good, they are true friends. The conclusion of the myth of the round men reinforces the moral of the *Phaedrus* that if love remains at the physical level, denied any common transcending other as the basis for the search for unity, it cancels autonomy.

Plato's principal point drawn from the *Phaedrus* and the *Symposium* seems to be that friendship is a necessary condition for realizing the Good. The passion, the eros, is a condition not of the friendship, but of the common desire for the rational ideals that the friendship augments and sustains.

We would offer a rehabilitated Plato as a means of preparing for a discussion of the Confucian idea of friendship. The received Plato needs rehabilitation with respect to the notion of friendship due to the manner in which the mystical and meditative traditions of the Hebraic-Christian sensibility have stressed the private, personal, individuated character of spirituality. Granted that the institutions of monasticism and congregational worship for the most part perpetuate this understanding of friendship as the ground of spirituality, there is the prominent belief among many of us that the sole relationship essential to the ends of spirituality is that between the individual and her God. It is this belief that leads to the interpretation of friendship as merely an instrument for the attainment of spirituality. The *philia* that binds friends does not really bind them at all; it is the means whereby the eros driving each separately toward the Good is augmented and sustained. Friendship allows friends to go about the business of being spiritual, which means seeking a personal, individual, relationship with that which lies beyond.

Evidence for the mitigation of the importance of friendship to spirituality is capsulized in the emergence of the concept of *agape* as a mode of divine love in early Christian theology. *Agape* comes to mean the love of God expressed through his creatures. So conceived, human beings are channels of God's love in the sense that the love of one individual for another is, in fact, God's love expressed through those individuals. The implication is that love, as *agape*, has a Divine origin as well as a Divine end. The importance of this type of love in the development of Christian spirituality led to a deemphasis upon the type of love associated with classical Greek notions of *philia*.

So far, we have raised two Platonic questions as a means of anticipating our discussion of the Confucian understanding of friendship. The first question is whether friendship can promote spirituality. On the Platonic model we have sketched in the simplest terms, this is clearly so. A second question is whether by so serving, it is denied any intrinsic value and is rendered merely instrumental. The evidence seems to lead us to that conclusion insofar as we rely on the Platonic sensibility.

If we now seek to compare the foregoing Platonic model of friendship to that of the Confucian understanding, we shall be able to see quite well how the friendship relation, which serves as one of the fundamental relationships contributing to the formation of community is, in Confucian China, not shaped by appeals to transcendent grounds or goals.

The *Xunzi* recalls a conversation between Confucius and several of his disciples on the central virtue of classical Confucianism, *ren* 仁, conventionally translated "benevolence," "humanity," "love," "altruism," and "goodness":

> Zilu came in and Confucius asked him, "... What does it mean to be a *ren* person?" He replied, "... A *ren* person is one who causes others to love him." Confucius remarked, "Such is called a refined person."

> Zigong came in and Confucius asked him, "... What does it mean to be a *ren* person?" He replied, "... A *ren* person is one who loves others." Confucius remarked, "Such can be called a consummately refined person."
>
> Yan Yuan came in and Confucius asked him, "... What does it mean to be a *ren* person?" He replied, "... A *ren* person is one who loves himself." Confucius remarked, "Such can be called the truly enlightened person."[5]

This passage invites considerable commentary. At least for the interpretation of Confucius proffered by the *Xunzi*, "love" as it originates in the project of becoming a truly enlightened *ren* person is a ground of mutual incorporation between oneself and other. Since the kind of love referenced in this passage requires consideration of the concerns of the other person, it is not entirely surprising that the term that translates it, *ai* 愛, also means "to grudge" or "to be sparing with." A person who loves another and assumes that person's concerns as her own, respects the uniqueness and integrity of the other, strives to take her on her own terms, and is circumspect in any demands she might make. She values the person's difference as the basis for their friendship, and wants the other to remain fully herself, without being distorted or reshaped in the relationship. Hence, in this classical Chinese sense of love, to love another is to be sparing of her.

The first and lowest level of personal achievement entails conducting oneself in such a manner as to occasion other people taking one's concerns as their own —使人愛己. While this in Confucius' eyes is praiseworthy conduct, it is still one-directional, focusing as it does upon the satisfaction of one's own needs. As such, there is a residual selfishness in this espoused goal.

The second level of personal cultivation requires that one take the concerns of others as one's own—愛人. While this is perhaps a higher level of development than the first, it is again only one-directional, focusing on the needs of the other rather than one's own. Such altruism, while admirable, is unfortunately self-abnegating. One's own legitimate concerns are not properly served.

The highest level, then, is necessarily reflexive, incorporating in one's own person the entire field of self-other concerns—自愛. *Ren* here does not refer to an isolatable agent or action; rather, *ren* describes a cultivated and mutually beneficial relationship between self and other. It references a complementarity grounded in the specific conditions of one's cultivated relationship with another person.

The cultivation of *ren* is thus irreducibly other-entailing. One cannot become *ren* in Descartes' closet. The relationality of *ren*—a graph comprised of "person" 人 and the number "two" 二—is underscored repeatedly in the *Analects*:

> The Master said, "... As for the *ren* person, in wanting to establish himself he establishes others; in wanting to succeed himself he helps others to succeed. Being able to take as one's correlations those near at hand can be said to be the method of realizing *ren*."[6]

Again, as argued in part I above, this process of cultivation is not an altruism that entails self-abnegation; on the contrary, it must entail the full self-other relationship:

> The Master replied, "Self-discipline and practicing the ritualized roles and relationships will make one *ren*.[7] If for the space of a day one were able to accomplish this, the whole empire would turn to him as a model of *ren*. Becoming *ren* is self-originating—how could it originate with others?"[8]

In interpreting this passage, it is important not to presume an "ego-self" that has to be overcome. Rather, *ji* 己 here references an incipient, inchoate self that is radically situational, and hence reflexive. It is the cultivation and extension of this reflexive self that brings with it both personal and communal realization.[9]

Ritual practices, *li* 禮 are the repertory of those formal roles, practices, actions, and institutions that continue the living culture. They are meaning-invested behaviors that, when properly enacted, conduce to communal harmony. These actions are a central concern in becoming *ren* because of their capacity to locate a person socially and culturally within a community.

Important here again is this notion of reflexivity. Ritual practice, like love (*ai*), is bidirectional. Ritual or "propriety" requires that cultural meaning be recovered in the formal role and performance, and also that the role be personalized and "made one's own" by investing it with oneself and one's own importances. Ritual is enacted by one person, and invokes a reaction in the community in which it is performed.

This brings us to a potentially problematic passage repeated in the *Analects* that helps us focus the peculiar conditions of Confucian friendship. It is because of the fundamental importance of "other" in this existential project of becoming *ren* that Confucius can say repeatedly: "Do not have as a friend anyone who is not as good as you are. And where you have gone astray, do not hesitate to mend your ways."[10] In the absence of some transcendent reference, persons must rely on the quality of their relationships as a resource for improvement. This exclusionary notion that a friend, to qualify as a friend, must be as good as or better than oneself seems to be contradicted in other passages in the text. For example:

> Master Kong said, "Having three kinds of friends will be a source of personal improvement; having three other kinds of friends will be a source of personal injury. One stands to be improved by friends who are true, who live up to their word, and who are broadly informed; one stands to be injured by friends who are ingratiating, who feign compliance, and who are eloquent talkers."[11]

On the surface, it would seem that ingratiating friends are still friends. But this is not really so. Ritual practice and music, in the absence of personal achievement, are hollow and meaningless; in fact, such conduct cannot be properly called ritual practice and music. As Confucius observes,

> What use is propriety (*li*) to one who in his person is wanting in character (*ren*)? What use is music to one who in his person is wanting in character?[12]

That is, ritual performed by a culturally vacuous person is not really ritual. Similarly, a Confucian "friend," a *you* 友, who is not better than oneself is not properly a friend. Unlike the English word "friend," *you* for Confucius cannot be used loosely for mere acquaintances or strangers, or as a mark of goodwill or kindly condescension. A distinction is usually made between the two terms conventionally translated as "friend (*you*)" in classical Chinese. *Peng* 朋 is someone who has a common master (*tongmen* 同門), and *you* is someone who has common purposes (*tongzhi* 同志). *You* is cognate with *you* 右, meaning the "right hand" and, by implication, "to honor, to esteem." It is further cognate with *you* 佑" to assist" and *you* 祐" a blessing." As such, "friend" in classical Chinese, like the expression "two" generally, entails hierarchy. It is an occasion to grow personally, and can only be assigned to the *ren* relationship in which one is able to express deference to another. Friendship is based upon appreciated differences between oneself and another person that present themselves as specific occasions for one's character development, rather than upon perceived commonalities with the other person.

You is also homophonous and defined paronomastically in the classical corpus with *you* 有—"having at hand." It is having someone at hand to whom one can defer, and take as one's model. *You* is going "hand-in-hand" with someone from whom one can benefit and learn, deriving as this term originally does from a graph that contains a representation of the human hand.

That Confucius insisted upon this restricted and specific use of "friend (*you*)" is suggested in a discussion on the meaning of "friend" that involves two of Confucius' closest protégés, Zixia and Zizhang. In the years following the death of the Master, these two disciples had matured into patriarchs in their own right with their own interpretations of what Confucius had said and meant.

> The protégés of Zixia asked Zizhang about friendship (*you*). Zizhang queried, "What has Zixia told you?" They replied, "Join together with those from whom you can learn; spurn those from whom you cannot."

It would seem from Zixia's definition of *you* that he is retaining the strictness with which Confucius wants to use this term. But such a narrow reading does not go unchallenged. Zizhang counters,

> This is different from what I have heard. The exemplary person exalts the worthy and is tolerant of the common, praises those who are capable and is sympathetic to those who are not. If in comparison with others I am truly worthy, who am I unable to tolerate? If I am not worthy in the comparison, and people are going to spurn me, on what basis do I spurn them?[13]

In evaluating these two very different interpretations of Confucius' attitude toward friendship, it is helpful to recall the profile of these two disciples that emerges from frequent reference in the *Analects* and elsewhere.

Zizhang with his free-wheeling altruism was repeatedly rebuked by Confucius for paying more attention to appearances than to substance, and for using language without due care.[14] In one telling passage,

> Zizhang asked about the way (*dao*) of the able person. The Master said, "Not following in the steps of others, one does not gain entrance to the inner chamber."[15]

Confucius is here criticizing Zizhang for not deferring sufficiently to moral exemplars, thereby precluding any entry into sagehood.

Zixia, on the other hand, is credited more than any other disciple for his scholarship, and played a major role in the transmission of the Confucian Classics.[16] On this basis, then, we can speculate that it is probably Zixia who is transmitting the more literal understanding of Confucian friendship (*you*).

In the peculiarly Confucian conception of friendship, then, we have certain conditions. First, a friend is a necessary condition for becoming consummately human (*ren*). Hence, when asked about how to become *ren*, Confucius replies,

> When living in a particular country, serve the most worthy of the high officials, and make friends with those scholar-officials who are most *ren*.[17]

One must love a friend as a complementary aspect of one's self, yet at the same time, allow such friends to retain their integrity. Again, although Confucius is clear that one cannot demand all-round perfection in a single person,[18] the friend must on balance and in important respects be qualitatively superior to oneself—an object of personal deference.

Given the central importance of *ren* in Confucian thought, the decidedly underdetermined status of this notion as it is presented in the *Analects* has been a source of concern for commentators over the centuries. On six different occasions, Confucius is called upon to define *ren*, and six times he gives a different answer. The best that Confucius can do in stipulating the content of *ren* is to point to historical exemplars.

If we interpret classical Confucianism as an aestheticism that begins from the coordination of insistently particular details, the vagueness of *ren* can be explained as the same uncertainty that attends any aesthetic achievement. Like any ritual or role (*li*) in the Confucian world, friendship is fundamentally aesthetic in the sense that it emerges as a harmony through the fruitful collaboration of unique details. Its formal aspects are always qualified and made contingent to specific social, cultural, and natural conditions by the investment of personal interest. Given these particularistic demands of *ren*, involving as it does the mutually enhancing coordination of *this* person with *this* friend, friendships are always unique relationships that cannot be captured in the language of formula or replication.[19]

Ren is conventionally translated benevolence, humanity, and goodness. The problem with "benevolence" is that it psychologizes *ren*, reducing a holistic and resolutely social conception of person to someone's particular moral disposition. "Humanity," a broader and hence more adequate term, still fails to do justice to the profoundly religious dimension of *ren*, and vitiates the uniqueness inherent in becoming *ren*. In fact, it tends to set up the opposition we find in the contrast between religion and humanism. Friendship, for Confucius, is grounded in *ren*, and is at the same time, the road to religiousness. Confucius does not appeal to transcendent beings or principles as the ultimate reference for growth; rather, he says of the process of personal cultivation: "I study what is near at hand and aspire to what is lofty."[20]

What is the relationship, then, between Confucian friendship and religiousness? Confucian religiousness begins from the assumption that there is a continuity and interdependence between *tian* 天, conventionally translated as "Heaven," and the human being (*ren* 人). This correlativity between *tian* and the particular person is often captured in the claim that *tianren heyi* 天人合一 (literally, "*tian* and human beings are continuous") used to summarize religious sensibilities during this period.[21] Hence, the *Mencius* observes:

> For a person to realize fully one's heart-and-mind is to realize fully one's nature and character, and in so doing, one realizes *tian*.[22]

Tian and "the way" (*dao* 道) are often associated if not used interchangeably in the classical Confucian corpus. And Confucius insists that "it is the human being who broadens the way, not the way that broadens the human being."[23]

The continuity and interdependence between *tian* and the human being is reflected in the familiar line from the *Mencius*: "All of the myriad things are here in me."[24] We can explain this claim in the following way. Persons are radically situated as persons-in-context, inhering as they do in a world defined by specific social, cultural, and natural conditions. Persons shape and are shaped by the field of things and events in which they reside. A person is fluid and multivalent in the sense that, in any particular situation, he or she is open to redefinition in many different ways by appeal to the roles of mother, sister, and so on. Articulated and brought into focus in any one of these roles, a person expresses the community from both a focal and a local perspective within the extended field of relationships.

An analogy might help here. The full value of any one note in a musical composition can only be assayed by understanding its place in the entire piece of music as performed. Any one note thus has implicate within it the entire score. That note may be said to focus the entire field of relationships constituted by the compositions. Important here is that the field of relationships is not circumscribed, but an unbounded reservoir of particular detail that remains open and available for further inclusion. The field of relevant detail for the particular note can be extended to include a movement in another piece by the same composer, or his entire corpus, or the musical product of a particular era, and so on.

"Persons-in-context," like the particular note in the musical performance, are multivalent, bringing the human community and its natural surrounds into focus from their particular perspective. As such, they are more or less distinguished, more or less articulated, more or less representative of the values and cultural importances of their communities.

This language of focus and field provides us with a way of talking about the continuity and interdependence of the human being and *tian* presupposed in the Confucian worldview. *Tian* is the field, the social, cultural, and natural context, and is in some sense greater than the particular person ("*Tian* has given life to and nourished excellence in me"),[25] as well as being implicate within and brought into focus by the particular person ("all of the myriad things are here in me").[26] As we have noted above, *tian* is frequently described in anthropomorphic terms. But the relationship is bidirectional, and works the other way as well. The human being is also theomorphic. That is, when a person is successful in focusing culture and its institutions in a manner that is exemplary, and emerges as a model for his community and future generations to which they defer, he has extended himself through their patterns of deference, and has become the object of reverence. Hence, in the Confucian vocabulary, cultivation enlarges one's person (*da ren* 大人), so that one becomes literally "larger than life."[27]

The sage is describable in nothing less than cosmic terms:

> Zhongni (Confucius) is the sun and moon, and there is no way of climbing beyond him.... The Master is unreachable, just as the sky (*tian*) cannot be divided and scaled.[28]

By contrast, a failure to cultivate oneself on the part of the person who enjoys opportunity and power results in moral retardation. He remains literally a "small" person (*xiaoren* 小人) and appears as a foil for the exemplary person (*junzi* 君子) throughout the *Analects*.

An analysis of the character *shen* 神 restates this analysis in religious terms. As we have noted above, *shen* means both human spirituality and divinity. Etymologically, its root meaning 伸 is "extension." As persons become increasingly spiritual through the effective performance of communal life forms (*li* 禮), and becomes increasingly inspirational for their communities, they are exalted, and move in the direction of divinity.[29] Cultural heroes, such as the Duke of Zhou, Guanzhong, Confucius, Laozi, are in one sense, dead, and yet are culturally alive and well, having ascended to become gods. The term "to perish" in Chinese (*wang* 亡) means "to be forgotten" (*wang* 忘). Hence ancestors, long entombed yet still remembered, are a continuing cultural resource for the tradition, and continuing objects of reverence.

Where then, is the friend (*you*) in this process of religious realization? Persons in this tradition seek personal growth in the community of other persons who are vital repositories of culture. Only those persons from whom one can learn and "increase" (*yi* 益), and who through inspired deference, provide a source of meaning for oneself, are conducive to personal growth. Early in the quest, such friends are undoubtedly many. But one's personal extension absorbs these persons into one's own field of selves, and those remaining persons representing the quality of difference necessary for continuing growth become more difficult to find.

Very well. Presupposing the above discussion, and given Confucius' insistence that a friend should be better than oneself, we may ask, "Whom would Confucius call his friend?" The *Mencius* is of some assistance here:

> Mencius said to Wanzhang, "The best scholar-official of one village will make friends with the best scholar-official in another village; the best scholar-official in one state will make friends with the best scholar-official in another state; the best scholar-official in the empire will make friends with other scholar-officials like him. And not content with making friends with the best scholar-officials in the empire, he further discusses the ancients respectfully. When one recites the poems and reads the writings of the ancients, how could it be that one does not know their persons? This is the reason one discusses the age in which they lived. This, then, is what it means to exalt friends."[30]

Confucius's first friend, then, is the Duke of Zhou:

> The Master said, "My how I have regressed! It has been a long time now since I dreamed again of meeting with the Duke of Zhou."[31]

Beyond "friends in history" such as the Duke of Zhou, Guanzhong, and Kings Wen and Wu, it is a question as to whether Confucius could have any friends.

Confucius, as he is portrayed in the *Analects*, is peerless, and hence, friendless. To assert that Confucius had friends would diminish him. On the other hand, he is described as learning from everyone and from no one:

> Gongsun Chao of Wei asked Zigong, "Who did Confucius learn from?" Zigong replied, "The culture (*dao* 道) of Kings Wen and Wu has not yet fallen to the ground. It resides in people. While none remain unaffected by it, those who are worthy have got it in great measure, while those who are not still have a modicum of it. Who then did Confucius *not* learn from? Again, how could there be a single, constant teacher for him?"[32]

Another way of viewing this peculiarly Confucian notion of friendship is to appreciate the extent to which family relationships dominated the social and political structure. We have alluded above to Ambrose King's argument that *all* relationships were ultimately construed in familial terms.[33] This meant that success within one's various social circles would eventually establish one as a patriarch, a position that would not reduce to friendship relations. It is significant that while D. C. Lau has Confucius referring to his disciples as "my young friends," the expression translated literally is "my little masters/sons (*xiaozi* 小子)." This paternalism was pervasive in the culture, and has remained unchanged as a model of order throughout the whole history of Confucianism.

If there is any exception to the observation that Confucius had no friends, it was his favorite disciple, Yan Hui, who most likely in death became available to Confucius as a friend. Confucius rarely and reluctantly used the term *ren* to describe anyone, including himself. In fact, he repeatedly side-stepped the use of *ren* to characterize people around him.[34] Yan Hui was the exception:

> With my protégé, Yan Hui, he could go for several months without departing from *ren* in his thoughts and feelings;[35] as for the others, only every once in a long while might *ren* make an appearance.[36]

Perhaps most telling was Confucius' comment to Zigong which repeats the same language as "Take as friends only those who are better than yourself":

> "Comparing yourself with Yan Hui, who is the better person?" Zigong replied, "How dare I have such expectations. With Hui, learning one thing he will know ten; with me, learning one thing I will know two."
> The Master said, "You are not his match. Neither you nor I are a match for him."[37]

While Confucius himself had no friends, it would seem to be the case that all who knew and loved Confucius took him as friend in the proper sense. The exclusiveness with which Confucius is willing to use the term "friend" (*you*) does not preclude other very positive relationships through which one expresses nurturance and caring. The Mencian dictum, "Try your best to treat others as you would be treated,"[38] means that the category *you* does not exhaust the people to whom one owes affection in the Confucian world.

It is difficult to think of two more distinct conceptions of friendship than those of Plato and Confucius. For Plato, true friendship is based upon the equality expressed by the need to hold all things, most particularly the search for beauty, truth, and goodness, in common. For Confucius, friendship is a one-directional relationship in which one extends oneself by association with one who has attained a higher level of realization. Further, the ironic self-effacement used by Socrates to permit an equality where none might otherwise exist is absent from the Confucian tradition.

The negative assessment of sexuality is absent from Confucius. Indeed, the theme of sexuality itself is effectively absent at the level of intellectual discourse. The absence of verbal reference to sexuality with regard to friendship, or any other relationship in the classical Chinese tradition, might be explained in the following way. The Great Preface to the *Book of Songs* states:

> Song is the result of dispositions. It resides in the heart-and-mind as dispositions and is articulated in language as song. One's feelings stir within one's breast, and take form in words. When words are inadequate, they are voiced in sighs. When sighs are inadequate, they are chanted. When chants are inadequate, unconsciously, the hands and feet begin to dance them.

Language, song, and body are three levels of discourse that differ in that as we move from words to music to dance, the discourse becomes increasingly personal and decreasingly referential. It is an investment of self. Dance or other bodily expressions, including sexual relations, cannot be reduced to language without profound depersonalization. People don't say "I love you" in Chinese because such a disposition is expressed in so many ways that the language, far from reinforcing the love relationship, depersonalizes it, and brings it into question. Sexual relations, when articulated in language, invite other people into the act—sexuality becomes public, and borders on the pornographic.

There is a clear reference to transcendent ideals in the Platonic understanding of true friendship, but no such transcendence is present in the Confucian tradition. The norm of Confucius is sagehood, a goal which is realized by becoming coextensive with the tradition. Such a realization, which at its extreme would be tantamount to becoming *tian*, remains an immanent norm, for *tian* itself is immanent.

For Confucius, friendship has more the quality of Platonic *eros* than *philia*. It is not only one-directional, but it is directed at that which is more realized. For Plato, the mutuality of joint inquiry is a presupposition of the individual attainment of the Good. For Confucius, to the degree that friendship is for the sake of realizing the goal of sagehood, it may be said to be instrumental. Nonetheless, friendship is an indirect route to the Good for Plato, while it serves as a direct path to sagehood for Confucius.

There is a poignancy in the conclusion that Socrates and Confucius could not be friends. Confucius, at a early stage of his development, might seek friendship based upon a perceived superiority in Socrates, while Socrates would solicit Confucius' participation in the joint inquiry after the Good. Socratic irony would not allow the inequality Confucius requires as a means of self-betterment. Confucius would not permit he and Socrates to hold all things in common.

RITES AND RIGHTS

One signal of profound difference between Chinese notions of community and Western liberalism is that in the latter, modern social and political theory has in large measure revolved about questions such as the relation of the individual to society, the realms of private and public activity, the status of natural and positive law, the character of rights and duties, the sanctioning powers of the state (legitimate authority), the meaning of justice, and so forth. By contrast, concerns relevant to discussion of Chinese social and political thought would include the cultivation of personal, familial, and communal life (*guanxi* 關係), the function of tradition-based ritual activity and social roles (*li* 禮) in reproducing sociopolitical harmony, the definition and attunement of social and political roles through the ordering of names, the efficacy of cultural modeling, modes of justifiable remonstrance, and so on.

The notion of *li* or "rites, ritual practice, roles and relationships" is very broad, embracing everything from manners to media of communication to social and political institutions. It is the determinate fabric of Chinese culture, and further, defines sociopolitical order. It is the language through which the culture is expressed. Ritual practice is not,

of course, a purely Chinese innovation, but its prominence and pervasiveness as an apparatus for ordering society, and its dominance over
formal legal institutions, gives the Chinese *li* a unique definition.[39]

Contemporary discussions of Chinese attitudes toward human rights,
influenced perhaps by the Western model, tend to be state-centered and
basically political in their orientation. The discussion of human rights in
Western philosophy, emerging out of the natural law tradition and essentialistic definitions of human agency, often entail a reliance upon the
language of transcendence. As an alternative, we want to examine *li*, the
traditional, primarily social, mechanism for constituting community and
generating its sociopolitical order. We then want to try to articulate ways
in which *li*, in its own peculiar way, has done some of the work expected
from human rights, and how it has influenced the way in which contemporary Chinese society has entertained the Western doctrine of universal human rights.

The character *li*, generally translated "rites," "ritual practice," "propriety," and "ceremony," has strong religious import in the sense of
"bonding." Clear from the graph, *li* 禮 is cognate with the character, *ti* 體,
which means "to embody, "to constitute a shape," and by extension,
"organic form." Angus Graham in his work on the *Later Mohist Canons*
has identified *jian* 兼 and *ti* 體 as a pair of technical terms that cover the
total/unit relationship, both as whole/part and collection/individual.[40] A
good argument can be mounted, however, that given the processional
assumptions of Chinese natural cosmology, *jian* and *ti* would be better
understood as a field/focus relationship. For example, the *Later Mohist
Canons* define *ren* 仁 as *ti ai* 體愛—"differentiated, individuated, or
focused loving" (as opposed to *jian ai* 兼愛 "collective loving" familiar in
the Mohist tradition).[41]

Ritual practices, then are "performances," social roles and practices
that, through prescribed forms, effect relationships. The etymology of the
English "rites" and "ritual" is suggestive for our understanding of both *li*
and its cognate *ti*. In Latin, *ritus*, derives from the base **ri-* "to count," "to
enumerate," which in turn is an enlargement of the base **ar-* "to join" as
in "arithmetic" or "rhyme." That is, ritual practice is the rhyme and
rhythm of society.

The translation of *li* as "propriety" also has its justification. It
indicates the "proprietorial" implications of ritual practice that involve
making a community "one's own." To perform ritual is, on the one hand,
to be incorporated as integral to the society such ritual practice defines,

and hence to be shaped and socialized by it. On the other hand, it is to contribute oneself to the pattern of relationships that ritual entails, and thereby to have determinative effect on society. Because of this contributory and participatory emphasis of ritual practice in the Chinese context, *li* does not carry with it the several pejorative connotations such as superficiality, formalism, and irrationality that often attach to the English term "ritual." *Li* is not passive deference to external patterns or norms; it is a "making" of society that requires the investment of oneself, one's judgment, and one's own sense of cultural importances.

Although ritual practices initially lure the performer into social relationships with the stability and acceptability of their authorized forms, they are not simply given standards of appropriateness sedimented within a cultural tradition that serve to shape its participants in predictable ways. Ritual practices also have a creative dimension. In this sense, they are more exhortative than prohibitive. Rituals inform the participant of what is proper only to the degree that they are performed by him. Beyond any formal social patterning is an open texture of ritual that is personalized and reformulated to accommodate the uniqueness and the quality of each participant. From this perspective, ritual is a pliant body of practices for registering, developing, and displaying one's own sense of cultural importances. It is a vehicle for reifying the insights of the cultivating person, enabling one to reform the community from one's own unique perspective, and ultimately, to leave one's own mark on the tradition.

There are variable degrees of personalization in ritual practices, and as a consequence, the roles they establish are hierarchical. These roles form a kind of social syntax that generates meaning through coordinating patterns of deference. And to the extent that worth is a function of interest and attention, the process of extending and deepening these roles brings with it a greater felt significance. It follows then, that individuality in the liberal democratic sense of autonomy and independence is anathema to ritually constituted society, suggesting even idiocy and immorality. To be socially unresponsive is to be irresponsible.

Ritual practice is not only synchronic, that is, constitutive of a given social present; it is also diachronic. A community's memory, its culture, is an inherited repertoire of formalized actions that display the cumulative investment of meaning and importance (*yi* 義) of one's precursors in the cultural tradition. Ritual both preserves and transmits cultural significances. For this reason, the performances and embodiment of the ritual tradition not only socialize a person to make one a member of a community, it further enculturates one. Ritual informs the particular person with a shared set of values and provides one with the opportunity to integrate in a way conducive to the maintenance and enrichment of community.

In what may be taken as the authoritative statement on ritually constituted community in the Chinese tradition, Confucius declares that the project of ritual practice is to effect social harmony:

> The exemplary person (junzi 君子) seeks harmony (he 和) rather that agreement (tong 同); the small person does the opposite.[42]

Ritual action is a pervasive condition of Confucius' vision of social harmony because, by definition, it not only permits, but actually requires personalization. This harmony is predicated on the premise that people are unique, and that they must be orchestrated into relationships that permit expression of this uniqueness.[43] A formal ceremony without this commitment is a hollow, meaningless, and even antisocial parody; on the other hand, a ceremony that coordinates and expresses the genuineness of its participants is a source of social cohesion and enjoyment.

Ritual actions are unique not simply because they require personalization, but further because they display the specific quality of the performers. The significance of ritual practice and its potential to produce social harmony is a direct function of the cultivated quality of several of its participants.[44]

Throughout the *Analects*, the truly harmonious community, relying as it does upon quality people to refine themselves in ritual action and to assume the internal perspective entailed by a sense of shame, is defined as fundamentally self-ordering:

> Lead the people with administrative injunctions (zheng 政) and keep them in line with penal law (xing 刑), and they will avoid punishments but will be without a sense of shame. Lead them with excellence (de 德) and keep them in line through roles and ritual practices (li 禮), and they will develop a sense of shame, and moreover, will order themselves.[45]

Where the order of a community is constituted by an internal network of interpersonal patterns of deference, and is, therefore, immanent and emergent rather than imposed, the ruler does not "rule."[46]

This "self-ordering" of community does not entail closure. It is neither compliance with some top-down decree nor replication of some predefined ideal. It is instead a project of disclosure, involving the co-ordination and mutual accommodation of members of community who, through ritualized roles and practices, pursue personal and sociopolitical realization simultaneously. This inseparability of personal integrity and social integration collapses the means/end distinction, rendering each person both an end in oneself, and a condition or means for everyone else in community to be what they are. The model is one of mutuality.

In ritual-ordered community, particular persons stand in relationships defined by "creativity" rather than "power." This distinction between "power" and "creativity" is essential for an understanding of community constituted by ritual action. Whereas "power" often suggests the correlative concepts of domination and control, "creativity" is a notion that can only be characterized in terms of self-cultivation and articulation. Unlike power relationships that require tensions among component elements be resolved in favor of one of the components, in relations defined by creativity there is no final "otherness," no separation or distancing, nothing to overcome. Instead, creativity requires that each participant in a relationship be continually in the process of creating the other.[47] Community thus defined through the creativity of its members is programmatic—a goal that is constantly pursued rather than an immediate reality or fixed ideal. It is an open-ended aesthetic achievement, contingent upon particular ingredients and inspiration. It is more like a work of art than a product of a formula or blueprint.

We have stressed the role of self-cultivation and personalization in the capacity of ritual practice to constitute community. Implicit in self-cultivation and communal deference to its achievements is cultural elitism. The identification of any particular person as authoritative in his performance of ritual entails the elevation of his conduct to the level of a cultural norm. This sort of cultural elitism is not coercive or authoritarian; it is a matter of deference rather than obedience. The dynamic of ritual practice is spontaneous social approval and respect, not enforcement. And the greater one's excellence, the more outstanding and determinate one becomes. The converse is also true: In the absence of self-cultivation and participation, one does not emerge as either culturally determinate or determinative.

As we have argued above and elsewhere,[48] in the Chinese tradition generally and Confucianism specifically, humanity itself is a progressive cultural accumulation and achievement. Humanity is a refinement of the animal world occasioned by the modeling efficacy of its cultural leaders. A qualitative ascendancy from brute (*qinshou* 禽獸) to indeterminate masses (*min* 民) to determinate person (*ren* 人) and ultimately to authoritative person (*ren* 仁), reveals the degree of one's refinement through ritual actions. With this cultural ascent of man, it follows that in one direction, those who violate social relations and the values they embody are truly, not metaphorically, brutes, and in the other, that humanity is open-ended, and can be ever increasingly refined.

Because ritual action can only take account of a person to the extent that one is differentiated and distinguished, the indeterminate masses (*min*) necessarily have a more passive and deferential role.[49] This same demand of ritual action for personal signature, while promising to make the most of available diversity, means also that the achieved community will in some important respect always be local, conditioned by the expectations and the imagination of its specific cultural leaders and the circumstances of its time and place. It thus falls to those who are the fullest participants in ritual practice, and thus the fullest members of community, to shape a future for their particular community, both in terms of goals to be achieved and minimal qualifications for participation.

It is important here to note the relationship between exhortative ritual action (*li* 禮) and prohibitive penal law (*xing* 刑). In the tradition defined by Confucius, the relation is correlative, and the conceptual content and function of penal law can only be understood against an appreciation for the way in which ritual practice works to constitute a person in society.[50]

Penal law establishes a minimum standard for what it means to be human and draws the external perimeter on what is acceptable at any time within the jurisdiction of ritual practice. It is significant in this respect that the term *xing* 刑 belongs to a set of cognates that have as their core idea "to form" or "to shape," including, of course, *xing* 形.[51] It is in this sense of shaping that penal law functions as an instrument for defining and sustaining communal harmony, distinguishing it from the notion of law as a basis for arbitrating conflicting claims.

Where ritual provides a direction for refinement and aspiration, law instructs with deterrent force in what is minimally acceptable. Where ritual action prompts creative cultural adventure and reifies what is most significant in cultural achievement, law secures the society, sets constraints on the existing social order, and surgically eliminates what is incorrigible. Just as the entire community as the web of relationships shares in and is improved by appropriateness in the performance of ritual action, so the entire community shares in and is culpable when penal law must be invoked. Appeal to law is a communal admission of failure. For this reason, when law is invoked, the problem is not as much one of guilt or innocence as of shame. It is a rupture in the outer limit of community that should be known, and should be redressed through concerted social effort.[52]

Although Confucius aspires to a state that is free of litigations,[53] he is keenly aware of the need for law.[54] On the other hand, focusing his attention and efforts on promoting the social apparatus that is productive of a harmonious community, Confucius has little interest in debating procedures for dealing with hypothetical lapses of order:

> The Master had nothing to say about strange happenings, the use of force, disorder, or the gods.[55]

Several reasons can be given for Confucius' reluctance to entertain "disorder" (*luan* 亂) as a topic for discussion, but perhaps the most important is preoccupation with the ritual structure of society. He saw this ritual structure as being both participatory and programmatic, as a set of formal behaviors and institutions through which a particular group of people can negotiate the goal of common harmony. Social order, in fact, order generally, is for Confucius "bottom-up," emergent from the mutual accommodation of specific participants in patterns of interweaving deference. Just as the conductor addressing his orchestra is not concerned to elaborate upon the innumerable possibilities for discord, so Confucius too has little interest in the topic of variations in social disorder.

The concepts of "human rights" and "ritual action" are functionally analogous to the extent that they are both social practices that establish and define the limits of relationships among persons and between a person and the state. It has been noted that although the English term "ritual" is often attended by negative formalistic connotations, the Chinese counterpart, *li* is generally free from such associations. The converse of this situation occurs with the concept of "rights" in English and its modern Chinese equivalent, *quanli* 權利: literally, "weighing up personal interests." *Quan* 權 has generally denoted "power," not in the positive sense of legitimate authority, but with the connotation of some provisional advantage that derives from exceptional circumstances. In contrast to its common antonym, *jing* 經, which means "regular" or "normal," *quan* indicates the "irregular and "expedient," even the "opportunistic." It suggests more of special privilege than of some common expectation. Its complement, *li* 利, is likewise a mixed term. Basically, it means "profit," "interest," or "advantage," but since classical times it has tended to convey a selfish preoccupation with personal benefit at the expense of what is "appropriate" (*yi* 義) for all concerned.[56]

The term, *quanli*, does have a history. The *Xunzi* brings these two terms together for the first time in the extant corpus with decidedly negative import:

> For this reason, neither contingencies (*quan*) nor personal advantage (*li*) can subvert the exemplary person.[57]

When, in the nineteenth century, *quanli* was employed as originally a Japanese translation of the notion of "human rights," the initial Chinese response to it must have been one of considerable bemusement. Nonetheless, this oblique approximation of "rights" made its formal entry into the Chinese world, and has achieved a technical prominence in the many constitutions promulgated in this century. Even so, the rhetoric of rights that dominates Western political discussions is still very foreign in the popular Chinese culture. Of course, this Chinese resistance to the notion of human rights is due to factors far more fundamental than bad translation. Appealing to our discussion of ritually constituted community with its presuppositions and its goals, we want to suggest that rights as defined in the classical Western tradition entail assumptions that are in many ways incompatible with Chinese social considerations.[58]

It is not necessary to scratch the surface of traditional Chinese assumptions that ground the notion of ritually constituted community very deeply to discern the reasons there is conceptual resistance to human rights defined as the *dominium* of the discrete individual. To begin historically, our conception of rights and its relevance has been influenced by the small familial community in which custom and tradition guaranteed fundamental dignities, and the modern nation-state in which the increasingly mobile and atomized population must claim their humanity from an impersonal and often oppressive government machine. While a persuasive argument can be made that the Industrial Revolution, for better and for worse, has altered our concept of community to the extent that human rights is a reasonable response for protecting personal worth, this same argument can be reversed to explain why the Chinese, given the relative durability of their traditional social and political profile, have not been under the same compulsion to develop a scheme of individual rights.

However, allowing that historical forces at work on culture have conspired to reinforce an existing conception of discrete individuality is considerably short of admitting that such a concept leapt wholly formed as a determined, necessary, and logical response to objective historical conditions. It is likewise less than self-evident that the forces of modernization must in all cases entail the rise of individualism and the disintegration of the community-centered order.[59]

The concept of the natural human condition that has held sway in the Chinese tradition is radically different, and in many ways anathema to individualistic notions in terms of which Western doctrines of human rights have often been framed. The classical formulation of human nature, *renxing* 人性, elaborated throughout the subsequent Chinese tradition, belongs to Mencius. For Mencius, strictly speaking, a human is not a sort of being, but a kind of doing, an achievement. The concept, *xing* 性, generally translated as "nature," is derived from and is a refinement on *sheng* 生 meaning the whole process of birth, growth, and the ultimate demise of a living creature. In the human context, it perhaps comes closer to the creative act of constituting "character," "personality" or even "constitution" than what we generally understand by "nature."[60] This human "nature" is to be distinguished from some innate physiological or psychological structure. In fact, the most commonly cited classical passage on human nature states:

> One's natural defining conditions (*tianming* 天命) are what is meant by "nature" (*xing* 性).[61]

That is, one's *xing* is one's life in the world, one's *tianming*. This particular passage has often been conceptualized with strong Western assumptions, understanding *xing* as an innate potential. Donald Munro, having translated this passage in precisely these terms, concludes:

> This means that a person's nature being so decreed, cannot be altered through human action; it is a "given" that exists from birth.[62]

Tang Junyi, however, has more appropriately understood *tianming* to be the relationship that obtains between *tian* and the human being, emphasizing the mutuality of the relationship and rejecting explicitly the very Western notion of irrevocable Fate or Destiny.[63]

Mencius suggests that the human being emerges in the world as a spontaneously arising and ever changing matrix of relationships through which, over a lifetime, one defines one's nature and character. At birth, this relationality is described as only faint "beginnings" (siduan 四端), tying one into the world in the same way as one's physical form.[64] This incipient relationality is defined in terms of interpersonal bonds (ren 仁), meaning and value disclosing bonds (yi 義), societal bonds expressed through the performance of roles and relationships that entail both deference and obligation—(li 禮), and intellectual and moral bonds (zhi 知), all of which are open to cultivation. Importantly, these bonds are more an ongoing process of deepening one's social relationships than the conditions that define one's initial dispositions. An infant in this tradition is thus not born in any sense an "individual." In fact, to call a person an "individual" would be to abstract one from the value invested network of particular familiar and cultural conditions and the immediate cognitive and practical relationships that define one and make growth possible.

This initial disposition is "good" in the sense that these bonds are elicited responses to the already formed dispositions of family and community. Consider the love focused upon and responded to by the new born infant. These bonds are then nurturable with varying degrees of deftness and style (shan 善).[65] Just as "rightness" (yi) as a norm emerges out of deference to personal achievements of appropriateness in ritually constituted relationships, so "goodness" (shan) as a description of character derives from deference to perceived facility in the cultivation and coordination of these same defining relationships. In both cases, they are fundamentally an aesthetic and derivatively a moral achievement. Nurturing these primordial ties sustains one as a human being and elevates one above the animal world.[66]

Given this dynamic conception of human "nature," Mencius is not moved to establish a distinction between nature as the actual process of being a human being, and nature as some superordinated capacity or faculty or set of categories that underlies and determines the process of becoming.[67] One means of understanding this relational conception of human nature and character (xing) is to reflect on the shared implications between it and its cognate, xing 姓, one's "family clan or name." Like xing, one's family name is a generalization shared by an historical group of people that both defines them and is defined by them. It signifies a set of conditions suggesting both a shared culture and the opportunity for cultivation in particular ways by each member. It produces a context within which to "make a name for oneself" by distinguishing one's personal name (*ming* 名) and adding to the distinction of one's family. Neither one's family name nor one's *xing* is an essential or innate faculty; both are a focus of historical relationships that one participates in and that becomes a repository for one's achievements over a lifetime. Where one might associate name with certain physiological similarities, these are surely less significant than the shared values that family members contribute to the sociopolitical order.

The fact that the Chinese tradition has been largely persuaded by the Mencian-based definition of human "nature" described above rather than by any theoretically fortified notion of discrete individuality has profound implications for the way in which the soil of China has responded to the human rights transplant.

First, there is no philosophical basis that will justify "self" as a locus of interests independent of and prior to society. Under the sway of a relational understanding of human nature, the mutuality of personal, societal, and political realization has been generally assumed.[68] Much if not most of the commentary available on Chinese attitudes to human rights has interpreted this fundamental presupposition as a kind of self-abnegation or "selflessness" that, in a very modern and subtle way, echoes Hegel's interpretation of Chinese culture discussed in part I above in which the Chinese are externally animated, and hence devoid of moral sensibilities.[69]

In China, political directives appear to take the form of broad and abstract slogans promulgated in the public institutions and the press. What is not apparent is the degree to which such directives require interpretation and application as they ramify back down through society. Communication and consensus is, in fact, arrived at by a much less abstract mechanism than would be characteristic of a society constituted of strictly autonomous individuals. This is true in a large measure because the Chinese conception of humanness does not presuppose any notion of a moral order transcending the consensual order that could justify either demagogic appeals or appeals to individual conscience, and that might disrupt the consensus. Said another way, supreme personalities in the Chinese tradition, for better and for worse, are a public responsibility.

In the Chinese tradition, morality is a cultural product that derives from the ethos or character of the society and is embodied in its ritual patterns of conduct, and human rights to have any meaning must be regarded as a kind of social practice. In place of a metaphysics of morals guaranteeing a concept of natural rights, there is in China a marketplace of morals where what is natural is open to negotiation. Given that order is defined from the bottom up, and concrete conditions temper generalizations to yield varying degrees of appropriateness, the notion of universalizability is problematic. In fact, the Chinese have approached doctrines of "universals" with the caution of a culture fundamentally reluctant to leave the security of immediate historical experience for the more tentative reaches of transcendent principles. And even when this language does seem to appear in the more contemporary Chinese literature through the influence of translation, one must always ask the question: What does the Chinese author or reader understand by these locutions? It is philosophically telling that the Chinese-English dictionary will define *pubian* 普遍 not only as "universal," but also as general, widespread, pervasive, and common.

Evidence for the absence of universals is everywhere in the culture: a euhemeristic mythology that evolves out of concrete historical events;[70] a concept of divinity as a direct extension of the spirituality of particular human beings; a concept of "reason" emerging out of and defended by appeal to concrete historical instances of reasonableness; a concept of morality articulated through analogy with particular historical exemplars;[71] a conception of knowledge inseparably bound to practical efficacy;[72] a self-originating cultural identity that is inward looking to the point of being xenophobic;[73] and so on.

A final most important illustration of this Chinese reluctance to universalize is a difficulty in accommodating the notion of equality as we understand it. It is our concept of "individual" as the social unit that permits our quantitative sense of equality. Equality thus understood tends to make qualitative assessments suspect if not even abhorrent, leading as they will to egoism, sexism, nationalism, racism, and so on. It is against an *essential* equality that we allow that people have *accidental* differences in rank, dignity, power, ability and excellence.

The Chinese conception of person as a specific matrix of roles will not tolerate any assertion of natural equality. The Chinese view is well reflected in the words of John Dewey, himself a strong critic of natural rights and strict equality:

> Equality does not signify that kind of mathematical or physical equivalence in virtue of which any one element may be substituted for another. It denotes effective regard for whatever is unique and distinctive in each.... [Equality] is not a natural possession, but is the fruit of the community when its action is directed by its character as a community.[74]

Although persons stand in irrevocably hierarchical relationships that reflect fundamental differences among them, ritual practice serves the notion of qualitative parity in several ways.

First, the dynamic nature of roles means that privileges and duties within one's community tend to even up across a lifetime. One's duties as a child are balanced by one's privileges as a parent. Thus one's field of relationships over time produce a degree of parity. Secondly, the notion of equality, like identity, is equivocal in that it can be used to mean sameness between two or more things, or when applied to one thing, can mean forbearance on the part of other things to allow it to be itself and not something else. The first sense of equality proceeds from empathy with perceptible sameness; the second from tolerance and enjoyment of perceptible difference. There is an important sense of parity in the assertion that all things are different, and yet are equal in that they ought to be allowed to realize their own premises. This sense of parity is not entirely altruistic; in fact, it is decidedly self-serving in that diverse elements in one's environment contribute to one's own creative possibilities. Ritual-based order seeks to guarantee tolerance, for it is the basic nature of harmony, the aspiration of ritual practice, that it is enhanced by a coordinated diversity among its elements.[75]

Given this long-standing preference for the substantive over the abstract and the immediate over the generalized, there is an inbuilt resistance to what must be perceived as the vagaries of the universal human rights rhetoric.

A typical Associated Press report under the headline "Human Rights Gaining Ground," tells the world:

> The human rights situation improved in both China and Taiwan in the past year, the United States Government said on Thursday, but it continued to rate both countries as autocratic and totalitarian.[76]

There is a strong element of this same attitude in the encouragement that our academics extend to the Chinese world. In the conclusion to his analysis of the human rights situation in China, Andrew Nathan also suggests that the Chinese have a long way to go in order to be like us:

> The Chinese intellectual tradition contains many of the building blocks of a more liberal, pluralistic theory of rights, and the new opening to the West has made many of the resources of foreign intellectual traditions available for fresh consideration.... But this essay suggests the burden of the past which any major change in the character of the Chinese rights system will have to overcome.... For individual political rights to gain a different kind of footing in China would require changes far beyond the legal codification and regulation of the same rights philosophy that has been dominant for nearly a century.[77]

Critics are wont to balance our judgment on the Chinese situation against the succession of campaigns in China to forestall "bourgeois liberal" influences. Our proposals, however, are directed toward sustaining the direction and the momentum of *their own* social and economic development, while our encouragements to embrace individual human rights is a further effort to reform *their* society.

With the surge in Chinese publications, official and otherwise, on the topic of human rights following the 1993 Bangkok Declaration, it seems clear enough that the Chinese are taking Western ideas seriously. What is not clear at all is that the reverse is true. In the final paragraphs of this chapter, then, we want to leave the Chinese to their own devices, and return to our conception of human rights to see if it cannot be strengthened in some way by an appeal to the Chinese model.

It is not necessary to rehearse the many benefits that we derive from our commitment to human rights. In our world today, these benefits are as obvious as they are important. We want rather to focus on certain of the weaknesses of rights theory.

The Confucian model of communal order brings into question certain uncritical assumptions that drive liberal democracy. A first, theoretical, issue has to do with a basic dissatisfaction we might have with the definition of individual that grounds much rights theory. Henry Rosemont Jr. has said it well:

Contemporary moral philosophy, the Confucian texts suggest, is no longer grounded in the real hopes, fears, joys, sorrows, ideas and attitudes of flesh and blood human beings. Since the time of Descartes, Western philosophy—not alone moral philosophy—has increasingly abstracted a purely cognizing activity away from persons and determined that this use of logical reasoning in a disembodied "mind" is the choosing, autonomous essence of individuals, which is philosophically more foundational than are actual persons; the latter being only contingently who they are, and therefore of no great philosophical significance.[78]

There is much in the substantive and relational definition of human being found in the Confucian tradition that might be a resource for rethinking our notion of "autonomous individuality." This is especially so with respect to the manner that notion effectively renders context a means to individual ends. An obvious weakness here is the priority of individual freedoms and privileges to communal and environmental duties. Taken to the extreme, it becomes the tyranny of the shameless individual, consuming precisely those communal resources that are necessary for the promotion of strong families, robust communities, and adequate education, while in exchange, inflicting unrelenting violence upon those who protect him, and the environment that provides him shelter and sustenance.

Corollary to a more contextual definition of persons would be to reflect on the often advertised negative consequences on discrete individuality, and ride herd on the possible abuses of an institutionalized egoism. In this regard, R. J. Vincent describes at least two important examples of these abuses:

> Just as nationalism tends to make states reluctant to give an inch of their fatherland, rights tend to make individuals insistent on all that is their due. They become righteous.... The second caution is against the self-righteousness of rights. This is the tendency to call *our* rights natural rights or human rights which others should also benefit from or conform to, when they have their own pattern of preferences in this regard (and no doubt their own tendency to universalize them).[79]

Individual autonomy does not necessarily conduce to human dignity. In fact, if dignity is felt worth, and if worth or value is a function of engagement with the diverse elements of one's community, the exaggeration of individuality might easily be seen as antithetical to the protection and fostering of human dignity. The Chinese concept of person might be useful in reflecting on and establishing a distinction between individual autonomy and self-fulfillment.

In this same vein, given our history as the descendants of dissidents, the inordinate emotive importance that we are inclined to focus on human rights might require a better sense of proportion. The celebration of human rights as a means of realizing human dignity is, of course, grossly overstated. To use human rights as a measure for the quality of life possible within community is like using minimum health standards as universal index for the quality of restaurants. While one would not want to sit down to dinner in the absence of these standards, they hardly guarantee a quality repast. Human rights as law is ultimately a minimum standard, a last resort, the invocation of which signals a gross failure in the community.

On the relationship between human rights and law, R. Randle Edwards observes that:

> respect for individual rights is closely associated with formal legality. While laws can exist without respect for rights, rights cannot long exist without laws.[80]

On the contrary, the Confucian alternative would suggest that almost all of the actual rights and duties that the sociopolitical order promotes are sustained by extralegal institutions and practices, and are enforced by social pressures rather than punishments. Japan is a good example of a Confucian country in which a high regard for human rights has been achieved in its majority population without significant recourse to the courts. In fact, reliance upon the application of law, far from being a means of realizing human dignity, is fundamentally dehumanizing, impoverishing as it does, the possibilities of mutual accommodation, and comprising our *particular* responsibility to define what would be appropriate conduct.

The introduction of obligation—the "power" mode of relatedness— has the effect of mediating and thus constricting the creative possibilities of the elements constituting a relationship. The emphasis on ritual, by contrast, is an effort toward the optimization of these possibilities. A careful and sympathetic look at the Chinese model might suggest alternative nonlegal mechanisms for resolving conflicts, and temper the readiness of the individual to pursue legal measures by providing reasonable alternatives. Movement away from formal procedures might also be a movement toward a greater practicability.

Another issue to be considered would be how to bring rights theory into a more general perspective. The basically Marxian criticism that rights select out only particular, primarily political aspects of human existence for special protection would be blunted by a more broadly cultural definition that recognizes the immediate and inseparable relationship between cultural conditions and the variable content of abstractly defined human rights. The fact is, the conceptual content of a given right, regardless of universal claims, is constantly being redefined by factors that intrude upon it, including every manner of social and political pressure. This realization might serve as a basis for tying the variable definition of human rights to the project of our own cultural refinement and to the realities of cultural differences.

Just as China's resort to the Western model is enabling it to establish more formal and clearly defined guidelines for its changing sociopolitical order, our recourse to the Chinese model might stimulate a clearer recognition of the ritual basis of human rights. It might provide us with a greater tolerance for cultural diversity and promote the capacity not only to recognize our own parochialisms, but to cherish them as the actual substance of our human rights.[81]

Notes

PROLOGUE

1. MacIntyre (1991):105.
2. MacIntyre (1991):105.
3. As MacIntyre (1991: 106) himself observes: "Confucius, it seems generally to be agreed, had a relatively small place for explicit theorizing within the moral life itself. And the end internal to that life, conceived in Confucian terms, is simply to live in an excellent way."
4. MacIntyre (1991):116.
5. MacIntyre (1991):115.
6. MacIntyre (1991):115.
7. Lloyd (1996):425–427.
8. Lloyd (1996):426.

1. PROBLEMATIC OF SELF IN WESTERN THOUGHT

1. For a discussion of the characteristic vagueness of philosophical notions, see Hall and Ames (1995):chapter 2, passim.
2. See Adkins (1970), Snell (1960), and Dodds (1951). These works testify to the gradual development of consciousness as the basis for an integral selfhood.
3. For an elaboration of the term "historical vagueness," see Hall (1994):103–108.
4. See Hall and Ames (1995).
5. Indeed Plato's *Theatetus* is the *locus classicus* for this development. The definition of knowledge as "true belief plus dialectical support"

depends upon the notion that essential definitions are necessary in order to secure the terms employed in argumentation.

6. See Hall (1973):23–29, Hall (1982b):chapter 3, and Hall and Ames (1995):93–99 for elaborations of these models.

7. Lactantius, *Inst. div.* vii.7.9 (DK 68 A 139).

8. For the general narrative that serves as the context for this sort of account, see Hall and Ames (1995), especially pp. 91–109.

9. For an elaboration of this narrative, see Hall and Ames (1995):75–90.

10. Charles Kahn (1988), Albrecht Dihle (1982), and Alasdair MacIntyre (1988), to name a few. The story of the development of the notion of 'will' is, of course, quite complex. See Kahn's discussion of the contributions of the Stoics to this enterprise.

11. See Blumenberg (1983) and Hall (1994):25–28;33–37 for discussions of the importance of the notion of self-assertion as a means of understanding the modern age.

12. See Jürgen Habermas (1987) and David Kolb (1987) for examples of this sort of analysis. See Hall (1994):chapter 1, for an elaboration of this account.

13. See Hall and Ames (1995):106–109 and 112–133 for a discussion of first problematic thinking.

14. See Donald Davidson (1982).

15. Hume (1960):415.

16. "Freud and Moral Reflection" in Rorty (1991b):147.

17. Rorty (1991b):147.

18. See Rawls (1971) and Rawls (1996).

19. Lucretius (1946): Book Four 1108–1110, 219–220.

20. See *The Symposium* 190e–193 in Plato (1978). This myth is discussed in slightly greater detail in part III below. See pp. 255–257.

2. FOCUS-FIELD SELF IN CLASSICAL CONFUCIANISM

1. Donald J. Munro (1979):40.

2. See R. Randle Edwards (1986):44. This position is widely held. Compare in the same volume Louis Henkin, "The Human Rights Idea in Contemporary China: A Comparative Perspective," p. 39 and Andrew J. Nathan, "Sources of Chinese Rights Thinking," pp. 141–147.

3. This is, of course, the language of George Herbert Mead. For the limitations of such language for the interpretation of Chinese notions of selfhood, see pp. 41–43 below.

4. Mark Elvin (1985):170.

5. This passage occurs in *Zuozhuan* Zhao 12 (Legge, p. 641) where Confucius says, "There is an ancient record which states, 'Self-discipline and practicing the rites will make you *ren* 仁'." The context is a king who comes to a bad end because he has no *zike* 自克 "self-control." Waley notes that *ke* can also mean "able," but the *Zuozhuan* passage is rather clear evidence for rendering this term "self-discipline."

6. *Analects* 12.1.

7. Graham (1990b):288–289 takes Ames to task for relying upon "relation" language. Graham observes: "As for 'relationships', relation is no doubt an indispensable concept in *exposition* of Chinese thought, which generally impresses a Westerner as more concerned with the relations between things than with their qualities; but the concern is with concrete patterns rather than relations abstracted from them, as Ames knows well." An entirely appropriate caution.

8. See Whitehead (1933).

9. See Victor H. Li (1978), especially chapter 4.

10. See Wm. Theodore de Bary (1985):332.

11. G. W. F. Hegel (1956):138.

12. Jacques Gernet (1985):147.

13. Michael LaFargue (1994), esp. 97–98, often translates *xin* as "feelings," particularly when translating the *Mencius*.

14. This is an irony in Charles Moore's *The Chinese Mind: Essentials of Chinese Philosophy and Culture* (1967) and more recently, Robert Allison's *Understanding the Chinese Mind* (1989), wherein most of their authors contradict the titles of these two collections by insisting upon the inseparability of "heart-mind."

15. See A. S. Cua (1985) for an excellent analysis of the dominant Chinese understanding of "type" and "category."

16. It is certainly true that many treatments of "body" in contemporary philosophy are pursued with the explicit intention of overcoming the mind-body dualism. This is true of both the phenomenological accounts of Merleau-Ponty, and others following his lead, as well as the social psychological accounts associated with John Dewey and George Herbert Mead. As we shall note below, Mead provides us with a

suggestive set of reflections for the development of a comparative treatment of self in the Chinese tradition.

For a careful employment of Mead's understanding of the social self
applied to Japanese Zen thinkers, see Steve Odin (1994). And for an explicit discussion of "body" in the classical Chinese tradition, see Thomas
P. Kasulis et al. (1993).

17. For a detailed discussion of this vocabulary and its use, see John
Hay (1993).

18. *Analects* 3.3.

19. We discuss in some detail the interpretative dangers entailed in
applying the organic model to Chinese understandings in general, in Hall
and Ames (1995):269–274.

20. Joseph Needham (1956).

21. See Schwartz (1985).

22. Needham (1978):248.

23. Needham (1956):302. Italics added.

24. Needham (1956):337.

25. Hall and Ames (1995):269–271.

26. This is particularly odd given the fact that Needham was himself
trained as a biologist.

27. Schwartz (1985):373.

28. See Munro (1985b):passim, and Schwartz, (1985):200, 416–418.
For our discussion of "genealogical cosmogony," see Hall and Ames
(1995):185–192.

29. See Hall and Ames (1994):85–88.

30. As we have suggested, the concept of "will" is a late arrival in the
West. Until the period of discussions of *voluntas* by Augustine and others,
one can find little evidence that such a concept as "will" is viably present.
See Alasdair MacIntyre (1988).

31. See Hall and Ames (1995):273–275 for a discussion of the
relationship of *ars contextualis* to the focus-field conception of order.

32. See Hall and Ames (1987):283–296 for a consideration of the
notion of *shu* as "deference" in the Confucian *Analects*.

33. See *Analects* 2.1 and 15.5.

34. Mead (1934):175–178.

35. Mead (1934):144.

36. Mead (1934):223n.

37. Mead (1934):144n.

3. FOCUS-FIELD SELF IN CLASSICAL DAOSIM

1. Those interested in the complex textual problems associated with the *Zhuangzi*, should consult Graham's "How much of *Chuang-tzu* did Chuang-tzu write?" in Graham (1990a); Graham (1982), *Chuang-tzu: Textual Notes to a Partial Translation*; and Harold D. Roth's "Who Compiled the *Chuang Tzu?*" in Rosemont (1991).

2. See the discussion of "correlative cosmologies" in Hall and Ames (1995):256–268.

3. Augustine (1949):VIII.158.

4. For an interpretation of Freud that avoids this sort of conflictual dynamic, see Donald Davidson's "Paradoxes of Irrationality" (1982), Richard Rorty's "Freud and Moral Reflection" (1991b), and the brief discussion of this interpretation above pp. 16–17.

5. See Hall and Ames (1995):85–88.

6. *Zhuangzi* 33.13.2; cf. Graham (1981):259.

7. See Hall and Ames (1995):183–197.

8. Cf. *Zhuangzi* 21.7.33 and 60.22.77.

9. *Huainanzi* 6.51.15. The translation is from a draft by Lau and Ames (unpublished).

10. *Huainanzi* 2.16.9. The translation is from a draft by Lau and Ames (unpublished). Cf. *Zhuangzi* 17.6.42 and 21.7.32.

11. *Zhuangzi* 15.6.1; cf. Graham (1982):84.

12. *Daodejing* 37.

13. *Daodejing* 17.

14. *Daodejing* 57.

15. *Daodejing* 3. We follow the Mawangdui text for the last line.

16. Thus, with some qualifications, we agree with Angus Graham (1989):194 in his claim that Zhuangzi "accepts without question that we have to take the world as it is, [and] denies only that analytic reason can show us how it is."

But Graham's further claim that Zhuangzi is a *naive* realist is perhaps misleading. The modes of discrimination employed by so-called "analytic reason" are built into many of our most naive responses to the world. Daoism says "lest you become as a little child" you shall in no wise achieve sagedom. The realization of such naiveté, and of seeing the world as it is, seems as formidable as that of, say, the Platonist who achieves true vision only by rigorous ascent to the Good permitted by a mastery of the dialectic. Characteristically, Daoist sages are appropriately naive only at the end, not at the beginning of their discipline and practice.

17. *Zhuangzi* 6.2.69; cf. Graham (1981):58.
18. *Zhuangzi* 4.2.31; cf. Graham (1981):52–53.
19. *Zhuangzi* 3.2.1; cf. Graham (1981):48.
20. *Zhuangzi* 3.2.8; cf. Graham (1981):49.
21. *Daodejing* 1.
22. See Hall (1982b):229–291.
23. See Graham (1990a):322–359.
24. *Zhuangzi* 45.17.87; cf. Graham (1981):123.
25. *Zhuangzi* 15.6.4; cf. Graham (1981):84.
26. *Zhuangzi* 19.6.89; cf. Graham (1981):92.
27. *Daodejing* 79.
28. *Zhuangzi* 7.3.2; cf. Graham (1981):63–64.
29. *Zhuangzi* 50.19.54; cf. Graham (1981):135.
30. See Rump (1979):17.
31. *Zhuangzi* 21.7.33; cf. Graham (1981):98–99.
32. The missionary sinologist, James Legge (1962):266–267, in a note to his translation of this passage, observes:

The little allegory is ingenious and amusing.... [I]t is in harmony with the Taoistic opposition to the use of knowledge in government. One critic says that an "alas!" might well follow the concluding "died." But surely it was better that Chaos should give place to another state. "Heedless" and "Sudden" did not do a bad work.

33. Graham (1982):20–22.
34. See the discussion of Daoist uses of correlative thinking in Hall and Ames (1995):225–237.
35. This is a possible translation of the title of the first chapter of the *Zhuangzi*.
36. The term is, of course, Matthew Arnold's.
37. Lenk (1987).
38. *Chou I* [*Yijing*] (1978):41.*xisheng*.5.
39. *Zhuangzi* 6.2.67; cf. Graham (1981):58.
40. *Zhuangzi* 17.6.53. Cf. Graham (1981):88.
41. Goethe, Wolfgang *Faust* Part I:1699–1700.
42. *Ibid*:1686–87.
43. Brooks (1975):209.

44. Whitehead (1978):338.

45. One may recall Socrates, at the end of the *Symposium*, arguing that the tragic poet should be capable of writing comedy as well. This claim is a consequence of the ironic Socrates' belief that comedy and tragedy are but masks of irony. The comic and tragic senses are superficial façades. Only irony allows us to see clearly.

4. CHINESE SEXISM

1. Dupre (1993):14.

2. See Hall (1982b) for a discussion of the reshaping of sex and gender identities by recourse to technological processes.

3. Black (1989):184.

4. Black (1989):184–185.

5. Adapted from Aristotle, *Metaphysics* 986a22–986b2. See Aristotle (1984):1559–1560.

6. See Gilligan (1982).

7. See Flax (1989):*passim.*

8. Grimshaw (1986):59; see also Grimshaw (1992).

9. Grimshaw (1986):203.

10. *Analects* 6.30.

11. An intelligent discussion of the role of this dualism in shaping the sexual symbolism associated with the Western tradition is Lloyd (1993).

12. See, for example, Flax (1989).

13. See, for example, Gilligan (1982).

14. Grimshaw (1992):228–229.

15. Not all poststructuralist thinking converges with feminist concerns. See the reservations with respect to certain aspects of post-modern thought in Tatyana Klemenkova (1992). An important conversation has been initiated by the pragmatist, Richard Rorty. In his "Feminism and Pragmatism" (Rorty [1991a]:231–258), Rorty provides an analysis of the manner in which pragmatism might serve as a resource for contemporary feminism. Rorty notes that if, as many feminists argue, language itself is largely a male product, some sort of intervention may be essential. Such intervention might take the form of a self-imposed exile of representative numbers of women from present social institutions, allowing, over some generations, for the production a more empowering language. Reading his essay, one can't avoid the suspicion that Rorty

might be offering this "solution" as a hyperbolic response to what he conceives to be extreme claims on the part of some feminists. We, however, think the proposal to be perfectly sound—even if difficult to imagine being implemented.

16. *Analects* 17.25.

17. Lu Xun (1981):117.

18. Female (*nü* 女) is distinguished from male (*nan* 男), but *nan* is not used to classify characters that identify specifically "male" gender traits. Rather the contrast is between "female" (*nü*) and "person" (*ren* 人), defining human traits. The fact that such a parallel exercise in the Chinese language cannot be carried out with respect to "male" supports our claim that the gender prejudice in the Chinese tradition has been that woman has not been allowed to be person. This observation is a response to a question posed by one of the SUNY Press readers of our manuscript, Lisa Raphals, to whom we are grateful. We cannot, however, hold her responsible for our answer.

19. We are using the "monoandrogynism-polyandrogynism" distinction of Joyce Trebilcot (1982).

20. For an earlier version of this argument, see Ames (1981).

21. Needham (1956):33. Other scholars who make this same association between feminine gender traits and the Daoist ideal are the following: Chan (1963):13; Kaltenmark (1969):58ff.; Waley (1958):57; E. M. Chen (1969):402–404.

22. Needham (1956):105.

23. See Needham (1956):59.

24. Needham (1956):57.

25. Needham uses the words "feminine" and "female" interchangeably in his discussion of Daoism. This is understandable, perhaps, given the absence of a female/feminine distinction in the classical Chinese language. We follow the convention here in distinguishing between biological sex (male/female) and psychosocial gender (masculine/feminine). Were we to enforce this distinction, "feminine" would be more appropriate in Needham's discussion.

26. Needham (1956):61.

27. Needham (1956):59.

28. The familiar alternative to this "feminine" interpretation of Daoism is the Creel (1970a) inversion of "feminine" and "masculine." These seemingly "feminine" qualities are simply a purposive device for effectively maintaining political control. "Not contending," for example, is the best way to contend. This basically *Hanfei* understanding of the

Daodejing reduces the text to a political stratagem whereby an ambitious and aggressive ruler can impose his will on his people, keep them ignorant, and manipulate them to his own ends.

29. Needham (1956):34.

30. *Daodejing* 25.

31. *Daodejing* 22. This translation is based on the Mawangdui text. The received *Daodejing* has: "Thus the sage embraces continuity to be the model of the world."

32. *Daodejing* 41.

33. *Daodejing* 28.

34. *Daodejing* 52.

35. *Daodejing* 42.

36. *Daodejing* 22, 28.

37. *Daodejing* 57.

38. Soon after Mao Zedong's assumption of power in China, he proclaimed the equality of the sexes. By all accounts some real changes did take place, and rather quickly. The gains in sexual parity have since been eroded under the weight of the persistent Confucian tradition.

39. See Ames (1990).

40. See the description of the relationship between the neo-Confucian Li Yong and his mother in which the mother on the death of the father becomes "father" to Li Yong in Anne Birdwhistell (1992).

41. Guisso (1981):59.

42. Guisso (1981):50.

43. Guisso (1981):59.

44. Guisso (1981):60.

45. *Analects* 9.23. See also 14.43 and 17.26.

46. Grimshaw (1992):227.

5. EXCURSUS ON METHOD

1. See for example Chad Hansen (1983) and (1985b). We have a brief discussion of this issue in Hall and Ames (1987):261–264, and a somewhat longer reflection in Hall and Ames (1991).

2. Graham (1989):3.

3. Chang Tung-sun (1939):180.

4. Of course, the same is true intraculturally: There are sufficient differences between the attitudes toward, and characterizations and uses

of, the term "truth" among Anglo-European philosophers as to signal that different terms ought be used. Part of the tension between the realist and some pragmatist understandings of truth is due to the fact that they are really talking about altogether different things.

5. See Hall and Ames (1995):155–158.

6. Pedersen (1959):339.

7. Ibid.

8. See Hall and Ames (1995):chapter 1, especially pp. 3–12.

9. Wender (1973):26.

10. Robinson (1968):108–109. Sextus Empiricus, *Adv. math.* vii.3, and Simplicius, *De caelo* 557.25 (DK 28 B 1).

11. For an elaboration of the paradoxes and their effects upon subsequent thought in the Western classical tradition, see Hall and Ames (1995):25–33, 37–38, 45–46.

12. By tradition, Xenophanes was believed to be Parmenides' teacher.

13. Robinson (1986):56; Strobaeus, *Ecl. phys.* i.8.2 (DK 21 B 18).

14. See the account of the victory of second-problematic thinking in Hall and Ames (1995):111–119.

15. See Hall and Ames (1987) and Hall and Ames (1995) passim.

16. For a discussion of *ars contextualis*, see Hall (1987) and (1994), and Hall and Ames (1987).

17. Graham (1989):394.

18. Sometimes it seems that Angus Graham believed in a "Grammar Heaven," where nouns, verbs, and adjectives flit and flutter in untarnished glory. It is his excessive (we believe) faith in morphology that leads him to import structuralist assumptions into his interpretation of correlative thinking. For our criticism of Graham on this issue, see Hall and Ames (1995):125–133. In a letter to Graham shortly before his death we addressed our concerns in this way: "Perhaps the only Western invention that is not easily exportable to China is Chinese grammar."

19. Graham (1989):395.

20. Graham (1989):395.

21. Graham (1989):395–396.

22. Graham (1989):396.

23. Graham(1989):394–95.

24. Graham(1989):394.

25. Graham (1989:155.

26. Hall and Ames (1987):364.

27. See Hall and Ames (1995):202–211.

28. Graham (1989):398.

29. Hall and Ames (1987):364n30.
30. See Bloom (1981).
31. Graham (1989):398.
32. Hall and Ames (1987):267.
33. Hall and Ames (1987):267.
34. Graham (1989):398.
35. Graham (1989):398.
36. See Graham (1989):30, 331–332 and Graham (1990b):287.
37. Graham (1989):410.

6. CULTURAL REQUISITIES FOR A THEORY OF TRUTH

1. For this discussion, see chapter 1 of Whitehead (1978), "Speculative Philosophy."

2. As we shall see later on, the so-called pragmatic theory of truth presumes to get along quite well without the notion of a single worldorder, as is well-expressed in the title of William James (1977), *A Pluralistic Universe*. And see Richard Rorty (1982): "The World Well Lost."

3. See Hall and Ames (1995):242–244; 268–278.

4. See Hall and Ames (1987):131–138 and (1995):116–119 for a discussion of the distinction between aesthetic and logical order and of the relevance of this distinction to the Chinese understanding of "World." See (1987):195–249, and part III below for a discussion of the senses of *tian, dao,* and *de*.

5. See Hall and Ames (1995):chapter 1, passim.

6. See Hall and Ames (1995):25-32.

7. See Hall and Ames (1995):chapter 1, passim.

8. For a discussion of Xunzi's understanding of argumentation, see Cua (1985):5–8, 43–87. See also Hall and Ames (1995):202–211.

9. This is an important point. In the twentieth century, the Mohist *Canons* and *Names and Objects* have been rehabilitated in order to aid in the attempts to translate the spirit of Western philosophical works into Chinese. The distinctly nonessentialist form that Mohist logic took in its original form militates against its straightforward use to translate Western texts.

Further, the (at present) limited *ability* to translate Western ontologies into Chinese language is an issue distinct from the *desirability* of employing exotic philosophies in a reconstruction of the Chinese sensibility. One thing is clear: The metaphysical colonization of China is no less suspect than its political, commercial, and technological counterparts.

10. See Graham (1989):155.

11. Mao Zedong (1951):287.

12. See Graham (1989):410 for his discussion of the philosophical implications of classical Chinese operating without the copular verb.

13. See *Hanfeizi* 36.4.20.

14. See Hall and Ames (1995):40–46, 62–65, 123–133.

15. See Hall and Ames (1987):298–312.

16. For a more protracted consideration of the meaning of "image" in the Chinese context, see Hall and Ames (1995):211–225.

17. Graham (1989):227–228.

18. Graham (1989):227.

19. Graham (1989):228.

20. Chang Tung-sun (1939):172.

21. See Derrida (1982).

22. See Rorty (1979).

23. Charles S. Peirce, John Dewey, and William James are responsible for the first two transitions. And each took part in the movement away from "mind" to the more naturalistic notion of "experience." The shift from experience to language is the work of later pragmatists such as W. V. O. Quine, Wilfrid Sellars, Paul Goodman, Hilary Putnam, Donald Davidson, and Richard Rorty.

7. A PRAGMATIC UNDERSTANDING OF THE WAY

1. Hall and Ames (1995):211–278.

2. See our discussions of models in Hall and Ames (1987):176–182.

3. In reflecting on the functional analog to the representational notion of truth dominant in Western philosophy, we have benefited from Eliot Deutsch's work on truth. Deutsch (1979), as is a signature of much of his creative philosophical reflection, reverses the familiar metaphysical and epistemological process of analysis to begin with aesthetic and religious resources, looking to the notion of "truth" as it is at work within these dimensions of the human experience.

4. Norman (1971):24.

5. Hershock (1996):15.

6. Chang Tung-sun (1939):178–179.

7. See Ames (1981), which argues against this characterization.

8. Needham (1956):59–61. See also Dubs (1946):266.

9. Smith (1983):121–123.

10. Yü Ying-shih (1985):176–177. See also our discussion of Schwartz (1985) in part III; he advances a similar distinction.

11. Yü Ying-shih (1985):175.

12. Rubin (1976):94, 96, 103.

13. *Analects* 18.5–8. See *Zhuangzi* 31.12.52; cf. Graham (1981):186. This passage seems to be an extended parody on these *Analects* passages. At least one interpretation of this *Zhuangzi* passage has Confucius as a spokesperson for the Daoist position that, like the *Analects*, also criticizes the recluse for abandoning the world.

14. For example, *Zhuangzi* 39.14.56; cf. Graham (1981):128.

15. *Analects* 15.29.

16. *Zhuangzi* 39.14.77; cf. Graham (1981):133.

17. *Xunzi* 79.21.22.

18. *Zhongyong* (conventionally translated as *Doctrine of the Mean*) 28. See also *Analects* 2.11, 2.15, and 13.4.

19. Hsiao Kung-chuan (1979):98.

20. *Daodejing* 28.

21. Needham (1956):33.

22. Parahomastic definition—namely, the process of defining a term by appeal to a term similar in sound that also possesses some semantic associations—is pervasive in the classical commentaries and glosses. Said another way, the classical Chinese commentators focus their interest on *how* a living term discloses its meaning within its various contexts, rather than assuming that terms have some univocal, essential meaning independent of how they are used.

23. Interestingly, *jun* 君 and *zun* 尊 both have cognates (*qun* 群 and *zun* 傅 respectively) that mean "many together." *Zun* 尊, has a homophonous cognate, *zun* 撙, meaning "to regulate, to have in hand." This is a range of meaning similar to *jun* 君. The *Shuowen* isolates the etymonic elements of 君, suggesting it is a "combined meaning (*huiyi* 會意)" character derived by combining *yin* 尹, "to regulate, to manage, regular," with the graph for "mouth: *kou* 口: the person who "regulates" communicates and commands. The *Xizhuan tonglun* 繫傳通論 commentary on the *Shuowen* states:

> *Jun* 君 means "to regulate, to order," a generic name for leaders.
> It is one who the world can take as its model for uprightness and

order. Where the model is upright, so is the shadow it casts; where it is bent, so is the shadow. His mouth is his means of issuing commands.... The *jun* is the one to whom the crowd below 群下 repairs.

The *yin* 尹 component in *jun* 君 is significant, defined in the *Shuowen* as *zhi* 治 "to bring proper order, to regulate, to govern well," and further, as "one who handles affairs."

24. See for example, Hsiao Kung-chuan (1979):118–119.

25. Hsiao Kung-chuan (1979):119.

26. Creel (1970b):335n62.

27. *Analects* 18.7.

28. *Analects* 8.13.

29. *Analects* 2.21.

30. See D. C. Lau (1983):appendix I. The designation of "uncrowned king" is found in *Huainanzi* 9.80.23; see Ames (1993):205.

31. Lau (1983):xi.

32. Chen Daqi (1964).

33. *Analects* 7.26.

34. *Analects* 6.30; see also 16.8 and 7.34.

35. *Analects* 14.6.

36. *Analects* 7.34.

37. *Analects* 7.33.

38. *Analects* 3.24, 7.31, 9.6, 9.14, and 10.6.

39. *Analects* 6.7.

40. *Analects* 5.3 and 14.5.

41. Beyond these frequently used categories of *shengren, renzhe*, and *junzi*, there are several other alternatives that, because they rarely occur, are more problematic. Confucius has never met a *shengren* (7.26), but allows that his favorite student, Yan Hui, is a *xianren* (6.11). Yan Hui is also described as a *renzhe* (6.7), a characteristic shared in common with the *xianren* of old (7.15). Hence, the *xianren* does not rank with the *shengren*, but is as least as high as the *renzhe*. Although *shanren* on occasion is associated with *shengren* (7.26), this category of personal achievement is described explicitly as being lower (11.19). *Chengren* occurs only once (14.12). The content and qualifications for this category seem to be a function of the times. Apparently standards were higher in the past. And finally, the *daren* also occurs only once as one of three things a *junzi* holds in awe (16.18). This being the case, *daren* is at least higher than *junzi*, and

since Yao, the revered sage-king is described as "*da*", *da* has a direct association with *shengren*.

This translation of qualitative difference into a qualitative ranking seems to have some textual justification, and certainly has a ready consonance with analytical scholarship. But at the very least, it is not illuminating, and at worst, it can be misleading.

First, the *Analects*, insisting that these several categories for personal achievement are intrinsically related, will not accommodate an exclusivity among them:

> In the way (*dao*) of the *junzi*, what is to be conveyed first and what is to be placed last? The way is analogous to the plant world in that it can be differentiated and classified. But how could there be any "error" in the way of the *junzi*? It is just that it is only the sage (*shengren*) who can travel the way from first step to last.

The way of the *junzi* and that of the sage do not differ in content or quality, but in compass. Again, apart from the comprehensiveness of the *shengren* category, the relative ranking of these other distinctions does not seem to hold. For example, although there might be a *junzi* who "on occasion fails to act with *ren*," *ren* is elsewhere clearly described as a defining condition that qualifies the *junzi* as *junzi*:

> Wherein does the *junzi* who abandons *ren* warrant that name? The *junzi* does not leave *ren* even for as long as it takes to eat a meal. In moments of haste and excitement, he sticks to it. In situations of difficulty and confusion, he sticks to it.

Further, and *contra* Chen Daqi, it is not at all clear that *renzhe* is a category of personal achievement higher than *junzi*. For example, in the following passage, *renzhe* and *junzi* are used interchangeably:

> "If the *renzhe* were informed that there was another person in the well, would he jump in after him?" The Master replied, "How so? A *junzi* can be sent on his way, but he cannot be entrapped. You can cheat him, but not confuse him."

Far from being exclusive categories, being *ren* and being *junzi* entail each other:

Zengzi said, "The *junzi* gathers friends through his refinement, and strengthens his *ren* through his friendships."

In fact, we can readily identify a whole list of passage in which *renzhe* and *junzi* are described in strikingly similar terms:

1. ... the *renzhe* is not anxious ... (14.28, 9.29)
    ... the *junzi* is not fearful or anxious ... (12.4)
2. Fanzhi asked about *ren*. The Master replied,
    "It is to love others." (12.22)
    ... the *junzi* in learning the *dao* loves others. (17.3)
3. Only the *renzhe* is able to like others and dislike others. (3.3)
    Zigong asked, "Does the *junzi* have his dislikes?" The Master replied, "He does indeed."
4. The *renzhe* in wanting to establish himself establishes others, in wanting to advance himself advances others. To be able to take the analogy from what is closest to oneself can be called the method of *ren*. (6.30)
    Zilu asked about the *junzi*. The Master replied, "Cultivating himself, he achieves respect.... Cultivating himself, he makes others content and secure.... Cultivating himself, he makes the people content and secure." (14.42)
5. Becoming *ren* is self-initiating—how could it come from others? (12.1)
    The *junzi* seeks for it in himself; the small person seeks for it in others. (13.21)
6. Sima Niu asked about *ren*. The Master replied,
    "The *renzhe* speaks with hesitation." (12.3)
    The *junzi* ... is careful in speaking.... (1.14)
    The *junzi* wants to be slow in speaking.... (4.24)
    When it comes to speaking, the *junzi* takes nothing lightly. (13.3)
    The *junzi* must be careful in speaking. (19.25)
7. Fanzhi asked about *ren*. The Master replied, "In where he abides, he is reverent; in handling affairs, he is respectful; in working with others, he does his best." (13.19)
    Confucius said, "The person who is able to encourage five dispositions in the empire is *ren*: ... reverence, tolerance, integrity, diligence, and generosity." (17.6)

> There are four ways in which he is consonant with the way (*dao*) of the *junzi*: he conducts himself with reverence; he serves his superiors with respect; he nurtures the people with generosity; he employs the people with appropriateness. (5.16)

42. For example *renzhe* and *junzi* can be described in terms of their dispositions and the quality of their deportment. See *Analects* 1.8, 6.7, 16.10, and 19.7.

43. *Mencius* 7B.25.

44. *Analects* 2.14, 4.11, 4.16, 6.13, 7.37, 12.16, 12.19, 13.25, 13.26, 14.23, 15.2, 15.21, 15.34, and 17.4.

45. *Analects* 13.23.

46. *Analects* 7.1.

47. *Analects* 1.14, 2.13, 4.24, 13.3, 14.27, 15.23, 16.1, 16.6, 19.9, and 19/25.

48. *Analects* 1.14.

49. Hall and Ames (1987):56–61.

50. For a more complete discussion of *cheng*, see Tu Wei-ming (1989), especially 76–82. See also Hall and Ames (1987):57–61.

51. *Zhongyong* (conventionally translated as *Doctrine of the Mean*) 25.

52. *Mencius* 4A.12.

53. Although *zhen* occurs once in the *Mozi* (7.6.35), scholars generally date this portion of the *Mozi* as late Zhou, and Sun Yirang (1975) even suggests that it is from the hand of Confucians rather than Mohists. The Lao-Zhuang partnership in originating and popularizing terms is, of course, not confined to *zhen*. The now familiar term, "self-so-ing (*ziran*)," for example, does not appear in any texts anterior to them, except for one occurrence again in a section of *Mozi* (70.42.50) that Lo Genze dates as post-*Zhuangzi* and pre-*Xunzi*. There is no doubt that by the time of Xu Shen (ca. 30–124), the compiler of the *Shuowen*, *zhen* had very strong Daoist connotations.

54. *Zhuangzi* 87.31.32. Cf. Graham (1981):251.

55. *Zhuangzi* 87.31.32. Cf. Graham (1981):251.

56. *Huainanzi* 2.14.21. Unpublished draft translation by D. C. Lau and Roger T. Ames.

57. *Zhuangzi* 19.6.92; cf. Graham (1981):92.

58. *Zhuangzi* 15.6.4; cf. Graham (1981):84. See *Huainanzi* 14.2.4 for an interesting revisioning of this passage.

59. *Zhuangzi* 15.6.4; cf. Graham (1981):84.

60. *Daodejing* 57.

61. *Zhuangzi* 19.7.4; cf. Graham (1981):95.

62. *Zhuangzi* 3.2.3; cf. Graham (1981):48.

63. *Daodejing* 64.

64. *Zhuangzi* 4.2.33; cf. Graham (1981):53.

65. *Daodejing* 54. See also 21 and 57. Another repeated expression that has the same import is "Therefore discarding that he takes this. (*gu qu bi qu ci* 故去彼取此)." See 12, 38 and 72.

66. *Zhuangzi* 4.2.27; cf. Graham (1981):52.

67. *Zhuangzi* 4.2.26; cf. Graham (1981):52.

68. See *Analects* 12.1.

69. *Daodejing* 22.

70. *Zhuangzi* 13.5.31; cf. Graham (1981):79–80.

71. Rubin (1976):98, 115–116.

72. *Zhuangzi* 19.7.2; cf. Graham (1981):94.

73. *Zhuangzi* 15.6.9; cf. Graham (1981):85.

74. *Xunzi* 79.21.22.

75. *Zhuangzi* 44.17.50; cf. Graham (1981):149.

76. *Zhuangzi* 15.6.3; Graham (1981):84.

77. *Zhuangzi* 64.23.72; cf. Graham (1981):106.

78. *Analects* 18.6. It is interesting that the passages that provide a Confucian rejoinder are located in the last five books of the *Analects*, which were probably compiled a full generation after the teachings of Confucius had begun to take root. See D. C. Lau (1983):appendix 3.

79. *Analects* 18.8.

80. *Analects* 4.10.

81. *Analects* 18.7.

82. *Zhuangzi* 31.12.52; cf. Graham (1981):186.

83. Watson (1968):136; see Fukunaga (1966):192–195.

84. Graham (1981):185–187 points out this *Huainanzi* parallel, and translates it accordingly.

85. The work of Graham (1990a) and Roth (1991) is an attempt of sort the composite *Zhuangzi* out thematically into various groupings: primitivist, Yangist, and syncretist documents. This effort is a recognition of the heterogeneity of the text, and the many divided and sometimes conflicting ideas that it expresses.

86. In the earliest form of this character, the mouth is on the left side.

87. Liu Buwei (1977):540. See also Hall and Ames (1987):165–166 for other examples of how *he* has been defined in the classical literature.

88. *Analects* 1.12.

89. This phrase was originally in chapter 63, but we have restored it to this chapter where it makes better sense.

90. *Daodejing* 79.

91. See Whitehead (1978):110–115. See also Neville (1974):10ff. and Grange (1997): 51–60 for useful applications of this vocabulary.

92. Whitehead (1978):4.

8. DECLINE OF TRANSCENDENCE IN THE WEST

1. See *Thinking Through Confucius* passim, where the claim is made that there is no operative sense of transcendence in classical China.

2. Hall and Ames (1987):13.

3. See the attempt of Hartshorne (1964) to develop a coherent doctrine of external relations in his *The Divine Relativity: A Social Conception of God* (1964).

4. The understandings of transcendence of God applied, of course, to Jewish theology as well. The contrast of the "names of God"—for example the ineffable ("transcendent") *Yahweh* and the approachable ("immanent") *Adonai*—is a case in point. See Edmond Jacob (1958).

5. For a discussion of the contrasting interests of the contemporary Chinese and Western scholars in one another's cultures, see Hall (1991) and Ames (1995).

6. Copernicus (1955):438.

7. Kepler (1955):278.

8. Kepler (1955):book five, section 9, proposition xxvi.

9. Newton (1952):541.

10. Newton (1952):542.

11. Newton (1952):542.

12. Calvin (1960):book III, chapter 23, section 2. For a brief discussion of the relation of Calvin's doctrine of God's Will to that of Occam and Scotus, see François Wendel (1963):127–129.

13. John T. McNeill (1960):926.

14. Calvin (1960):book I, chapter xvii, Section 2 (our italics).

15. Weber (1958).

16. *Metaphysics* 1072b.

17. *Metaphysics* 1072b.

18. Harvey Cox (1966).

19. Cox (1966).

20. We certainly do not wish to dismiss Spinoza's most subtle and profound system in such an apparently perfunctory manner. Suffice to say that he has had his dedicated defenders. Still one of the best defenses of Spinoza is Wolfson (1934). For an analysis of Spinoza which resonates with the one we have suggested, see Hartshorne and Reese (1953):189–191, 194–197.

21. See, for example, Mark C. Taylor (1984).

22. Whitehead (1978):346.

23. Whitehead (1978):346–347.

24. Whitehead (1978):348.

25. Whitehead (1978):7.

26. For this distinction, see Hall and Ames (1995) passim.

27. Augustine (1950):book XXII, chapter 29.

28. Jan van Ruysbroek (1951):245.

29. Bernard of Clairvaux (1987):195.

30. John of the Cross (1958):182.

31. Teresa of Avila (1979):89.

32. Teresa of Avila (1979):88–89.

33. Pike (1992).

34. Pike (1992):35.

35. See Stace (1960).

36. See, for example, the preface to John of the Cross (1958) for a discussion of the often willful corruption of John's mystical writings.

37. Pike (1992):212.

38. James (1929):418–419.

39. See Stace (1960):130ff.

40. See Zaehner (1961).

41. See Smart (1965).

42. For fuller discussion of the classification of mystical experiences briefly treated here, see Hall (1982a):242–250 and Hall (1982b):230–240.

43. This word was coined by R. C. Zaehner.

44. Whitehead (1925).

45. See Hall and Ames (1995):3–12.

46. It is not just in physical sciences that one notes the decline of traditional rational appeals. Debates in the biological sciences which challenge the notion of "natural kinds" represent yet another manner in which rationality of science has been threatened. See Dupre (1993).

47. Bentham (1843).

48. Dewey (1927):102.
49. Dewey (1973):151.
50. Sandel (1982), (1996), and Bell (1993).

9. TIAN AND DAO AS NONTRANSCENDENTAL FIELDS

1. Schwartz (1975b):59. The transcendent conception of *tian* and *dao* that we find in this somewhat earlier essay is developed in even stronger terms in Schwartz (1985) *passim*.

2. Schwartz (1975b):59.

3. Ibid.

4. Schwartz (1975b):60–61.

5. Schwartz (1975b):64.

6. Ibid.

7. Schwartz (1975b):65.

8. Mou Zongsan (1963):20.

9. Ibid.

10. We have benefited in our appreciation of Mou Zongsan's contribution to this debate by John Berthrong's (1994) detailed account of it. In describing our own position on transcendence as it is presented in *Thinking Through Confucius*, our only qualification would be to disassociate ourselves from Berthrong's claim that we allow that transcendence becomes part of the picture beyond the classical Chinese tradition in later philosophical speculation—neo-Daoism, Buddhism, neo-Confucianism. We simply suspend judgment on this issue until we have had further time to study the original sources.

11. Berthrong (1994):117. See Ames (1991a) passim, in which he makes a similar case for Tang Junyi's interpretation of *renxing*, conventionally translated as "human nature."

12. Mou Zongsan (1963):21.

13. Berthrong (1994):114. Berthrong is appealing to Hartshorne's version of process theism, which does not make the same metaphysical claims with regard to the primordiality of "creativity." There is no reason, therefore, for him to interpret Mou's rather elaborate and expansive speculations on "unbounded creativity itself" in metaphysical terms. On a Whiteheadian model, however, one might easily proceed to elaborate Mou's claims concerning "creativity" along ontological lines.

14. Li Minghui (1994):148.

15. Ibid.

16. For an elaboration of this way of understanding relationships, which we term *ars contextualis*, the "art of contextualization," see Hall and Ames (1987) and (1995).

17. Li Minghui (1994):142.

18. Li Minghui (1994):143.

19. Li Minghui (1994):144, citing Mou Zongsan (1963):21.

20. Li Minghui (1994):145–146.

21. Mou Zongsan (1963):21.

22. Li Minghui (1994):142.

23. Hall and Ames (1987):13 and passim.

24. Mou Zongsan (1963):94–95.

25. Ryle (1949):149–153.

26. See Hall and Ames (1995):183–197.

27. See Hall and Ames (1987):12.

28. See Lau and Ames (1996) for the military application of this idea.

29. *Yijing* 43.*xishang*.9.

30. *Yijing* 47.*xixia*.4.

31. *Zhuangzi* 45.17.81; cf. Graham (1981):122.

32. Taylor (1990).

33. See Cook and Rosemont for their revised translation of this work: Leibniz (1994).

34. Schwartz (1975a) and (1975b).

35. Bodde (1961).

36. See Graham (1990b):288.

37. Graham (1990b):287.

38. Richards (1932):87 recognizes the possibility that "concept" might be a culturally specific instrument: "The problem seems to grow still more formidable as we realize that it concerns not only incommensurable concepts but also comparisons between concepts and items which may not be concepts at all."

39. See Graham (1990b):287. See also Graham (1990a):7–66, "The Background of the Mencian Theory of Human Nature." Graham's point here is that we end up assigning Mencius a notion of teleology endowed in human being in the act of creation that does not fit. As Sandel (1982):50 observes, "To speak of human nature, for example, is often to suggest a classical teleological conception, associated with the notion of a universal human essence, invariant in all times and places."

40. Richards (1932):86–87.

41. Richards (1932):89, 91–92.

42. Graham (1990a).

43. Graham (1990a):322.

44. Nietzsche (1966):20.

45. Richards (1932):92–93.

46. See Tang Junyi (1988):95–127.

47. The Han dynasty has always been taken seriously when scholars have reflected on the political and social construction of China, but has not attracted the same degree of attention with respect to culture. The examples of this neglect are legion. What John Major (1993:5–11) says of the "relative obscurity" of the *Huainanzi* applies equally to most of the textual materials from this syncretic period. Major's own self-initiated conversion from the "Needhamesque" search for scientific "might-have-beens" to an appreciation of the formative importance of Han cosmology in shaping the Chinese perception of its place in the world is part of an ongoing sea change in our perception of this era. Li Zehou (1987:38–81) makes an argument that the Han dynasty is far more important to the foundations of cultural and intellectual China than has previously been acknowledged. We make the same argument in *Anticipating China*.

48. An example of the animated aspect of *qi* is *Zhuangzi* 46.18.18; cf. Graham (1981):124:

> *Qi* transforms and there is shape; shape transforms and there is life.

49. An example that illustrates this spiritual aspect is *Mencius* 7A.1:

> Mencius said: "For a person to realize fully one's heart-and-mind is to realize fully one's nature and character (*xing*), and in so doing, one realizes *tian*."

There is an immediate line between human realization and spirituality as a human contribution to the world.

50. See Hall and Ames (1995), especially chapter 3.

51. See Allan (1979) and Ahern (1981).

52. *Analects* 16.8.

53. *Analects* 8.19.

54. *Analects* 19.24.

55. *Zhongyong* 32.

56. Thus it bears some similarity to Derrida's "impossible sign." See Derrida (1976):234.

57. See *Daodejing* 42.

58. See Hall and Ames (1995):chapter 1; also Hall (1978), and Hall (1982b).

59. See Tang Junyi (1988):95–127.

60. *Zhuangzi* 54.20.61; cf. Graham (1981):118.

61. *Zhuangzi* 5.2.40 and commentary on it in 63.23.58; cf. Graham (1981):54 and 104 respectively.

62. For both Plato and early Aristotle, *kosmos* was the "visible God" (*horatos theos*).

63. See Hall and Ames (1995):chapter 2 for the development of this terminology.

64. This does not mean that "time-space" are *necessary* conditions of the world—as we will see below, even these are surrendered in the description of the Chinese emergent cosmos.

65. Textual examples that emphasize the world as flux are *Analects* 9.17:

The Master was standing on the river bank, and observed, "Isn't its passing just like this, never ceasing day or night!"

and *Yijing* 34.55.*tuan*:

The heavens and the earth fill and empty, and with the seasons wax and wane. How much more so human beings? the gods and spirits?

66. We saw an example of this assumption above in *Daodejing* 25:

Soundless, formless,
It stands solitary and is not corrected.
It revolves without pause.
This can be considered the mother of the world.

67. An illustration of this sensibility is *Yijing* 45.*xixia*.2:

Coming and going without end is called "getting through." To transform is to get through, and to get through is to be enduring.

68. The expression "focus" is derived etymologically from the Latin meaning "fireplace" or "hearth," as in "hearth and home."

69. François Jullien (1995) makes a similar observation on the cosmological dimension of any particular work of art in the Chinese tradition.

70. A discussion of some of these analogies is to be found in Hall (1982b):247–250 and *passim*.

10. CHINESE COMMUNITY WITHOUT TRANSCENDENCE

1. See Hall and Ames (1995):268–278.
2. Plato (1956):75.
3. Ibid.
4. Plato (1978): *Symposium* 191b–c.
5. *Xunzi* 105.29.29.
6. *Analects* 6.30; see also 3.3, and 15.39.
7. See part III chapter 2 note 5 above.
8. *Analects* 12.1.
9. See Ames (1991c) and Fingarette (1991) for an engagement on the reflexivity of the focal self.
10. *Analects* 1.8; see also 9.25. The point here is that real friends (*you*) who are better than you lead you in the right direction—the opposite of erring in what you do.
11. *Analects* 16.4. See also 19.3.
12. *Analects* 3.3. Note the place of this passage immediately following Confucius' criticism of the Three Families of Lu for their inappropriate use of ritual.
13. *Analects* 19.3.
14. Especially *Analects* 12.20.
15. D. C. Lau (1983):258–260. Zizhang seems to be rash, and is criticized by other protégés. In *Analects* 11.16, we read:

> Zigong inquired, "Who is of superior character, Shi [Zizhang] or Shang [Zixia]?" The Master replied, "Shi oversteps the mark, and Shang falls short of it."
> "Does this make Shi better?" asked Zigong.
> "One is as bad as the other," replied Confucius.

16. D. C. Lau (1983):256. Pu Shang, known as Zixia, was a man of letters, and is remembered by tradition as having had an important role

in establishing the Confucian canon. Although Zixia tries to compensate for his image as a pendent by insisting that virtuous conduct in one's personal relationships is what learning is all about, Confucius criticizes him at times for a being petty and narrow in his aspirations. He has a major place in the last five chapters of the *Analects*, where he underscores the importance of learning. Confucius allows that he himself has gotten a great deal from his conversations with Zixia.

17. *Analects* 15.10.

18. *Analects* 13.25, 18.10.

19. We have argued for the particularity of *ren* at some considerable length in Hall and Ames (1987), especially pp. 110–130.

20. *Analects* 14.35.

21. See Hall and Ames (1987):chapter 4, especially pp. 241–246 for our argument that this is a fair characterization of Confucian religiousness.

22. *Mencius* 7A.1.

23. *Analects* 15.29.

24. *Mencius* 7A.4.

25. *Analects* 7.23.

26. *Mencius* 7A.4.

27. On the covers of *Thinking Through Confucius* and *Anticipating China*—a Tang dynasty Han Huang painting and a detail from a later Five Dynasties handscroll respectively—the Confucian scholars are portrayed as twice the size of their attendants.

28. *Analects* 19.24 and 19.25. See also 2.1 and 8.19, and *Mencius* 3A.4.

29. See *Mencius* 7B.25.

30. *Mencius* 5B.8.

31. *Analects* 7.5.

32. *Analects* 19.22.

33. See Ambrose King (1985).

34. See, for example, *Analects* 5.8.

35. Following the "functional" rather than "anatomic" implications of *xin*, it is translated here as "thoughts and feelings."

36. *Analects* 6.7.

37. *Analects* 5.9. The grammar is equivocal here. The translation suggested by Zhu Xi is "You are not his match. I grant you, you are not his match." But the *yu* also appears in the first phrase of this passage.

38. *Mencius* 7A.4.

39. Herbert Fingarette (1972) and Tu Wei-ming (1979a, 1985, 1989,

1993) have done a lot to bring out both the centrality and the uniqueness of ritual as it has functioned in the Confucian tradition.

40. See Graham (1989):145 and (1978):265.

41. Graham (1978):270.

42. *Analects* 13.23. See also 1.12, 2.14, and 15.22.

43. *Analects* 3.12.

44. *Analects* 3.3.

45. *Analects* 2.3.

46. *Analects* 15.5; see also 2.1.

47. See Hall (1982b):249.

48. Ames (1991a).

49. See Hall and Ames (1987):chapter 3 passim for this distinction between *ren* and *min*.

50. *Li* is frequently used as shorthand for several conceptual clusters, the most familiar being *li, ren,* and *yi*; and *li* and *yue*. See Hall and Ames (1987):chapter 2 *passim,* and Kenneth DeWoskin (1982):174ff. For a discussion of the role of penal law in Confucian philosophy, see Ames (1991b).

51. See Karlgren (1957):213.

52. See McKnight (1981). McKnight demonstrates that imperial amnesties occurred every few years in the broad sweep of Chinese history. This being the case, China was in fact relying upon pressures within the community to restore all by the most egregious violations of social order.

53. *Analects* 12.13.

54. *Analects* 13.11 and 13.12. See Ames (1991b) for an argument against the opinion that Confucius was antagonistic toward law.

55. *Analects* 7.21.

56. *Analects* 4.16.

57. *Xunzi* 3/1.49.

58. See Rosemont (1988) for a discussion of the relatively negative value of rights talk within Chinese culture. For a more recent assessment, see Ames (1997).

59. We are responding here to Jack Donnelly's remarks on the alternative traditions. See especially Donnelly (1985):82–83.

60. See Graham (1990a):8 in which he is keen to correct his earlier understanding of *xing* as "that which one starts with" to make it more representative of the whole process of one's existence. Ames (1991a), relying on Graham and Tang Junyi, develops this further.

61. *Zhongyong* 1.

62. Munro (1979b):19–20, 57.

63. See Tang Junyi (1961–62).

64. See *Mencius* 2A.6: "A persons's having these four beginnings (*siduan*) is like having four limbs."

65. The *Shuowen* lexicon defines *shan* as "synonymous with 'appropriateness/rightness' (*yi*) and 'beauty' (*mei*)." This aesthetic sense is also apparent in the cognate refinement of *shan* (to make good =) "to repair," "to put in order."

66. In 4B.19, Mencius observes that "what distinguishes the human being from the brutes is ever so slight, and where the common run of people are apt to lose it, the exemplary person preserves it."

67. Graham (1991a:15) in worrying over this distinction between faculty and process, concludes:

We need not look too closely at this distinction, because Hsun-tzu [Xunzi] in the 3rd century BC seems to have been the first to recognize it, and he tells us that the word is used to mean both.

68. See *Analects* 6.30, and the *Great Learning* (*Daxue*), which is the classic statement for this coextensive relationship.

69. Hegel (1956):111–112.

70. Note the absence of a developed mythology in the early tradition and its emergence in the Han dynasty. Also it is remarked that both Daoism and Confucianism developed from fundamentally philosophical traditions to become formalized religious movements—"From Philosophy to Religion," as it were. In fact, such a characterization is an untenable separation of secular and sacred in the classical tradition. Philosophical and religious sensibilities have been coterminous and mutually entailing in the culture.

71. Rosemont (1986) and Fingarette (1972). The insights of these two scholars with respect to the nature of morality also apply to rationality—witness the relative minor role of rational skepticism as a motive force in the tradition.

72. See Ames (1988) and (1991).

73. Hegel (1956):117 comments: "This empire [China] early attracted the attention of Europeans, although only vague stories about it had reached them. It was always marvelled as a country which, self-originated, appeared to have no connection with the outer world."

74. Dewey (1927):150–151.

75. This notion of parity can be traced back in the tradition to both Daoism and Confucianism. In Daoism, parity is implicit in the *wu-wei* posture, and in Confucianism, the central methodology of *shu*, "deference" likewise requires the entertainment of other persons on their own terms. See Ames (1989) for this argument.

76. *South China Post* (Hong Kong), February 21, 1987.

77. Nathan (1986b):163–164.

78. Rosemont (1988):175.

79. Vincent (1986):17–18.

80. Edwards (1986):41.

81. See Ames (1997).

Works Cited

Adkins, A. W. H. (1970). *From the Many to the One*. Ithaca: Cornell University Press.

Ahern, Emily (1981). *Chinese Rituals and Politics*. Cambridge: Cambridge University Press.

Allan, Sarah (1979). "Shang Foundations of Modern Chinese Folk Religion." In *Legend, Lore and Religion in China*, ed. Sarah Allan and Alvin P. Cohen. San Francisco: Chinese Materials Center.

Ames, Roger T. (1997). "Continuing the Conversation on Chinese Human Rights." *Ethics and International Affairs*, April.

Ames, Roger T. (1995). With Lin Tongqi and Henry Rosemont Jr. "Chinese Philosophy: a Philosophical Essay on 'the State-of-the-Art.'" *The Journal of Asian Studies* 54.3.

Ames, Roger T. (1994). With W. Dissanayake and T. Kasulis, editors. *Self as Person in Asian Theory and Practice*. Albany: State University of New York Press.

Ames, Roger T. (1993). *The Art of Rulership: A Study of Ancient Chinese Political Thought*. Albany: State University of New York Press.

Ames, Roger T. (1991a). "The Mencian Conception of *Ren xing*: Does it Mean 'Human Nature'?" In *Chinese Texts and Philosophical Contexts: Essays Dedicated to Angus C. Graham*, ed. H. Rosemont Jr. La Salle, Ill.: Open Court.

Ames, Roger T. (1991b). "From Confucius to Xunzi: An Ambiguity of Order in Classical Confucianism." In *Interpreting Culture through Translation*, ed. R. T. Ames, S. W. Chan, and M. S. Ng. Hong Kong: Chinese University of Hong Kong.

Ames, Roger T. (1991c). "Reflections on the Confucian Self: A Response to Fingarette." In *Rules, Rituals, and Responsibility: Essays Dedicated* to *Herbert Fingarette*, ed. Mary I. Bockover. La Salle, Ill.: Open Court.

Ames, Roger T. (1991d). "Meaning as Imaging: Prolegomena to a Confucian Epistemology." In *Culture and Modernity: East-West Philosophic Perspectives*, ed. E. Deutsch. Honolulu: University of Hawai'i Press.

Ames, Roger T. (1989). "Putting the *te* Back in Taoism." In *Nature in Asian Traditions of Thought*, ed. J. Baird Callicott and Roger T. Ames. Albany: State University of New York Press.

Ames, Roger T. (1988). "Confucius and the Ontology of Knowing." In *Interpreting across Boundaries: New Essays in Comparative Philosophy*, ed. G. Larson and E. Deutsch. Princeton: Princeton University Press.

Ames, Roger T. (1981). "Taoism and the Androgynous Ideal." In *Women in China*, ed. Richard W. Guisso and Stanley Johannesen. Youngstown, N.Y.: Philo Press, 1981.

Ames, Roger T., and Wimal Dissanayake (eds.) (1996). *Self and Deception: A Cross-Cultural Philosophical Enquiry*. Albany: State University of New York Press.

Analects (*Lun-yü*). (1940). Peking: Harvard-Yenching Institute Sinological Index Series, Supplement 16.

Aristotle (1984). *The Complete Works of Aristotle*. 2 vols. Edited by Jonathan Barnes. Princeton, N.J.: Princton University Press.

Augustine, Saint (1950). *The City of God*. Trans. by Marcus Dodds. New York: Modern Library.

Augustine, Saint (1949). *The Confessions of Saint Augustine*. Trans. by Edward Pusey. New York: Modern Library.

Bell, Daniel E. (1993). *Communitarianism and Its Critics*. New York: Oxford University Press.

Bentham, Jeremy (1843). "Anarchical Fallacies." In *Collected Papers*, reprinted in *Human Rights* 32 (A. I. Meldin ed. 1970).

Ban Gu, *Hanshu*. Peking: Zhonghua shuju, 1962.

Bernard of Clairvaux (1987). *Bernard of Clairvaux: Selected Works*. Trans. by G. R. Evans. New York: Paulist Press.

Berthrong, John H. (1994). *All under Heaven: Transforming Paradigms in Confucian-Christian Dialogue*. Albany: State University of New York Press.

Birdwhistell, Anne (1992). "Cultural Support for the Way of Mother and Son." In *Philosophy East and West* 42:3.

Black, Alison H. (1989). "Gender and Cosmology in Chinese Correlative Thinking." In *Gender and Religion: On the Complexity of Symbols*, ed. C. W. Bynum, S. Harrell, and P. Richman. Boston: Beacon Press.

Bloom, Alfred H. (1981). *The Linguistic Shaping of Thought: A Study in the Impact of Language and Thinking in China and the West.* Hillsdale, N.J.: Lawrence Erlbaum.

Blumenberg, Hans (1985). *Work on Myth.* Cambridge: MIT Press.

Blumenberg, Hans (1983). *The Legitimacy of the Modern Age.* Cambridge: MIT Press.

Bodde, Derk (1961). "Myths of Ancient China." In *Mythologies of the Ancient World*, ed. Samuel Noah Kramer. Garden City, N.Y.: Anchor Books.

Book of Changes. See *Chou-i.*

Borges, Jorge Luis (1981). *Borges: A Reader.* Edited by Emir Rodriguez and Alasdair Reid. New York: E. P. Dutton.

Brooks, Cleanth (1975). *The Well Wrought Urn.* New York: Harcourt, Brace, and World.

Calvin, John (1960). *Institutes of the Christian Religion.* Edited by John T. McNeill. Trans. by Ford Lewis Battles. Philadelphia: Westminster Press.

Chan, W. T. (1963). *The Way of Lao Tzu.* Indianapolis: Bobbs-Merrill.

Chang Tung-sun (1939). "A Chinese Philosopher's Theory of Knowledge." *Yenching Journal of Social Studies* 1.2.

Chen Daqi (1964). *Kongzi xueshuo.* Taibei: Chenggong.

Chen, Ellen Marie (1969). "Nothingness and the Mother Principle in Early Chinese Taoism." *International Philosophical Quarterly* 9.

Chou-i (1935). Peking: Harvard-Yenching Institute Sinological Index Series, Supplement 10.

Chuang Tzu (1947). Peking: Harvard-Yenching Institute Sinological Index Series, Supplement 20.

Copernicus, Nicolaus (1955). *Epitome of Copernican Astrology.* Trans. by C. G. Wallis. Chicago: Encyclopedia Britannica.

Cox, Harvey A. (1966). *The Secular City: Secularization and Urbanization in Theological Perspective.* New York: Macmillan.

Creel, H. G. (1970a). *What is Taoism?* Chicago: University of Chicago Press.

Creel, H. G. (1970b). *The Origins of Statecraft in China.* Chicago: University of Chicago Press.

Cua, A. S. (1985). *Ethical Argumentation: A Study in Hsün Tzu's Moral Epistemology*. Honolulu: University of Hawaiʻi Press.

Davidson, Donald (1982). "Paradoxes of Irrationality." In *Philosophical Essays on Freud*, ed. B. Wollheim and J. Hopkins. Cambridge: Cambridge University Press.

de Bary, Wm. Theodore (1985). "Neo-Confucian Individualism and Holism." In *Individualism and Holism: Studies in Confucian and Taoist Values*, ed. Donald J. Munro. Ann Arbor: University of Michigan Press.

Derrida, Jacques (1982). "White Mythology." Reprinted in *Margins of Philosophy*, trans. Alan Bass. Chicago: University of Chicago Press.

Derrida, Jacques (1976). *Of Grammatology*. Trans. by Gayatri Chakravorty Spivak. Baltimore: Johns Hopkins University Press.

Deutsch, Eliot (1979). *On Truth: An Ontological Theory*. Honolulu: University of Hawaiʻi Press.

Dewey, John (1973). *John Dewey: Lectures in China 1919–21*. Honolulu: University of Hawaiʻi Press.

Dewey, John (1927). *The Public and Its Problems*. Athens, Ohio: Ohio University Press.

DeWoskin, Kenneth (1982). *A Song for One or Two: Music and the Concept of Art in Early China*. Ann Arbor: University of Michigan Press.

Dihle, Albrecht (1982). *The Theory of Will in Classical Antiquity*. Berkeley: University of California Press.

Dodds, E. R. (1951). *The Greeks and the Irrational*. Berkeley: University of California Press.

Donnelly, Jack (1985). *The Concept of Human Rights*. London: Croom Helm.

Dubs, Homer (1946). "Taoism." In *China*, ed. H. F. McNair. Berkeley: University of California Press.

Dupre, John (1993). *The Disorder of Things: Metaphysical Foundations of the Disunity of Science*. Cambridge: Harvard University Press.

Edwards, R. Randle (1986). "Civil and Social Rights: Theory and Practice in Chinese Law Today." In *Human Rights in Contemporary China*, ed. R. Edwards, L. Henkin, and A. Nathan. New York: Columbia University Press.

Elvin, Mark (1985). "Between the Earth and Heaven: Conceptions of the Self in China." In *The Category of the Person*, ed. Michael

Carrithers, Steven Collins, and Steven Lukes. Cambridge: Cambridge University Press.

Fairbank, John (1987). *China Watch*. Cambridge: Harvard University Press.

Fairbank, John (1983). "Review" of John Lubot's *Liberalism in an Illiberal Age*. *China Quarterly* 96.

Fingarette, Herbert A. (1991). "Comment and Response." In *Rules, Rituals, and Responsibility: Essays Dedicated to Herbert Fingarette*, ed. M. Bockover. La Salle, Ill.: Open Court.

Fingarette, Herbert A. (1979). "The Problem of the Self in the *Analects*." *Philosophy East and West* 29.2 (April 1979).

Fingarette, Herbert A. (1972). *Confucius: The Secular as Sacred*. New York: Harper & Row.

Flax, Jane (1989). *Thinking Fragments: Psychoanalysis, Feminism and Postmodernism in the Contermporary West*. Berkeley: University of California Press.

Fukunaga Mitsuji (trans.) (1966). *Sōshi: Gaihen*. Tokyo: Asahi shinbun.

Gernet, Jacques (1985). *China and the Christian Impact: A Conflict of Cultures*. Trans. by Janet Lloyd. Cambridge: Cambridge University Press. This book was originally published in 1982 as *Chine et christianisme*. Paris: Editions Gallimard.

Gilligan, Carol (1982). *In a Different Voice*. Cambridge: Harvard University Press.

Graham, A. C. (1992). *Unreason within Reason: Essays on the Outskirts of Rationality*. Lasalle, Ill.: Open Court.

Graham, A. C. (1990a). *Studies in Chinese Philosophy and Philosophical Literature*. Albany: State University of New York Press.

Graham, A. C. (1990b). "Reflections and Replies." In *Chinese Texts & Philosophical Contexts: Essays Dedicated to Angus C. Graham*, ed. Henry Rosemont Jr. La Salle, Ill.: Open Court.

Graham, A. C. (1982). *Chuang-tzu: Textual Notes to a Partial Translation*. London: School of Oriental and African Studies.

Graham, A. C. (1989). *Disputers of the Tao*. La Salle, Ill.: Open Court.

Graham, A. C. (trans.) (1981). *Chuang-tzu: The Inner Chapters*. London: George Allen & Unwin.

Graham, A. C. (1978). *Later Mohist Logic, Ethics and Science*. Hong Kong: Chinese University Press.

Grange, Joseph (1997). *Nature: An Environmental Cosmology*. Albany: State University of New York Press.

Grimshaw, Jean (1992). "The Idea of the Female Ethic." In *Philosophy East and West* 42.2.

Grimshaw, Jean (1986). *Philosophy and Feminist Thinking*. Minneapolis: University of Minnesota Press.

Guisso, Richard W. and Stanley Johannesen (eds.) (1981). *Women in China: Current Directions in Historical Scholarship*. Youngstown, N.Y.: Philo Press.

Guisso, Richard W. (1981). "Thunder over the Lake: The Five Classics and the Perception of Woman in Early China." In *Women in China: Current Directions in Historical Scholarship*, ed. R. Guisso and S. Johannesen. Youngstown, N.Y.: Philo Press.

Habermas, Jürgen (1987). *Philosophical Discourse of Modernity*. Trans. by Frederick Lawrence. Cambridge: MIT Press.

Hall, David L. (1998). "On Looking Up 'Dialectics' in a Chinese Encyclopedia." In *Being and Dialectics*, ed. William Desmond and Joseph Grange. Albany: State University of New York Press.

Hall, David L. (1997). "The Way and the Truth." In *Companion to World Philosophy*, ed. Eliot Deutsch and Ron Bontekoe. Oxford: Blackwell.

Hall, David L. (1996). "Our Names Are Legion for We Are Many: On the Academics of Deception." In *Self and Deception: A Cross-Cultural Philosophical Enquiry*, ed. R. Ames and W. Dissanayake. Albany: State University of New York Press.

Hall, David L. (1994). "Buddhism, Taoism and the Question of Ontological Difference." In *Essays in Honor of Nolan Pliny Jacobson*, ed. S. Puligandla and David Miller. Indianapolis: Indiana University Press.

Hall, David L. (1994). *Richard Rorty: Prophet and Poet of the New Pragmatism*. Albany: State University of New York Press.

Hall, David L. (1991). "Modern China and the Postmodern West." In *Culture and Modernity: East-West Philosophic Perspectives*, ed. Eliot Deutsch. Honolulu: University of Hawaii Press.

Hall, David L. (1989). "Dancing at the Crucifixion," *Philosophy East and West* 39.3 (July).

Hall, David L. (1987). "Logos, Mythos, Chaos: Metaphysics as the Quest For Diversity." In *New Essays in Metaphysics*, ed. R. Neville. Albany: State University of New York Press.

Hall, David L. (1982a). *Eros and Irony*. Albany: State University of New York Press.

Hall, David L. (1982b). *The Uncertain Phoenix*. New York: Fordham University Press.

Hall, David L. (1978). "Process and Anarchy—A Taoist Vision of Creativity." *Philosophy East and West* 28.3:271–85.

Hall, David L. (1973). *The Civilization of Experience*. New York: Fordham University Press.

Hall, David L., and Roger T. Ames (1995). *Anticipating China: Thinking through the Narratives of Chinese and Western Culture*. Albany: State University of New York Press.

Hall, David L., and Roger T. Ames (1991). "Rationality, Correlativity, and the Language of Process." *The Journal of Speculative Philosophy* 5.2:85–106.

Hall, David L., and Roger T. Ames (1987). *Thinking Through Confucius*. Albany: State University of New York Press.

Hansen, Chad (1985a). "Individualism in Chinese Thought." In *Individualism and Holism: Studies in Confucian and Taoist Values*, ed. D. Munro. Ann Arbor: University of Michigan Press.

Hansen, Chad (1985b). "Chinese Language, Chinese Philosophy, and 'Truth.'" *Journal of Asian Studies* 44:491–517.

Hansen, Chad (1983). *Language and Logic in Ancient China*. Ann Arbor: University of Michigan Press.

Hartshorne, Charles (1964). *The Divine Relativity: A Social Conception of God*. New Haven: Yale University Press.

Hartshorne, Charles, and William L. Reese (eds.) (1953). *Philosophers Speak of God*. Chicago: University of Chicago Press.

Haudricourt, A. G. (1962). "Domestication des animaux, culture des plantes et traitement d'autrui." *L'Homme* 2.1.

Hay, John (1994). "The Persistent Dragon (*lung*)." In *The Power of Culture: Studies in Chinese Cultural History*, ed. W. Peterson, A. Plaks, and Y. S. Yu. Princeton: Princeton University Press.

Hay, John (1993). "The Human Body as a Microcosmic Source of Macrocosmic Values in Calligraphy." In *Self as Body in Asian Theory and Practice*, ed. T. P. Kasulis, R. T. Ames, and W. Dissanayake. Albany: State University of New York Press.

Hegel, G. W. F. (1956). *Philosophy of History*. Trans. by J. Sibree. New York: Dover.

Henkin, Louis (1986). "The Human Rights Idea in Contemporary China: A Comparative Perspective." In *Human Rights in Contemporary China*, ed. R. Edwards, L. Henkin, and A. Nathan. New York: Columbia University Press.

Hershock, Peter (1996). *Liberating Intimacy: Enlightenment and Social Virtuosity in Ch'an Buddhism*. Albany: State University of New York Press.

Hsiao Kung-chuan (1979). *A History of Chinese Political Thought*. Trans. by F. Mote. Princeton: Princeton University Press.

Hsün Tzu (1966 rep.). Harvard-Yenching Sinological Index Series, Supp. 22. Taipei: Chinese Materials Center.

Huainanzi (unpublished). Draft translations of chapters 1 and 2 by D. C. Lau and Roger T. Ames.

Hume, David (1960). *The Treatise of Human Nature*. Edited by L. Selby-Bigge. Oxford: Clarendon Press.

Jacob, Edmond (1958). *Theology of the Old Testament*. New York: Harper & Row.

James, William (1977). *A Pluralistic Universe*. Cambridge: Harvard University Press.

James, William (1929). *Varieties of Religious Experience*. New York: Modern Library.

John of the Cross (1958). *Ascent of Mount Carmel*. Trans. by E. Peers. Garden City, N.Y.: Image Books.

Jullien, François (1995). *The Propensity of Things: Toward a History of Efficacy in China*. New York: Zone Books.

Kahn, Charles (1988). "Discovering the Will: From Aristotle to Augustine." In *The Question of "Eclecticism": Studies in Later Greek Philosophy*, ed. J. Dillon and A. Long. Berkeley: University of California Press.

Kaltenmark, Max (1970). *Lao Tzu and Taoism*. Trans. by Roger Greaves. Stanford: Stanford University Press.

Kasulis, Thomas P. (1993). With R. Ames and W. Dissanayake, editors. *Self as Body in Asian Theory and Practice*. Albany: State University of New York Press.

Karlgren, Bernhard. (1957). *Grammata Serica Recensa*. Stockholm: Museum of Far Eastern Antiquities, Bulletin No. 29.

Kepler, Johannes (1955). *The Harmonies of the World*. Trans. by C. Wallis. Chicago: Encyclopedia Britannica.

King, Ambrose (1985). "The Individual and Group in Confucianism: A Relational Perspective." In *Individualism and Holism: Studies in Confucian and Taoist Values*, ed. D. Munro. Ann Arbor: University of Michigan Press.

Klemenkova, Tatyana (1992). "Feminism in Postmodernism." *Philosophy East and West* 42.2.

Kolb, David (1987). *The Critique of Pure Modernity.* Chicago: University of Chicago Press.

LaFargue, Michael (1994). *Tao and Method.* Albany: State University of New York Press.

Lau, D. C. (trans.) (1983). *Confucius: The Analects.* Hong Kong: Chinese University Press.

Lau, D. C. and Roger T. Ames (1996). *Sun Pin: The Art of Warfare.* New York: Ballantine.

Lau, D. C., and Chen Fong Ching (eds.) (1992). *A Concordance to the Huainanzi.* ICS Ancient Chinese Text Concordance Series. Hong Kong: Commerical Press.

Leibniz, Gottfried Wilhelm (1994). *Writings on China.* Trans. by D. J. Cook and H. Rosemont Jr. La Salle, Ill.: Open Court.

Lenk, Hans (1987). *Kritik der Kleinen Vernunft.* Frankfurt: Suhrkamp.

Lewis, Mark Edward (1990). *Sanctioned Violence in Early China.* Albany: State University of New York.

Li Minghui (1994). *Dangdai ruxue zhi ziwozhuanhua (The Transformation of Self in Contemporary Confucianism).* Taibei: Academia Sinica.

Li Zehou (1987). *Li Zehou zhexue meixue wenxuan.* Taibei: Gufeng Publishers.

Li, Victor H. (1978). *Law without Lawyers.* Boulder: Westview Press.

Liu, Buwei (1977). *Lushi chunqiu.* Edited by Yang Jialo. Taibei: Dingwen shuju.

Lloyd, Genevieve (1993). *The Man of Reason.* Minneapolis: University of Minnesota Press.

Lu Xun (1981). "Wo de jielieguan" (My Views on Chastity). In *Lu Xun quanji (Complete Works of Lu Xun).* Peking: Peoples' Press.

Lucretius (1946). *De Rerum Natura (On the Nature of Things).* Trans. by C. Bennet. Roslyn, N.Y.: Walter J. Black.

Mao Zedong (1951). "Maodunlun (On Contradictions)." In *Mao Zedong xuanji (Selected Works of Mao Zedong),* vol. 1. Peking: Peoples Press.

MacIntyre, Alasdair (1988). *Whose Justice? Which Rationality?* Notre Dame, Ind.: University of Notre Dame Press.

McKnight, Brian E. (1981). *The Quality of Mercy.* Honolulu: University of Hawaii Press.

McMullen, David (1987). "Bureaucrats and Cosmology: The Ritual Code of T'ang China." In *Rituals of Royalty*, ed. D. Cannadine and S. Price. Cambridge: Cambridge University Press.

McNeill, John T. (ed.) (1960). *Institutes of the Christian Religion*. Trans. by F. Battles. Philadelphia: Westminster Press.

Major, John S. (1993). *Heaven and Earth in Early Han Thought: Chapters Three, Four, and Five of the Huainanzi*. Albany: State University of New York Press.

Mauss, Marcel (1985). "A Category of the Human Mind: The Notion of Person; the Notion of Self." In *The Category of the Person*, ed. M. Carrithers, S. Collins, and S. Lukes, trans. W. Halls. Cambridge: Cambridge University Press.

Mead, George Herbert (1934). *Mind, Self and Society*. Edited by C. Morris. Chicago: University of Chicago Press.

Mead, George Herbert (1938). *Works of George Herbert Mead*, vol. 3: *The Philosophy of the Act*. Edited by Charles W. Morris. Chicago: University of Chicago Press.

Mencius (*Meng Tzu*). (1941). Peking: Harvard-Yenching Institute Sinological Index Series, Supplement 17.

Mou Zongsan (Mou Tsung-san) (1963). *Zhongguo zhexue de tezhi*. Taibei: Xuesheng shuju.

Munro, Donald J. (1985a). "Introduction." In *Individualism and Holism: Studies in Confucian and Taoist Values*, ed. D. Munro. Ann Arbor: University of Michigan Press.

Munro, Donald J. (1985b). "The Family Network, the Stream of Water, and the Plant." In *Individualism and Holism: Studies in Confucian and Taoist Values*. Ann Arbor: University of Michigan Press.

Munro, Donald J. (1979a). "The Shape of Chinese Values in the Eye of an American Philosopher." In *The China Difference*, ed. R. Terrill. New York: Harper & Row.

Munro, Donald J. (1979b). *Concept of Man in Contemporary China*. Ann Arbor: University of Michigan Press.

Nathan, Andrew J. (1986a). "Political Rights in the Chinese Constitutions." In *Human Rights in Contemporary China*, ed. R. Edwards, L. Henkin, and A. Nathan. New York: Columbia University Press.

Nathan, Andrew J. (1986b). "Sources of Chinese Rights Thinking." In *Human Rights in Contemporary China*, ed. R. Edwards, L. Henkin, and A. Nathan. New York: Columbia University Press.

Needham, Joseph (1978). *The Shorter Science and Civilisation in China*, vol 1. Abridgement by C. Ronan. Cambridge: Cambridge University Press.

Needham, Joseph (1956). *Science and Civilisation in China*, vol. 2. Cambridge: Cambridge University Press.

Neville, Robert Cummings (1981). *Reconstruction of Thinking*. Albany: State University of New York Press.

Neville, Robert Cummings (1974). *The Cosmology of Freedom*. New Haven: Yale University Press.

Newton, Isaac (1952). *Optics*. Edited by R. Hutchins. *Great Books of the Western World*, vol. 34. Chicago: Encyclopaedia Britanica.

Nietzsche, Friedrich (1966). *Beyond Good and Evil*. Trans. by W. Kaufmann. New York: Vintage.

Norman, K. R. (trans.) (1971). *The Elders' Verses II: Therīgāthā*. Pali Text Society Translation Series No. 40. London: Luzac and Company.

Odin, Steve (1994). *The Social Self in Zen and Mead*. Albany: State University of New York Press.

Owen, Stephen (1992). *Readings in Chinese Literary Thought*. Cambridge: Council on East Asian Studies, Harvard University.

Pedersen, Johannes (1959). *Israel: Its Life and Culture*, vol. 2. London: Oxford University Press.

Peters, F. E. (1967). *Greek Philosophical Terms: A Historical Lexicon*. New York: New York University Press.

Pike, Nelson (1992). *Mystic Union: An Essay on the Epistemology of Mysticism*. Ithaca: Cornell University Press.

Plato (1978). *The Collected Dialogues of Plato*. Edited by E. Hamilton and H. Cairns. Princeton: Princeton Univerity Press.

Plato (1956). *Phaedrus*. Trans. W. C. Helmbold and W. G. Rabinowitz. Indianapolis: Bobbs-Merrill.

Rawls, John (1996). *Political Liberalism*. New York: Columbia University Press.

Rawls, John (1971). *A Theory of Justice*. Cambridge: Harvard University Press.

Richards, I. A. (1932). *Mencius on the Mind*. New York: Harcourt, Brace and Co.

Robinson, John M. (1968). *Introduction to Early Greek Philosophy: The Chief Fragments and Ancient Testimony, with Connecting Commentary*. Boston: Houghton Mifflen.

Rorty, Richard (1991a). *Objectivity, Relativism, and Truth.* Philosophical Papers, vol. 1. Cambridge: Cambridge University Press.

Rorty, Richard (1991b). *Essays on Heidegger and Others.* Philosophical Papers, vol. 2. Cambridge: Cambridge University Press.

Rorty, Richard (1982). *Consequences of Pragmatism.* Minneapolis: University of Minnesota Press.

Rorty, Richard (1979). *Philosophy and the Mirror of Nature.* Princeton: Princeton University Press.

Rosemont, Henry, Jr., (ed.) (1991). *Chinese Texts and Philosophical Contexts: Essays Dedicated to Angus C. Graham.* La Salle, Ill.: Open Court.

Rosemont, Henry, Jr. (1988). "Why Take Rights Seriously? A Confucian Critique." In *Human Rights and the World's Religions,* ed. L. Rouner. Notre Dame, Ind.: University of Notre Dame Press.

Rosemont, Henry, Jr. (1986). "Kierkegaard and Confucius: On Following the Way." *Philosophy East and West* 36.3.

Rosemont, Henry, Jr. (ed.) (1984). *Explorations in Early Chinese Cosmology.* Chico, Calif.: Scholars Press.

Roth, Harold D. (1991). "Who Compiled the *Chuang Tzu?*" In *Chinese Text and Philosophical Contexts: Essays Dedicated to Angus C. Graham,* ed. H. Rosemont Jr. La Salle, Ill.: Open Court.

Rubin, Vitaly (1976). *Individual and State in Ancient China.* Trans. by S. Levine. New York: Columbia University Press.

Rump, Arrienne, in collaboration with Wing-tsit Chan (trans.) (1979). *Wang Pi's Commentary on the Lao tzu.* Honolulu: University Press of Hawaii, Society for Asian and Comparative Philosophy monograph, No. 6.

Ryle, Gilbert (1949). *The Concept of Mind.* London: Hutchinson.

Said, Edward (1978). *Orientalism.* New York: Random House.

Sandel, Michael (1996). *Democracy's Discontent: America in Search of a Public Philosophy.* Cambridge: Harvard University Press.

Sandel, Michael (1982). *Liberalism and the Limits of Justice.* Cambridge: Harvard University Press.

Saussy, Haun (1993). *The Problem of a Chinese Aesthetic.* Stanford: Stanford University Press.

Schwartz, Benjamin I. (1985). *The World of Thought in Ancient China.* Cambridge: Harvard University Press.

Schwartz, Benjamin I. (1975a). "The Age of Transcendence." *Daedalus* 104 (Spring):1–7.

Schwartz, Benjamin I. (1975b). "Transcendence in Ancient China." *Daedalus* 104 (Spring):57–68.

Smart, Ninian (1965). "Interpretation and Mystical Experience." *Religious Studies* I:75–87.

Smith, Richard J. (1983). *China's Cultural Heritage: The Ch'ing Dynasty, 1644–1912.* Boulder: Westview Press.

Snell, Bruno (1960). *The Discovery of the Mind: The Greek Origins of European Thought.* New York: Harper & Row.

Solomon, Robert C. (1992). *The Bully Culture: Enlightenment, Romanticism, and the Transcendental Pretense 1750–1850.* Lanham, Md.: Rowman and Littlefield.

Stace, Walter (1960). *Mysticism and Philosophy.* Philadelphia: Lippincott.

Sun Yirang (1975). *Mozi jiangu.* In Yan Lingfeng (ed.), *Mozi jicheng* 12–15. Taibei: Yiwen yinshuguan. First published 1894.

Tang Junyi (1988). "Zhongguo zhexue zhong ziran yuzhouguan zhi tezhi (The defining conditions of natural cosmology in Chinese philosophy)." In *Zhongxi zhexue sixiang zhi bijiao lunwenji.* Taibei: Xuesheng shuju.

Tang Junyi (1968). *Zhongguo zhexue yuanlun: yuanxing pian.* Hong Kong: New Asia Press.

Tang, Junyi [T'ang Chün-i] (1961–62). "The T'ien Ming (Heavenly Ordinance) in Pre-Ch'in China." *Philosophy East and West* 11.4 (October 1961); 12.1 (January 1962).

Taylor, Mark C. (1984). *Erring: A Postmodern A/Theology.* Chicago: University of Chicago Press.

Taylor, Rodney L. (1990). *The Religious Dimensions of Confucianism.* Albany: State University of New York Press.

Teresa of Avila (1979). *Interior Castle.* Trans. by K. Kavannaugh and O. Rodriquez. New York: Paulist Press.

Trebilcot, Joyce (1982). "Two Forms of Androgynism." In *"Femininity," "Masculinity," and "Androgyny".* Totowa, N.J.: Rowman and Littlefield.

Tu, Wei-ming (1993). *Way, Learning, and Politics: Essays on the Confucian Intellectual.* Albany: State University of New York Press.

Tu, Wei-ming (1989). *Centrality and Commonality: An Essay on Confucian Religiousness.* Albany: State University of New York Press.

Tu, Wei-ming (1985). *Confucian Thought: Selfhood as Creative Transformation.* Albany: State University of New York Press.

Tu, Wei-ming (1979). *Humanity and Self-Cultivation: Essays in Confucian Thought*. Berkeley: Asian Humanities Press.

van Ruysbroeck, Jan (1951). *John of Ruysbroeck*. Edited by Evelyn Underhill. Trans. by C. A. Wynschenk. London: John M. Watkins.

Vincent, R. J. (1986). *Human Rights and International Relations*. Cambridge: Cambridge University Press.

Waley, Arthur (1934). *The Way and Its Power: A Study of the Tao Te Ching and Its Place in Chinese Thought*. London: George Allen and Unwin.

Watson, Burton (trans.) (1968). *The Complete Works of Chuang Tzu*. New York: Columbia University Press.

Weber, Max (1958). *The Protestant Ethic and the Spirit of Capitalism*. New York: Scribners.

Wendel, François (1963). *Calvin—Origins and Development of His Religious Thought*. Trans. by P. Mairet. New York: Harper & Row.

Wender, Dorothea, (trans.) (1973). *Hesiod and Theognis*. New York: Viking Penguin.

Whitehead, A. N. (1978). *Process and Reality* (corrected edition). Edited by D. Griffin and D. Sherburne. New York: The Free Press.

Whitehead, A. N. (1968). *Modes of Thought*. New York: Capricorn Books.

Whitehead, A. N. (1967). *Science and the Modern World*. New York: The Free Press.

Whitehead, A. N. (1933). *Adventures of Ideas*. New York: Macmillan.

Wolfson, Harry (1934). *The Philosophy of Spinoza: Unfolding the Latent Process*. Cambridge: Harvard University Press.

Wu, Kuang-ming (1990). *The Butterfly as Companion: Meditations on the First Three Chapters of the* Chuang Tzu. Albany: State University of New York Press.

Xunzi. See *Hsün Tzu*.

Yang, C. K. (1959). *Chinese Communist Society: The Family and the Village*. Cambridge: MIT Press.

Yijing. See *Chou-i*.

Yü Ying-shih (1985). "The 'Philosophic Breakthrough' and the Chinese Mind." *Zhexue niankan* (Bulletin of the Chinese Philosophical Association) 3.

Zaehner R. C. (1961). *Mysticism Sacred and Profane—An Inquiry into Some Varieties of Preternatural Experience*. New York: Oxford University Press.

Index

331